Citizenship in an Enlarging Europe

Also by Barbara Einhorn

CINDERELLA GOES TO MARKET: Citizenship, Gender and Women's Movements in East Central Europe

CITIZENSHIP AND DEMOCRATIC CONTROL IN CONTEMPORARY EUROPE (*editor, with Mary Kaldor, Zdenek Kavan*)

WOMEN AND MARKET SOCIETIES: Crisis and Opportunity (*editor, with Eileen Janes Yeo*)

Citizenship in an Enlarging Europe

From Dream to Awakening

Barbara Einhorn

Professor of Gender Studies
Department of Sociology
School of Social Sciences and Cultural Studies
University of Sussex, Brighton, UK

© Barbara Einhorn 2006

All rights reserved. No reproduction, copy or transmission of this publication may be made without written permission.

No paragraph of this publication may be reproduced, copied or transmitted save with written permission or in accordance with the provisions of the Copyright, Designs and Patents Act 1988, or under the terms of any licence permitting limited copying issued by the Copyright Licensing Agency, 90 Tottenham Court Road, London W1T 4LP.

Any person who does any unauthorized act in relation to this publication may be liable to criminal prosecution and civil claims for damages.

The author has asserted her right to be identified as the author of this work in accordance with the Copyright, Designs and Patents Act 1988.

First published in 2006 by
PALGRAVE MACMILLAN
Houndmills, Basingstoke, Hampshire RG21 6XS and
175 Fifth Avenue, New York, N.Y. 10010
Companies and representatives throughout the world.

PALGRAVE MACMILLAN is the global academic imprint of the Palgrave Macmillan division of St. Martin's Press, LLC and of Palgrave Macmillan Ltd. Macmillan® is a registered trademark in the United States, United Kingdom and other countries. Palgrave is a registered trademark in the European Union and other countries.

ISBN-13: 978–1–4039–9840–8 hardback
ISBN-10: 1–4039–9840–X hardback

This book is printed on paper suitable for recycling and made from fully managed and sustained forest sources.

A catalogue record for this book is available from the British Library.

Library of Congress Cataloging-in-Publication Data

Einhorn, Barbara.
   Citizenship in an Enlarging Europe : from dream to awakening / Barbara Einhorn.
      p. cm.
   Includes bibliographical references and index.
   ISBN 1–4039–9840–X (cloth)
      1. Women – Europe, Eastern – Political activity. 2. Sex discrimination against women – Europe, Eastern. 3. Sex role – Europe, Eastern. 4. Europe, Eastern – Social conditions – 1989– I. Title.
HQ1236.5.E852E36 2006
305.430947′09049—dc22   2006041675

10 9 8 7 6 5 4 3 2 1
15 14 13 12 11 10 09 08 07 06

Printed and bound in Great Britain by
Antony Rowe Ltd, Chippenham and Eastbourne

To Paul, for his love and support

Contents

Acknowledgements ix

1 **Democratization and Reinvented National Identity: Contradictory Trends?** 1
   Introduction 1
   Difficulties in 'transition' 5
   Gender in transformation/transforming gender 8
   Gendered nationalisms 12
   Feminist sightings: prospects for citizenship 14
   Structure of the book 16

2 **Issues of Governance: Contested Strategies for Gender Equity** 21
   Introduction 21
   Strategies for gender equitable citizenship 23
   The role of the nation state in political representation 27
   Civil society activism as political strategy 30
   European Union enlargement and gender mainstreaming 33
   Conclusion 40

3 **Gender in Mainstream Politics: Scaling the Structures** 42
   Introduction 42
   What counts as 'politics' and where does it occur? 44
   The discursive focus on civil society 46
   Gender in mainstream politics 47
   Moving gender from margin to centre: the quota debate 56
   Conclusion 59

4 **Civil Society or NGOs: Empowerment or Depoliticization?** 61
   Introduction 61
   Civil society and gender 64
   Feminism in East–West dialogue 69
   Grassroots activism 74
   Eastern European feminism within the global context 87
   Conclusion 90

5 Family, Nation and Reproductive Politics: Between the Private and the Public 94
Introduction 94
Debates about the public–private divide 96
Altered family and social policy models 99
Demographic shifts and the question of childcare 104
Reproductive politics and discourses of the nation 108
Conclusion 122

6 Femininities and Masculinities: Gender Re-presented 124
Introduction 124
Media images and market realities 126
Superwoman teetering on a tightrope 129
Glamour puss sweeps the market 131
Gender and national identity 136
Hegemonic femininity: a conclusion 139

7 Labour Market Access: Persistent Patterns of Inequality 144
Introduction 144
Male bias in economic restructuring? 148
Gender-unequal access to the labour market 151
Marketization and occupational segregation 156
Experiencing unemployment 163
The impact of social policy changes 166
Conclusion 169

8 Citizenship in an Enlarging Europe: Towards Gender Equity? 171
Introduction 171
Civil society and the language of empowerment 172
Which institutional framework? 175
Citizenship: agency or capabilities, rights or entitlements? 178
Identity, differences and the capacity for joint political strategies 186

Notes 191

Bibliography 204

Index 241

Acknowledgements

This book has been long in the gestation. It has benefited greatly from various kinds of support, both professional and personal. The list of those to whom I am indebted is not exhaustive. For brilliant research and editorial assistance, perceptive readings and constructive critique as well as warm friendship I thank Charlie Sever. Jelena Đorđević has also contributed valuable research assistance. For invaluable help with formatting the final product, I am particularly grateful to Mary Shiner. Special thanks go to those scholars from the region itself who provided key information, or read and commented on individual chapters, giving extremely useful feedback on the accuracy of their portrayals, especially Sandra Bitušiková, Marina Blagojević, Kinga Lohmann, Daniela Ritossa, Kornelia Slavova and Małgorzata Tarasiewicz. Other scholars in East and West whose work has inspired me and whose feedback and friendship have enriched me include Cynthia Cockburn, Irene Dölling, Cynthia Enloe, Mary Evans, Małgorzata Fuszara, Susan Gal, Elena Gapova, Sander Gilman, Hana Hašková, Hana Havelková, John Holmwood, Larissa Lisyutkina, Sonja Lokar, Jasmina Lukić, Swasti Mitter, Maxine Molyneux, Hildegard Maria Nickel, Spike Peterson, Shirin Rai, Sasha Roseneil, Sheila Rowbotham, Silke Steinhilber, Júlia Szalai, and Nira Yuval-Davis. I am grateful also to Jen Nelson, my editor at Palgrave Macmillan, for editorial advice and enthusiastic feedback, to Gemma Darcy Hughes and Clare Lawson of Palgrave, and to Vidhya Jayaprakash of Newgen Imaging Systems for her helpful efficiency in the production process. My very warm appreciation and gratitude goes to my steadfast and ever insightful friend Diane Neumaier.

1
Democratization and Reinvented National Identity
Contradictory Trends?

Introduction

> Others and frontiers, these are the two conceptual points around which Europe has built its identity. ... A certain unease follows the disappearance of the opponent, the mirror in which Western Europe contemplated itself for so long, nurturing its narcissism.
>
> Ugrešić, 1998a: 244, 1998b: 304

More than fifteen years have passed since the Fall of the Berlin Wall heralded the official end of the Cold War, and with it the demise of Western Europe's 'Other'. Central and Eastern Europe, the 'Cinderella' societies, were to come to the ball, to be granted access to the freedoms, the pleasures, the opportunities of West European liberal democratic market societies. Indeed the imagery with which this process has been depicted, especially in the case of German unification, is that of a marriage between the materially and spiritually impoverished East (as petitioner or would-be bride) with the affluent and morally superior West (as the strong and protective prince).

Novelist and essayist Dubravka Ugrešić refers to the 'love between East and West Europe', as a 'story' in which 'Eastern Europe is that sleepy, pale beauty, although for the time being there is little prospect of an imminent marriage' (Ugrešić, 1998a: 236, 1998b: 297). Susan Gal and Gail Kligman write of the 'Cold War shadow boxing' in which 'frequently, the rivalry between East and West was veiled and indirect, each side assuming instead of mentioning the other's existence as a competitive or negative model' (Gal and Kligman, 2000a: 9). The removal of this political 'Other' has been uncomfortable for both sides, but especially for the West, since it was after all the West (exemplified in Ronald Reagan's description of the Soviet Union as 'the Evil Empire') that was responsible for reinforcing the binary already implicit in Lenin's and Stalin's concepts of the 'class enemy'. Obviously the East–West binary constructed twin monoliths, obscuring multiple other layers of difference, between and within countries in Central and Eastern Europe such as those of culture, national identity, gender and class.

Even today, East and West continue to serve as mutual foils, mirroring each other in discourses that reinforce mutual prejudices. These oppositions testify to the apparent inability to define 'Our' identity without the existence of Another constructed as inferior to us. Dubravka Ugresic notes that 'Europe has rarely integrated, rather it has tended to banish. So the inhabitant of Europe has adopted ... the basic notions: *us*, Europeans, and *them*, people from beyond the border' (Ugrešić, 1998a: 243–4, 1998b: 303–4). She cites Zygmunt Bauman feeling 'tempted to say that the post-war creation (or, rather, re-creation) of Europe proved to be ... thus far the most lasting consequence of the communist totalitarian episode', from which a 'new European self-identity re-emerged, in an almost textbook fashion, as a *derivative of the boundary*' (Bauman, 1995: 244). The 'Wall in our heads', as East German dissidents earlier named it, still remains. The 'loss of the opponent' has not eliminated the gendered imagery of the East as a woman, and a poor, disadvantaged one at that. Nor has it led to a culture of reciprocity, or lessened mutual misunderstandings in constructions of the 'Other'.

Current Western media discourses about Central and Eastern Europe reflect these continuing prejudices. They tend to take one of two forms. The first centres on fears fomented by European Union enlargement. Media reports indulge in scare-mongering about the possibility of a mass migration of labour from the poorer East to the purportedly more affluent Western labour market. The second makes more explicit the tendency already implied here to foment a 'moral panic'. By playing on prejudice focused on questions of ethnicity and gender, it whips up primitive fears of a loss of national identity through being engulfed by the 'Other', specifically by Roma on the one hand and by East European prostitutes and/or trafficked women on the other. Media accounts construct an opposition between Russia and Eastern Europe as the main sending countries and West European countries as the principal destinations for trafficked women in the sex industry, sometimes depicted as being a larger and more profitable industry worldwide than the drug trade.

The gender specificities of such scenarios are rarely acknowledged, being overshadowed by fearful constructions of transnational organized crime. Rather, the focus is the potential harm to the labour markets, the welfare regimes and the moral climate of Western European countries. Julia O'Connell Davidson points out that the United Nation's protocol on trafficking adopted in 2000 'appears to approach trafficking as a sub-set of illegal migration'. She poses the question in this context as to why international agencies such as the UN as well as the European Union and individual countries have made 'trafficking' their focus, rather than squarely addressing the larger issue of migration and particularly the treatment of migrants in receiving countries. Davidson highlights the 'conceptual, definitional and methodological problems associated with the term "trafficking" ' and argues that 'it is the woolly and imprecise nature of the term "trafficking" that allows EU governments to state a commitment to combating the abuse and exploitation of migrant women and children whilst simultaneously setting in place an immigration system that is widely regarded as threatening fundamental human rights such as the right to asylum' (Davidson, 2003; see also Anderson and Davidson, 2004).[1]

Media-fomented 'moral panics' about potential swamping by East European 'Others' are particularly ironic in the light of the widespread political recognition that large-scale migration is an essential, though partial, solution to the problem of shrinking and ageing populations in Western Europe. Calling this a 'moral panic' is not intended to ignore, nor to belittle, the very real social, economic and political issues arising from European Union enlargement. It is worth pointing out, however, that the political and media treatment of such issues often fails to acknowledge their frequently highly gendered ramifications. In the case of East-to-West migration, it is not the well-being or otherwise of trafficked women which underlies Western European media and government concern, but rather the wish to defend Fortress Europe from an 'alien' East European 'Other'.

Mutual mistrust continues to characterize not just media and political discourses within broader geo-political East–West constellations. It has also loomed large in East–West dialogues about gender, often mired in mutually hostile imaginings. Laura Busheikin writes that 'the space for this relationship is already occupied – by preconceptions, ingrained habits of thought on both sides, and a panoply of various myths' (Busheikin, 1997: 12). Given the level of prejudice in Western depictions of Eastern European populations and social conditions, it is not surprising that East Europeans for their part reject Western analyses of their situation as distortions or caricatures.

Feminists in Central and Eastern Europe have resisted what they experience as Western ignorance, arrogance and complacency expressed in the presumption that Western feminist theoretical models could have relevance to the very different life experiences of women in the region.[2] Throughout, this book seeks to demonstrate the difficulties in analysing often contradictory data and interpreting trends across a range of countries which manifest differential rates and directions of change. This is a delicate process, especially from a perspective that seeks to be receptive and sensitive to analyses of social change as documented by the social actors and scholars who are themselves direct actors in and observers of those changes. Clearly I acknowledge that I write from the perspective of a Western feminist scholar, albeit one who has conducted research and worked closely with scholars and activists in the region for several decades. My prime concern has always been to try to avoid imposing from the outside an analysis that does not ring true to those whose experiences form the basis of it. For this reason I have privileged the voices of actors and the studies of scholars from the region, allowing them to speak for themselves.[3]

Reviewing the difficult dialogue between feminists from East and West in 1997, Hana Havelková suggests that 'the fault is on both sides' and that the 'the core of the misunderstanding in the dialogue between Eastern and Western European feminists is ... that we were assuming that a focus on women must necessarily mean the same thing in all contexts' (Havelková, 1997: 56–7).[4] In other words, the problem lay in a failure to take into account the different cultural and historical specificities in Eastern and Western Europe during the Cold War period. This critique echoes earlier criticisms by women from the South, in which Western feminists stood accused of a 'colonialist gaze' and hegemonic discursive presumptions. In her most recent contribution to this debate, Chandra Talpade Mohanty, author of the seminal 'Under Western Eyes', revisits her earlier article and concedes a potential for feminist solidarity in struggles against the increasing globalization of capital (Mohanty, 2003). In my view, the dialogue between feminists in East and West Europe, difficult as it has been at times during the past 15 years, has the potential to produce creative joint responses to the gendered constraints of the current (neo-liberal) model that continues to dominate current, new and future members of the European Union. It is in the spirit of contributing to understandings of the place of gender in the 'new' world order and to conceptualizations of the strategies best placed to achieve gender equitable societies that this study is written.

This monograph adopts a cross-cultural and comparative perspective on the potential for citizenship in an enlarging Europe. In so doing, it is unique both in its range and in its interdisciplinary approach.[5] It deploys gender as the category of analysis in evaluating the impact and direction of ongoing processes of social, economic and political transformation in Central and Eastern Europe. It considers the prospects for gender equitable citizenship and social justice under the twin impact of democratization and marketization within the larger frameworks of European Union enlargement and economic globalization. Individual chapters focus (as detailed at the end of this introductory chapter) on strategies of mainstream political participation versus civil society activism; gender inequalities in economic restructuring; the redrawing during transformation of the public–private divide; the influence of discourses of nation and identity and of gendered representations of masculinity and femininity.

The book's discussion of the prospects for gender equitable citizenship centres on gender as a structuring principle of the transformation process (Einhorn, 1993; Gal and Kligman, 2000a; Young, 1999: 226). Individual identities and the social relations to emerge from the transformation have been shaped by gendered inequalities of power. Gender norms – in other words dominant discourses around what constitutes masculinity and femininity – have been shown to colour discursive representations of nation and identity. Beyond that, gender has influenced the contours of labour markets, the climate of political cultures, indeed the very forms of citizenship on offer within the new social, economic and political formations in the region.

Difficulties in 'transition'

Before introducing further this book's arguments about the gendered nature of the 'transition' in Central and Eastern Europe, it is important to underline three ways in which the very notion of 'transition' is flawed when applied in this context. First, the descriptor 'transition' presumes prior knowledge of the outcome of these fundamental changes (from one known quantity: state socialism in this case, to another: Western-style capitalism), constructing change as a simple *shift* that in effect *ends* with the adoption of the neo-liberal market model, as opposed to a lengthy, complex and multi-layered *process* with both considerable country-specific variations and an uncertain and possibly quite diverse set of outcomes (Outhwaite and Ray, 2005: 22, 87). Second, it assigns positive value to this allegedly desirable – but in effect deadly – outcome embodied in the so-called Washington consensus that has been externally imposed on the region. It is noteworthy here that the process has not involved a 'transition' to West European or Scandinavian-style social market economies. Joseph Stiglitz writes of 'the challenges and opportunities of transition', but concludes that 'seldom has the gap between expectations and reality been greater than in the case of the transition from communism to the market'. For this failure in Russia, but also in most of the other countries in the region, he attributes at least part of the blame to those 'Western advisers, especially from the United States and the IMF, who marched in so quickly to preach the gospel of the market economy' (Stiglitz, 2002: 133, 136, 151).[6] Third, and most importantly for our argument here, however, the notion of 'transition' elides gender as a structuring dynamic of the economic, social and political transformations in the region (Gal and Kligman, 2000a: 10–13).[7]

Some analysts assert that the neo-liberal paradigm, sometimes known as the 'Washington consensus' is 'dead' (Rodrik, 2002, quoted in *The Economist*, 2002), hence that there may be a global 'transition' away from this model of governance. With its focus on three areas of economic reform – liberalization, deregulation and privatization – it dominated global development theory and practice during the 1980s and 1990s. This version of the neo-liberal model, the fundamentalist as opposed to the pragmatic approach, privileged market forces to the virtual exclusion of state intervention or regulation. Fundamentalists 'believe that the state is inevitably the key threat to liberty; that free enterprise is good in itself, not only for the growth it will bring; that markets are realms of freedom, and that promotion of entrepreneurship and innovation is not only key to efficiency and growth but is also good in itself' (Elson, 2002: 82).

Small wonder then, that it was the 'recipe' for transformation from a centralized state-led economy to a market economy prescribed for the countries of Central and Eastern Europe after the collapse of state socialist regimes in 1989 (Broad, 2004: 131). During this period 'the Washington Consensus became the only way; the desirability of its policies was presented as an objective economic truth' (Broad, 2004: 132). However, these policies did not necessarily result in the economic growth promised by their proponents. And their adverse effects became immediately apparent in the form of 'expanding inequity, increased environmental damage, decreased worker rights and benefits' (Broad, 2004: 132).

This interpretation of marketization as privatization has had particularly pernicious effects in Central and Eastern Europe. The negative impact of this form of neo-liberal agenda was further exacerbated during the 1990s, argues Robin Broad, when 'the Washington Consensus pushed its privatization plank further, this time into public services'

(Broad, 2004:141). Those disproportionately disadvantaged by neo-liberal policies include women, all workers and the poor. Broad identifies the 'vast unemployment ... and social havoc wreaked as governments shed control to the private sector', arguing that these policies also undermined human rights and democracy (Broad, 2004: 132, 141-2). This would suggest that the twin processes of democratization and marketization, heralded as the solution to all past problems in the region, in practice worked against each other, with predictably negative effects for both citizenship and gender equity.

Robin Broad asserts further that 'there is no question that, as of 2004, the era of "market fundamentalism" has ended' (Broad, 2004: 134). The campaign for debt relief and the opposition of anti-globalization activists provide testimony to its ongoing force as well as to the growing impetus of a movement to counter it. Increasingly, some economists such as the former World Bank chief economist and 2001 Nobel Prize laureate Joseph Stiglitz are also speaking out about its malign influence. Stiglitz has stressed 'the fallacy of letting the free-market rule without government intervention and regulation' (Stiglitz, 2002: 73, cited in Broad, 2004: 140). Yet despite such indications that acceptance of the need for state regulation is growing, this insight remains so far confined to an elite critique which has yet to be translated into a substantial policy shift, as Broad concedes (Broad, 2004: 146, 148).

On the other side of the state-market debate, a significant factor in Central and Eastern Europe that undoubtedly aided the introduction of 'market fundamentalism' in many of the countries in the region was the anti-state reaction which inevitably followed the previous years of state intervention into every sphere of life. This reflex was reinforced by three further currents flowing in the same direction. First, this anti-state stance was shared by Western feminist questioning of the merits of state intervention in the quest for gender equality (Allen, 1990). Second, globalization theorists argued that the nation state was losing its power in the face of global capital accumulation and the resulting transnational corporate power. Broad concedes that one reason the paradigm shift away from 'market fundamentalism' has so far had minimal policy impact is 'in part a tribute to the continuing grip of corporate interests over political institutions' (Broad, 2004: 148).

Third, as Margaret Somers powerfully argues, the newly charismatic concept of social capital dangerously elides acknowledgement of power and rights, in short the realm of the state and citizenship, from the agenda. It is itself a tool of neo-liberalism, signalling 'not the sociologizing of the market model but a *marketizing of the social*' (Somers, 2005: 7;

emphasis in original). The concept of social capital plays straight into the neo-liberal agenda of individual responsibility, ignoring the twin role of 'the decline of the welfare state and its ancillary social supports on the one hand, and the privatizing restructuring of the economy on the other' in fomenting increased poverty and inequality, and undermining understandings of democracy and citizenship. This has led in Central and Eastern European transformations to a corresponding degradation of the concept of civil society, such that 'the civil society concept has come to represent less rights-oriented democratic politics than merely an anti-statist appendage for the "compassionate" side of market society' (Somers, 2005: 17–18).

Clearly, then, there is growing scepticism on a number of grounds about the neo-liberal model as an unquestioned good to which the countries of Central and Eastern Europe should aspire. This scepticism underlines the doubtful value of the terminology of 'transition' as opposed to 'transformation' in studies of the region and informs much of the analysis that follows.

Problematic in itself is the tendency in the political discourse of 'transition' to equate democratization with civil society activism. International agencies, national governments and supra-national governments like the European Union alike have rhetorically invested civil society with immense power in the process. A European Commission report of June 2005 on civil society dialogue between the European Union and candidate countries pledges the European Union to 'support the further development of a lively and vibrant civil society in the candidate countries', which it sees as 'key to the consolidation of human rights and democracy, in line with the political criteria for accession' (EC, 2005a: 3). In practice this commitment has been less evident. The report acknowledges that in the first round of enlargement, 'citizens ... were not sufficiently informed or prepared'. In proposed dialogues with the next candidate countries, Turkey and Croatia, 'civil society should play the most important role' (EC, 2005a: 2). Chapter 2 explores further both the equation of democracy with civil society and the failure to involve civil society organizations in preparations for the first round of accession. Chapter 4 looks at the pitfalls of idealizing civil society organizations and their degradation within the neo-liberal market model.

Gender in transformation/transforming gender

Gender as a structuring dynamic of transformation was and continues to be conveyed in many countries through traditionalist discourses that re-emerged in the vacuum left by the demise of state socialist ideology (Outhwaite and Ray, 2005: 17). Discourses about the family re-inscribed notions of appropriate masculinity and femininity, simultaneously circumscribing the potential social, political and economic roles open to men and women. Such discourses went hand-in-hand with – and indeed justified, either prospectively or retrospectively – a modified social policy model that attempted to legitimate the need to shed labour by propounding a traditional family regime characterized by gender hierarchy and a male-breadwinner model.

The problem lies not simply in the fact that the chosen model of transformation constructs – and constrains – the identities available to individuals (Gal, 1997: 32). The gender stereotypes discursively deployed by this model have in turn influenced the shape and direction of the social, economic and political changes themselves. The reciprocal relationship between political discourses and the policies that emerge from them on the one hand, and individual citizens in their social roles and relationships on the other, is therefore mediated by gender. As Susan Gal and Gail Kligman write: 'Not only do state policies constrain gender roles, but ideas about and differences between men and women shape the ways in which states are imagined, constituted and legitimated' (Gal and Kligman, 2000b: 4).

In a transformation process shaped by the market-led neo-liberal model of democratization, notions of both the political subject and the economic actor tend to be construed as neutral and universal, yet are in practice gendered male. There have been a number of critiques within and outside the region of emerging 'masculine democracies' and the negative impact on social justice of exclusionary polities (Einhorn, 1991, 1995b: 15; Heinen, 1992: 135; Posadskaya, 1991, 1994: 168; Sperling, 1999: 98–145). Anne Phillips underlines this point when she argues that 'societies cannot confidently establish which policies are most just without the equal involvement of women and men, young and old – of the less as well as the more powerful members of the society' (Phillips, 2002: 132).

If the process of democratization has led to politics 'being redefined as a distinctively masculine endeavour', so too the process of marketization has resulted in 'the "defeminization" of waged labour' (Alsop, 2000: 85–116). In the early period, women bore a disproportionate share of the high unemployment that followed the introduction of market forces in most countries of the region. Extreme disparities between male and female unemployment rates have lessened in the intervening period in many countries, but the trend has persisted. In addition, women face much greater difficulties in finding re-employment, for a variety of reasons ranging from the closure or prohibitive pricing of formerly free and widely available childcare facilities, to discriminatory hiring practices on the part of both foreign and domestic firms. This means that women were during the 1990s disproportionately represented among the long-term unemployed. Such difficulties apply particularly to mothers with young children, and to women in the post-45 age bracket (Alsop, 2000; Lokar, 2000; Ruminska-Zimny, 2002; Steinhilber, 2001).

Mutually exclusive discourses on what constitutes masculinity and femininity after 1989 were accompanied by re-definitions of what constitutes 'men's work' and 'women's work'. This meant that women were unable to maintain the modest incursions into formerly male-dominated occupations that they had made during the state socialist period. Nor, however, have they been – as some economists had predicted they might be – able to compensate for these losses via growth within female-dominated sectors of the economy. The process of marketization in Central and Eastern Europe was treated as synonymous with a process of privatization. Women have been under-represented in the new private sector, not, as the economist Liba Paukert has argued in a paper for the International Labour Organization, because of presumed gender-specific reluctance to take risks. Rather they were structurally more tied to the public sector in terms of their predominance in clerical and administrative jobs or in education and the caring professions (Paukert, 1995).

Simultaneously with marketization came a structural shift from an industrial to a post-industrial economy. A similar shift has been faced by West European economies, but in a more gradual process. In Central and Eastern Europe this shift was telescoped into a much shorter space of time and its impact was heightened by the fact that it was part of a triple process involving marketization and privatization at the same time. The resulting expansion of the retail and service sectors was predicted in some quarters to benefit women because of (1) their existing predominance in these sectors; (2) their relatively high level of education and qualifications gained in the state socialist period; and (3) their experience in the earlier second or black economy (Fodor, 1997; Fong and Paul, 1992; Szalai, 2000). This prediction has not been borne out. Indeed, as jobs in the service sector, and in new IT-based clerical and administrative occupations became more attractive and better paid, so there was a shift towards male employment (Alsop, 2000; Steinhilber, 2001: 208). This trend is not confined to Central and Eastern Europe but has been noted earlier in relation to the field of information technology in Western Europe (Sutherland, 1990). It is a trend that might appear paradoxically to present a reversal of gender stereotypes with regard to 'men's' and 'women's' work. As new technology makes jobs cleaner and more highly skilled, requiring less physical effort, men opt to move into them, leaving women to perform the simple and repetitive tasks or the lower-status jobs which do not offer career-enhancement opportunities (Khotkina, 1994).

This discussion exemplifies the role of gender as both cause and effect in the development of new democratic polities and market economies, hence as a key component structuring the transformation process itself. Central to these processes is the role of political discourse. Here there is a gap between rhetoric and reality not dissimilar to that which featured centrally in the state socialist period (Einhorn, 1993, 1996: 223, 2000b: 108; Gal and Kligman, 2000b: 6). The paradigm of women in a dual role as workers and mothers in state socialist ideology was replaced in newly emergent traditionalist political discourses by an idealized vision of women in a unitary and sacred role as mothers. It is obvious that in practice, women's earning capacity is crucial to the survival of the families for which they are attributed primary responsibility. It should not therefore come as a surprise that while the level of female labour market participation has indeed fallen dramatically, it is still high by West European standards and continues to play a central role in women's sense of identity and worth (Alsop, 2000; Ashwin and Bowers, 1997; Einhorn, 1993, 1997; van Hoven-Iganski, 2000). Many personal testimonies by women link their sense of identity in large part to the social context of the workplace. Nonetheless, the discursive devaluation of women's paid employment has led in some cases, as an article on Bulgaria illustrates, to self-deprecation on the part of women themselves who suggest that what they do is not 'real' work (Petkova and Griffin, 1998).

These examples show the pernicious effect of the 'new' political discourses which effectively redraw the boundaries between the public and the private, with women discursively if not in practice displaced from the public spheres of mainstream politics and the labour market (Sperling, 2000). The corrosive effects of such discourses in the context of revived 'pre-Communist patriarchal attitudes' in some countries are evident in the view that 'women are considered second-rate both by men and by themselves'(Roman, 2001: 55).

Many studies have documented the importance of family and friendship networks as a kind of substitute civil society during the state socialist era, when they functioned as havens from the long arm of the state. Hana Havelková writes that the family 'assumed a special function as the refuge of moral values. ... It substituted for the public sphere. ... As the private sphere became more important, so did the role of women' (Havelková, 1993: 68–9). Slavenka Drakulić spoke about how apartments were 'mythical cult objects' during state socialism and about the need felt at that time 'to set a boundary between private and public' when 'the state wants it all public' (Drakulić, 1992: 91–2). Thus whilst state socialist rhetoric vaunted the public sphere and promised to socialize all aspects of life, ironically the citizens of these regimes erected boundaries which enshrined the public–private divide. Mira Marody has written of an 'us' (the people) versus 'them' (the state) dichotomy (Marody, 1990: 268, 1991: 112–13, 1992: 2–3). It is this legacy that explains women's current reluctance to politicize the personal (Duhaček, 1998a).

There is a dual paradox here, contrasting both with Western Europe, where feminists busied themselves in the 1970s and 1980s demolishing the public–private divide, and with the reversal of values ascribed to the public and the private during the transformation period. The private, prized in the state socialist past as the sole site of individual autonomy, has lost its value in a landscape that discursively elevates the public spheres of the polity and the market. The devalued currency of the private is not revalued by the discursive moral gloss painted over it. Rhetorical 'elevation' to responsibility for the private sphere serves merely to mask women's demotion from public political and economic status. One could say that both the state socialist period and the period of social, economic and political transformation are not simply characterized by, but actually constructed and legitimized by gendered discourses of the public and the private. Perhaps the sole difference is in the signifiers, the contrary ideological meanings attached to those spheres and to the gender-'appropriate' roles within them ascribed to both men and women. Where state socialist ideology prioritized women's productive over their reproductive role, democratization and marketization have opened up the public sphere, but encoded it as the sovereign space of men, with women allotted economically and politically secondary status.

Gendered nationalisms

Discourses that prevailed in some countries in the region towards the end of the state socialist period and beyond ascribed to women prime responsibility not simply for the individual family, but also for the family of the nation. Depending on the specific cultural context, women have been respectively allotted a life of sacrifice 'taking comfort in the Virgin Mary's example' (Harsanyi, 1993: 40); cast as heroic women mediating for their men and children the harsh burdens of the transformation, for example in the mould of strong, 'brave women' during the 150 years of Polish partition (Graff, 2002; Titkow, 1993: 253); seen as icons of motherhood with a 'symbolic mission' as saviours of the nation (Bracewell, 1996; Lisyutkina, 1993: 282); or given the task of bearing babies for the nation (*The Guardian*, 7 June 1990). Nationalist discourses rely on rigidly gender-divided roles that allow women 'a strictly limited sphere of action – to reproduce the nation – and men are instructed to defend it' (Milić, 1993: 120). In such constructions, women have a symbolically important function but are disempowered as citizens. Nationalist discourses are in fact not just gendered, but also discriminatory in class and ethnic terms in dictating which women are entitled to become mothers of the nation, and which men's children they may bear (Yuval-Davis, 1996).

Emergent discourses of national identity have been particularly marked reactions, not only to the earlier political and economic hegemony of the Soviet Union, but also to the universalist rhetoric employed by regimes that subsumed differences under the presumption that socialism's driving force was egalitarianism. The attraction of a politics of difference sits comfortably with the individualist discourses of liberal democracy, but can also be explained in terms of this reaction, just as the strong pressures for regional autonomy and/or devolution into smaller national units in parts of Western Europe can be seen as a reaction against the feared development of the European Union as super-state.

In a manner similar to the gendered political discourses already discussed, nationalist discourses expose a reciprocal relation between rhetoric and its impact on people's lives. If the nation is imagined as a woman, women are also thought to embody the nation. Narrowly framed notions of appropriate masculinity and femininity equate femininity with maternity and construe women as 'mothers of the nation' whose duty it is not only physically to reproduce the nation but also to embody and pass on the nation's moral, cultural and spiritual values to the next generation. Such gendered discourses have very real consequences for individual men and women living within the states that espouse them. Thus the ethnically defined national identities imposed on the citizens of former Yugoslavia led to rape being deployed as an instrument of war by all sides in the war in Bosnia-Herzegovina, but primarily by Serb men seeking to destroy the property and the very cultural identity of Bosnian Muslims (Enloe, 1998; Salecl, 1994; Seifert, 1996). When symbolically women signify as Mother Earth, the body and territory of the nation, actual conflicts are played out on real women's bodies (as has occurred in many earlier historically documented cases, such as that of the German women raped after the Second World War or the Korean comfort women tortured and maltreated by Japanese government edict during the Second World War). Symbolic representations of the homeland are transformed into bloody reality. Militarized nationalism presents an extreme case of the instrumentalization of gender, and through it, of people's lives. It illustrates the very real danger that rigid and reactionary imaginings of masculinity and femininity pose in practice in terms of bodily as well as emotional harm to real women and real men.

Another arena in which gender has demonstrably acted as a structuring principle of the transformation is that of reproductive politics. This is often linked with discourses of nationalism in that fears of demographic decline fuel racist discourses when the dominant ethnic group perceives itself as threatened by a minority, as in the case of the Roma in Hungary or the Ukraine. A striking, related phenomenon in the rush to introduce democracy and the rule of law was the attack in many countries on laws legalizing access to abortion. This at first sight surprising and apparently counter-intuitive fact inspired Gal and Kligman's multi-country study of 'reproduction as politics' (Gal and Kligman, 2000b). Here was an apparent paradox: given the severe economic and social upheaval caused by the twin processes of democratization and marketization, why should an aspect of (reproductive) life seemingly so firmly located within the sphere of private moral and ethical decision-making have been something which in the case of Germany almost derailed the process of unification, in Poland led to years of political campaigning, and in both resulted in markedly more restrictive legislation than in the past? The rush to restrict access to abortion clearly demonstrates one thing: reproductive rights – and specifically abortion – raise the political temperature precisely because they are located at the very apex of the public–private divide (Einhorn, 1993: 74; Gal and Kligman, 2000a). Who has the right to decide on reproductive issues? Individual women, or the state? If it is the latter, surely this not only negates women's capacity to act as moral beings in their own right; more than that, it denies them full political subject status as equal citizens.

Feminist sightings: prospects for citizenship

Notwithstanding the gendered constraints identified in many of the developments to date, it would be a mistake to see only the difficulties and not the undoubted opportunities offered by the fundamental processes of social change in Central and Eastern Europe. New political and social spaces have opened up, enabling women to construct challenges to the prevailing gendered relations of power. Politicians, NGOs, regional networks and new Gender Studies programmes are all contributing to the formulation of alternative discourses and political strategies. East–West discussions and joint research projects are on the increase, many of them funded by international agencies or supranational instances like the European Commission.

Whether through lobbying for quotas to increase the level of female political representation and influence legislation and policy, or through the advocacy of civil society networks such as Karat at the regional and international level, women in Central and Eastern Europe have stepped into the arena of the public political realm and are making themselves heard and seen as a force to be reckoned with.

Groups exerting pressure on their national governments are able successfully to draw on the language of international standards set out in CEDAW (Convention on the Elimination of all Forms of Discrimination Against Women) or EU directives, or on the shared experiences of groups and research from West European or Southern countries. The resourcefulness and sheer determination of several regional projects and networks, their analytical clarity and the speed of their success in having quotas adopted or national machineries made more effective in some cases and countries, sets a standard that women's networks in Western Europe and elsewhere can only admire and wish to emulate. It is this activism and its successes, especially in coalitions formed across cultural, ethnic or national boundaries with other civil society organizations, political parties, scholars and other social groupings that embody real hopes of achieving a more gender equitable citizenship, both within and beyond the region of Central and Eastern Europe.

The analysis of trends evident in the transformation process from a standpoint of over 15 years after the Fall of the Berlin Wall allows us to extend theoretical discussions about the public–private divide, the role of civil society and the potential for gender equitable citizenship in Central and Eastern Europe and beyond. This study is based on recent empirical and qualitative data emanating in the main from within the region itself. Its aim is to show how discourses, representations, policies and practices deployed during the transformation process continue to reveal gender as constitutive of the identities available in the new economic, social and political environments. Detailed analyses contained in each chapter demonstrate the sometimes paradoxical, contradictory and ambivalent ways in which the transformation has been and is being both conceptualized and implemented. The constraints on and opportunities for gender equitable citizenship within an enlarging Europe provide the core focus of analyses crossing a wide range of contexts: mainstream politics, civil society activism, the public–private divide, discourses of national identity, media representations and the labour market.

Structure of the book

A key influence shaping the pace and direction of political, social and economic transformation during the past five years has been the process of European enlargement. Eight countries from the region became members of the European Union in 2004.[8] Bulgaria and Romania are due to join in 2007, and Croatia is currently a candidate country, together with Turkey. Chapter 2 discusses issues of governance in an enlarging Europe, including debates surrounding gender mainstreaming as an EU policy. It also considers two alternative strategies for pushing policymaking in a gender equitable direction: increasing the level of female representation in mainstream politics and civil society mobilization.

Among the contradictory potential effects of accession to the European Union for Central and Eastern European countries, it is worth noting four here. First, positive pressure is being exerted on accession countries to adopt a gender mainstreaming strategy. Yet this is a contested policy, and one that existing member states are themselves far from implementing fully. Even in the European Union itself, 'in no policy area ... has gender mainstreaming been firmly established' (Bretherton, 2001: 61). Second (directly undermining the positive potential of using EU standards as leverage on national governments), during discussions about European Union enlargement, 'a strong argument was made that aspects of the *acquis*, including social policy areas such as gender equality and safety at work, should be set aside to facilitate accession'. Gender analysis was notable by its absence from the European Commission's 1995 White Paper on enlargement, generating fears 'that CEE governments would be encouraged to regard gender inequality, and other social problems, as unimportant (marginal)'. Third, the policy of gender mainstreaming was not integrated into the European Commission's strategy for a future, enlarged European Union. This 'failure to mainstream gender in *Agenda 2000* fuelled strong fears that enlargement will entail a general weakening of EU equality policy' (Bretherton, 2001: 69–70; see also Mazey, 2000 and Watson, 2000b). Fourthly and finally, a gender mainstreaming approach can be seen as inadequate in countries like Poland where there were no existing parallel equal opportunities policies (Heinen and Portet, 2002: 159).

Gender mainstreaming is itself a contested policy. Some analysts argue that it is only under pressure from transnational institutions – in this case the European Union – that national governments feel compelled to comply with gender equality norms. Yet in the case of Poland, there was evidence of non-compliance which did not impede or delay the accession process.[9] An alternative argument asserts that many EU gender equality policies themselves only exist as the direct result of grassroots pressure from women's and feminist activist groups. Jacqui True and Michael Mintrom maintain that the findings of their quantitative study of Central and Eastern European countries in the run-up to accession show clearly that the adoption of gender mainstreaming policies and machineries is directly linked to the strength of women's civil society activism (True and Mintrom, 2001; see also Hoskyns, 1996). Yet gender mainstreaming can also be seen as paying lip service to gender equity targets that are then undermined by the inadequate power or insufficient funding base of the institutional structures responsible for implementing the policy at national level. This reveals in many countries a lack of political will underpinning the move towards gender mainstreaming.

The third chapter moves from theoretical debate to examine the arena of mainstream politics and the quest for gender equitable political representation. Prior to EU accession negotiations, gender was marginal on the political agenda of the democratization process. Indeed what counts as 'political' had been narrowed in the process to denote formal party and parliamentary politics alone. This chapter explores the contradiction between this definition and the discursive validation of civil society involvement, both within the region and by international donor organizations. Finally, it discusses strategies such as the introduction of quotas that are designed to overcome the hurdles limiting women's capacity to become active citizens in the public sphere of politics.

The fourth chapter explores how the parameters of the civil society to emerge from economic liberalization not only categorize and circumscribe those activities considered 'political', but also affect the very formation of political identities and the spaces within which those identities can be mobilized. It identifies the deeply gendered nature of both the processes of political identity formation and the spaces available for political activity.

This chapter analyses the relationships of civil society theory to gender and feminism as well as to liberal democratic politics. Further, it critiques the propensity on the part of both governments and international agencies to idealize the realm of civil society, in part to the detriment of developing a political culture that could promote women's interests or an agenda incorporating gender equity. It elaborates the notion of a civil society 'trap' in which civil society becomes a euphemism for NGOs run by women that fill the gap in welfare provision left by the retreating state. Finally, it suggests that even in the best-case scenario where NGOs and civil society associations are valued for their creative contribution to political culture, there is the danger of a civil society 'gap' characterized by a lack of mechanisms for, or readiness to engage in, dialogue between state-level policy institutions and civil society associations.

The chapter provides empirical data on women's movements and NGOs in the region within the context of theoretical discussions about practical versus strategic gender interests (Molyneux, 1998/2001) or women's versus feminist movements (Alvarez, 1999). Many groups in the region during this period have been involved in 'social' rather than 'political' activism and as such occupy a 'parallel' space in avoidance of mainstream politics (Jalušić, 2002: 105). Yet there are signs of emerging feminist trends (Graff, 2001). Finally, the chapter discusses how NGO dependence on donor funding can influence the issues around which they mobilize. Gender equality directives of the European Union have provided groups with the discursive 'armoury' with which to make their claims. Yet this has also had the potential to dictate the issues that would gain approval (and funding) from Brussels (Regulska, 2001).

Chapter 5 of this volume examines how the transformation process has transformed the relationship between the public and the private. The issues it singles out for consideration are: debates about and shifts in the public–private divide; the impact of altered social policy models on gender roles in the family, looking specifically at the question of domestic labour; demographic changes and the question of childcare provision; issues of reproductive politics, including the cases of abortion and violence against women (at both the personal and the national level). The re-creation of national identities based on nostalgic ideals of femininity and masculinity reinforced women's primary responsibility for the private sphere, thus restricting any collective action they potentially undertook within the discursive limits of the public–private, political–non-political divide: 'Post-socialist transitions ostensibly to liberal capitalism and democracy have been able to rely on prior gendered social arrangements in the family and at the heart of civil society' (True, 2000: 75; see also Roman, 2001). Moreover, experiences of conflict and nation-building since 1989 have served in some countries to reproduce fixed and unchanging essentialist gender identities. Attempts to achieve greater gender equality in this context have sometimes appeared fruitless (Jalušić, 2002).

Chapter 6 looks at the way individualist consumer culture and the media influence the possibilities of identity formation. The death of state socialism's ideal type, self-sacrificing Superwoman, able to juggle a career, motherhood and political involvement has ushered in images of femininity that present new versions of the old virgin–whore duality. With the exception of the new female entrepreneur, Superwoman's successor, women are represented either as idealized symbols of chaste but subservient motherhood or as Westernized fashionistas or sexualized objects of pornography. This binary may exaggerate how limited the range of images of femininity available in the market are. Yet advertising and the new print media manifest strong trends towards sexualization on the one hand and traditionalization on the other. Thus the chapter exposes contradictions between the ostensible opening up of choice implied by the newly acquired freedom of the press, and processes of closure in which the available images of acceptable femininity imply conformity rather than difference and individuality.

Chapter 7 considers as an important factor affecting the transformation process the radical shift in the global historical and geo-political contexts, particularly in terms of the growing power of global capital. In place of the old binary confrontation of would-be socialist states based on a centrally planned economy on one side of the Cold War divide, and democratic market economies on the other, economic restructuring to conform with the neo-liberal market model is now the globally dominant paradigm. This paradigm privileges the market as the sole regulator of society, at the expense of the state and hence also of social safety nets. It can be expressed as the dominance of economic reform over political direction and social welfare. Western European societies, perhaps especially Britain, have to differing extents been in the grip of this model for 20 years longer than the countries of Eastern and Central Europe. Yet this model has obvious implications for gender relations, for equal opportunities, and for social justice that either are already – or will become – shared experiences between women and men in Eastern, Central and Western Europe.

The chapter discusses the gendered character of unemployment during the transformation process; discriminatory advertising and hiring practices; the gender pay gap; occupational segregation; and the impact of social policy changes on pension entitlements.

The final chapter (Chapter 8) returns to the central question running through the entire book, namely that of the utility of the concept of citizenship in striving towards a society characterized by gender equity. It begins with a discussion of the discourse of 'empowerment', sometimes preferred in the development literature to the notion of citizenship status, as an alternative to citizenship's undue focus on state institutions, mainstream political parties and legislative instruments. It proceeds to discuss the relative merits of discourses of rights as against discourses of capabilities and finally of entitlements, in theorizing a form of citizenship most amenable to producing gender equity. The book concludes with a celebration of the activities of regional networks and the positive potential of coalition politics to transcend gender, national and regional divides.

2
Issues of Governance
Contested Strategies for Gender Equity

Introduction

This chapter is concerned with the opportunities for and constraints on gender equitable governance in Central and Eastern Europe.[1] It elaborates theoretical concerns and debates about the most propitious strategies to achieve this end. One of the facets of this discussion concerns the distinction between feminist, movement-based campaigns for social justice, and the acceptance of gender equality as a political goal that can be approached bureaucratically, for example by top-down state-led policies such as gender mainstreaming. This theoretical discussion sets the scene for the two subsequent chapters, which present detailed country-based data and analysis on two specific arenas for the implementation of gender equity: mainstream politics (Chapter 3), and civil society mobilization (Chapter 4).

The theoretical discussion of this chapter focuses on three key issues in the quest for gender equitable citizenship, all of which illustrate the complexity of what is at stake, the varying pace and scope of change, and some of the factors influencing these changes. The three issues are

- hindrances to and mechanisms for increasing female political representation and introducing gender-sensitive policies into mainstream politics;
- contestations about the role and efficacy of civil society activism in contrast to mainstream political involvement;
- pros and cons of gender mainstreaming as the EU-sponsored policy for the achievement of gender equality outcomes.

The transformation process in Central and Eastern Europe to date has been undertaken – as have political restructuring processes in Western European 'old' EU member states – under the aegis of an assumed consensus around the neo-liberal market model. This version of the 'convergence theory ' is the result of a transition from a bi-polar to a uni-polar world dominated by the processes of economic globalization on the one hand, and US-led neo-liberal rhetoric affecting politics, economics and social policy on the other. In Central and Eastern Europe it marks the policy outcome of political abandonment of the socialist rhetoric of egalitarianism and social justice in favour of the liberal discourse of individual liberty and (economic) opportunity.

The fundamental nature of this transformation has resulted in profound social as well as economic and political dislocations. The relative retreat of the state from welfare provision within the externally imposed neo-liberal paradigm has exacerbated the impact of economic restructuring. Some of the negative effects have been huge increases in poverty, and a widening income gap (Daskalova, 2000: 339). Some authors would claim that one of the most definitive effects has been the re-emergence of class as a social determinant in the region (Gapova, 2002; Regulska, 2002). Economic losses are presented as more than matched by new opportunities, both in terms of entrepreneurship and the freedom (not always matched by the capability) to organize politically. Yet in several countries the increased space for individuation and the establishment of differentiated identities has encouraged discrimination, marginalization – and in extreme cases – conflict based on ethnic or religious 'otherness'.

Clearly there have been differences in approach and in the implementation of the neo-liberal agenda. Poland's radical economic restructuring strategy contrasts with the Czech Republic's mix of neo-liberal and social democratic elements of reform (Steinhilber, 2006). In social policy terms, this is reflected in 'the tension between a tradition of – and in some countries continued commitment to – extensive welfare provisioning and substantive income redistribution through the state on the one hand, and the residualist social policy set-up advocated by the currently dominant global neo-liberal economic framework on the other' (Steinhilber, 2006). Nonetheless, the currently dominant influence of IMF/World Bank neo-conservative ideology – combined with the pressures of EU accession – has led to a level of 'real' convergence between Eastern and Western Europe that could facilitate the acknowledgement of common issues among feminist scholars across Europe.

The discursive accompaniment to transformation has highlighted gains in civil and political rights, while the process itself has been, in material terms, almost entirely focused on economic restructuring: marketization, interpreted as privatization. Thus, while EU accession embodied hopes because of the European Union's formal commitment to gender equality through gender mainstreaming, it has in practice meant a process of economic alignment and integration. In this process, concerns not only for gender equality, but also for citizenship and social justice are marginalized. The political is seen as secondary to the economic, and hence issues of gender justice, always an add-on to central EU concerns about the labour market, are marginalized (Jezerska, 2003: 172). Indeed, in the aftermath of the 'no' votes in the referenda on an EU Constitution in Holland and France in 2005, the talk is of a retreat from a politically united Europe, and a return to the free trade association of the original EEC (European Economic Community). This scenario constitutes a further threat to concerns for gender equality – in terms both of social justice and parity in political representation.

Uncertainty about the future of the European Union compounds existing doubts about how genuine EU commitment to social and gender justice is. Ironically, it was concern to protect their superior welfare state in France and the Netherlands that in part prompted their 'no' vote. In the UK, by contrast, the possibility of appeal to the European Court of Justice, or the European Court of Human Rights has been seen by feminist activists as giving them leverage, providing a mechanism by which the supra-regional government of the EU could apply pressure on the more reactionary national state, thus forcing implementation of EU gender-equality directives. In Britain, the beginning of the Thatcher government in 1979 had signalled the end of the consensus about the post-Second World War welfare state based on universal entitlements, and the end therefore also of assumptions about citizenship being based on social as well as economic and political rights.

Strategies for gender equitable citizenship

Regardless of their adherence to particular versions of feminist theory, feminists in East and West, North and South deliberate on the optimal strategies for the achievement of more gender equitable polities and societies. There is debate about whether an increased level of female political representation is indeed a sufficient, or even a necessary condition for achieving that end (Lépinard, 2005). Two particular approaches that currently loom large on the international agenda but whose relative merits are contested, are: gender mainstreaming as a top-down policy designed to achieve gender equality in public policy, and quotas as a movement-advocated means to increase the level of women's political representation. Discussions about these strategies in some sense replay older debates concerning the merits of top-down versus bottom-up approaches.[2] Mihaela Miroiu has critiqued the introduction of anti-discriminatory legislation in Romania in the run-up to EU accession as 'feminism from above', or 'room-service feminism' bringing with it uncomfortable echoes of the past (Miroiu, 2004: 96). Such debates also symbolize the difference between gender-neutral approaches to equality of opportunity and gender specific positive action policies designed to overcome the legacy of culturally reinforced social hierarchies of gender inequality.

Both these strategies are relevant mainly at the national level. Another approach is the policy of gender mainstreaming, adopted by the United Nations at the 1995 Beijing World Conference on Women and very much favoured by the European Union. Gender mainstreaming is highly relevant to discussions and developments within the region of Central and Eastern Europe, since it – at least formally – formed part of the negotiations and preparations for the 2004 accession to the EU of the first eight countries from the region. This third approach to increasing gender equity in turn raises questions as to what is the most appropriate frame for addressing equalities issues: the nation-state or supra-national bodies such as the European Union. This chapter therefore discusses the three strategies for gender equity described above and also raises questions about the most relevant framework for achieving them.

The Beijing Platform for Action called for the introduction of gender equality legislation and the establishment of National Women's Machineries to facilitate and monitor their implementation. International agencies such as the United Nations and supra-national governmental bodies such as the European Union have since then favoured gender mainstreaming strategies utilizing these mechanisms, especially in relation to development and structural adjustment policies. Gender mainstreaming has been defined in a variety of ways, not always consistent with each other, nor with clarity of meaning. The UK's Department for International Development describes it as 'a commitment to ensure that women's as well as men's concerns and experiences are integral to the design, implementation, monitoring and evaluation of all legislation, policies and programmes so that women and men benefit equally and inequality is not perpetuated'. It stresses that 'gender mainstreaming does not preclude women-only projects. It shifts their focus from women as a target group, to gender equality as a goal' (Derbyshire, 2002). BRIDGE, the gender research and information unit at the Institute for Development Studies, UK, shifts the emphasis from an ideological commitment to gender equality, to a more narrow institutional focus.

It sees gender mainstreaming as 'an organisational strategy' designed 'to bring a gender perspective to all aspects of an institution's policy and activities, through building gender capacity and accountability' (Reeves and Baden, 2000: 11).

In many regions of the world, as well as in the context of European Union enlargement, this strategy is hampered by the lack of women in legislatures. Women's rights or gender equality as a goal is, with few exceptions, not the priority of political parties so that political parties do little to foster increased levels of female representation.[3] During the run-up to EU accession, for example, the Polish Centre for Women's Rights stated that 'Poland has done nothing to adjust its legislation to EU standards in the field of equal status of women and men and that issue is probably the last item on the government priorities list' (Nowakowska and Piwnik, 2000: 114).

Suspicion of top-down statist approaches that was prevalent in the early years of transformation has persisted in some countries and goes some way to explaining the enhanced status of NGO activity in the region as opposed to mainstream political involvement. This suspicion was a perfectly understandable reaction to the experience of an all-powerful and invasive state during the socialist period (Szalai, 1990). Nor is anti-statism peculiar to East European feminisms (Mansbridge, 2003). When Western or Southern feminists ponder whether or not to 'give up on the state' they are (with the exception perhaps of Latin American countries re-establishing democratic institutions after the end of authoritarian rule) not speaking from a position of experiences of the state similar to those in Central and Eastern Europe. The resistance to state-led solutions has – until recently – expressed itself, among other ways, in rejection of the use of quotas as a political strategy.

Quotas seem to many feminists from the region to smack of the undemocratic manipulation of the political process by the previous regimes through the installation of puppet 'representatives' in parliaments, whose job it was merely to rubber-stamp decisions taken elsewhere, that is in the Central Committees and Politburos of the ruling Communist Parties (with women notably absent from those higher echelons of political power) (Einhorn, 1993; Jezerska, 2003: 171). However, the experience of dramatic falls in the level of female political representation in early democratic elections in several countries in the region eventually led to shifts in this attitude.[4] Women activists in Georgia, Latvia and Poland, for example, now advocate the adoption of quotas for women as the necessary short-term strategy for achieving some level of critical mass of women, and thus as a mechanism for the achievement of gender equality in parliaments and legislatures. In Poland, strong lobbying by the Women's Pre-election Coalition (comprising women's groups and NGOs from all over the country) led to the adoption by three political parties of a 30 per cent quota rule. This was probably influential in attaining an increased percentage of female parliamentarians, with their share rising from 13 per cent in 1997 to 20 per cent in 2001 in the Sejm (Lower House) and from 12 per cent to 23 per cent in the same period in the Senate (Upper House) (Fuszara, 2000; Spurek, 2002). At the same time, interviews with women politicians in Slovakia still reveal a 'deep distrust towards quotas and in several cases also lack of gender awareness and sensitivity' (Bitušiková, 2005c: 9).

Drude Dahlerup and Lenita Freidenvall (2005) point out that quotas are not the only, or even necessarily the optimal route to equal representation for women. The doubling of women's share of seats in the UK Parliament in 1997 from 9 per cent to 18.9 per cent on the basis of some 'women-only' candidate lists (Lovenduski, 2001: 744) counters the argument that 'many historical leaps in women's parliamentary representation can occur without quota provisions, just as the mere introduction of quotas has not resulted in uniform increases in the number of women parliamentarians worldwide'. Nevertheless, despite the complex difficulties associated with implementation, introducing 'electoral gender quotas as an affirmative action measure to increase women's representation', adopted now in many countries worldwide, is a first step towards equality in political representation (Dahlerup and Freidenvall, 2005: 27).

A further reason for seeking to increase levels of women's political representation in national legislatures is particularly pertinent in the case of Central and Eastern Europe. There is a need to address the loss of social entitlements that followed the transformation process (Daskalova, 2000: 346–7). During a 1995 political debate in Hungary, the proposal to dismantle remaining universal social welfare entitlements was justified by arguments that 'social expenditures have to be brought down to secure a "healthy" economy, while welfare universalism had to be abolished to ensure economic "growth"' (Haney, 2002: 186). Women's relative loss of access to the labour market has been well documented (Einhorn, 1993, 1997; Lokar, 2000). So also have the issues of discriminatory hiring practices and sexual harassment that have followed. (Daskalova, 2000: 340, 342; Einhorn, 1997; Lokar, 2000; NWP/OSI, 2002; see also Chapter 7 for further discussion of these issues).

The neo-liberal market paradigm empowers the male economic actor as the citizen with the capacity to exchange contracts in the marketplace. Without publicly provided social entitlements, for example to adequate and affordable childcare, in a context where they are still seen as primarily responsible for looking after children, women do not have an equal capacity to access the public spheres of either the market or the polity. This situation is exacerbated by the nationalist and religious discourses paramount in several countries of the region which allot women sole responsibility for the private sphere and enjoin them to produce babies for the nation (Daskalova, 2000: 350; Gapova, 1998; Slapšak, 1997; Zhurzhenko, 2001b). Such discourses insidiously both reinforce the economy's need to shed labour and legitimize the closure of childcare facilities.

In these contexts, it is necessary to rethink the optimal modality for the achievement of gender equitable outcomes, particularly in relation to the question of women's full participation in determining the policies and practices that affect their lives, exerting influence as active political subjects. I have expounded elsewhere (Einhorn, 1995a: 218–28, 2000a: 110–16, 2000b: 110) a theory of social *entitlements* rather than one of individual *rights* as best facilitating conceptual and practical linkages between state, market and household. It is necessary to reiterate here that the state, historically the locus of welfare and social provision, and the actor with regulatory power over working conditions, has a crucial role to play in enabling women to develop the capacity to access both market and polity on an equal basis with men. Obviously the nation state's power to enforce decent working conditions is waning in the face of powerful transnational corporations. In future, therefore, there will be a need to develop transnational regulatory bodies for the protection of citizens' and workers' rights. However, for the short- to medium-term, in the absence of easily recognizable or accessible bodies of this kind, political participation at the nation state level will remain important. Moreover, the national state is both more accessible and more accountable than international institutions. The extent to which the regulatory role in relation to issues of social justice and gender equity hitherto played by the nation state is increasingly taken on by supranational legislative and enforcement bodies such as the European Parliament or the European Court of Justice, is a development to be watched.

The role of the nation state in political representation

The mutual influence and two-way effects – in East and West – of European Union enlargement has repercussions for the question to be discussed in this section. The issue is whether the relevant frame for rights claims in the era of EU enlargement (and in the wider context of globalization) is the nation state or supra-national institutions such as the European Union. Nancy Fraser argues that today, 'the Keynesian-Westphalian frame is losing its aura of self-evidence' (Fraser, 2005: 2). For her, this loss of self-evidence denotes the demise of West European social democratic welfare states as a result of neo-liberal policies. Simultaneously, it represents challenges to the nation state as the unquestioned address for citizenship claims by supra-national institutions of governance such as the EU and the UN, but also, more powerfully still, by corporate economic power. Fraser asserts therefore that in the post-social democratic era 'it is no longer axiomatic that the modern territorial state is the appropriate unit for thinking about issues of justice, nor that the citizens of such states are the pertinent subjects' (Fraser, 2005: 3; see also Walby, 2003).

Fraser argues that greater social justice can be achieved through transnational solidarity, backed up by supra-national institutions of governance that are in a position to mediate between local (or national) claims and the forces of economic globalization. This is a very attractive proposition, and some evidence of it exists already in the form of the very effective transnational networking among NGOs that has emerged since the 1995 UN Conference on Women in Beijing. Nevertheless, the jury is still out on whether the nation-state has been superseded by regional or international institutions in terms of its ability to confer citizenship rights or implement human rights. It is still indisputably the nation-state, for example, that has the power of inclusion and exclusion, particularly in terms of permitting immigrants and refugees to gain access to nationality and hence also to citizenship rights.

Despite the evident difficulties of engagement with state institutions, the argument that feminists should not give up on the state, 'not least because it will not give up on women' (Stewart, 1996: 39) is still powerful. A recent Hungarian study demonstrates clearly the continuing relevance and power of the national – or indeed in many cases the local – state as the address and the implementing authority for welfare claims (Szalai, 2005). The local state in Hungary (and elsewhere) has the power, not merely to distribute benefits in a social welfare regime based on residual needs rather than universal entitlements, but also to act as the arbiter of eligibility. In so doing, the state also *structures* social inequality. This study illustrates clearly that the local state is not a monolithic, faceless bureaucracy, but in fact consists of 90 per cent female officials who discriminate against female claimants on the grounds of their perceived 'otherness'. In judging who qualifies as 'deserving' poor, local women welfare officials apply gendered and racist discourses in judging Roma women as 'irresponsible' for having too many (of the wrong kind of) children. Excluding them from welfare entitlements has the effect of denying them full political and social rights, hence equal citizenship status with the majority Hungarian population. Júlia Szalai argues convincingly that this example demonstrates how discourses of *cultural* otherness become translated into *structural* discrimination (Szalai, 2005).

In 2004, a special issue of the *International Feminist Journal of Politics* was devoted to exploring issues of gender and governance in the era of globalization (Waylen and Rai, 2004). In it, Shirin Rai argues persuasively that 'comparative feminist scholarship provides key insights into the constitutive, gendered nature of the state in the global political economy and thus challenges the "declining state" thesis'. She documents the 'decisive shift' in the 1990s 'from scepticism and caution towards the state to an engagement with and embrace of state institutions' on the part of feminists (Rai, 2004: 584, 586). She had argued earlier that the danger of co-optation of the national machineries and their 'gender agenda' by the state does not negate 'the importance of the state as an arena for furthering gender justice' (Rai, 2003: 19). Of particular pertinence to this chapter is the centrality of women's movement efforts to change state policy both by arguing for quotas for women in state legislatures, and through engagement with the national machineries for gender mainstreaming.

Discussing the relevance of the nation state to gender equality aspirations in Central and Eastern Europe, Joanna Regulska observes that 'neither the official "sameness" imposed by the communist political culture nor the "difference" engendered by differing degrees of democratization has liberated women as fully participating political actors' (Regulska, 2002: 11–12). She therefore poses the question: 'Will the fact that women have not found significant opportunities in formal, domestic political structures make them more likely to search for alternative ways to act politically beyond the nation-state?' The impressively effective international lobbying activities of Karat, a coalition of NGOs in Central and Eastern Europe and the former Soviet Union, might suggest an affirmative response. Yet this transnational networking complements rather than supplants the nation state's role as addressee for citizenship claims, at least for the present time.

Whilst it is true that the existence of the European Court of Human Rights has enabled some individuals within the European Union to take their own governments to court, this is costly and difficult, and surely represents the exception. This possible route for remedying gender injustice is an example of negative political freedom, in the tradition of nineteenth- century liberal democratic theory. It also exemplifies the way that human rights discourse – and indeed classical liberal citizenship discourse – focuses on the individual, rather than on social groups, whereas gender equity – despite the multiple differences and inequalities among women fostered by the neo-liberal market model – demands the overcoming of structural disadvantage as opposed to mere individual difficulty. Most women in Western Europe, whether they are exercised about the continuing gender pay gap, the glass ceiling, occupational segregation in all its forms, parental leave, domestic violence, lesbian rights, or the rights of migrant women and female asylum seekers, possess neither the social nor the financial capital to access such supra-national institutions. For the majority then, the nation state remains the only address to which they have access and to which they can address claims for citizenship rights, social entitlements and greater gender justice.

Civil society activism as political strategy

Most feminist scholars stress the necessity for both increased levels of female political representation, *and* pressure from below, to make gender mainstreaming strategies effective (Hoskyns, 1996; Rai, 2003; Stratigaki, 2005). The transformation process has seen a veritable explosion of 'civil society' activity in Central and Eastern Europe, at the same time as the role of civil society associations and NGOs is the focus of funding and policymaking by international donor agencies and governments alike. Political theory has long established that women – and not only those adopting the anti-state stance specific to this region in the post-communist period – find grassroots and local, single-issue politics to be more in tune with and compatible with their commitments and lifestyle than mainstream political party involvement. An enormous number of NGOs has emerged in the region, many of them initiated and managed by women. However, in the particular context of a rigidly applied neo-liberal market model and the loss of social provision this entails, such political involvement takes on particular meanings, constitutes particular political subject positions, and is accompanied by particular risks (Einhorn and Sever, 2003, 2005).

Specifically, there is a danger of what I have called elsewhere the civil society 'trap' (Einhorn, 2000a; Einhorn and Sever, 2003, 2005). This is where women's NGOs in effect provide some of the welfare functions abandoned by the state. This problem is highlighted by a young Polish woman reflecting on her work with the local women's refuge and hotline over a period of three to four years:

> Yes, maybe you do undertake work at the grass roots, so to speak .... But in a way we're doing the job of the Ministry of Health or the Ministry of Education. We're simply doing the job of the government institutions who should be dealing with these problems. ... Without changes from the top, you can have as many telephone hotlines as you like, or refuges for battered women, but without changes in the law, in political thinking, without rules, laws and so on from the top, nothing will change – really (U.P. interviewed in Nowa Huta, November 1998, quoted by Watson, 2000b: 380)

Karat, an advocacy coalition of women's NGOs in the region formed in 1997, states that women are active in NGOs on an equal basis with men, and that NGOs have been successful in influencing government policy in several countries. However, they also document the lack of capacity-building and expertise, the dependence on foreign donors and the distortions this can produce in NGO priorities and activities (Barendt, 2002; WAD, 2002). Karat recognizes the need for NGO advocacy work to be professionalized; Sabine Lang argues in contrast that the 'NGOization of feminism' dilutes its political and dynamic impact (Lang, 1997). There is a danger that state retrenchment reduces NGOs and other civil society organizations to acting as service providers, rather than as political activists and social advocates.

Karat's executive director Kinga Lohmann feels that the role of NGOs in the young democracies of Central and Eastern Europe must be understood as differing from that of NGOs in Western Europe. This is because they also contribute to the development of the rule of law in each country through detailed knowledge of international agreements and the mechanisms for their monitoring, as well as of national legislation. Such a role underlines the need for professionalization (Lohmann, personal communication July 2005). Debates about professionalization, and about the impact of donor dependence on civil society mobilization, are discussed in further detail in Chapter 4 below.

My theory of a civil society 'trap' (Einhorn, 2000a) relates to the ways in which it is women's unpaid labour – often performed by women made redundant who have difficulty in finding re-employment – that provides social supports such as childcare or care of the elderly. This labour remains invisible, simultaneously depended upon yet unrecognized by state agencies. Women's NGOs and grassroots activist groups are filling the vacuum where the state has withdrawn from public service provision. This 'trap' at least in part derives from the idealization of civil society that followed the fall of state socialism. Civil society was seen as the epitome of the democratic space that had earlier been lacking, both by dissident activists and theorists within the region, and by Western analysts and international donor agencies.

There are debates around the conceptualization of civil society and its relationship to autonomous women's or feminist movements. In the context of the transformation process in Central and Eastern Europe, an apt comment was made by Ferenc Miszlivetz, a Hungarian academic and former dissident activist: 'We dreamed of civil society. What we got was NGOs' (Miszlivetz, 1997). It could be argued that in order to overcome the donor dependency and potential loss of political edge faced by NGOs in the region, and thus to avoid the civil society 'trap', the imbalance between the market and the state needs to be overcome. While regional resistance to statist solutions is perfectly understandable given the recent history of all-controlling state socialist regimes, Western and Southern critics of the Washington Consensus see the neo-liberal paradigm as having seriously under-estimated the necessary and constructive place of government regulation in economic development, not to mention its role in the quest for social justice.

Compounding the civil society 'trap' is the civil society 'gap' (Einhorn, 2000a; Einhorn and Sever, 2003, 2005). This relates to the lack of channels of communication between NGOs and social movements on the one hand, and political power structures and state agencies on the other. How does civil society activism by women translate into gender-sensitive policymaking? Both the Beijing Platform for Action and subsequent recommendations have stressed the 'need for greater consultation between NGOs and national machineries'. In this context, 'the question of access to government becomes critical' (Rai, 2003: 35).

Karat Coalition for gender equality in Central and Eastern Europe identifies two problems that precisely exemplify this 'gap': 'Despite the fact that a process of opening the state authorities to the public has started, NGOs are kept outside mainstream policy formation. ... The main obstacle is the unresponsiveness and unwillingness of the administration to engage in a dialogue with civil society or even with other departments and governmental institutions' (WAD, 2002). This demonstrates the risks involved in focusing on bottom-up strategies or grassroots activism to the exclusion of involvement in conventional party politics and the policies of gender mainstreaming. The only way to ensure there is effective transmission of views from civil society to government, and efficient translation of grassroots insights and demands into new legislation and state policy, is to institute mechanisms for regular two-way communication. Overcoming the civil society 'gap' also requires some level of commitment on the part of national governments to take seriously – to the point of adopting and institutionalizing – some of the measures proposed by civil society organizations.

European Union enlargement and gender mainstreaming

As has already been mentioned, the transformation process in Central and Eastern Europe, in all its complexity, multi-layeredness, and inter-country variations, is occurring within a framework of dual supra-regional processes. Both processes exert a direct influence on the shape and direction of the political, social and economic changes within individual countries and the region as a whole. The first of these is economic globalization, a process that has the potential to weaken national polities in relation to powerful transnational corporate interests, yet seems at the same time to be strengthening international grassroots campaigning networks. The second, currently more central, process is that of European Union enlargement. Like the fall of the Berlin Wall and the end of the Cold War that it symbolized, what should be borne in mind is that European Union enlargement is a dual process that involves change in the West as well as in the East.[5]

The way in which the process is being conducted has implications for citizenship and gender equality in the region. There is a very real danger of creating second class status for those countries relegated to the second round of accession such as Bulgaria and Romania, third class status for candidate countries, and marginal status for those left out in the cold, now named 'neighbouring' countries. This could widen already existing gaps in levels of female political representation and gender equality between an 'in' group of countries in Central Europe and the Baltic states, relegating countries in Eastern and Southeastern Europe (with the exception of Slovenia) to the second tier, and effectively marginalizing Russia and Central Asian countries.

A further danger is that the European Union's exclusive focus on the economic sphere of the market will simply elide many of the most crucial problems of gender equality in relation to political and social rights. In EU policy 'from the beginning the social has been subsumed within the economic and only given a separate focus when this appeared functional or necessary to economic integration' (Hoskyns, 1996: 207). If the social has been excluded by this narrow economic focus, the political has disappeared from view entirely. This poses clear dangers for the achievement of gender equality, but these dangers have not been adequately addressed within EU policy. Women in Central and Eastern Europe have long experience of this kind of limited policy focus. In a conference paper delivered in 2002 as spokesperson for the Karat Coalition of women's NGOs from the region, Regina Barendt asserted that 'if state intervention remains limited to the labour market, as was the case under socialism, the most immediate impact is to intensify the exploitation of women on the one hand, and fail to alter the traditional gendered division of labour on the other. We in the region have known this for 25 years, but it is only now slowly gaining recognition in the EU' (Barendt, 2002).

Joanna Regulska maintained in 2002 that the persistent privileging of economic over social and political concerns undermined the hopes of Central and Eastern European countries that they might join the EU as equal partners. She found that the evidence from the negotiations around accession reinforced 'the impression that there is a lack of EU commitment to carry gender discourse as a part of accession negotiations'. While the Polish government had felt obliged (admittedly only in May 2001) to introduce the requisite equal pay and equal treatment legislation, this was confined to measures in the sphere of the labour market, and remained 'purely instrumental' to the goal of achieving EU member status (Regulska, 2002).

The Czech government has failed fully to implement the equal opportunities legislation it introduced as an amendment to the Labour Law in 1999 for the purposes of harmonization with EU requirements (True, 2003b: 98–100). After the June 2002 elections, the government founded a Permanent Commission on the Family and Equal Opportunities in the Chamber of Deputies. First, it is noteworthy that equal opportunities is bracketed with family matters; second, a year later the Commission had done nothing other than organize training sessions for its own members (Marksová-Tominová, 2003: 14). The evidence from these two countries would seem to suggest that neither national governments in the region nor the European Union treated gender as a measure of readiness for accession. In the run-up to the first round of enlargement, it seemed that compliance or non-compliance with the gender norms of EU legislation was likely neither to impede, nor to delay accession for those countries that joined in 2004 (Steinhilber, 2002a).

The EU gender mainstreaming approach – in existing EU countries too – itself hides a lack of conceptual clarity in terms of meaning, intentionality and purpose.[6] The current European Commission mission statement on gender equality interprets gender mainstreaming as 'integrating the gender equality objective into all Community policies' (European Commission, 2005b). Yet this leaves much unclear. Is the goal, for example, equal treatment, equality of opportunity, or equality of outcomes? Does it necessitate equal opportunity legislation, anti-discrimination legislation, or positive measures to promote women in order to create a level playing field where equal opportunities might gain purchase? (Lovenduski, 2001)[7] Is there a problem in the fact that gender mainstreaming is a top-down strategy? Might the crucial political impetus of feminist goals of social transformation be lost through the co-optation and institutionalization of gender implied by this strategy? (Rai, 2003: 19).

Mieke Verloo, keynote speaker at an international conference on gender mainstreaming in 2002 warned that 'gender mainstreaming should not replace politics' (Verloo, 2002). Gender mainstreaming policies should not become an alibi, masking violations of women's rights as human rights. Nor should they be used as a means of making budget savings by withdrawing funding from specific women's projects or terminating affirmative action programmes. Ute Gerhard argues that there is no cause for rejoicing at the paradigm shift from a women's politics to an equal opportunities approach, especially when the latter is often used to sideline policies and projects designed to promote women's equality. She feels that the European policy of gender mainstreaming can only ever be useful as an additional policy, not one that replaces either the promotion of women or active participation 'from below'. She points out that the history of women's movements demonstrates the ongoing need for those who swim against the 'mainstream' (Gerhard, 2003: 97).

Maria Stratigaki describes, from her eight-year experience of working in the Equal Opportunities Unit of the European Commission, the conflict during the development of gender mainstreaming between two different policy frames. One frame emphasizes the transformative potential of GM in 'complementing and reinforcing positive action and equality legislation'. The other uses GM 'as an alternative to positive action' which can be 'used to downplay the final overall objective of gender equality' (Stratigaki, 2005: 165–6, 168). As Stratigaki asserts, 'without simultaneously tackling the accumulated inequalities between the sexes and reinforcing gender-specific policies, GM effectiveness cannot be assured' (Stratigaki, 2005: 169; see also Rees, 1998: 197).

Gender mainstreaming does have positive potential when it is implemented as part of a dual strategy acknowledging that women and men do not start out from positions of equal power. German government ministries are required (albeit with inadequate financial and personnel resources) both to 'mainstream' gender in every department and in every policy instrument, and to prioritize and support affirmative action schemes for women. This positive approach is hampered by two factors. First, gender mainstreaming as understood here is solely geared to labour market needs. Only one of five definitional clauses actually mentions equal opportunities and the need for improvements in work–life balance. Second, as in many other countries, the office entrusted with implementation of the policy lacks an adequate budget and sufficient personnel to guarantee compliance. For the accession countries, such a dual strategy is crucial (Heinen and Portet, 2002: 159). It involves not just respect for the principle of gender equality as integral to all policy-making, but also the implementation of equal opportunities policies and positive discrimination programmes.

The lack of conceptual clarity at the heart of EU policy produces two problematic results in practice. The first is that relevant EU directives have thus far been framed in terms of economic efficiency. They are conceived as mechanisms for integrating women into the labour market effectively, rather than as strategies for political transformation designed to create gender equitable societies. Maria Stratigaki claims that there is evidence of 'cooptation by economic priorities' and that 'the use of GM to eliminate positive action can be found in EU labour market policy texts' (Stratigaki, 2005: 176, 180; see also Rai, 2003: 29).

The second problem is that – as in existing member countries – the gender mainstreaming machinery in the accession countries remains systemically weak. In fact, the establishment of national machineries was part of the commitment to National Plans of Action that all governments in Central and Eastern Europe and the former Soviet Union took upon themselves to comply with the UN's Beijing Platform for Action. Yet the process of EU accession, whilst lending moral support, has not directly contributed to the strengthening of national machineries. Karat, the campaigning Coalition of women's NGOS in the region, notes that whilst national machineries have been established in most countries, and while they do increasingly cooperate with local NGOs, NGOs remain concerned that 'progress has been too slow and too inconsistent to counteract negative economic and social trends and to have a substantive impact on the real situation of women' (Karat, 2005b: 1).

Weaknesses in the machinery designed to institutionalize gender mainstreaming policies echo the experience in many of the older member countries. In the UK, for example, the first fully paid Minister for Women was appointed as late as 2001 (Lovenduski, 2001). However, there has as yet been little sign of effective gender mainstreaming policies emanating from this office and adopted by the government. Few countries acknowledge the need for state institutions to institute a dual strategy, combining gender mainstreaming policies with positive measures to enhance gender equality.

The political limitations of gender mainstreaming as a policy approach are therefore replicated in both conceptual and practical problems in Central and Eastern Europe. Hence 'almost all accession countries have commissions or departments on equal opportunities, but, with very few exceptions, they hardly understand the concept, not to mention the initiative they may take or the competence they have to carry out activities in this respect' (IHF, 2000: 17). The national machinery for women takes a wide range of institutional forms 'from NGO status to a very strong mandate within the government' (Jezerska, 2003: 167).

Poland provides an illustrative example of the difficulties in introducing both national machineries and gender equality legislation. Following the election success of the left (post-communist) political alliance in September 2001, Izabela Jaruga-Nowacka was appointed in November 2001 as Government Plenipotentiary for the Equal Status of Women and Men.[8] She held the rank of secretary of state in the Prime Minister's Chancellery. This status in itself represented the success of lobbying by women's NGOs who met with the Prime Minister immediately after the autumn 2001 elections. The government had proposed locating the Plenipotentiary in the Ministry of Labour and Social Affairs and designating it the Plenipotentiary for the Equal Status of Women, Men and the Family. Location in the Prime Minister's Chancellery lent the Plenipotentiary the authority to initiate legislative drafts as well as to verify whether all new legislation complies with the equal treatment of men and women (Lohmann, personal communication, August 2005).

Nevertheless, the Plenipotentiary did not at first have an automatic right to attend cabinet meetings, nor to insist that her recommendations be translated into legislation or government policy. Moreover, the brief has subsequently been widened in order to fulfil EU requirements (but without increased human or financial resources) to include not only gender-based discrimination, but *all* forms of discrimination. This means in effect that the position has remained symbolic, in that it commands neither the political status nor the budget to bring about substantive change in political policies or social practices (Chołuj, 2003: 213). In spring 2000, the Parliamentary Women's Group had proposed the establishment of a Parliamentary Commission on the Equal Status of Women and Men. This Commission was finally brought into being in April 2005 (Lohmann, personal communication, August 2005).

In a sharp reversal, however, the newly elected conservative Polish Prime Minister in November 2005 closed down the office of the Plenipotentiary for Equal Status of Women and Men and appointed instead a Family Consultant. In January 2006 a group of women's organizations from the vibrant NGO sector met to consider the situation and their strategy. They composed a letter to the Prime Minister demanding the reinstatement of the Plenipotentiary and adequate resourcing of the post, plus the dismissal of the Family Consultant 'whose declarations are a threat to the state's neutrality in matters of religion'. They also made demands regarding implementation of the EU's policy of gender mainstreaming; for the end of continuing discrimination against sexual minorities; for the provision of pre-school childcare facilities and the involvement of women's NGOs in the creation of a National Program to Counteract Violence in the Family; for the elimination of stereotypes that undermine women's access to the labour market; and for the introduction of a national programme designed to increase the participation of women in the 2006 local elections (NEWW-Polska, 2006).

The first draft of an Act on the Equal Status of Women and Men in Poland was presented to the Parliament (Sejm) in December 1996, after five years of lobbying. Further drafts were submitted in 1997 and 1998. On 4th March 1999, admittedly before the 2001 elections,[9] a further draft Equal Status Act met with laughter and derision in the Polish Sejm (Lower House). Prompted by the Parliamentary Group of Women, the Senate (Upper House) presented a new draft to the Sejm in January 2003. At this time, women activists lent the draft bill cautious support despite its shortcomings, out of a conviction that this would ensure the establishment of a permanent office responsible for gender equality issues.

The Draft Act provided for the creation of Anti-Discrimination Offices at both central and local government levels. Although this Office would represent an institutionalized National Women's Machinery (albeit within the context of a single anti-discrimination body), the draft Act remained weak in that it lacked sanctions against non-compliance (Chołuj, personal communication, 2003; Lohmann and Seibert, 2003: 26–7). The most recent draft Equal Status Act (again presented by the Senate) in June 2005 was rejected by a majority of MPs in the Sejm. This time around the draft Act was neither supported nor lobbied for by women activists and academics. They felt it had been so emasculated that it retained nothing of the law's original intent. In fact it contributed nothing that did not already exist in the provisions of the Constitution or the Labour Code (Lohmann, personal communication, August 2005). As of September 2005 the Anti-Discrimination Office had not been established in Poland, nor had legislation pertaining to Equal Status or Non-Discrimination been passed.

Yet one subsequent positive development appeared to demonstrate the increased influence of women activists. This was that as of July 2002 the Office of the Plenipotentiary for the Equal Status of Women and Men acquired an Advisory Board to facilitate taking into account NGO expertise (Lohmann, 2005). An important influence was undoubtedly the need to comply with EU standards on equal opportunities, since Poland was one of the first group of candidate countries to join the European Union in 2004. This example would seem to counter the theory of a civil society 'gap', in that a specific mechanism has been set up for the transmission of civil society views to the Plenipotentiary, the government minister responsible for equality issues.

In the Czech Republic, NGOs were completely sidelined in the EU accession process. Moreover, none of the state institutions involved in the process addressed issues of gender equality, nor were they held to account on this front by EU negotiators. Several women's NGOs which applied to national bodies for a share of the EU funding they had received to facilitate preparation for accession, were turned down. When the organization Gender Studies applied for funding to participate in a regional project on women's political education, the Czech government was the only one in the region to refuse funding support, using the argument that 'women and men are equal in this country and therefore political education of women is not a priority'. At state level the National Training Fund in 2003 published a draft document on a strategy for human resources development in the Czech Republic in which gender issues did not appear once in its 53 pages (Marksová-Tominová, 2003: 12–13).

Lithuania was the first country in the region to appoint an ombudsperson responsible for gender equality issues. In June 2002 it also introduced amendments to its Equal Opportunities legislation allowing measures of 'positive discrimination' in order to ensure compliance with EU equal rights directives. (NWP/OSI, 2002: 14). In taking this step, Lithuania is several years ahead of Britain, which plans to introduce such amendments to the Sex Discrimination Act only in 2006.

It is obvious from the evidence cited that the formal mechanisms and legislation vary from country to country, but that even where they are in place, there are questions about the level of actual rather than merely formal implementation. As in Western Europe, many of the countries in Central and Eastern Europe lack sufficient numbers of women in positions of power in legislatures and in trade unions who are committed to gender equality and might ensure that legislation or gender-related EU directives are translated into practice. Although the European Union has stated its commitment to gender equality and hence compliance with EU norms as a precondition for EU membership, there is evidence that compliance was not in fact monitored, so that gender did not impede or delay accession for those countries who joined in 2004 (Bretherton, 2001; Steinhilber, 2002a).

Moreover, there is a danger that European Union enlargement could result in harmonization downwards, whereby women in Central and Eastern Europe are forced to accept lower levels of political representation, labour force participation, childcare provision, pay equity or reproductive rights than those to which they have been accustomed. This danger was borne out in some aspects of the German unification process. Another example is the case of abortion in Poland. During the accession process Polish feminism was seen 'as a hostage to EU negotiations', in a process whereby Polish women were required 'to remain silent on the question of reproductive choice so that Poland may join the EU unhampered by the Catholic Church' (Graff, 2002: 16, 26).

Conclusion

It is clear that the implementation of gender mainstreaming policies and the effectiveness of national women's machineries depends in large part on the existence of 'strong democratic movements holding these bodies accountable' (Rai 2003: 19), in other words 'the dynamic involvement of political, social and civil actors with high visibility' (Stratigaki, 2005: 172; see also Einhorn, 2000a; Hoskyns, 1996; Jezerska, 2003). Jacqui True and Michael Mintrom validate the key role of social movements and particularly the transnational feminist movement in 'the diffusion of gender-mainstreaming mechanisms' (True and Mintrom, 2001: 27). In her later study of the efficacy and transformative potential of gender mainstreaming as a strategy, True concludes that 'gender mainstreaming is an open-ended and potentially transforming project that depends on what feminist scholars, activists and policy-makers collectively make of it' (True, 2003b: 368).

Without support from mainstream politicians and the institution of properly supported mechanisms for their implementation, gender mainstreaming policies can not succeed. Shirin Rai cites the paucity of resources available to most national machineries as an inhibiting factor (Rai, 2003: 35). The key to adequate resources for the full implementation of gender mainstreaming strategies is political support at the highest levels (Rai, 2003: 34, 37). Yet Zuzana Jezerska argues that in most Central and Eastern European countries, political will is precisely what is lacking. This explains 'the rather patchy growth of women's national machineries' in the region (Jezerska, 2003: 182). Such unevenness in part results from the widespread belief among politicians and the public that gender equality already exists as a relic of state socialist legislation and policy. There is therefore a strong feeling that specific mechanisms such as national machineries are unnecessary, even superfluous, since women's status in the region is not a matter for concern.

Political will needs to be generated, and maintained. Only pressure from below can ensure that issues of gender equity are kept on the agenda of national, supra-national and international institutions and that gender-sensitive policies are not merely written into legislation, but also given weight in terms of the human and financial resources necessary for their implementation. While national machineries have an 'agenda-setting role', 'their legitimacy derives from the close contact they are able to maintain with women's groups' (Rai, 2003: 25). Both political will and grassroots activism are therefore necessary but not sufficient preconditions for the achievement of gender equality. Beyond this combination, the crucial catalysts for effectivity are communication and influence in both directions. In other words, the channels open for transmission of grassroots demands to the politicians, and the influence to ensure their passage into legislation, are crucial if policies such as gender mainstreaming or quotas are to make a real difference, not only to women's lives, but to the life and health of societies as a whole, both nationally and internationally.

It is therefore important to consider the integrally related issues of women's representation in mainstream polities on the one hand, and grassroots activism and lobbying on the other. Where this chapter has focused on theoretical debates around different policy approaches, the next two chapters will deal with the policy discussions and political practices adopted in Central and Eastern Europe. Chapter 3 concentrates on representation in political parties and state legislatures, while Chapter 4 turns to civil society mobilization.

3
Gender in Mainstream Politics
Scaling the Structures

Introduction

> Young lady, you seem to think with your glands. Yes, we have primarily men, from the local mayors to representatives up to the parliamentarians, from business owners – who hire only uneducated but good-looking young girls – to taxi drivers. ... Particularly after 1989, most of the men that I have had the opportunity to discuss the problem with endorse the emancipation of women ... within given parameters in social, civil, and political life – except when it comes to their own wives and daughters.
> (Prominent male representative of the Romanian National Liberal Party, cited by Grunberg, 2000: 319)

> The mission of building gender-inclusive democracies is far from being fulfilled. ... As part of the funding community, we must continue to advocate for increasing resources for women's empowerment. As a part of the global women's movement, we must ensure that women's voices are a vital part of global politics. Simply put, if women are excluded from democracy, democracy fails.
> (Posadskaya-Vanderbeck, 2002: 7)

The transformation process in Central and Eastern Europe has been simultaneously economic, involving marketization and privatization, and political, involving democratization. Yet it is significant that both processes have been constructed within the parameters of neo-liberal understandings that privilege the economic over the political, and hence the individual economic actor over the citizen as political subject. This goes some way to explaining the relative scholarly and activist neglect until recently of political representation in state legislatures in the region as a key gender equality measure.[1]

This chapter considers how the economic changes were embedded in – and have themselves shaped – an altered political landscape, in which the discourses used to describe and understand the accompanying social and cultural changes were fundamentally reworked. Early insights into the intrinsically gendered nature of both the economic and political transformations in the region are developed further here with reference to mainstream politics, specifically to issues of gender equitable political participation and representation (Einhorn, 1993; see also Gal and Kligman, 2000a).

What makes political participation and representation key measures of gender equitable citizenship status? First, the fundamental nature of the transformation in Central and Eastern Europe has thrown political discourse back onto old certainties encapsulated in traditional gender regimes. In such regimes, the public sphere – and hence politics – is men's business, while women's realm is the private sphere of the family (and the wider family of the nation). Second, gender parity in elected assemblies, or at least the achievement of a 'critical mass' of female parliamentarians, are necessary steps towards equality of representation. 'Critical mass' or a 'threshold level' of women in legislative bodies is an essential mechanism for effecting gender-sensitive legislation, as well as shifts in the political agenda and in the social and cultural discourses that construct women as secondary citizens, in order to take account of women's interests and incorporate women's perspectives (Phillips, 1995: 82; see also Lovenduski 2001: 744, 746; Rai 2003: 38).[2]

This chapter first discusses the potentially disabling definition of what counts – or is publicly acknowledged – as politics. It then considers some of the reasons for the current privileging of civil society involvement, itself a contributing factor to the relative lack of attention paid by scholars and activists both within and outside the region to the importance of mainstream politics. The main body of the chapter is then concerned with women's political participation, with the gendered barriers to that participation, and with strategies to overcome those barriers. It includes discussion of levels of representation at national and local level in individual countries in the region. Finally, it presents the views of both politicians and the public on women as politicians, and on the deployment of temporary special measures such as quotas to increase gender balance in mainstream politics.

It is important in this analysis to pay heed to three complicating factors. The first concerns emerging differences in political developments between and within individual countries in the region (Havelková, 2000: 120). The second relates to problematizations of the category 'woman' (Butler, 1990; Gal, 1997: 31). Judit Acsády notes the lack of identification of women in the region with gender-based group interests (Acsády, 1999: 406). Nevertheless, the refusal to analyse systematic gender disadvantage can be politically disabling. A group of Czech sociologists stress the necessity of women's active political participation as a group in order to effect change in social and media discourse constructing them as inferior (Čermáková *et al.*, 2000: 133,135). Beyond that there is the question of distinguishing political participation as women from feminist activism. This is discussed in Chapter 4. The third factor is perhaps even more fundamental than theoretical debates about the definition of women-in-politics, or inter-country differences in political developments. This concerns the contested issue of what counts – conceptually and empirically – as political activity. The next section deals with this issue.

What counts as 'politics' and where does it occur?

Feminist scholars have stressed the need to redefine what counts as 'political' and to rethink the space in which this occurs in order to measure the true level of women's political participation (Benn, 1993; Graham and Regulska, 1997: 65). This was a response to earlier ostensibly gender-neutral political theory that rendered women invisible as political subjects and especially as political actors. Alternatively, this theory cast female political subjects as both lacking independence – led by their husbands in their voting behaviour – and as more conservative than men. In opposition to such views, feminist theorists argue that politics is not a discrete activity occurring somewhere 'out there', far from the arenas of women's daily lives, but indeed that these very lives, and in particular the gendered power relations inherent in all institutional structures, including those of the family, are deeply political, and hence that 'politics' occurs in all social relations in both public and private realms.

Feminist political theorists have thus countered the discursive marginalization of women as somehow less political than men by drawing attention to the restrictive understandings of political participation and the political sphere that underpinned it (Lovenduski and Norris, 1993). They showed clearly that women *are* politically active, but not necessarily at national level or in mainstream party politics. Rather, women tend to engage with issues at the local government level rather than in national legislatures, and to become involved in grassroots civil society associations in preference to mainstream political parties.

This insight has strong relevance to any analysis of women's political participation in Central and Eastern Europe in the years since 1989. Civil society activism in particular has been dominated by women, as the next chapter demonstrates. It would be absurd to deny such NGO activism the status of 'political' activity (Heinen and Portet, 2002: 162–3). A study conducted for the Council of Europe has also demonstrated relatively high levels of active female involvement in local politics, beginning with the 1990 local elections, although there are contradictory trends. The level of female representation in local politics rose between 1990 and 1994 in the Czech Republic and Poland, but fell in Hungary over the same period. More recent data remains mixed.[3]

The relatively high levels of female political representation attained in several countries in the 1990 local elections demonstrate continuity from the state socialist past. Under those regimes women had been fairly well represented at local level in most countries across the region (Einhorn, 1993). Indeed in Hungary, a Politburo member György Marosan defined local, as opposed to mainstream and state-level politics, as 'women's task' (Fodor: 2002: 257). This could be interpreted negatively – as relegating women to a level of politics that was considered inconsequential by the regime – or positively, as an acknowledgement of women's preferences for local-level involvement. Either way, despite this historical legacy on the one hand, and the current statistically positive levels of female representation in local politics on the other, there are still barriers and hurdles to women's participation even at the local level. These include lack of time, the persistence of the double burden giving women prime responsibility for the family in addition to their paid work, and lack of trust in women politicians (Bitušikova, 2005c: 2). In Poland, this seems to have led women to abandon participation in the local state in favour of civil society activism (Graham and Regulska, 1997: 73).

NGO involvement too, however, reveals gender-specific drawbacks. The ways in which political identities have been discursively constructed in the transformation process have in some cases acted to discourage women's use of civil society spaces for collective action. Case studies of local initiatives in three small- and medium-sized Polish towns showed the persistence of political barriers that prevented women influencing local public policy (Graham and Regulska, 1997: 74). Although the majority of NGOs in the Czech Republic were female-led by 1995, they were perceived as politically weak and ineffective

(Kligman, 1996: 72). That the NGO experience is not unproblematic is explored in further detail in the next chapter.

The discursive focus on civil society

The empirical observation that women are active in local and grassroots rather than national and mainstream politics is given particular force in Central and Eastern Europe by the somewhat extravagant hopes pinned on civil society as a space with great potential for political mobilization. In the immediate aftermath of the demise of state socialism, civil society appeared paradoxically as both an un-political and a political space. It tended to be cast simultaneously as the arena whose development was urgently necessary to counteract the over-politicization of society through an intrusive and all-powerful state, and as the arena that provided a measure of the success of democratization.

It is possible to perceive three contributory causes to this preoccupation with civil society as the theatre of democratization – to the exclusion from the analysis of the institutions and structures of political parties and the state (Howell and Pearce, 2001: 69). The first lies in the idealization of the concept of civil society that emerged from its pre-1989 development by (male) dissident theorists in the region. 'Antipolitical' theorists such as György Konrad, Adam Michnik and Václav Havel countered the universalist conceptions of citizenship and actual surveillance of individual citizens in state socialist societies with the notion of civil society as the space in which individual autonomy, authenticity and creativity could flower (Einhorn, 1993).

The understanding of civil society as the locus of political critique based on individual moral responsibility was powerfully persuasive within the politically repressive context within which it arose. It echoed classical liberal political theory in its focus on the individual (as opposed to the group, or the working classes) as political actor. However, it was subsequently mapped somewhat uncritically onto the ostensibly empty and gender-neutral democratic political context that followed. In reality, of course, civil society constitutes a space that is neither neutral, nor free of gendered relations of power (Einhorn and Sever, 2003, 2005; Gal and Kligman, 2000a: 92; Watson, 1997, 2001). The idealization of civil society as politics- and power-free space was thus driven by circumstances particular to the region, subsequently reinforced by the discursive and policy predominance lent it by Western governments and international donor agencies alike.

The second contributory factor is that 'the political' was relatively neglected in the region during the initial (and understandable) fixation on the exigencies and impact of economic reform. The pre-dominance of the economic is of course endemic to the neo-liberal agenda, which assumes the market as the sole regulator of society and hence relegates the polity to a back seat. In Western European countries like Britain where this model has dominated since the late 1970s, it has also been responsible for a fiscal skew and relative neglect of both the social and especially the political dimensions of change. This process is ostensibly being countered in the Central and Eastern European context by understandings of the political as a precondition for EU accession. Yet it can be argued that the European Union is itself constituted in terms of – and driven by – primarily economic considerations.

A third factor lies in the discourse of post-structuralist thought. As in the West, this theoretical trend tends to prioritize socio-cultural phenomena and non-institutional activities to the detriment of the political. In themselves, these are extremely important elements eminently worthy of analysis. Yet the resulting neglect of the mainstream political realm presents dangers from the point of view of gender equity. It remains true that without a critical mass of women in political parties, national legislatures and state executives, the likelihood of political shifts in the direction of gender mainstreaming, gender-sensitive legislation, and the achievement of gender equity more generally remains low (Einhorn, 2000b: 109; for the application of this insight to other contexts, see Hoskyns and Rai, 1998; Lovenduski, 2001; Molyneux, 1988/2001; Rai, 1996, 2000; Randall, 1998).

Gender in mainstream politics

Gendered discourses about what constitutes the realm of the 'political' are one of the elements of continuity, rather than rupture with the past (Einhorn, 1993). This view is reinforced in an increasing number of micro-analyses of the region. A study of local politics in Poland notes that the elaboration of group interests and political priorities tends to be articulated by men who are blind to gender as a structuring principle of unequal power relations. In a phrasing very reminiscent of the past, men in power insist that 'women's issues' must wait until other more critical problems are resolved (Graham and Regulska, 1997; cited in Rueschemeyer, 2001: 168). The discourses adopted by political parties in Hungary after 1989 defined what counts as political in a deeply gendered manner (Gal, 1997).

This is a perspective familiar to women in Western Europe, both in its suggestion that 'women's issues' are minority and/or marginal issues, and its echo of the discourses that prompted women in the late 1960s in

Western Europe and the USA to leave New Left politics in favour of setting up autonomous ('Second Wave') feminist groups. It is a perspective internalized to an extent by many women themselves, which reinforces their political disempowerment. A study of differences between women in a small Hungarian town asserts that 'women's sense that their womanhood is antithetical to politics has most likely been influenced by the emerging definition of political activity itself' (Kovács and Váradi 2000: 182–3).

Gender is viewed in most countries of Central and Eastern Europe as secondary to more critical political and especially economic developments (as though these were themselves gender-neutral). Gender equity is treated as secondary to a catalogue of other priorities such as economic reform, democratization, civil society and political institution-building (Roman, 2001: 53). Human rights, if considered, are perceived as gender-neutral. Consequently, most political parties in the region have omitted from their party platforms and policies women's interests or any mention of gender as a structuring element of the transformation process itself. Perhaps as a reflection of the postmodern 'cultural turn', favouring theoretical rather than empirical analysis, there are few current studies of the impact of gender as a variable at the macro-political level in the countries of Central and Eastern Europe. Indeed the majority of analyses of democratization in Central and Eastern Europe omit gender altogether from the frame of analysis.[4] Even studies that do identify gender as a key variable tend to focus on the re-articulation and re-construction of the public–private divide, or on civil society and NGO activities. What is problematic about this is that neglect of the macro-political level – including the obligatory and often peremptory nod in the direction of 'gender mainstreaming' – tends to leave structurally gendered polities and policies untouched.

The relatively high levels of female political representation achieved by women in some Western European or Nordic countries are often cited by both Western and Eastern analysts as examples of aspirational goals.[5] A cynical view might hold that the only reason for such high levels of female representation is that the power and influence of national legislatures is falling in relation to supra-national bodies such as the European Union on the one hand, and the power of global economic and political institutions on the other (Lokar, 2005: 26). In the early period of political transformation, by contrast, the level of female political representation in the region dropped, prompting Polish sociologist Małgorzata Fuszara to remark that 'women's presence in Parliament appears to be significantly lower when Parliament acquires real power' (Fuszara, 2000: 272; see also Sperling, 1996: 50).

Despite the role played by new supra-regional or global constellations of political and economic power, many feminist theorists writing on other contexts defend the validity of a focus on the national state as the institution still responsible for the legislation and social policies that impact most directly on women's lives (Goetz, 2003; Rai, 2004; Waylen, 1998). During the transformation period in the region, parliamentary politics has remained dominant, underlining the importance of getting women promoted to leadership positions within political parties or placed high on candidacy lists (Bitušiková, 2005c: 3). By contrast, the network of grassroots women's organizations was initially relatively weak and split in terms of prioritizing the issues (Gaber, 1997: 150). Małgorzata Fuszara acknowledges the prime importance of mainstream politics for Poland. Despite 'the redefinition of what is "public" and "political" ', the very real political influence exerted by women through civil society activism does not alter the fact that 'most decisions that affect women, and that shape women's situation and opportunities, continue to be made in traditionally defined, male-dominated political bodies, such as Parliament and government' (Fuszara, 2000: 261; see also Heinen and Portet, 2002: 162).

Nor does the relatively high level of civil society activism necessarily reflect an equally high level of political consciousness about gender equality issues. While women constitute the majority in many NGOs and other grassroots organizations, many of these organizations are not actually concerned with defending women's interests or addressing gender issues. (Havelková, 2000: 131; Kostova, 1998: 217). Part of the reason for this lies in the persistence of state socialist socialization and the internalization of a rhetoric that proclaimed equality between the sexes as already achieved within a context where dedication to the common good was paramount. This legacy tends to mitigate against women conceiving of themselves either as individuals, or as political subjects with a claim to the realization of equal rights (Gal, 1997; Havelková, 2000: 132). As a result, there is no sense of urgency emanating from women themselves regarding gender equity as a political goal.

Once the legitimacy of focusing on national legislatures is accepted, the question then becomes: Have political discourses and mainstream political institutions in Central and Eastern Europe become more gender-sensitive and gender-equal respectively in the 15 years since the Fall of the Wall? The dramatic drop in the level of female political representation in national parliaments in the first democratic elections after 1989 has been much discussed. In a number of countries, the level plummeted even further in the second elections a year or so later (Einhorn, 1993: 153).

The striking suddenness of the plunge in levels of female political representation led both activists and commentators to apply the term 'male democracies' to what was happening in the process of democratization (Sonja Licht, cited in Einhorn, 1993: 148; see also Eisenstein, 1993; Heinen, 1992: 135; Kligman, 1996; Posadskaya, 1994; Sperling, 1996; Young, 1999). Others have used similar terminology, speaking of 'incomplete democracies', of 'masculinism', or expressing the idea that 'if women are excluded from democracy, democracy fails' (Fuszara, 2000: 271; Posadskaya-Vanderbeck, 2002: 7; Renc-Roe, 2003: 6; Waters and Posadskaya, 1995; Watson, 1993).

It must be conceded, notwithstanding this trend, that the dramatic post-1989 drop in levels of female political representation in the region is perhaps less of an abrupt change than first appeared. First, it is important to bear in mind that the initial fall to 10 per cent or less lowered female representation to average Western European levels.[6] Second, as I have argued earlier, the fall was less real in its impact than the raw figures suggested, given the token nature of parliaments within the previous state socialist regimes. Real power lay with the upper echelons of the Communist Party, in the Central Committees and especially the Politburos of the Party, in which women had a level of representation diminishing to vanishing point, despite forming on average 30 per cent of Party members (Einhorn, 1993: 151–2; Fodor, 2002: 258).

Plunging levels of female political representation during the first ten years of the transformation therefore presented – contrary to appearances – an element of continuity beneath the apparent rupture as presented by the raw data. In her study of internal Hungarian Communist Party documents, Éva Fodor posed a question about whether the political subject in state socialist times was truly genderless. Her response claims that 'the discursive foundations of male domination were transformed but never eliminated under state socialism'. In this context, she therefore argues that while women *were* regarded as political subjects in their own right, they were nevertheless construed as inferior to men, indeed as less trustworthy politically. Their gendered disadvantages (such as the 'heroic triple role of worker, political functionary and mother' Bitušiková, 2005c: 1) made them structurally less able than men to devote themselves to party political activities. Fodor concludes from this that there was 'explicit gender differentiation and male bias embedded in the concept of the ideal communist subject' (Fodor, 2002: 241, 243, 252, 257–8, 260; see also Gal, 1997).[7]

Pessimistic conclusions drawn from the downturn in female political representation cited the pervasiveness of both persistent and emergent discriminatory rhetoric. The evidence boded ill for the achievement of the 'critical mass' necessary to influence legislation and policymaking in a gender-sensitive direction (Lovenduski, 2001; Renc-Roe, 2003: 6–7). The low level of female representation in Bulgaria appeared to reflect not only the removal of the quotas associated with the previous political regime, but a legacy of inertia, passivity and little awareness that political rights were rights that required defending (Kostova, 1998: 217). Women's relative absence from the Czech political scene was attributed to lack of recognition of any gender-specific issues that might motivate them to engage with mainstream politics (Havelková, 2000: 124–5). Alexandra Bitušiková regrets more forcefully the phenomenon of '(in)visible women in political life in Slovakia', and the persistence of the 'stereotype that women do not understand politics and should not *"poke their noses into it"*' (Bitušiková, 2005b: 1; emphasis in original). In Poland it is evident that 'the clear decline in women's participation in traditional political arenas has undermined women's influence on the decisions and regulations that directly affect women's scope of freedom and ability to shape their own lives and actions' (Fuszara, 2000: 261).

Differing explanations have been offered for women's relative lack of visibility or apparent lack of interest in mainstream politics. These include the dominance of the economy over politics on the neo-liberal agenda and – particularly in the first years of economic restructuring – the sheer struggle to adapt and survive (Heinen and Portet, 2002: 160). People saw unemployment and the retrenchment of the state from the provision of services as the main problem. They relied blindly on the market to improve the economic situation, in the belief that this – rather than political changes – could provide the solution (Havelková, 2000: 129). Here it is worth noting that the lack of adequate public services is not a shortcoming of the neo-liberal market economy, but one of its structuring principles, as will be discussed in Chapter 7.

Some analysts in the region claim that the sense of political powerlessness engendered by state socialist regimes persisted in the democratization process. The manner in which the dissolution of Czechoslovakia was decided by government fiat in late 1992 exacerbated this sense for citizens of the Czech Republic and Slovakia. No referendum was held, and the government ignored opinion polls showing that 70–80 per cent of the public wished the Federation to continue. Such disregard of the popular political will may help to explain reactions of anger and antipathy to politics in those countries. Darina Macková claims that this disenchantment was responsible for a drop of 25 per cent in voter participation in the following general elections in Slovakia (Macková, 2000: 50).

Many authors still refer to the pervasive sense that politics is a 'dirty business' best left to men (Einhorn, 1993; for more recent evidence of the persistence of this view see Chimiak, 2003; Heinen and Portet, 2002: 160 and Kovács and Váradi, 2000: 181). Political passivity on the part of women is interpreted variously as complacency carried over from the past experience of legislatively enshrined equality, material struggles for family survival, or collusion with the discursive pre-eminence attributed to women's responsibility for the private sphere, itself reinforced by nationalist rhetoric (Heinen and Portet, 2002: 160).

As is clear from the country-based evidence cited above, speculation about the causes of low female participation rates ranges from the stress of dealing with the transformation to disenchantment carried over from the past and expressed in the present as either disinterest or active rejection of political involvement. These causes are compounded by structural factors such as the nature of the electoral system, the lack of quotas in most countries and political parties, the arbitrary and unpredictable influence of political party list gatekeepers on women's inclusion on electoral slates, women's lack of public profile or of the networks of influence that constitute political capital, and the unfavourable positioning of women on electoral lists (Bitušiková, 2005b; Gaber, 1997: 148, 2003; Fuszara, 2000; Graham and Regulska, 1997; Macková, 2000: 50). Such factors suggest that feelings of disempowerment and disillusion with politics are not just remnants from the past, but have emerged as a reaction to the particular ways in which the political has been defined during the transformation process. Some analysts suggest that women's lack of engagement with mainstream politics is no greater than that of men, and that their apparent collusion with their relative political marginalization may be temporary (Havelková, 2000; Rueschemeyer, 2001).

Consensus is lacking about whether women's actual voting patterns show them as conservative or progressive, or even about whether left-of-centre parties really are more likely to include women on their lists as has historically been assumed. Renata Siemieńska (1998) maintains that women were more likely to support Conservative parties in Poland during the early to mid-1990s. This finding was supported in data from local elections in Hungary (Kovács and Váradi, 2000: 181). Yet in Slovakia, more women voted for Left parties, and left-of-centre political parties also returned higher percentages of women deputies in the 1994 elections (Macková, 2000; Wolchik, 1998: 169). Incremental increases in the number of female deputies in the Czech Republic since 1996 – so that they held 17 per cent of seats in the Chamber of Deputies in 2002 compared with 9.5 per cent in 1994 – can be attributed to the success of left-wing parties, which are also the parties that more often place women in electable positions on their party lists (Rakušanová, 2003: 21).

Polish opinion polls offer contradictory evidence. One survey showed as many as 70 per cent of respondents who expressed greater trust in male politicians, while another indicates that many people would give preference to female candidates 'and would trust them in particular to represent issues relevant to women'. The second result contradicts the frequently propagated view that voters do not trust, and hence do not vote for, women candidates. This appears to provide evidence that the low level of female politicians in Poland reflects the prejudices of male party leaders rather than voter resistance (Siemieńska, 1998: 136–7). It also suggests that it might be in the self-interest of Polish political parties to promote the election of more women (Fuszara, 2000: 273, 283; see also Heinen and Portet, 2002: 161–2).

Those women who do wish to become politically active in mainstream structures face considerable structural hurdles that make it difficult for them to succeed. These include the difficulty of gaining access to favourable positions on electoral lists, the substance of political party programmes, and the nature of political discourse, especially evident in electoral broadcasts. Female candidates report either actual or perceived pressure to subordinate women's interests or gender issues to more pressing 'party issues' in order to be included on candidate lists (Daskalova, 1997: 168; 2000). When they do succeed in being placed on the lists, they tend to be ranked so low that their chances of actually being elected are minimal (Bitušiková, 2005b: 6; Heinen and Portet, 2002: 160–1; Rakušanová, 2003: 22; Renc-Roe, 2003: 13; Siemieńska, 1998).

It is still far from standard procedure for gender issues to be included in political party programmes and women politicians often feel their voices are not heeded (Gaber, 2003; Daskalova, 1997: 169; Fuszara, 2000; Graham and Regulska, 1997; Siemieńska, 1998). Women's relatively high party membership level in Slovenia is not reproduced in a corresponding presence in decision-making committees (Gaber, 1997: 148–9, 2003). Czech female MPs and Senators are perceived as less competent than their male equivalents, and are routinely assigned responsibility for and hence membership of parliamentary committees dealing with less prestigious issues such as welfare, health, education and culture. Frustration at the lack of women government ministers led in 2000 to the formation of the 'Women's Shadow Cabinet' in the Czech Republic. Despite some negative media coverage, this action was influential in establishing the Government Council for Equal Opportunities for Men and Women in October 2001, as required for EU accession (Rakušanová, 2003: 21–4).

Małgorzata Fuszara analysed the political broadcasts and the electoral programmes of individual political parties during the 1993 Polish elections, in which women gained 13 per cent of seats in the Sejm (Lower House). The decisive majority of parties, including both moderate and right-wing parties, as well as Solidarity, at that time made no mention whatsoever of women's or gender issues in their campaign materials. A second group mentioned women in the context of family policy, advocating an increase in maternity leave and benefits, and espousing the extension of opportunities for part-time work. A third set of parties, the smallest group, representing left of centre parties including the Democratic Left Alliance and the Labour Party, did raise issues of gender discrimination. They favoured the liberalization of abortion and measures to counteract high female unemployment and the feminization of poverty, albeit also in the context of supporting women-as-mothers, especially single mothers. Most tellingly, however, even this group did not raise gender issues such as abortion, labour market discrimination, or women's political presence in the media. All mention of gender in party political media broadcasts was framed within the dominant traditionalist discourse of a male-breadwinner model. Women appeared solely in relation to their ' "calling" as mothers and homemakers'. One right-wing party invoked religious discourse connected with the nationalist myth of the 'Polish Mother' in referring to 'the "cross" carried by Polish women' (Fuszara, 2000: 277–9).

In Lithuania, a similar pattern emerged in the 1996 parliamentary election campaign, during which no political parties either advocated or practised gender mainstreaming policies. Political party programmes fell into three groups on gender issues: those (four parties, mainly conservative) that had no explicit policies on women's rights or equal opportunities; those (Christian Democrats and the Lithuanian National Union) that paid a lot of attention to family questions, subsuming the interests of women as individuals to the group interests of the family; and those (four centre and left parties, including the Lithuanian Women's Party) that formulated clear policies on equal opportunities and gender equality. Nevertheless, a local study claims that the inclusion or exclusion of gender issues in electoral platforms was not the decisive factor affecting voting behaviour (Lithuanian Women's Issues Information Centre, 1999: 37–8, 58–9).

These analyses of televised party political broadcasts in Poland in 1993, and of electoral platforms in the 1996 Lithuanian elections suggest a political climate that marginalizes women and discounts gender as a political issue. Yet this is belied by voting behaviour in some countries suggesting that far from public opinion lagging behind legislation or political practice, the public are actually more in favour of women politicians than the (largely male-dominated) political parties. In the 1997 Polish elections a higher number of women was actually elected than their level of representation on party lists would seem to make possible; also more women were elected in individual precincts through direct elections than from party lists (Fuszara, 2000: 280; see also Heinen and Portet, 2002: 161–2; Siemieńska, 1998; Spurek, 2002).

There are some suggestions that after the early downturn, levels of female political representation in the region have been rising since 1994. In fact the data so far is inconclusive and contradictory, both within and between countries. Nor can a neat divide be drawn between Central and Eastern European countries. Neither has actual or aspiring EU accession candidacy necessarily improved gender equality in political representation. Recent data show that while there have been gradual improvements in the Czech Republic, Slovakia, Croatia, Bulgaria and Poland (the level dramatically doubling in the latter two between 1995 and 2001), by contrast levels of female representation have actually fallen since the mid-1990s in Hungary, Romania and Lithuania.[8]

Poland forms an illustrative case study in which divergent and contradictory trends demonstrate the difficulty of interpreting the available data, both empirical and analytical. In Poland the percentage of women MPs had already fallen in the period 1980–89. The level was halved again in 1991, but rose again to its 1989 level in 1993. In the 1997 elections the number of women elected to the Sejm (the Parliament) stayed constant, but the number in the Senate fell slightly. Małgorzata Fuszara interprets the fall since 1989 as the exact reverse of the trend in Western Europe where the number of women elected to Parliament has risen in the last few years.[9]

However, after Fuszara's analysis was published in 2000, there was another election in Poland in September 2001. This saw a dramatic increase in the number of female politicians elected from 13 per cent to 20 per cent in the Sejm (Lower House), and from 12 per cent to 23 per cent in the Senate (Lohmann, 2005: 3; Renc-Roe, 2003). This testifies mainly to the positive effects achieved by lobbying, especially by the Pre-Election Coalition formed by women's groups and NGOs specifically to support female parliamentary candidates. The group came together in reaction to the lack of policymaking on gender equality by the right-wing government that had held power from 1997 to 2001. That government dismantled National Women's Machinery, replacing it with an Office for the Family promoting a traditionalist patriarchal family model.

In response, the Coalition's strategy consisted of attending pre-election hustings to ask candidates about their attitudes and intentions with regard to gender equality issues. The campaign received considerable media coverage and contributed significantly to raising awareness amongst politicians and the public about gender issues (Lohmann, personal communication, August 2005; Lohmann and Seibert, 2003: 19).

Partly as a result of this lobbying, three left-of-centre political parties introduced a voluntary 30 per cent quota for women candidates. This resulted in 34.6 per cent of women on the Social Democratic coalition list and 30.3 per cent on the Freedom Union list, compared with only 12 per cent on the right-wing Solidarity Alliance (Heinen and Portet, 2002: 161).[10] In addition, while Solidarity Electoral Action (AWS) had no women among its top 30 candidates, and the Polish Agrarian Party (PSL) placed no women in the top 20 list places, the Freedom Union (UW), the Democratic Left Alliance (SLD) and the Union of Labour (UP) placed a number of the women in the top ten on their candidate lists, where they had more realistic chances of being elected. Between them, the winning coalition of the Democratic Left Alliance and the Labour Union had 36 per cent of women on their candidate lists, and 17 per cent of those in the first five positions were women (Renc-Roe, 2003: 13, 18).

There is debate about the impact of these quotas. Was the increase in female parliamentarians actually the direct result of lobbying by the Pre-Election Coalition? Did the positioning of some women high on candidate lists affect it? Or was it simply the numerical effect of election victory by a coalition of the Democratic Left Alliance and the Labour Union (accounting for the election of 55 women MPs)? (Renc-Roe, 2003: 17–20; Spurek, 2002). Whatever the principal cause, the 2001 elections in Poland contributed to changing political party positions on gender issues, and raised public awareness of and support for mechanisms to increase gender equality in political representation. An exit-poll survey of voters in the town of Nysa carried out by the Electoral Research Institute found that 84 per cent of women and 66 per cent of men felt there were too few women in politics, while 69 per cent of women and 52 per cent of men agreed with political parties adopting quotas for women on electoral lists (Renc-Roe, 2003: 21–2).

Moving gender from margin to centre: the quota debate

The previous chapter presented theoretical debates on the relative merits of different strategies for overcoming persistent gender bias in politics. The goal is the creation of gender equitable polities. This section presents debates and further data from Central and Eastern Europe pertaining to quotas. Quotas represent what the United Nations Convention on the Elimination of All Forms of Discrimination against Women (CEDAW) terms 'temporary special measures' which aim to overcome the legacy of inequality in political representation. A report published by the British Council suggests that the main reason the use of quotas remains controversial may well be the fact that they are so undeniably successful. Indeed they represent 'the most effective method in the short term to increase levels of women's representation' (Stephenson, 2004: 16).

Campaigning for quotas or parity in political representation may seem to some to represent a renunciation of feminist politics. This is because quotas appear to focus exclusively on the mechanics and the parameters of liberal democratic institutions, in the process renouncing substantive, not to speak of socially transformative political agendas.[11] Yet many concede that without quotas, it remains difficult to achieve a 'critical mass' of female representatives in national legislatures. The lack of such a 'critical mass' hinders the possibility of introducing gender-sensitive legislation, not to speak of achieving a truly representative form of democracy that speaks for, and utilizes the strengths of, its female as well as male citizenry (Renc-Roe, 2003: 6–7). An example can be found in Britain, where the Labour Party's introduction of 'women-only' candidate lists in some electorates doubled the percentage of female members of Parliament from 9.2 per cent in 1992 to 18.2 per cent in 1997 (Lovenduski, 1996, p. 9 table 2; Lovenduski, 1999, table 11.1, p. 191). Ironically it was male Labour Party candidates who contested this practice of 'women-only' lists as discriminatory in terms of the Sex Discrimination Act, which does not currently allow for affirmative action. There are plans to introduce such provision into the Act in 2006. In the meantime, the successful challenge resulted in lower levels of female representation after the 2001 elections, before it was overturned again for the 2005 elections. The argument for quotas is that they have the potential to overcome accumulated prior disadvantage that results in gender inequalities which 'would otherwise exclude women from political influence and power' (Phillips, 2002: 118).

The initial reaction of feminists in Central and Eastern Europe to quotas was one of hostility. Certainly 'quota' 'was a dirty word' at the beginning of the 1990s in the nine countries of Southeastern Europe that participated in 2001–02 in a training programme with a wide remit for the political empowerment of women (Lokar, 2003: 39). This was understandable within the historical and political context of a strong negative reaction to the past 40 years of state socialist political domination.

Quotas seemed reminiscent of the interventionist and undemocratic manipulation of the political process by the previous regimes, where token female representatives were installed in parliaments whose function was in any case restricted to the rubber-stamping of decisions taken elsewhere (Chimiak, 2003; Einhorn, 1993, 1996; Renc-Roe, 2003: 11).

Nonetheless, the experience of drastically lowered levels of female political representation has led to a gradual shift in attitude in some countries. A number of political parties in some countries in the region have adopted voluntary quotas. The Hungarian Socialist Party (the successor party to the Communist Party) has introduced a quota of 20 per cent for women and for people under 35 (Global Database of Quotas for Women, 2005). Of course this is less than the 30 per cent quota for women during the state socialist period in Hungary and elsewhere in the region that itself falls far short of representational parity (Fodor, 2002: 258). The Social Democratic Party in the Czech Republic has introduced quotas for women occupying party offices, and for women on its electoral lists (Rakušanová, 2003: 21). As already discussed above, three political parties in Poland adopted voluntary quotas in the run-up to the September 2001 elections.

In Bulgaria, a survey conducted by the Bulgarian Gender Research Foundation reported that a majority of respondents were opposed to the principle of quotas. Arguments included suspicion of the token representation of different categories of women through top-down imposition of quotas in the past. Negative attitudes of this kind are highest among women who are already active in politics, as the following quotation from a female MP demonstrates: 'I'm definitely against the application of quota models and regulations. ... Everyone has to find his/her own place and to be worthy of it no matter what sex' (Bulgarian Gender Research Foundation, 2000; Lokar, 2003: 40). Interestingly, public opinion in Bulgaria is less hostile. Another survey conducted in 2000, this time by the Bulgarian National Public Opinion Centre, found 49 per cent overall, and 59 per cent of women, in favour of quotas for women in parliament (Bulgarian National Public Opinion Centre, 2000; see also Chimiak, 2003: 17).

Resistance to special measures such as quotas is often couched in terms of the neo-liberal paradigm with its belief in individual political rights and the power of the market (Gaber, 2003; Havelková, 2000). Yet there seems to be a fairly wide consensus showing that the ground is shifting in favour of quotas. It is said that Czech women would now be more favourably disposed towards quotas than they were in the immediate post-state socialist period (Wolchik, 1998). In 1999, 63 per cent of Poles came out in favour of quotas for female political candidates (Heinen and Portet, 2002: 160). An unequivocal voice in favour of quotas comes from Karat Coalition of women's NGOs in the region founded in 1997. In their statement to the UN General Assembly in June 2000, Karat demanded that their governments introduce 'measures of affirmative action to overcome obstacles to women's equal participation in politics' (Karat, 2001).

A project initiated by the Stability Pact Gender Task Force in South Eastern Europe from the late 1990s aimed to improve the political empowerment of women through a whole range of measures. These included gender awareness building, training of women in political skills, campaigning for women to vote, lobbying for the establishment of national gender equality mechanisms, but also advocating the adoption of positive measures such as quotas in order to increase the number of female politicians at both national and local level (Lokar, 2003: 7). Ultimately their aim was to move via quotas to a situation of parity in political representation (Lokar, 2005). In the short space of time until early 2003, the project was already able to chalk up some remarkable successes. Even their defeats testified to intensive political campaigning by and on behalf of women.[12] Quotas were successfully implemented in four countries. Their defeat in another five was probably only the first step in a longer necessary campaign. The conclusions drawn by the project's leaders were that it is necessary to introduce quotas or other positive measures both in electoral legislation and on party statutes (Lokar, 2003: 43). A second project to establish quotas in social democratic parties was conducted between 1995 and 2005 by the Central and Eastern European Network for Gender Issues. Whilst acknowledging that there are many pros and cons related to the use of quotas as a gender equality mechanism, the Network has already seen both short- and longer-term positive effects from their introduction (Lokar, 2005).

Conclusion

The experience of both projects for women's political empowerment in South Eastern Europe suggests that even when quota rules have been instituted, they are often not observed. Many social democratic parties in Central and Eastern Europe introduced the quota rules solely in order to qualify for membership in the Socialist International, but once on the statutes, proceeded to ignore them. The process of European Union enlargement and elections for the European Parliament were helpful in applying pressure (Lokar, 2005: 10). The project leaders conclude that the only means of ensuring political party adherence to the implementation of quotas is through a broad coalition of forces. This includes cross-party alliances within legislatures as well as close cooperation between women parliamentarians and women's NGO networks at both the national and transnational level. What becomes clear is that positive strategies to increase women's political representation must be buttressed by civil society mobilization. It is to this that the next chapter turns.

4
Civil Society or NGOs
Empowerment or Depoliticization?[1]

Introduction

> Woman does not constitute a 'we' group. ... This may be one of the reasons why women's self-organizing and their capacity to (defend) their interest is still weak.
>
> Acsády, 1999: 406
>
> The truth is that Polish feminism can and does exist, though it is often tormented by self-doubt. As a movement – cultural, political, and intellectual – we are growing in numbers and becoming radicalized by the hour.
>
> Graff, 2002: 1

The parameters of the civil society to emerge from economic liberalization not only categorize and circumscribe those activities considered 'political' (Acsády, 1999; Gal, 1997; Gapova, 2001). They also affect the very formation of political identities and the spaces within which those identities can be mobilized (Einhorn and Sever, 2003, 2005; Young 1999: 226). This chapter identifies the ways in which both the processes of political identity formation and the spaces available for political activity are deeply gendered. It explores the impact of both material conditions and discursive trends on the political and other identities constructed during the transformation process. It asks how these factors have encouraged or discouraged women's use of civil society spaces for collective action.[2]

The first section elaborates the relationship of civil society theory to gender and feminist theory as well as to liberal democratic politics. Debates about the usefulness or applicability of Western feminist theory set the scene for discussion of the ongoing East–West feminist dialogue. This is followed by presentation of the kinds of women's and feminist groups that have emerged in Central and Eastern Europe. This section discusses the donor focus on NGOs rather than autonomous grassroots groups and asks whether this is encouraging the development of service provision rather than groups with an agenda of political and social transformation. The final section considers the role and importance of regional and transnational networking in strengthening the political agency of women's civil society associations in Central and Eastern Europe.

The new civil and political freedoms promised by democratization were themselves gendered, as the previous chapter has already demonstrated. Unequal access to political power was augmented by the stark social (gender, class, ethnic) differentiations that emerged in the course of the social and economic transformation process. The cumulative effect of massively increased gender inequalities encouraged expectations, especially on the part of Western feminist scholars, that strong women's and/or feminist groups might emerge in response to this turmoil. These expectations were in part an acknowledgement of the intensive involvement of women in independent peace and human rights groups, and dissident activity more generally during the late state socialist period (Kaldor, 1991; Einhorn, 1991, 1993, 1995). The high level of women's involvement at that time led some scholars to venture the theory that fundamental political change such as that in Central and Eastern Europe presents not only crises in gender relations or threats to women's rights, but also opportunities for feminist activism (Bystydzienski, 1992; Randall, 1998). However, contrary to expectations, no large-scale mobilization by either women's or explicitly feminist groups eventuated in the immediate aftermath of the transformation (Bystydzienski, 2001; UNRISD, 2005; Watson, 2001).

This chapter discusses the reasons for this apparent 'absence' of feminist mobilization. In so doing, it questions the idealization of the term 'civil society' and examines some 'myths of transition'.[3] The first of these myths suggests that despite – or perhaps precisely because of – their officially proclaimed 'equality', women were politically passive under state socialism. The myth perpetuates the construction of women as the objects of state socialist policy by presenting them as the 'victims' or 'losers' of the transformation process. In the second 'myth of transition' women are portrayed as undertaking very little to mobilize in defence of their rights out of the view that not only feminism, but all 'isms' and indeed politics in general is a 'dirty' or 'even shameful' business best left to men (Grunberg, 2000: 310).

It will be shown that these myths are inaccurate as well as simplistic. Not only do they fail to address differences in national and cultural contexts within the region, but more substantively, they under-estimate the actual existence of much grassroots activity before as well as after 1989. In so doing, they also tend to perpetuate 'traditional' definitions of political activity as exclusively occurring within political parties and legislatures. In this way they render much of women's activism invisible and rely on an a-historic conceptualization of the operation of civil society. The particular nature of the civil society 'created' by economic liberalization not only categorizes what it considers 'political', but also affects the formation of particular political identities and forms of mobilization. This process differs in the post-state socialist context in Central and Eastern Europe from that of the post-welfare state context in Western Europe (as well as from that within different national contexts in the region itself).

If one accepts the basic premise that feminism constitutes theorized experience, then the differing social realities, cultural traditions and varied experiences of the transformation process within the region will be theoretically formulated in a manner that differs fundamentally from British or US feminism (Havelková, 2000: 119–21). In 1990, a Czech (female) politician spoke of 'an allergy to feminism' in the region (Einhorn, 1993). This view remained remarkably persistent during the 1990s, provoking reluctance on the part of activists to be identified as feminists. A Polish survey in March 1996 revealed a majority of respondents who rejected the term 'feminism' without having any idea what it means (Fuszara, 2000: 282, and note 27). Views prevalent in Russia in the mid-1990s construed feminism as something unnatural (Bridger, 2000b). Even women activists were affected by this climate. A participant at a seminar for activists in Novocherkassk said: 'For a long time I did not know the exact definition of feminism. I always heard that feminist is a kind of term of abuse' (Ferree *et al.*, 1999: 103). In the Czech Republic, feminism is still today described as 'anti-family, anti-child and anti-feminine' (Hašková and Kolarová, 2003: 51). Research into the roots of strong anti-feminist attitudes in Hungary blames the media for 'misogynist ideas' that portray feminists as 'masculine, man-hating lesbian[s]'. Such abusive notions go hand in hand with pre-existing ideas of women as less than fully independent political subjects (Petö, 1997: 159). In Romania there is widespread hostility to both feminism and women's rights issues, characterized as 'Western concerns that are inappropriate to the Romanian context'. The majority of interviewees from Romanian women's NGOs interviewed in 1995–96 hastened to distance themselves from the label feminist (Grunberg, 2000: 323–4).

This chapter re-examines the antipathy towards feminist discourse in the region, especially in the light of ongoing debates between feminist activists and scholars in East and West. Charges levelled against Western feminist theory by women in Central and Eastern Europe echo earlier critiques of hegemonic Western feminist discourse raised by women of colour and women from the South. As in the earlier debates, part of the problem in East–West dialogues lies in the (largely unacknowledged) unequal power dynamics between East and West. These have seen Western – particularly American – feminists assume the ability to define the very nature of feminist politics as it is 'expected' to arise. This makes it difficult for feminists within the region to generate indigenous theories that might better fit their understanding of their own circumstances. This difficulty at one stage reached a point where some of those in the region who challenge the issues and analyses around which feminists in the UK and the US have mobilized, felt that they were accused of 'attacking democracy itself' (Gapova, 2001: 1).

Civil society and gender

Civil society theory too is subject to misunderstanding. The false assumption that its meaning is static fails to recognize that when concepts travel between different geographical, historical and cultural contexts, this inevitably affects the way they are interpreted and applied (Gal and Kligman, 2000a: 93; Gal, 1997: 32). Failure to acknowledge this results in the attempt to apply an a-historical concept to specific historical contexts. It also denies the fact that neither civil society space nor civil society discourse are neutral; above all, they are gendered. An example of such gendered relations of power in Romania is that 'civil society discourse ... is anti-state, and is elaborated by men, often as a means to launch their political careers' (Grunberg, 2000: 320). Peggy Watson asserts that 'it is the representation of civil society as an absolute political space rather than a socially specific domain of power relations ... that underlies the limits to mutual understanding of East and West, since what it means is the unwarranted universalization of the identities inherent in liberal civil society' (Watson, 1997: 27).

The concept of civil society was originally developed as part of liberal democratic theory during the eighteenth century to describe a space for the exercise of negative rights. It was defined as the embodiment of the right to 'freedom from' state interference, rather than an enabling or empowering space facilitating the 'freedom to' indulge in political action. The notion of civil society has subsequently come in political theory to define the space that exists between the state and the household in a democracy (Gal, 1997; Gal and Kligman, 2000a; Hann and Dunn, 1996; Keane, 1988, 1998). It is thus discursively placed at the boundary between the public (state and market) and the private (family, household) spheres. Seen in this light, 'civil society' represents the space between the legislative and regulatory power of the state and its institutional structures on the one hand, and the supposedly unregulated arena of the private sphere on the other. In the Cold War period, Western European second-wave feminist movements applied it to their attempts to re-work the public–private divide. Despite the negative freedom of its origins, then, 'civil society' came to represent a discourse of independent mobilization in a space both allowing and enabling political resistance to the state.[4]

In the latter years of state socialist regimes in Central and Eastern Europe, therefore, the concept of civil society became inextricably linked with the practice of political dissidence. The relationship between the state and its citizens was analysed at the time in terms of a 'lack' of the discursive space of civil society. The long arm of the state reached directly into every aspect of individuals' lives, leaving little space for the formulation of alternative discourses. 'Civil society' defined as a form of 'anti-politics' (an expression coined by György Konród) became virtually a code word for political opposition. Dissident groups active in the late 1970s and the 1980s such as Charta 77 in Czechoslovakia, the Hungarian Democratic Opposition, and Solidarity in Poland used the term as a 'rallying cry' (Gal and Kligman, 2000a: 91).

It was not only theorists and activists who became enamoured of the concept of 'civil society' following the end of state socialist regimes in the region. International agencies and funding bodies, the EU, the UN and national governments as well as policy analysts also apostrophized it as *the* space par excellence for the building of democracy in the region. A 1999 UNICEF study, for example, defines women's participation in civil society as 'vital for [their] well-being and, no doubt, for the success of the transition itself', since 'a strong civil society can provide a sound foundation for economic and political development in the transition countries' (UNICEF, 1999: 100). Yet it is important to recognize that the concept of civil society is itself an ideological construct of liberal democracy (Duhaček, 1998a; Gapova, 2001). Indeed it can be argued that its anchoring in this context may constitute a constraint on autonomous political organizing as a politically effective form within the different context of transformation in Central and Eastern Europe. Vlasta Jalušić cautions that 'the ambiguous acceptance of a simplistic liberal-democratic agenda with its limited view of politics, rules out the rethinking of the structural relations between public, private and intimate spheres and issues'. Nevertheless, she judges women's group activities to be building 'the groundwork for new definitions of the boundaries between the private and public, state, civil society and the family' (Jalušić, 2002: 104–5).

Ironically, the incorporation of former (male) dissidents into the parliaments and the consequent valorization of state power over civil society, inscribed the discursively vaunted civil society as in practice female-dominated and weak in comparison to (male) state power. Indeed in some cases, the new political institutions began to see civil society mobilization as a threat to their power. Lech Wałęsa, for example, disempowered the women's section of Solidarity before dismantling many citizens' committees in Poland, just as grassroots movements were beginning to gain force (Tarasiewicz, 1991).

The tendency to marginalize civil society organizations in relation to state institutions was compounded for women's groups by hostility to the concept of gender equality as a political issue, to women's organizing in general, and to feminism in particular in both popular discourse and the media (Acsády, 1999; Havelková, 1997; UNICEF, 1999). The Romanian media often ignore or trivialize the women's movement, thereby contributing to its marginalization before it has been able to establish itself strongly (Grunberg, 2000: 309). In her analysis of this, Laura Grunberg appears herself to accept the secondary status of civil society activism, asserting that 'adopting a politics of anti-politics is not appropriate for post-1989 circumstances'. She chides women activists for not recognizing their activities as political, yet feels that a lack of gender awareness is hardly surprising given the legacy of state socialist rhetoric about women's 'emancipation' as something already achieved (Grunberg, 2000: 313).

The next chapter returns to an earlier argument about how the private sphere was valorized during the state socialist period as a kind of civil society in embryo (Einhorn, 1993). Within this space, conceptualized as the sole locus of individual autonomy and independence from state interference, gender-neutral solidarity reigned. This solidarity excluded any discussion of gender-based inequalities or intra-household conflict. Consequently 'there is no tradition of women asserting their interests independently of men's, whether in the public or in the private sphere' (Bast-Haider, 1993:13, cited in Chamberlayne, 1995: 30). It is striking that Jan Kubik's categorization of four main types of civil society organizations under authoritarian regimes does not include the private sphere of extended family, kinship and friendship networks in which women played so large a role in Central and Eastern Europe. The four groupings are: official associations or a pseudo-civil society (which would include the former official Women's Associations or Unions); networks anchored in informal economic activities (often mediated through the private sphere, and hence the category that could in theory encompass the embryo civil society defined above); 'opposition', or 'dissident' groups; and organizations sponsored by religious institutions (Kubik, 2000, cited by Hašková and Kolarová, 2003: 45–6).[5]

Women's political subjectivity was formed by a system that had already granted them formal political equality, and thus rendered mobilization around 'women's issues' secondary to other political goals. Issues that mobilized West European feminists, such as demands for abortion rights, increased political representation, childcare facilities, or welfare provision were invisible for Eastern European women because such rights and social entitlements were granted from above by a paternalist socialist state. The enjoyment of social provision 'as of right', stigmatized in recent Western discourse as 'welfare dependency', tended to provoke inertia and political apathy (Dölling, 1991; Duffy, 2000; Einhorn, 1993; Gapova, 2001; Havelková, 2000; Szalai et al., 1990). Nor was there awareness that such provisions – taken for granted because they were part of the 'givens' of the regime – in fact embodied rights that could be lost (Dölling, 1991). Seen against this background, the level of women's activity in civil society associations and NGOs since 1989 can be interpreted as surprisingly high, rather than as a disappointing 'retreat' from politics.

There is also more continuity of activity than would at first appear. As is already clear from the argument above that civil society space is not neutral, the idea that its development would be simple once state restraints were removed, turns out to be erroneous. Nor is it straightforward to assert that civil society activism was previously impossible or non-existent because the politically repressive state did not allow it. While it is true that autonomous political activity was frowned upon and actively restricted, a certain level of community involvement was by contrast explicitly supported by the regimes. One example was the neighbourhood or apartment block committees, held responsible for tending the collective gardens of apartment blocks or cleaning the communal spaces of stairwells (Chamberlayne, 1990). These could be seen as civil society activities, even if they did not represent strictly self-organized initiatives at their inception. Similarly, there was parental involvement in schools. Such activities differed fundamentally from those of official, pseudo-civil society organizations like the National Fronts or the Women's Councils in most countries in the region.

Nevertheless, these activities have usually been downplayed or interpreted negatively. Some analysts have felt that people's retreat into the haven of the private represented an abdication of social responsibility rather than a recourse to a social or political resource. In this interpretation, the officially legitimized (rather than spontaneously generated) neighbourhood and work collectives are seen as empty shells, or at best, social collectivities devoid of political impact. Still others have argued that any collective action or networks that did exist arose from the need for goods and services not satisfied by the shortage economies of state socialism. In this view, the embryo civil society of extended family and friendship networks were formations driven by economic necessity. Hence they were thought unlikely to survive the transformation, since the assumption was that in the future the market would satisfy such needs. In a more positive interpretation, Prue Chamberlayne argues that 'an ethic of mutual self-help, backed by trust and a sense of physical security, was strongly and proudly upheld in East Germany' (Chamberlayne, 1995: 28–9, 1990). Susan Gal hypothesizes that despite the tokenistic nature of women's involvement at the level of state structures, they may have felt that their power to make individual choices and decisions, while not extensive, was at least equal to that of men, but exercised differently, through their role in the family. Thus 'we must see the gendered aspects of post-1989 organizational change in Eastern Europe as the ideological effect of shifting boundaries in a social field that was not only already occupied, ... but also already structured by discourses and practices developed during state socialism and already focused on ideas about privacy, sexual difference, and nature' (Gal, 1997: 35).

Most of the theoretical literature on civil society is remarkably silent on issues of gender inequalities, and on the gender-specific nature of access to this space. This theoretical silence has material consequences when the concept is applied to the transformation situation. The individual who has the capacity to mobilize politically within civil society is based on liberal democratic theory's gender-blind definition of the citizen as untrammelled by social responsibilities. The rigid separation of the public and the private spheres that provides the basis of patriarchy remains unchallenged by the concept of civil society that, despite ambiguity, is in fact located in the public sphere. Civil society thus emerges as a space structured by gendered relations of unequal power (Einhorn and Sever, 2003, 2005; Lang, 1997: 103; Watson, 2000a). The utilization of civil society spaces by women's movements is therefore subject to the same constraints as the involvement of women in state structures. There is also a question as to whether the goal of civil society organizing should be 'equality' within the existing institutional structures or rather the re-definition and re-formation of these institutions and their underlying discourses. The concluding chapter of this book considers whether discourses of 'empowerment', rights, 'capabilities' or 'entitlements' might prove more effective than civil society discourse in enabling women to exercise their rights and responsibilities as citizens and members of social collectives.

Feminism in East–West dialogue

A central and ongoing feature of the transformation period has been the process of constructive yet often difficult dialogue between feminists in East and West. Several scholars have noted that it would be both inappropriate and politically unacceptable simply to map existing Western feminist theories onto the experience of societies in Central and Eastern Europe undergoing radical economic, social and political transformation (Einhorn, 1993: 211–12; Havelková, 2000: 118). Second-wave feminism in Western Europe and the US itself emerged from a quite different set of social realities and historically specific experiences. Feminist theories and feminist movements must therefore be seen as politically, culturally and historically contingent (Basu, 1995; Gal, 1997: 31–2).[6]

Earlier, I wrote that a 'joint adventure to reformulate the feminist project necessitates a process of listening in a spirit of openness and mutual tolerance' (Einhorn, 1993: 212). It may be that this project is now becoming possible, following the exploration of differences and disagreements that was its necessary precursor. Kornelia Slavova denotes the first stage of the 'feminist East-West encounter' as one of two-way 'translation', both literal and metaphorical. In this process, feminists in Central and Eastern Europe were literally translating Western feminist theories: 'we borrowed feminist methodologies, models of women-centred institutions or gender/women's studies educational programmes, models for legal and policy reform, conceptual apparatuses'. At the same time, Eastern feminists attempted to ' "translate" back into English our different experience as postcommunist women, trying to explain to the West our situation in Western theoretical terms (which did not work really well because of the drastically different social and economic setting and the meaning behind established concepts)' (Slavova, 2006:2).

As a result, in the 1990s the debate often mirrored – or re-constructed – the Cold War East–West binary in new feminist clothes. Western feminists perceived activists in Central and Eastern Europe as adopting or colluding with 'regressive' traditional images of femininity and self-sacrifice that prevented the exercise of active citizenship. In turn, women in the region were critical of what they saw as the individualistic and selfish nature of feminism in Western Europe (Gal, 1997: 31; Havelková, 1997, 2000; Kulczycki, 1999; Šmejkalová, 2001). As in all debates and misunderstandings, there was some truth on both sides. In this context, the early German–German dialogue with its manifestation of conflicting conceptions of feminism was particularly illuminating for the ways it revealed persistent mutual misperceptions and mistrust, even in a situation of shared language and shared cultural heritage (Einhorn, 1995b; Ferree, 1995; Gerhard, 2003; Lang, 1997; Lennox, 1995; Maleck-Lewy, 1997; Rosenberg, 1996; Teschner, 2000).

If feminism is a movement that has arisen in and constitutes its political subjects within specific historical and cultural contexts, then the expectation that feminist political activism would emerge in Central and Eastern Europe was actually inappropriate *in advance of* the creation of feminist political identities within the newly prevailing economic and political conditions. The incomprehension of some Western feminists faced with what they saw as the failure of women in Central and Eastern Europe to mobilize politically within the new spaces of civil society was therefore matched by the resentment of feminists in the region at the imposition of what they perceived as culturally hegemonic criteria unsuited to capturing their very different life experiences and delivered in a patronizing, even 'colonialist' style (Bassnett, 1992; Einhorn, 1993, 1995; Fábián, 2003; Nash, 2003; Petö, 2003: 194; Roman, 2001: 61; Šmejkalová, 2001; Watson, 2000b: 379).[7] In the twenty-first century it is necessary to move beyond this vicious circle of mutual recrimination (Havelková, 2000: 119). To achieve that, however, necessitates a further process. 'Before we can know which aspects of Western feminist theories can be applied to Eastern European realities or whether feminist concepts should be reformulated entirely before being applied there, it is necessary to delineate the differences between Western feminist theories and Eastern European realities' (Havelková, 2000: 120).

This book attempts to contribute to this ongoing dialogue, relying heavily – as did my earlier book – on the voices, the views, and the analyses of women from the region, in order to listen, to understand and to convey their perspectives (Einhorn, 1993). At the present time there is perhaps greater preparedness on both sides to acknowledge commonalities and shared problems as well as differences and misunderstandings. In the early years, East European feminists bridled at what they experienced as 'the "colonialist" comportment' of some 'Western experts' advising NGOs in the region: 'The phenomenon of idealizing the benefactor has led to some resentment of Western specialists who travel from what are assumed to be lush offices in their home institutions to the improvised offices of the recipient NGOs' (Grunberg, 2000: 316–17). While such descriptions are undoubtedly apt for some of the international donor agencies operating in the region, they were usually less likely to apply to Western feminist organizations with whom there has been much successful cooperation.

Hana Havelková believes that 'Eastern European women tend to over-emphasize the differences between Western theories and post-communist realities'. Even though she finds it methodologically 'imperative ... to keep working with the consciousness of difference between Western and Eastern European experiences', she also believes that there are 'basic commonalities in gender relations between the Czech lands and Western culture' (Havelková, 2000: 120). Polish feminists too felt by the end of the 1990s less of a need 'to distinguish their brand of feminism from western and Marxist feminisms' (Bystydzienski, 2001: 509). A particularly positive approach is offered by Denise Roman, who argues that the very social, historical and cultural contingency of Western theories of gender makes gender a useful tool of analysis applicable to *any* context and *any* historical situation (Roman, 2001: 62). This spirit of understanding and respecting differences, while also recognizing common interests in analysing the specificities of gender relations in different countries and regions makes constructive dialogue both possible and necessary in the quest to develop strategies conducive to the achievement of gender equity. This dialogue could be facilitated through recognition and acknowledgement of the impact of shared specific contexts. These include European Union enlargement, and the neo-liberal agenda that currently dominates the frame of economic globalization.

The difficulty is to formulate theories and strategies that might be deemed more appropriate to the specific situation of societies undergoing such fundamental processes of transformation. Daša Duhaček refers to the danger of replicating binary oppositions when she asks: 'How do we speak of feminism which is other *than* Western feminism, if not as a feminism which is the other to it, which would presuppose Western feminism as the parameter?' (Duhaček, 1998a: 129; emphasis in the original; see also Gapova, 2001: 1). Elżbieta Kaczynska, a member of the Polish Feminist Association in Warsaw stated in 1995: 'We tend to talk about our [Polish] feminism as what it's not – it's not like what the communists meant by gender equality or what it's like in the West – but we seldom state positively what Polish feminism is, or could be about' (Kaczynska, cited by Bystydzienski, 2001: 508). One important step in the development of societally specific theories – as it was for West European feminisms – is the rediscovery of earlier women's movements in each country, that is the history of the feminist 'foremothers'. An especially significant contribution to this history is the biographical dictionary of women's movements and feminisms in the region during the nineteenth and twentieth centuries (de Haan *et al.*, 2006)[8]

Despite disavowals of identification as feminists, there is in practice evidence of a thriving feminist discourse in the region. This has been particularly evident in the veritable explosion of academic Women's Studies and Gender Studies programmes. Many have been set up by independent providers, such as the Women's Studies Centres in Belgrade and Zagreb, which offer an impressive array of courses and work in cooperation with – or working towards successful accreditation by – universities. Successfully institutionalized university courses and programmes have been established in Warsaw, Berlin, Prague, Bucharest and Cluj, Vilnius and Riga among others.[9] The process of acceptance of Gender Studies as an academic discipline has, however, not always been easy, as documented for Ukraine (Kupryashkina, 1997; Pavlychko, 1997; Zherebkina, 2001; Zhurzhenko, 2001b). Particularly impressive has been the expansion in Russia from the lone Moscow Gender Studies Centre within the Academy of Sciences in 1990, to Women's Studies Centres and university courses in over 60 cities and universities across Russia and the CIS (Grünell, 1998; Khotkina, 2001: 345; Lipovskaya, 2001; Lisyutkina, 2003; Posadskaya, 1994; Posadskaya-Vanderbeck, 1997). Another particularly important and successful initiative has been the electronic sharing of information and scholarship via the electronic library of the Women's and Gender Studies Association of Countries in Transition (http://www.zenskestudie.edu.yu/wgsact/electronic-library.html). Vera Mackie points out that the internet has transformative potential in supporting transnational feminist linkages, through 'the potential to challenge notions of community based on simple geographical proximity, and the potential to force a rethinking of the "politics of location"' (Mackie, 2001: 193).

A relatively recent initiative that integrates feminist theory with practice is the Bulgarian Gender Research Foundation (BGRF). This is an independent NGO which 'promotes gender equality and women's human rights in Bulgaria through research, education and advocacy programmes' with the goal of 'promoting and facilitating the achievement of a gender balanced society in Bulgaria based on equal representation of women and men'. One could question 'equal representation' as the ultimate goal of gender equality. Yet the research, education and advocacy of the foundation target three specific issues: violence against women, especially domestic violence and sexual harassment at work; women's socio-economic rights; and women's political participation. 'These are all issues new for Bulgaria, difficult to work on and controversial in our society' (Bulgarian Gender Research Foundation, 2000).

The bodies of feminist theory that became the academic disciplines of Women's Studies, and later Gender Studies, can be said in the West to have emerged from reflexivity about women's grassroots activism and experience. It seems that their establishment in the region of Eastern and Central Europe in some cases mirrors this trajectory, but more often initiates rather than reflects feminist activism. In Russia, the 1996 conference organized by the Moscow Centre for Gender Studies discussed precisely the relationship between Women's/Gender Studies on the one hand, and feminism/women's activism on the other. Anastasia Posadskaya-Vanderbeck points out that this discussion *followed* the earlier need for immediate political activism in view of the fact that 'perestroika was happening without women'. This meant that 'politics, not education, was the entry point for feminism. Before teaching feminism ... we had to do feminism. We first had to create Russian women's experiences in contributing to and challenging the processes of democratization in order to be able to learn from and teach about those experiences' (Posadskaya-Vanderbeck, 1997: 374). Yet in the Baltics, Irina Novikova remarks on the opposite trajectory, commenting on the ' "marketization" of the field from the very beginning' in terms of having to seek funding and resources, usually from Western foundations, to guarantee successful institutionalization in the academy. She also points to the fact that 'the factor of grass-roots activism, so important for women's studies, was absent in our situation' (Novikova, 2001: 325).

Irene Dölling makes an important contribution to the future of Women's and Gender Studies based on the understanding of 'gender as a structural category' affecting all social relationships. This leads her on the one hand to espouse gender mainstreaming in the academy as well as in state institutions and policymaking processes. On the other, she argues compellingly that an exclusive focus on East–West relations and the transformation process is too narrow. Instead, she asserts, Women's and Gender Studies need 'to address gender relations and the general effects of "gender" in all the relations of a globalized world' (Dölling, 2001: 64).

Grassroots activism

Since the beginning of the transformation process, women's civil society activism has burgeoned. What is clear, however, is that – just as elsewhere in the world – this activism was very often not aimed at advancing women's rights, nor sought to establish gender justice. Much less was it explicitly feminist in challenging gender-based discrimination and unequal gender roles (UNRISD, 2005: 167). Women's political mobilization depends upon prior recognition of common interests. These common interests are not necessarily or always gender interests (Molyneux, 2001: 152).

The discussion that follows refers back to Maxine Molyneux's distinction, first formulated in 1985 and re-cast in 1988/2001, between practical and strategic gender interests. Practical interests derive from the immediate conditions that disadvantage women, such as poverty, domestic violence, childcare and reproductive health issues, seen as a major factor in the analysis of state intervention. Action to address these issues is largely undertaken by charities or grassroots NGOs providing services for specific groups. Strategic gender interests often arise from these practical needs, but rest on recognition of the structural and systemic causes of gender-based disadvantaging within a given culture. They thus involve a longer-term view and the wish to bring about systemic change (Molyneux, 1985, 2001: 153). Crucial in this process is the political intention, involving the 'capacity ... for questioning, undermining or transforming gender relations and the structures of subordination' (Young, 1993: 156).

A study of gender issues in Central and Eastern Europe published by UNICEF in 1999 identifies four main areas of women's civil society mobilization during the 1990s (UNICEF, 1999). These were: political participation; the promotion of business and professional activities; the provision of social services such as health care and education; and action to eliminate violence against women both in gender relations in the private sphere, and in military conflict. Of these, groups dedicated to achieving political change through increased gender equality in politics were clearly a tiny minority. Patrice McMahon identifies five types of women's NGOs in Poland and Hungary: liberal or feminist groups; conservative or religious groups; women's sections in political parties or trade unions; professional women's associations; and research institutes or Gender and Women's Studies Centres (McMahon, 2002: 40–1).

The UNICEF study lists 50 women's NGOs in Romania,[10] 70 in Ukraine, 160 in Estonia, and 600 in Russia in 1997/98 (UNICEF, 1999: 102, table 6.2; on Russia, see also Kay, 2000; Marsh 1996; Sperling, 1999). The *Directory of Women's Organizations and Initiatives in Poland*, published in 1995, listed more than 70 organizations, ranging from feminist and women's rights groups to church groups, and from professional groups, especially supporting women entrepreneurs, to groups supporting families, single mothers and battered women (Fuszara, 2000: 281–2). By 2000, there were 150 registered women's organizations in Poland, and by 2005 this had grown to more than 300 (Bystydzienski, 2001: 506; Lohmann, 2005: 3). Of 65,000 non-profit organizations registered in Hungary in 1997, 60 were labelled women's groups (Petö, 2002: 367). Women's NGOs in Hungary tend to be divided between professional and political groups. The latter also divide into those addressing – and supporting – women in their traditional roles within the family, and groups like the Hungarian Feminist Network, who remain somewhat isolated (Petö, 1997: 157,159). Women headed 84 per cent of NGOs in the Czech Republic in 1995, but at that time, NGOs were still considered politically weak (Kligman, 1996: 72). By 2003 there were 59 women's organizations in the Czech Republic, plus a further 21 projects committed to supporting women's rights or gender equality (Hašková and Kolarová, 2003: 48). By 1995 there were 35 women's organizations in Bulgaria. The majority of these, particularly the most influential groups, were those closely linked with political parties, at a high cost in terms of the subordination of gender concerns to party interests and party discipline (Daskalova, 2000: 353, 359).

One of the discussions about women's movements concerns the differences between women's and feminist groups (Alvarez, 1999; Beckwith, 2000; Molyneux, 1988/2001). Sonia Alvarez has defined the latter in a manner that in fact bears a strong resemblance to Molyneux's identification of groups following strategic gender interests. In Alvarez's view, feminist as opposed to women's movements see themselves as 'working to alter gender power relations that circumscribe their own lives as women' (Alvarez, 1999: 186; see also Beckwith, 2000: 437). Women's organizations in Romania fall into three main types: feminist organizations; women's organizations; women-friendly organizations. All of them share the view that 'feminism as a label must be avoided as compromising, and that gender policies should be redirected toward social assistance, not toward consciousness raising and emancipation' (Roman, 2001: 59–60). The Romanian Centre for Political Studies has divided Romanian NGOs differently, according to the focus of their activities, categorizing them as either 'institutionally-oriented NGOs' focused on politics; community-oriented groups largely concerned with culture, education and religion; or 'everyday-oriented NGOs' which are in effect service providers operating in the voluntary sector. The first type – which one might see as having a political and socially transformative agenda – are in a minority and significantly less active than other types of NGOs. Only three of 29 organizations studied between 1995 and 1996 were directly concerned with women's rights. Romanian NGOs address human rights rather than women's rights, which 'have been virtually silenced in the public sphere. It is more customary – even among women themselves – to speak about the rights of homosexuals, Roma or Gypsies, the Hungarian minority, or street children, than about the rights of women'. The women's movement in Romania is still weak because 'women represent a genuine force in civil society whose potential has not yet been adequately recognized or realized' (Grunberg, 2000: 312, 328, 331).

It is clear in all countries that specifically political groups taking a longer view on feminist goals such as gender equity form a minority compared with what one might call first aid or social welfare groups geared to issues of women's professional, emotional and social survival (Daskalova, 2000: 360; Fábian, 2003; Grunberg, 2000; Nash, 2003; UNICEF, 1999). The Bulgarian Women's Association – set up in 1993 and seeing itself as the heir to the largest pre-Communist women's organization – largely operates within an older model of charity, responding to the exigencies of transformation (Daskalova, 1997: 165). While the existence of prostitution, violence against women, and labour market discrimination are acknowledged, these issues tend to be treated as social problems emerging from economic restructuring rather than as examples of gender discrimination (Corrin, 1996; Havelková, 1997: 57; Mršević, 2000). In the Czech Republic most groups treat violence against women as a health care issue. They focus on the family and on childcare issues; women's professional development and labour market activity; and issues of environmental protection. The persistent prevalence of anti-feminist prejudice seems to explain why only a small proportion of women's groups in the Czech Republic define themselves as feminist or deal with issues of women's status in society. (Hašková and Kolarová, 2003: 48).

In the early post-communist period, some of the former official women's councils managed to survive, metamorphosing into new political groupings, or becoming part of new umbrella organizations. Two examples are the Union of Women of Russia, and the League of Polish Women (Buckley, 1997; Fuszara, 1997; Posadskaya, 1991, 1994; Sperling, 1999; UNICEF, 1999). The Czech Union of Women is still able to draw on its pre-1989 networks, making it a large organization in a landscape otherwise characterized by women's groups of around ten activists (Hašlková and Kolarová, 2003: 49). In Romania too, a Women's National Forum, established in 1993, and the Council for Social Dialogue among Women's NGOs, set up in 1996, 'appear to have reconstituted the structure and mentality of the now defunct Communist era National Union of Women' (Grunberg, 2000: 318). In Bulgaria, the sizeable Democratic Union of Women (DUW) is heir to the official Women's Union of the Communist period and is strongly linked with the Bulgarian Socialist Party, itself the renamed successor to the former Communist Party. The DUW's programme is welfarist, and brackets women with the family. Krassimira Daskalova asserts that 'the long patriarchal tradition of the Communist Party here hides behind the thin veil of women's activism' (Daskalova, 2000: 354–5).

Such reincarnations of the old regime-dependent official women's councils tend to be viewed with suspicion by the new autonomous movements (Einhorn, 1993). In Russia, their impact was also short-lived. The Union of Women of Russia was one of three members of a new political party called 'Women of Russia', which succeeded in getting 23 deputies elected to the Lower House of the Russian Parliament in 1993. In 1995, only three of its deputies were elected. This drop has been attributed to a variety of factors, including lack of funding, an anti-women bias in politics, and voter disenchantment with 'their lack of a clear set of policies' (Buckley, 1997: 166; Kay, 2000: 60). Nevertheless, some analysts stress that the effective demise of Women of Russia as a political force to be contended with 'should not be confused with the level of support for institutionalized political participation or commitment to building an autonomous women's movement in Russia' (Ferree *et al.*, 1999: 102; see also Sperling, 1998).

In Hungary, independent, self-help and grassroots groups were still a rarity in the late 1990s, particularly those with any kind of feminist agenda. Most women's groups mobilized around women's role as mothers, while others attempted to defend social rights by fighting to keep nurseries open or to maintain childcare leave provisions (Acsády, 1999). In Bulgaria, the women's movement in the late 1990s was conspicuous by its absence. Krassimira Daskalova interprets this 'failure' as 'due to the fact that public space is now occupied by the discourses of "femininity"'. Further she claims that women's organizations themselves contribute to the problem with their 'dogged support for motherhood'. This leads to the discursive marginalization of issues of identity, rights, domestic violence or other forms of gender inequality (Daskalova, 2000: 362).

Such 'dogged support for motherhood' is consonant with the ideal of the mother/eternal feminine that emerged in nationalist and traditional or religious discourses at the beginning of the transformation process, and significantly influenced the nature of women's activism in the early years in several countries (Alsop and Hockey, 2001; Bracewell, 1996; Bystydzienski, 2001; Gapova, 1998; Heinen, 1995; Janova and Sineau, 1992; Ostrowska, 1998; Pine, 1994; Reading, 1992; Zajović, 2005). Yet some have argued that it is mistaken to see activism constructed in terms of motherhood as necessarily retrograde in feminist terms. Women's groups in the region have consciously chosen to deploy their role as mothers as a political stance. This echoes the very successful campaigning of women's groups like the Madres de la Plaza de Mayo who were instrumental in the transition from military rule to democratic regimes in Latin America (Feijoo, 1998: 33–7; Jaquette, 1989, 1994). Groups like the Prague Mothers or the South Bohemian Mothers deliberately conduct their activities in opposition to environmental degradation in the name of their children's health. Many such groups deny that they are political organizations at all (Hašková and Kolarová, 2003: 50; Wolchik, 1998: 171–2). In Russia, women's organizations campaigned to rescue their sons from bullying and intimidation during military service, or to resist their deployment in Afghanistan (White, 2000). The parents who invaded the Yugoslav Parliament in 1991 also sought to bring their sons back from the front (Lukič, 2000).

These kinds of groups hoped to translate their enhanced status as mothers within the discursively and materially elevated private sphere of late state socialism into political capital in the post-state socialist present. Their activities embraced a reconstructed 'feminine' identity within newly dominant traditionalist discourses around gender. They used motherhood as a moral basis for public demands. Yet this stance tended to obscure women as political actors and – in the case of Serbia – simultaneously rendered them susceptible to co-optation by the very divisive ethno-nationalist political project they sought to oppose (Lukič, 2000; Žarkov, 1997). Motherhood deployed in an anti-war protest that was initially united across ethnic and national boundaries was 'transformed into mothers demonstrating to support nationalistic politics' and the war itself (Nikolič-Ristanovič, 1998: 235; Ugrešić, 1998a: 120–1).

Tatiana Zhurzhenko argues that 'in the former socialist countries, emerging new identities are domesticated by the authorities and used by political elites for their own interests in order to manipulate new social movements' (Zhurzhenko, 2001a: 30). In focusing their political activities on the family (protecting their children's health or saving their sons) or the nation (opposing divides along ethnic national lines), these women activists were represented by those in power, and by the media, as in no way challenging traditional gender hierarchies. Consequently, their activities further entrenched socialized gender identities, but did not transfer into recognizable new political identities.

There is a growing awareness of the intersection of various forms of difference in women's subordination. This is particularly relevant for minority groups suffering dual discrimination, where gender intersects with and is augmented by discrimination on the basis of ethnicity. New civil society groupings in several countries deal specifically with discrimination against Roma women (Petö, 1997; Szalai, 2005). Acknowledging that the shape of the transformation process in each country has its roots in the recent past, women in several initiatives collect oral history accounts of life under state socialism (Beck, 2000; Dölling, 1992, 1994a; Dölling et al., 1992; Schendler, 2001; True et al., 1999; Věšinová-Kalivodová, 2005: 426).

The national context obviously influences the issues and priorities of local women's movements. In the early 1990s, for example, the traditionalist-nationalist image of woman-as-mother-of-the-nation, which itself reflected the influence of the Catholic Church over Polish civil society, had the effect of stifling political debate on women's issues other than those linked to the family and reproduction. The abortion issue was the one question that galvanized groups with more broadly political goals within a context where it was male politicians and Church leaders who assumed the right to decide (Fuszara, 2000; Siemieńska, 1998; Zielińska, 2000). Two Polish organizations to arise in response to the attack on women's reproductive rights were the Federation for Women and Family Planning (formed in 1992) and Ośka, the National Women's Information Centre launched by 12 women's NGOs in 1995. Specific historical and cultural constructions of civil society and political activity have operated in the Ukraine too, dictating the formation of certain types of organizations while inhibiting the identification of a widespread women's movement or feminist politics at this time (Pavlychko, 1992, 1996, 2000; Rubchak, 1996, 2001; Zhurzhenko, 2001c).

One of the few explicitly feminist groups to be formed immediately at the time of the changes was the Independent Women's Association of eastern Germany (UFV). Resourceful self-help groups formed to combat the worst effects of the mass female redundancies. Two main issues split the UFV: the first concerned engagement in mainstream politics as opposed to single-issue projects (which one could interpret as addressing strategic versus practical gender needs); the second raged between women close to the PDS (Party of Democratic Socialism), successor party to the ruling East German Communist Party, and those wishing to reject that heritage (Behrend, 1995; Einhorn, 1991, 1995b; Maleck-Lewy, 1997; Young, 1999). Feminist groups that still exist today include the Polish Feminist Association and the Hungarian Feminist Network. The early surge of feminist activism in Hungary, Poland and Eastern Germany quickly showed signs of suffering from: hostility to feminism, activist burnout and political conflict respectively (Acsády, 1999; Einhorn, 1995b; Jankowska, 1991; Maleck-Lewy, 1997; Petö, 2002: 368). Groups in many countries subsequently concentrated on small, single-issue campaigns. Telephone hotlines and women's shelters were urgently necessary initiatives (Corrin, 1996; Fuszara, 1997: 135–6; Korać, 1996; Mlađenović and Matijašević, 1996; Mršević, 2001; Šribar, 2002). In their more limited focus, these groups could be said to have rejected the monolithic structures and universalized objectives of the state-led women's 'movement' of the past. It is important to note, however, that this was also a trend characteristic of Western women's groups during the same period.

Sabine Lang (1997) discusses the trajectory though which feminist aspirations were in her view side-tracked into single-issue campaigns in eastern Germany. She also documents a trend in united Germany – via the employment at institutional, local and national level of Equal Opportunities Officers – towards the professionalization of autonomous women's groups. Lang feels that the acknowledgement of gender equality concerns through such job creation was not necessarily synonymous with the incorporation of these concerns into policy. In other words, the German experience shows that between the acknowledgement of gender as a social determinant and the implementation of gender mainstreaming, there is a time lag.

Lang calls this trend the 'NGOization of feminism'. The transition from grassroots movement politics to professionalized NGO brings with it a structural tendency to move from a rejection of hierarchies to the establishment of new forms of hierarchy. Similarly, there is 'a tendency to translate the "traditionally" complex feminist agenda of emancipation and equality into specific single issues and a form of politics with a predominantly state-oriented focus'. Women's NGOs and single-issue projects become a source of potential careers rather than mobilizing around ideas of feminism and gender equality. In other words, 'NGOization' results in feminist priorities and activities becoming skewed towards state dependency and hence towards the implementation of political agendas dictated from above. 'Feminist NGOs are in danger of adapting to the vertical structure of current political life'. This is particularly problematic, Lang argues, in situations where there is a simultaneous decrease in the level of female political participation (Lang, 1997: 102, 113–15). Other commentators have by contrast welcomed the professionalization of women's NGOs, partly because of the way it has strengthened their ability to exert a more direct influence on legislative and political processes, but not least because it may help them develop the expertise to access external funding via complex application processes (Hašková, 2005).

The predominance of NGOs raises three key problematic issues. The first is the tendency for civil society activism to be reduced to NGO activities (Howell and Pearce, 2001: 91). Democratization in the region has been construed as dependent on the development of a vibrant civil society sector, which has in turn been seen as involving NGO activity (Hann and Dunn, 1996: 7). Yet such reductionism can have a de-politicizing effect, shrinking the political horizon from the quest for gender (and social) justice within the democratization process to immediate short-term issues demanding urgent attention. In the process, rather than empowering women politically, NGO activism could contribute to their marginalization and invisibility (Tinker, 1999: 88, 94). A more radical critique of this reduced civil society raises the question whether 'because "civil society" has become the fashionable concept of the 1990s it is reasonable to ask how far the growth of these activities is genuinely independent and how far it represents an artificially created demand in response to the various programmes established to support NGOs by Western governments, European institutions and private foundations' (Kaldor and Vejvoda, 1999/2002: 18).

The second problem is that in a context of marketization, privatization and state retrenchment, as dictated by the IMF and the World Bank (in the so-called Washington Consensus), the role of civil society organizations in general and NGOs in particular becomes service provision and thus the maintenance of the social status quo rather than political critique or advocacy for social change. Such service provision relies on the labour of women, labour that tends to remain invisible, certainly from labour market statistics, in that it is either voluntary (unpaid) or remunerated by short-term project funding. I have elsewhere called this the civil society 'trap' (Einhorn, 2000a, b; see also Chapter 2 and Chapter 8). This 'trap' reinforces the twin dangers just outlined, namely de-politicization (through the need to focus on fulfilling immediate social needs) and political marginalization. Discussing the role of NGOs as service providers in the realm of health, Rosalind Petchesky claims that the issues are 'not so much about NGO capacity – which in fact is often superior to that of public agencies – but rather about equitable allocation of resources and responsibility between predominantly female NGOs and male-dominated state authorities' (Petchesky, 2003: 221).

Even in the case of NGOs or other civil society organizations focused on longer-term socially transformative goals, there is an issue about how political insights gained and policy recommendations formulated at the grassroots level can be transmitted to the policymakers, let alone actually integrated into policy. This is a pitfall I have labelled the civil society 'gap', a gap in communications and political impact (Einhorn, 2000a; see also Chapter 2 and Chapter 8). Although EU enlargement directives and UN gender policy in relation to the Beijing Platform for Action require national governments to consult with 'social partners', reports suggest that in practice this is rarely implemented as a process of genuine two-way communication. More often, governments call consultative meetings that *inform* civil society organizations in a top-down manner of new policy developments.

The third problem with NGO-dominated civil society activism concerns the impact of donors on the political priorities and strategies of NGOs in the region. Not only do Western governments and international agencies have their own political, economic and social agendas, leading them to promote particular kinds of projects (Bruno, 1998: 186; Verdery, 1996: 205). Donor dependence and the unequal relationships between donors and recipients can also shape – and skew – knowledge-production, information-circulation and decision-making processes (Ishkanian, 2003: 3, 26; Kay, 2000: 193–4). A clear example is the dilemma – in conflict and post-conflict situations – of whether to concentrate on 'core response' activities or to divert attention from immediate crises in order to ensure funding. The Urgent Action Fund for Women's Human Rights highlights the acute nature of this dilemma, since in such situations, there is not enough time to do both (Barry, 2005: 7).

Trafficking provides a very clear example of the way that international donor agendas can unduly influence NGO priorities. A study of trafficking completed for Save the Children Sweden points to 'the trouble with trafficking' as presenting a multiple level problem involving political, definitional and methodological elements. At the political level, government concern with trafficking is often fuelled by the fear of inordinate levels of (illegal) migration and associated problems of transnational (organized) crime (Anderson and Davidson, 2004: 14). Governments therefore tend to respond by imposing tougher immigration controls. Yet the International Labour Office has stated clearly that restrictive migration policies are actually a factor fuelling markets for the smuggling and trafficking of migrants (ILO, 2002, cited by Anderson and Davidson, 2004: 15). At the definitional level, the term 'trafficking' reflects an essentialist model of social relations, casting only men as active agents capable of deciding voluntarily to migrate, while women appear solely as the passive victims of third party business ventures at their expense (Anderson and Davidson, 2004: 22; Outshoorn, 2005: 144–8).

Trafficking as a priority for funding by Western governments and international agencies therefore reflects the over-riding desire to stem illegal migration flows rather than care for trafficked women. Nor is European Union policy underpinned, it seems, by concern to ameliorate the economic and social conditions in the sending countries that might foster forced migration and prostitution (the 'sex trade'). Measures by the European Union to combat trafficking tend to stigmatize Central and European countries as the countries of origin. When the European Union funds anti-trafficking NGOs in Central and Eastern Europe, this reflects self-interest and a concern to fortify its own boundaries, not any kind of commitment to ensuring gender justice in the region. This exclusionary attitude to migration has led the European Union to be described as Fortress Europe (Cannan, 1996; Kofman and Sales, 1998).

The impact of supra-national government agendas on donor agencies and by extension on NGOs in Central and Eastern Europe is very considerable, as this example makes transparently clear. Instead of being handled within a framework of labour migration or even forced labour, trafficking is classed as a manifestation of international criminal activity. This in turn encourages an abolitionist agenda on the part of donor agencies, deterring or preventing Central and East European NGOs from dealing with the resulting prostitution as a form of work requiring regulation. Far from treating transnational sex workers as economic actors needing protection from exploitation and illegal treatment, international donors construct trafficked women solely as victims in need of 'rescue' and repatriation. Indeed the binary of abolition versus normalization of sex work often tends to obscure the perspectives and experiences of the illegal workers themselves (Agustín, 2005: 96–7). Clearly the political, definitional and methodological problems associated with trafficking make it difficult to establish the boundaries between prostitution, labour migration and trafficking, as well as the relation between trafficking and militarization (Kligman and Limoncelli, 2005: 121, 127). Clearly it remains the case that trafficking in Europe is rarely dealt with within the EU's frame of commitment to gender equality or women's human rights.

On the plus side, the potential benefits of financial and institutional support from transnational donor agencies or feminist networks can provide the space and resources for building effective civil society organizations in the region. Yet the short-term nature of most funding and the unpredictability and shifting nature of donor priorities make it difficult for groups to develop their institutional capacity or to plan effective longer-term projects (McMahon, 2002: 39). There is a strong danger that NGOs can become mesmerized by the need to adapt their priorities to fit available sources of funding rather than developing independent goals in direct response to the needs of their local communities. This can hinder their effectiveness, and even force smaller groups out of existence (Barry, 2005: 95; Ishkanian, 2003: 25, 27).

Many commentators have therefore criticized the 'double-edged sword' of NGO dependence on external financial assistance. In the Russian context, Rebecca Kay asks whether the impact of Western funding constitutes a 'pot of gold or poisoned chalice?' (Kay, 2000: 187–209). It is felt that regardless of whether the funds stem from feminist, governmental or international agency sources, they have the potential to distort the priorities of local-level women's NGOs (Cockburn *et al.*, 2001; Kramer, 2004; Roman, 2001; Sperling *et al.*, 2001). In Pakistan 'often activities also get defined by the agendas and the constraints of funding agencies. This also leads to professionalism, since management and efficiency become important, and to a *competition for resources and financial support*' (Khan, 2000: 7, emphasis added; Kay, 2000: 191–2). Žarana Papić has taken Sabine Lang's notion of the 'NGOization of feminism' one step further in her critique of the 'projectization' of civil society. This term describes the reduction of civil society activites to fund-raising in order to survive and carrying out limited activities within rigid parameters set by the donors. Projects are usually one-off and set short-term goals rather than creating the building blocks for longer-term political objectives (Papić, cited in Sali-Terzić, 2001: 144).

Bosnia-Herzegovina and Kosovo provide striking examples of mismatch between donor priorities – themselves influenced by dominant models of economic restructuring and privatization – and the actual activities of women's grassroots groups in response to the exigencies of the post-conflict situation (Barry, 2005: 164–7; Cockburn and Žarkov, 2002; Cockburn *et al.*, 2001: 166–7; Pupavac, 2005; Sali-Terzić, 2001; Walsh, 1998). Yet in many countries, those women's NGOs that do receive financial support of any kind are the fortunate minority. In Romania in 1995,

56 per cent of NGO financing came from foreign governmental and NGO sources, but only four of 29 women's organizations were actually receiving financial support of any kind (Grunberg, 2000: 315–17; 324).

The aspiration to become a member of the European Union has itself exerted a major influence both on the direction of national government policies and on women's civil society activities. On the positive side of the balance sheet, pressure to comply with EU directives on gender equality gave women's groups in the first eight accession countries the discursive tools with which to formulate claims. On the downside, the enlargement debate had a direct bearing on the choice of issues prioritized by women's groups in the hope that they would find favour (and funding) in Brussels (Regulska, 2001).

There is currently very real anxiety that previous sources of funding are drying up as donors move eastwards out of the new EU member countries. At the same time organizations have either not yet identified new sources of money, or feel unable to take advantage of them because of the complex application processes or conditionalities involved, especially with EU funding. Most women's NGOs in the Czech Republic feel ill-equipped to make this transition to EU funding which involves managing much larger budgets, and meeting the requirement to establish extensive partnerships (Hašková and Kolarová, 2003: 52; also Hašková, 2005). There has also been a shift in donor funding from long-term, flexible and inclusive financial support enabling capacity-building, for example, to short-term, one-off, individual project-based grants involving more limited funding yet demanding far higher entry requirements. This type of funding pressure can mean strategic changes of focus and political priorities by successful groups on the one side, and the demise of more politically radical, autonomous groups on the other (Hašková, 2005).

Some of the most inspiring examples of women's activism in the region have come from groups in former Yugoslavia that emerged under the duress of the ethno-nationalist conflicts of the early 1990s. Women in Black were formed in Belgrade in October 1991. Since then they have held a silent vigil every week in central Belgrade. They transformed their mourning during the conflict in the early 1990s from a private event to a public act of remembering *all* victims of war, defying ethnic nationalist discourses that constructed a binary of heroic versus shameful war deaths. They also made connections between military violence and increases in domestic violence (Korać, 1996; Nikolić-Ristanović, 2001). This broadening of focus from the individual to the collective and strategic formed an important element in the redefinition of women's political activity and use of the public sphere. Women in Black publicly challenged both the definition and the location of what counts as political. The group deliberately celebrates diversity, stating that 'we want to advocate new forms of solidarity within our own differences'. Non-violence is conceptualized as a political act, of resistance and of 'feminist solidarity'. They maintain and foster links, not only across ethnic and national divides within their own country, but with Women in Black internationally, in Israel, Italy, London, New York and Spain and with other groups dedicated to 'a pacifist and international feminism' (Women in Black, 1998: 31–2; Women in Black 2001; Zajović, 2005: 21).

Initial fragmentation of women's groups along the lines of the ethno-nationalist conflict in former Yugoslavia has been transcended. Many groups have gone on both to address strategic gender issues and to form networks with other service providers. The Autonomous Women's Centre against Sexual Violence in Belgrade established the Women's Information Centre in 1999. This aimed to increase women's participation in civil society through the provision of resources and networking. B.a.B.e. (Be active, Be emancipated) is a strategic lobbying and advocacy group located in Zagreb, dedicated to the affirmation and implementation of women's human rights. Funding by UNIFEM, CIDA-Canada, and the Open Society Institute enabled B.a.B.e. (among their many activities) to coordinate a study of 10 Southeastern European countries entitled SEELINE which monitored legislation between 2001 and 2003 from a gender perspective. Žena BiH (Women of Bosnia and Herzegovina), originally founded in Zagreb to support Bosnian refugees, expanded their remit after returning to Bosnia to incorporate income generation projects that had the potential to address the structural inequalities facing women refugees.

The Medica Women's Therapy Centre began in Zenica in 1998 to give rape victims treatment and care in a safe women-only environment. They offered medical, psychological and social support in dealing with the trauma of war, in the process transforming women victims of war into political and social agents capable of rebuilding their lives and the lives of their communities. In the years since the war ended, they have been activating as well as reflecting upon post-conflict development and networking. In this, Medica Women's Association has made a path-breaking contribution to gender-focused, ethnically inclusive work. A report on Medica's qualitative, participatory action research project concludes that such local integrative women's organizations 'are potentially a social space (and a rare one) in which a genuinely transformative, progressive revisioning of the social might happen after catastrophic societal failure' (Cockburn *et al.*, 2001: 14–18; 186–7; see also Cockburn, 1998;

Cockburn and Žarkov, 2002). Such findings – and indeed the group's activities in acknowledging and yet transcending differences – can be viewed as heartening and prophetic in the context of gender's centrality to the development of truly inclusive democratic polities.

Eastern European feminism within the global context

It is possible to argue that establishing networks that work through and reach out across differences can be seen as quintessentially feminist practices, regardless of whether or not the groups involved define themselves as feminist. The key feature of women's mobilization in both regional and global contexts since the late 1990s has been transnational women's networking. The Fourth United Nations World Conference on Women held in Beijing in 1995 gave the impetus to this development. It provided a forum for women's groups from all over the world to meet and network. It also placed pressure on governments, including those in Central and Eastern Europe, to implement measures for gender equality by signing up to the Beijing Platform for Action (UNICEF, 1999: 101). Participation in the Beijing conference not only set off an explosion in national, regional and transnational networking, but also gave local and national groupings the legitimacy and the strength to address transnational issues within their own country context (Cohen and Rai, 2000; WAD, 2002; Mackie, 2001: 192). Networking can produce what Inderpal Grewal and Caven Kaplan have termed 'transnational feminist practices', in other words actions dedicated to common struggles (Grewal and Kaplan, 1994: 438–9; Mackie, 2001: 198).

In an examination of the discourses and practices of transnational feminisms in the Asia-Pacific region, Vera Mackie makes points that could be applied to other regions and indeed to common struggles across regions. She differentiates two bases of such affiliations: the first involves similarity of social location across national boundaries; the second may involve differences of social location, nationality, ethnicity, class or sexuality, but does not exclude the possibility of acknowledging 'a recognition of mutually imbricated histories' within and beyond a specific region (Mackie, 2001: 195, 198). An example of the first is the success of international networking among home-workers, traditionally seen as the most powerless workers because of their often socially unprotected working conditions and their ostensible lack of access not only to financial resources, but also to social capital (Rowbotham, 1998). An example of the second type of affiliation is groups like La Strada in Poland (whose members may not themselves necessarily be trafficked or migrant women) which use regional and transnational networking to assist sex workers and involuntary migrants forced into prostitution (Anderson and Davidson, 2004; Buchowska, 2000).

The influential Network of East–West Women (NEWW) was formed in 1990 by feminists from the USA and former Yugoslavia. It has fostered activist and academic initiatives, and networking by feminists throughout Central and Eastern Europe. It now links 40 countries, sponsors an online network, a legal coalition, and a book and journal project. It has hosted several conferences in the region. In addition to 'sister-to-sister' networking such as NEWW, 'joint-venture' initiatives such as the United States-Newly Independent States (US-NIS) Women's Consortium or the Network Women's Programme of the Open Society Institute (NWP/OSI) channelled foreign funding into the region. Local groups have also received bilateral funding from foreign donor agencies or from women's groups in Western Europe and the US (NWP/OSI, 2002; Sperling *et al.*, 2001: 1160). The Söros Foundation has been instrumental in supporting women's groups throughout the region, specifically through the Open Society Institute's Network Women's Programme set up in 1997. Its director Anastasia Posadskaya-Vanderbeck was herself one of the most influential feminist academics and activists in the early post-socialist period in Russia and former Director of the Moscow Gender Studies Centre (OSI/NWP, 2002).

The continuing need on the part of women's groups in the region for support from these external networks and foundations is evident. Moreover, it is becoming increasingly necessary to seek multiple donors, rather than being able to rely on a single funding source. In the Czech Republic there are four types of sources: Czech state resources (ministries etc); the European Union and other foreign donors (governments, foundations, women's NGOs, UN agencies); group-specific resources (membership fees, fund-raising); and commercial sources (sponsorship, advertising) (Hašková and Kolarová, 2003: 52).

One network that has emerged with particular significance for developments in the region is Karat. Karat is a coalition dedicated to regional initiatives promoting gender equality. The name derives from the Warsaw hotel where the group was formally constituted in February 1997. At that time it comprised women's NGOs from ten Central and East European countries. Karat's aim has been to make the regionally specific needs of women in Central and Eastern Europe and the CIS more visible at the international level. Its first three years were spent monitoring the progress of various governments in the region in implementing the requirements of the Beijing Platform for Action. In the framework of the Beijing plus 5 reviews in 2000, Karat presented reports and recommendations to the UN. Its remarkable successes in such a short period, in lobbying as well as research, have enabled member organizations to gain a profile as actors and advocates for gender equality at both national and international level. Karat provides an example that could well be emulated by lobbying groups in Western Europe.

The main focus of Karat's programme for 2001–04 concerned the process of European Union enlargement. In partnership with NEWW Polska, it implemented the UNIFEM-sponsored project for 'Gender and Economic Justice in European Accession and Integration'. At a conference in Warsaw in November 2003, Karat launched four country-based reports for Bulgaria, Czech Republic, Hungary and Poland. Karat's objectives for 2004–05 centred on women's economic opportunities in the context of globalization. Activities for the period included lobbying and advocacy on a regional level (including EU structures), and strengthening the advocacy capacity of individual Karat member organizations at a national level (Karat News, November 2004). Through alliances and partnerships between women in the European Union and in Central and Eastern Europe, the project also hopes to foster better understanding and cooperation between the European Union and other European countries.

Karat formulated a clear set of demands in relation to EU accession:

- Equality within Europe, rather than a three-tier system (with second-class citizens in accession countries and third class citizens in non-accession countries);
- Gender equality in Europe;
- Improved understanding and cooperation between institutions, countries and regions;
- Greater legal guarantees of equal opportunities for women, in the sense that national states should be compelled to translate *de jure* regulations into *de facto* realities;
- Increased economic and social justice through the introduction of state mechanisms for a 'social market economy', rather than the unfettered capitalism of simple accumulation combined with the restructuring measures imposed by the IMF and the World Bank, which are presently dragging our countries without control into the wake of globalization;
- Initiatives, information and strategic partnerships for public debates on topics of sustainable development and gender equality;

- The right to self-determination and the right to be heard – nationally, regionally and throughout Europe.

Regina Barendt, a spokesperson for the Coalition, noted in 2002 that the EU accession process had until then been seen as the province of the state alone. Civil society organizations were excluded and individual citizens not kept informed. Furthermore, the European Union regards the status of women in the region as relatively good. In Karat's view, this leads to complacency whereby countries deal with EU directives in a purely formal manner, without regard to the actual situation of women in each country. The Women's Committee of the European Parliament has only recently begun to take seriously independent reports on the status of women and gender equality in the individual countries (Barendt, 2002).

At a conference in Prague in June 2005, Kinga Lohmann, Karat's executive director, confirmed that Karat now has 50 members in 21 countries. She expressed concern at new developments unveiled by the European Union. While the process of European Union enlargement had been helpful in reinforcing the role and influence of women's NGOs and their civic participation in the new member states, it had also created a new and largely artificial political divide in Europe. Draft policy documents had just been released on the Financial Instruments governing the further European Union enlargement process from 2007–13. The documents divide the region into candidate countries (Croatia and Turkey), potential candidates (Albania, Bosnia and Herzegovina, Serbia and Montenegro, Macedonia), and so-called neighbouring countries, namely those to be excluded for the foreseeable future (Belarus, Ukraine, Moldova, Georgia, Armenia, Azerbaijan). These financial instruments potentially re-create the East–West divide, only further to the east than the original Cold War divide. This could substantially impede the inter-country and regional cooperation between women's NGOs in Central and Eastern Europe so successfully established over the past ten years by the Karat Coalition (Lohmann, 2005: 4–5).

Conclusion

Although there is a plethora of women's associations in the region, many of them do not prioritize gender issues, nor do they consider their activities as political. At this point it is necessary to note that the definition of what is or is not a gender interest will also vary according to the historical and cultural context. Recent analysis, made with the benefit of hindsight, has questioned whether the presence or absence of a strategic definition of women's issues is in fact too simplistic an indicator in the context of fundamental social upheaval (Duffy, 2000; Watson, 2000a). The moment at which women's groups – initially established in reaction to the immediate negative effects of the transformation, such as groups lobbying to keep kindergartens open, or hotlines dealing with domestic violence – might become 'feminist' groups aiming to change systemically based gender inequalities, will also shift along these lines.

What becomes necessary therefore is not so much evidence that women in the region *are* in fact mobilizing, as analysis of the way that ideological discourses *produce* collective identities and political movements according to dominant and resistant forces within politics and society. We have seen how the specific historical and cultural constructions of civil society and political activity during the transformation process initially inhibited the emergence of a broader feminist politics. We have also seen a multiplicity of signs that this may be changing. There is encouraging evidence for this at multiple levels: in the emergence of Women's and Gender studies programmes; in increased levels of research on gender emanating from the region; in cross-border organizing by women in post-conflict situations; and in effective regional lobbying networks like the Karat Coalition.

For the moment, it appears that civil society activism is still preferred, at least by NGO actors, to top-down political solutions like gender mainstreaming or even an increased presence in polities facilitated by quotas. In some countries, it is clear that there has been a marked shift from purely reactive women's groups concerned in the main with mitigating the worst effects of the transformation process, to more proactive and consciously feminist groups targeting societal change. Recent Polish accounts claim that feminism is alive and active, and that earlier gloom about its prospects as well as anti-feminist traditions are fast becoming history (Bystydzienski, 2001: 509; Graff, 2002: 3).

Regional and supra-regional networking can be beneficial to the strengthening of local women's initiatives, as has been established above. Valerie Sperling *et al.* point out in the Russian context that West–East networking is 'not a unidirectional process', but one that generates reciprocal benefits (Sperling *et al.*, 2001: 1155–6). An example of this can be seen in the four country-based assessments completed in 2003 on the gender impact of EU accession on women in the labour market. Karat commissioned these reports, financed by UNIFEM. Far from this external funding destroying Karat's independence or distorting policy priorities, Karat was able to utilize the reports as part of its lobbying strategy. Moreover,

UNIFEM itself was able to benefit from Karat's advocacy during 2004 in order to secure its own threatened funding base. The East–West transactions between Karat and UNIFEM illustrate how transnational networking – and even external funding – can be of mutual benefit (Karat, 2004; True, 2003a: 152–61).

This positive example does not alter the fact that the discourses and policy requirements of external funders and supporters involve constraints as well as opportunities in terms of their impact upon the capacity, direction and objectives of women's groups in the region. Thus EU attention to and funding of women's initiatives can have knock-on effects on gender equality and women's rights in both social movements and the labour market. The context within which some issues such as trafficking are prioritized to the detriment of others by supra-regional bodies like the European Union may even skew what eventually comes to be seen as constituting feminism in the region.

This chapter has revisited some of the debates around what constitutes feminism within the East–West dialogue. It has also examined whether or not women activists in East Central Europe have been self-consciously forming collective political identities within the newly established space of civil society, and to what extent these groupings can be said to be, or see themselves as, 'feminist'. It has documented the more striking factor that many women's initiatives sprang out of reactions to an immediate need. In both public and private domains, women's grassroots groups and NGOs stepped in to plug the gap left when the welfare and social services previously provided by the state were either privatized or ruthlessly culled by the incoming regimes. These groups included charities, domestic violence hotlines, health care provision and poverty relief (Acsády, 1999; Bystydzienski, 2001; Fábian, 2003; Grunberg, 2000: 321).

To return here to Molyneux's notion of 'strategic' as opposed to 'practical' gender needs, civil society action designed to address strategic gender needs seeks to change perceptions, but also to influence policy, and thus engages more directly with male-dominated state structures (Molyneux, 1985, 2001). The leap from identifying disadvantage as the result of a personal failing to the identification of a discriminatory social arrangement is crucial to the formation of political identities, and to the way that civil society groups will address both 'practical' and 'strategic' gender needs. In the Central and East European context, the distinction may in fact be blurred. Russian women's movements focus on pragmatic issues and specifically the need to alleviate social need, but according to Myra Marx Ferree *et al.* this approach is integrated with a desire to effect social change (Ferree *et al.*, 1999: 94–6). The work of Medica and other groups referred to above also demonstrates the shift from practical to strategic needs and the development in the process of a feminist stance.

The democratization process – which has itself followed one particular paradigm – has created specific political identities shaped by the historical and cultural context within which transformation occurred in the region. Thus to speak of 'civil society' as a universal and neutral space which 'appeared' after 1989, and which shared the same features as the corresponding space in the liberal democracies of Western Europe, is fundamentally flawed. Indeed it could be asserted that the notions of civil society to which funding applicants from the region must conform mask a normalizing agenda of liberal democracy that inhibits criticism of the currently dominant neo-liberal capitalist agenda. Consequently, the concept of women's movements and discussion of the types of strategies that might emanate from the democratization process must be subject to the same caveats. Up to now, such conceptualization has often, in the view of East European feminists, simply reflected the ideological presuppositions of Western feminists, who have themselves been formed in different historical circumstances. The notion that there might emerge in Central and Eastern Europe broad-based feminist movements akin to those in Western Europe or the USA in the 1970s or 1980s betrays a fundamental misreading of the current historical conjuncture. The fact that many women's groups in the region are single-issue and/or lobbying groups in fact to a large extent mirrors the current position of the women's movement in Western Europe and indeed elsewhere in the world. This can, nevertheless, be interpreted positively.[11] The shared attributes of women's mobilization in Eastern and Western Europe, as well as globally in the north and the south, should provide the basis for increased mutual understanding and hence facilitate the development of cross-regional coalition politics.

5
Family, Nation and Reproductive Politics
Between the Private and the Public

Introduction

> One cannot have justice in the private without having it in the public [sphere], and the other way round.
>
> Gheaus, 2001: 188

> Abortion is the only good thing that democracy has brought us. Men have gained the right to be involved in politics and business; we have gained the right to abort! What else have we gained with the change to democracy ...? Food and things we cannot afford to buy?!
>
> 31 year old Romanian woman, cited by Băban, 2000: 233

The new political, economic and social structures in Central and Eastern Europe are intimately linked with notions of 'correct' gender roles and identities. These in turn have been naturalized in the service of newly dominant ideological and cultural positions. In other words the political, social and economic transformation was accompanied by discursive shifts and a reconfiguration of gender dynamics so fundamental that even what constituted 'masculinity' and 'femininity' was questioned (Duhaček, 1998a).

Traditional gender hierarchies formulated in essentialist terms were especially evident in discourses of the family and women's primary responsibility for it (Roman, 2001: 56). Of course these developments were not universal, but emerged particularly in those countries with strong nationalist trends or where institutionalized religion played an important role. Such discourses often construed the individual family as the microcosm of a rediscovered national community. National identity was to be defined through gender, mapped onto the bodies of women, defined and defended by men. Long before the convulsions of 1989, Eric Hobsbawm described with great prescience the symbolic equation of the nation with a woman as part of the process of 'inventing traditions ... [which] we should expect ... to occur more frequently when a rapid transformation of society weakens or destroys the social patterns for which "old" traditions had been designed' (Hobsbawm, 1983: 4, 7).

The sudden demise of state socialist regimes – notwithstanding the weak social cohesion of the societies they ruled – left an ideological blank slate on which a discourse of (gender and national) difference was inscribed as an antidote to the apparent pall of uniformity and sameness represented by the remaindered rhetoric of egalitarianism. Constructing the nation as a woman raises the spectre of a male 'warrior-hero' expected to defend her (Steans, 1998: 81). Such gendered visions of national identity breach the realm of the purely mythological or merely metaphoric. Rather, they signal material, politicized gender relationships, in which access to power and resources, control over reproduction and sexuality, and the authority to define the nation are all usually the province of men (Mayer, 2000: 2).

As I have noted elsewhere, the transformation process manifests elements of both continuity and change in gender relations (Einhorn, 1993). Several analysts from the region stress that the reappearance of naturalized notions of masculinity and femininity itself constituted continuity rather than change. Essentialist identities were therefore not so much to be interpreted as a sign of leap-frogging backwards to nostalgic nineteenth-century notions of nation that promised certainty through gender hierarchies. Rather, they were simply manifestations of a traditional, gender unequal regime that had never disappeared completely during the state socialist period. This regime was being explicitly re-established from the beginning of the 1980s in Hungary, Bulgaria and Romania, and even earlier in Czechoslovakia as part of the post-1968 attempt to establish a regime of 'normality' through a 'retreat into the private sphere' (Fodor, 2002; Havelková, 2000: 134–5; Petrova, 1997: 186; Roman, 2001: 56). The exclusionary inequalities of nationalist definitions of identity map easily onto re-emerging class differences as another salient feature of the post-1989 transformations. Both nationalism and class differentials are predicated on gendered representations and hierarchical gender regimes (Gapova, 2002: 641).

96 *Citizenship in an Enlarging Europe*

Continuity and change can be observed within the discourses and practices surrounding the family, as well as in discussions of the public–private divide. The family is a prime site for the investigation of gender inequalities. Gender relations in the family are, in turn, important indicators of gender equity and citizenship within the public sphere. Indeed the United Nations defines gender relations within the family as a key human development indicator (UNICEF, 1999: 57). Progress towards development and social justice requires greater gender equality in both the public and the private sphere (Gheaus, 2001: 187).

This chapter explores gender equality within the private sphere in relation to discursive constructions of the relationship between the public and the private. The issues it singles out for consideration are: debates around the public–private divide; shifts in family models and the gender relations they imply, with special reference to domestic labour; demographic change and the question of childcare; reproductive politics in the context of discursive constructions of the nation, highlighting the specific cases of abortion and violence against women.

Debates about the public–private divide

The transformation process has re-inscribed rather traditional discourses about the family and women's role within it. This has produced what I have elsewhere called 'ironies of history' (Einhorn, 1995a). By this I mean that there are contradictions between the promise of democracy in terms of the individual's development as a political subject, and the way that it has been implemented within a neo-liberal policy agenda. Women's citizenship potential is hedged in by naturalized gender discourses, producing a male-dominated, market-based polity. Thus the transformation process has tended to reinforce the public–private divide. Although the extent and expression of these developments varies across the different countries and cultures of the region, there are paradoxes inherent in the shift from the discourses and practices of the past state socialist to the current democratic regimes. Such paradoxes can best be understood, as I have argued earlier, by analysing the reversal of signification attributed to the public–private divide (Einhorn, 1993).

State socialism allotted women a dual role as workers and mothers (or a triple role as workers, mothers and political subjects), but in fact focused mainly on their role as workers. Prioritizing the productive over the reproductive sphere meant state neglect of gender inequalities within the family. In many countries the socialization of domestic labour and childcare promised as the quid pro quo for women's labour market participation was sorely lacking, in terms of both availability and quality. By contrast the traditionalist discourses that help to legitimize the neo-liberal market model idealize women's singular role within the family. In practice, this model prioritizes the ability to become an economic actor. Positing a dichotomy between women's roles as worker in the public sphere and mother in private in reality constructs a false binary. This is because economic exigencies make it necessary for most women in the present, just as in the past – in Central and Eastern Europe just as much as in Western Europe – to work outside the home.[1] Reproductive politics – standing as they do at the apex of the public–private divide – provide a very clear indicator of gender equality and women's citizenship, as will be discussed below. Yet it is in constructions of the private sphere that we find the most striking contrasts between past and present discourses, and the most obvious paradoxes with regard to the values attached to public and private domains in state socialist and democratic regimes.

In state socialist discourse, the world of production enjoyed higher status than the world of social reproduction. The opposite was true of people's life experience. Here the family took precedence over all else. People valued what has been called the private 'niche' society and family well-being far above any kind of commitment to the economic and political goals of the regime (Nickel, 1993: 147). The family was thus symbolically vested with authority, at the same time as it became materially important as the source of networks of barter and exchange in a shortage economy. This process entrenched the symbolic value of both femininity and masculinity in gender-divided family roles while also attributing considerable political status to women's role as the keeper of the household and facilitator of family and friendship networks. From the mid- to late 1970s onwards, the private sphere gained an additional aura, being seen not only as the one autonomous space not intruded upon by the over-politicized public realm of the state, but also as a site of resistance and hence an alternative space, an embryo civil society which could not exist in public. Larissa Lisyutkina encapsulates this understanding of the private sphere in Russia:

> The house, and especially the kitchen, in the 1960s, 1970s, and 1980s was the only free sphere. In Russia, to aspire to the kitchen does not have the same connotation as in the West. The Russian kitchen was a front of massive resistance to the totalitarian regime and is perceived with sentimental nostalgia today. Here, for the first time in post-revolutionary history, an alternative lifestyle for many Soviet people was formed. ... Here, heated arguments about culture and politics take place. From here people go directly to huge meetings in the square with banners and placards. In the kitchen one is surrounded by intimacy, publicity, and intellectual creativity (Lisyutkina, 1993: 276).

As I have argued earlier, the 'us' versus 'them' mentality implied in this construction of the private sphere meant that a kind of gender-neutral solidarity took precedence over any examination, acknowledgement or critique of gender inequalities within the household (Einhorn, 1993; Heinen and Portet, 2002: 145). Ironically, therefore, gender relations within the private sphere remained invisible in both official discourse and alternative practice. Yet women's pivotal role within this embryo civil society gave them, de facto, a status and importance which women within traditional family structures in Western Europe did not necessarily enjoy at that time. From a comparative perspective it is important to remember this. It was only through feminist lobbying from the 1970s onwards in Western Europe that women's subordination within the private sphere of the family, and specific issues such as childcare, the now much vaunted 'work–life balance', domestic violence or rape within marriage began to become visible, and it was much later that they became the subject of public scrutiny by state institutions.

Paradoxically, some scholars in the region have argued that in the context of countries undergoing transformation, there may be understandable reasons for wishing to maintain the public–private divide despite the gendered relations of unequal power within the private sphere. First, the fact of women's relative economic independence (despite their generally lower wages) meant they did not perceive material reasons for the existence of gender hierarchies within the family, nor feel that they might be entrapped within it (Gheaus, 2001: 185–6). Second, the degree of over-politicization of the public sphere during the state socialist period left many jealously guarding what they had experienced as the sanctity of privacy as a site of moral value and political freedom (Einhorn, 1993: 60; Gheaus, 2001: 185–6). Women in the region were thus reluctant to support legislation governing the domestic sphere when they felt they had only just gained confirmation of this realm's freedom from state intervention. They were not deterred by recognition that this might entail the re-inscription of traditional gender regimes inherited from the pre-communist period (Duhaček, 1998a; Einhorn, 1996; Gheaus, 2001: 186). Nor did this stance take cognizance of the fact that in West European welfare states too, the private sphere is not fully autonomous, but politically constituted and regulated.

To summarize, then, the private sphere held a secondary status in state socialist rhetoric, but pride of place in popular constructions of it as a site of individual conscience and embryonic civil society activism. During the transformation, this value hierarchy has been reversed, with a corresponding devaluation of women's status. While the family was discursively vaunted as the site of renewed moral and spiritual values in societies seen as having been dehumanized by the former state socialist regimes, in practice it lost legitimacy and value in direct relation to the recuperation of the public spheres of the polity and the market (Heinen and Portet, 2002: 147).

The gap between the discursive and material values attributed to the private and public spheres has therefore widened since the establishment of market-driven democracies in the region began. Discursively, women's role within the family has been lent an almost sanctified aura, whether in religious discourses or those with a nationalist flavour. The recuperation of masculinity and femininity is seen as the solution to family breakdown (the high divorce rate during state socialism), the falling birthrate, and societal ills in general. Many social problems were attributed retrospectively to women's labour market participation as evidence of their 'over-emancipation' (Sperling, 2000: 182). In this 'new' discourse, femininity becomes equated with maternity, while masculinity retrieves a kind of hunter-gatherer connotation.

Meanwhile it is in the marketplace that the citizen is construed. Within the neo-liberal agenda that prioritizes the market over the state, hence the economic over the political, the citizen occupies centre stage as economic actor and consumer. Taken in juxtaposition with high levels of female unemployment, the idealization of a 'return home' for women looks purely instrumental. Once again, reality jars with discourse. While most women have continued to participate in the labour market, the discursive shifts render their involvement in it just as invisible as their naturalized duties in the private sphere. As a result, issues of gender-based discrimination tend to disappear from discourses of both the family and the market. This discursive invisibility offers one explanation for the relative absence – at least until imposed by EU requirements – of gender issues from the political agenda in most Central and Eastern European countries.

Altered family and social policy models

The family continues to loom large in both past and present gender regimes. In the discourses of state socialism, as in those of both nationalism and neo-liberal democracy, the family features as the smallest unit of society, with strongly prescribed social responsibilities. State socialist regimes promised release from domestic drudgery through labour market participation and the socialization of domestic labour and childcare. The promise faded in the delivery. In practice, gender blindness in relation to the private sphere ensured the perpetuation of gendered roles and responsibilities. Since 1989 an explicitly patriarchal model of the family has been reinvented. This arises both from the neo-liberal market model which privileges male economic actors, and from (re-)emerging conservative religious and/or nationalist forms of discourse (Macková, 2000: 59). In this way the discourses of two diametrically opposed systems, despite their completely different political provenance, have both to some extent facilitated the perpetuation of a traditional gender hierarchy within the family and a focus on women-as-mothers. Traditional gender contracts of the kind currently being re-valorized are also not easily amenable to alteration by mere legislative change.

The adoption of a neo-liberal agenda has direct implications for the type of social policy and family models emerging in Central and Eastern European countries. Some similarities emerge with trends in Western Europe, for example in the shift from universalist to residual social welfare regimes in countries that have espoused neo-liberal solutions. The shift from universal entitlements to a social 'safety net' for the most vulnerable reflects a shift in conceptions of citizenship. Neo-liberals distance themselves from the social or economic rights of citizenship as constituent of the well-being of society, stressing instead the individual's duties and responsibilities for his or her own well-being. Society and social responsibility is pushed to the margins in favour of the individual who strides into the economic arena as self-reliant entrepreneur (in practice relatively powerless in the face of transnational corporate might).

In social policy terms, this shift in conceptions of the relationship between the individual, the state and the market is reflected in the devolution of responsibility for social welfare from the (national or local) state to the individual and the family. In practice, as many theorists have pointed out, this means that care for those with (emotional, mental or physical) special needs, as well as children and elderly dependents, falls to the unpaid labour of women, labour which Margaret Thatcher euphemistically de-personalized and de-gendered as 'care in the community'. Those who fall into unemployment or poverty by no fault of their own, but as a direct result of economic restructuring, many of them women, are stigmatized in a system that individualizes responsibility in this way.

Where there are striking differences with West European trends is in the type of family model emerging in many Central and East European countries. In Western Europe, there is a shift from the 'male-breadwinner' model lurking behind post-Second World War social welfare regimes to an adult earner model in which all adults are expected to participate in the labour market (Crompton, 2002: 540; Elson, 2002; Lewis 2003). There are further discussions to be had about the ways in which the unregulated labour markets envisaged in some neo-liberal economic theory undermine labour conditions through their espousal of labour market flexibility, often a euphemism for casual, part-time or short-term contracts without social protection. What is striking for our context, however, is the way that social policy in much of Central and Eastern Europe is following the opposite trajectory to that in Western Europe. Echoing traditionalist discourse, but running counter to actual labour market behaviour, social policy models in the transformation process have moved from a dual-earner model back to the assumption of a male-breadwinner model.

The German case highlights this shift perhaps most starkly, and the clash, for East Germans, of two fundamentally different family models. The state socialist model was predicated, like the social democratic model typical of Scandinavian countries, on a dual role for women as workers and mothers. It thus implied a dual-earner model, underpinned by an extensive system of state-subsidized services and universal welfare provision. By contrast, the conservative traditionalist male-breadwinner model promulgated in West Germany presupposes women in a singular role as full-time housewife-mothers. It therefore offers very little publicly funded childcare, and according to the principle of subsidiarity, holds the family responsible for the welfare of its members. It thus offers a residualist form of welfare regime.[2]

Gender and domestic labour

What actually does go on within the four walls of the newly sanctified family? How are traditional notions of masculinity and femininity enacted? Is there a gender hierarchy along traditional lines? Data on the division of domestic labour from the region offers contradictory evidence, but some indications of continuity with the state socialist past. Fieldwork in the region in the early 1990s suggested that in the past, within their legislatively enshrined dual role as workers and mothers, women in the region had still remained overwhelmingly responsible for the burden of domestic labour and childcare, spending up to four hours per day on it compared with just over an hour per day for men (Einhorn, 1993; see also Attwood, 1996). This came on top of full-time paid employment, which was the norm right across the region. In other words, traditional gendered divisions of labour within the family were never overcome, indeed never seriously addressed, by the state socialist regimes. More recent data suggests little change there. Two examples from the region are Poland and

Slovakia. In 1994, Polish women spent 4 hours 30 minutes on housework daily, while men spent 53 minutes. In a 1997 opinion poll, 74 per cent of both men and women in Poland felt that housework and childcare were women's responsibility. And in 1998, 79 per cent of men and 70 per cent of women believed that mothers of young children should not go out to work. Thus women themselves appeared to internalize and hence subscribe to the notion of their primary responsibility for the family (Heinen, 1995: 91; Heinen and Portet, 2002: 146). Potentially more optimistic findings emerge from a 2002 survey in Slovakia, in which 68 per cent of women and 55 per cent of men expressed the conviction that both partners should share childcare and household chores. Yet in practice, 88 per cent of Slovak women did most of the cooking, 81 per cent took responsibility for cleaning, 68 per cent did the shopping, and 67 per cent looked after the children (Bitušiková, 2005b).

The rediscovery of traditional notions of masculinity and femininity in the post-state socialist period suggests a potential intensification of this state of affairs. The Czech Ministry of Labour and Social Affairs in 1990 and 1991 proposed incentives – in the form of increased maternity leave and other social provisions – to persuade women to return home to their 'natural role as mothers' (True, 2003a: 59). A report by the Institute of Sociology of the Academy of Sciences asserts that in the Czech Republic, 'the asymmetry of the division of labour has only deepened in the course of the 1990s. ... Children are the sole responsibility of women ... . In the course of the 90s, the state has transferred a portion of its responsibilities (and related childcare) to the family. And the family, compliant with the redistribution of social roles and activities, has transferred them to the woman' (Čermáková et al., 2000: 133). An increase in women's self-exploitation in terms of household labour has to an extent helped cushion the worst impact of the social and economic transformations (True, 2003a: 111).

This data demonstrates that traditional gender hierarchies in the private sphere are being reinforced not merely at the level of discourse, but are materially and structurally determined. The adoption of macroeconomic structures privileging the market has led to political decisions involving the retrenchment of public childcare provision. Invoking the principle of subsidiarity effectively absolves the state of responsibility for care in relation to the future generation of workers and citizens, devolving it instead to individuals (effectively, in most cases, to women as mothers). Societal responsibility is borne individually rather than socially. This is a shift well known in Western Europe, especially Britain, where the neo-liberal paradigm was pioneered. Most famously,

Prime Minister Margaret Thatcher declared in the early 1980s that 'there is no such thing as society'. This invocation of individual responsibility negates the notion inherent not just in state socialist ideology, but in the practice of Western welfare states, that childcare is a public and social responsibility, an entitlement that demonstrates a commitment to social reproduction more than to gender equality.

Despite the structurally conditioned reinforcement of traditional gender roles demonstrated in the data cited from Poland and Slovakia, the picture is not straightforward. Data on household labour in Slovenia suggests a distinct improvement in terms of the equitable distribution of tasks. It shows a significant increase between 1989 and 1995 in shared responsibility for cooking, shopping and cleaning, as well as childcare (Lokar, 2000: 23). Yet this report seems rather to point to Slovenia as the exception. Another report from Slovakia suggested that the sharing of tasks was true only of the 16–30 per cent of couples in dual-earner partnerships, whereas the higher female share of unemployment meant that the unequal division of unpaid domestic labour is perpetuated in the majority of families (Macková, 2000). In Romania, social expectations had women doing the majority of household work and childcare, even when they were employed in paid work (Gheaus, 2001: 186). In Hungary too in the mid-1990s, women still shouldered three quarters of all housework and spent three times more time on childcare than men (Kovács and Váradi, 2000: 184; Haney, 2002: 210).

The apparent discrepancy between Slovenia on the one hand and Hungary, Romania and Slovakia on the other may in part be explained by a difference observed in earlier data between a 1988 survey of attitudes to domestic labour in the GDR, and a 1985 GDR survey of the actual division of domestic tasks (Einhorn, 1993). The Slovenian statistics seem to be based on self-reporting, albeit of both women and men (although the source of the data is unclear). The idea that people report what they think researchers wish to hear is well known to sociologists. A comparative East–West German study in the mid-1990s also documents contradictory trends, or at least contradictory self-reporting. The German survey results suggest that shopping and the care of sick children is mostly shared between spouses, while 90 per cent of both men and women in East and West Germany report that women still do the family wash. The German study also demonstrates the re-inscription of traditional roles as a result of the transformation process. A comparison with statistics from the GDR in 1988 shows that by 1994, there had been a marked increase in the gendered division of labour within the family in East Germany (Hartmann, 1998: 150, 152).

It is of course also possible that male unemployment is a relevant variable. Interviews conducted in Brandenburg, East Germany, set out to investigate whether the results of a study at the beginning of the 1990s in Northeast England would be replicated. This study had shown that the unemployed husbands of working women *did* perform more household tasks, although this participation in domestic labour did not impact on their attitudes to gender roles. They still felt that in 'normal' circumstances, domestic labour was 'women's work'. The Brandenburg interviews corroborate these findings. In general, women remained responsible for the vast majority of domestic labour including childcare. In circumstances where male partners were unemployed, the men did take on more of the domestic labour. However this was seen as strictly temporary and circumstantial. As soon as the male partners returned to work, there was a reversion to a more traditional gendered division of labour in the home (Alsop, 2000: 170–1).

It is indeed conceivable that there has been more positive change in attitudes towards gender equality in Slovenia that in the Czech Republic, Hungary, Poland, Romania, Slovakia or East Germany. Nevertheless, in view of the contradictory nature of the data in surveys from the region, the shift towards a partnership-based family model suggested by the Slovenian data should perhaps be read with caution. A further indicator which underlines the need for caution here is the domestic violence reported by one in seven women in Slovenia, according to a study by the local SOS Helpline for Battered Women and Children (Shircel, 1998, cited in UNICEF, 1999: 84). Clearly, it needs to be borne in mind that violence against women is a global issue and certainly not one confined to either Slovenia in particular or the region under discussion in general. Nevertheless, it does give us caution in relation to data suggesting an equitable sharing of household tasks.

Demographic shifts and the question of childcare

One clear indicator that all is not well with the post-socialist family can be found in altered patterns of demographic behaviour during the transformation period. The statistics show sharp declines in both marriage and divorce (Dölling *et al.*, 2000: 121; Macková, 2000; Wolchik, 2000: 67). UNICEF reports that marriage rates have halved in both the Baltics and the Caucasus (UNICEF, 1999: 45). In the past, high levels of marriage at a comparatively young age were matched by extremely high divorce rates. Now it seems that economic insecurity and social dislocation have led to a hesitancy both to marry and to divorce. In Hungary, the proportion of single-parent households had risen from 10 per cent in the mid-1980s to over 15 per cent in the mid-1990s. The impact of marketization and privatization left 40 per cent of lone mothers in Hungary in poverty by the mid-1990s (Haney, 2002: 220).

However equivocal their motivation, however lacking their quality, the falling away of earlier social supports in terms of credits for young couples, childcare benefits, maternity and childcare leave schemes, and available and affordable public childcare, has had palpable effects (Haney, 2002: 221; Heinen and Portet, 2002; True, 2003a: 22). Poland provides just one example of a residualist social welfare model in which 'the cost of social security is increasingly being transferred from the state to the household' (Nowicka, 2000: 70). UNICEF has documented the palpable erosion in the value of per-child family allowances in all countries in the region (UNICEF, 1999: 50). The fact that maternity leave in most countries in the region is still generous by comparison with many Western European countries does not compensate for its financial inadequacy (Goven, 2000; Heinen and Portet, 2002: 154; Macková, 2000). As a result, the proportion of women who take up the maternity leave to which they are entitled dropped by two-thirds in Poland between 1990 and 1996 (Heinen and Portet, 2002: 153). And in the context of neo-traditional family discourses, legislating for parental rather than maternity leave is problematic (Gheaus, 2001; Heinen and Portet, 2002).

There has been a marked drop in availability of pre-school childcare facilities across the region. Closure of workplace-linked facilities, devolution of provision from the national to the local state or the private sector, together with the loss of state subsidies have meant that existing facilities are both inadequate and/or priced out of reach. This contributes to a situation not untypical of Western Europe, where there is a trade-off between the woman's wages and the cost of childcare (UNICEF, 1999: 56). The drop is most striking in both the availability and the take-up of nursery places throughout the region, where there are few places for children under three. In the early 1990s, childcare fees rose by 86 per cent within one year in the Czech Republic (Heitlinger, 1993: 99). In Poland, the number of municipal crèches dropped by two-thirds, and the number of kindergartens by one-third, between 1989 and 1996. And the cost of the private childcare facilities that replaced them is prohibitive, such that they do not benefit those families most in need of them. By 2001–02 only 2 per cent of Polish children under 3 attended nurseries, and 33 per cent of pre-school children (but only 14 per cent in rural areas) attended kindergartens (Heinen and Portet, 2002: 154; Lohmann and Seibert, 2003: 70–1).

Elsewhere, kindergarten enrolment rates made a recovery after the first decade of the transformation, despite the decline in the number of places available. This is partly attributable to the decrease in the birthrate which reduced infant and young child populations by 10–50 per cent during the transformation (UNICEF, 1999: 55). UNICEF has urged that both state and market should contribute to the creation of new and flexible childcare policies that give all parents more choice and enhance their capacity to achieve a sustainable work–life balance. UNICEF argues that this is necessary firstly, because investing in children represents an investment in society's future. From the point of view of gender, the more significant argument coming from an international agency is the trenchant argument that 'responsibility for raising children is a fulcrum about which gender equality pivots' (UNICEF, 1999: 56–7).

The difficulty of managing a 'work–life balance', as the British Labour government calls it, is a gender issue for both Eastern and Western Europe, despite variations in social attitudes and childcare provision in individual countries (Begenau and Helfferich, 1997). *The Guardian*, a leading British daily newspaper, carried the headline in April 2002: 'Women are being told that they can't have a career and a child. Why not?' (Ashley, 2002: 16). In January 2003, the conservative *Times* newspaper printed an article on the balance between parenthood and work entitled: 'A Fairer World for Women? We're on the Nursery Slopes' (Sieghart, 2003: 20). A comment piece in *The Guardian* praised the Chancellor's budget speech for putting the issue of childcare on the public agenda. The article points out that regardless of whether the care is provided by the state or the private sector, public funding is necessary. This point counters the extreme neo-liberal view that the market can regulate supply and demand and hence supplants the need for public funding. In words reminiscent of those used by UNICEF in relation to Central and Eastern Europe, the article concludes in relation to Britain: 'The country needs to decide whether childcare is a public good, or a private problem' (Ashley, 2002). An individualized, market-based system of care provision reinforces gender inequalities in access and usage. This is one area where the state has a clear role in determining the institutional framework for the reconciliation of work and family life (Rubery *et al.*, 1999: 167).

A 'birth strike'?

Another change in demographic patterns has been the striking fall in the birthrate across the region and the sharp rise in the number of sterilizations performed (UNICEF, 1999: 45). This dual phenomenon was dubbed a 'birth strike' by the media (Einhorn, 1993: 67). It has been described as observable throughout the region (see for example True, 2000a: 85 and Zielińska, 2000: 43). The 'birth strike' was initially thought by in-country analysts and political commentators to be a reaction of women in the region to high levels of unemployment, and the difficulty in finding re-employment, exacerbated by the withdrawal of state support for families and specifically the loss of public childcare facilities that underpinned women's ability to access the public sphere of the market.

'Birth strike' was the term used in the German media to describe the allegedly enormous increase in the early 1990s in the number of sterilizations performed on young, childless women – providing a shocking and dramatic illustration of women's disadvantaging by the exigencies of economic restructuring. Two East German studies sift through the statistical data and deconstruct through interviews what turns out to be another 'myth of transformation' (Dölling *et al.*, 2000; Hornig, 1995). Their deflation of the 'birth strike' phenomenon provides a salutary example of how apparently observable, empirically documented sociological trends should not necessarily be viewed as objectively verifiable indicators of social change. Rather, they often reflect (ideological) preconceptions or expectations on the part of those reporting them. A UNICEF study reminds us, for example, that the decline in fertility was not the outcome of transformation, but part of a process that had begun earlier (UNICEF, 1999: 46).

The East German studies, conducted in the state of Brandenburg, show that although there *was* a drastic fall in the birth rate (in 1993, there were two-thirds fewer births than in 1989), and the number of sterilizations *did* increase dramatically in the first years after 1989 (from c. 800 in 1991 to c. 7000 in 1993, representing a 750% increase), in fact the two phenomena were not necessarily causally linked (Dölling *et al.*, 2000: 126, 132; Hornig, 1995: 184, 187). It seems that early, widely reported stories of employers demanding proof of sterilization at interview were perhaps examples of media hype, or a 'moral panic'. 'Moral panic' describes how an issue is inflated by the media at times of social change and economic insecurity to focus people's anxieties, diverting them from the real social and economic issues they need to grapple with (Thompson, 1998, 2001).

The context of this particular 'moral panic' was tht in October 1992, unemployment in Brandenburg reached 16 per cent, with estimates that if hidden forms of unemployment were included, the level would be 38.5 per cent. Women made up over 60 per cent of the unemployed (Dölling *et al.*, 2000: 121). In addition, the 1972 East German law allowing for abortion on demand within the first three months of pregnancy had been eliminated by the German Constitutional Court decision of 1992, making abortions fundamentally illegal and much more difficult to obtain. This context led early analysts to give credence to media reports at the time about childless women between the ages of 19 and 33 undergoing sterilizations in order to access the job market.

In reality, as both studies document through qualitative interviews, the average age of women who decided to become sterilized was 36, and the great majority of them were women in long-term partnerships who had at least one child already. In other words, these were women deciding not to have any *more* children, rather than not to have *any* children. This is exactly the same motivation given for sterilizations by women in West European countries (Dölling *et al.*, 2000: 120, 137; Hornig, 1995: 185). The later of the two studies highlights contradictions between media representations of women virtually being forced to 'choose' sterilization by dire economic circumstances, and women's self-professed motivations, indeed 'a contradiction between sterilization as a discursive event on the one hand and as a woman's decision on the other'. The authors conclude that the discrepancy 'itself reveals the discursive marginalization of eastern German women' (Dölling *et al.*, 2000: 119).

The increase in sterilizations can nonetheless be interpreted as an indicator of significant change in life chances for East German women once they found themselves located within the discourses and social practices of united Germany. For with unification came a social policy model that located women firmly within the family, to the detriment of what became defined as a secondary role as worker. Under state socialism East German women had been able more or less successfully to combine full-time work with motherhood, due largely to one of the most comprehensive systems of childcare provision in Central and Eastern Europe. In united Germany they are faced much more squarely, as their sisters in Western Germany always have been, with the fact that combining these two roles presents a *problem*. This problem is both discursively and materially underpinned by the conservative corporatist male-breadwinner family model that prevails in unified Germany (Cannan, 1995, 1996; Esping-Andersen, 1990). Hence, increased sterilizations can be viewed, if not as a 'birth strike', then still as an indication of a structural problem, symbolizing 'the price that women must pay for their careers' (Dölling *et al.*, 2000: 145).

Reproductive politics and discourses of the nation

Reproductive politics stand at the very apex of the public–private divide. As such, they provide a strong indicator of women's citizenship status.

It was both striking and at first glance surprising that in many countries the first piece of state socialist legislation to be attacked by the new democratic legislatures – after the reintroduction of private property – was the law governing access to abortion (Einhorn, 1993). In the context of political upheaval, acute macro-economic problems, high unemployment and the resulting severe social dislocation, it seemed strange that abortion – ostensibly a matter of individual conscience confined to the private sphere – should have been the focus of government attention. Indeed in Germany's case the issue of abortion delayed the entire unification process for some weeks (Alsop and Hockey, 2001; Clements, 1994; Einhorn, 1993; Maleck-Lewy, 1995; Maleck-Lewy and Ferree, 2000; Prützel-Thomas, 1995). Susan Gal and Gail Kligman identify four ways in which 'reproduction makes politics': first, debates about reproduction 'contribute to recasting the relationship between states and their inhabitants'; second, 'narratives of nationhood rely ... on reproductive discourses and practices to make and "remake" the category of "nation" and its boundaries'; third, 'debates about reproduction serve as coded arguments about political legitimacy and the morality of the state'; and finally, 'such debates constitute women as a political group' (Gal and Kligman, 2000a: 15–16).

British feminists fought during the 1970s for 'a woman's right to decide' as an expression of the right to bodily integrity, individual autonomy and self-development. In the post-state socialist context, debates about who has the right to decide have favoured state legislatures and in some countries the Catholic Church, rather than individual conscience within a human rights framework. In a tradition with a long history, reproduction has become defined as a matter of national interest, over which the state, not individual women, should have jurisdiction. Thus many of the new democratic governments in the region first flexed their muscles by demonstrating their power to limit women's reproductive rights. The extremely restrictive abortion law in Poland seemed to signal the limits being set on public debate as a signifier of a democratic civil society, setting limits ultimately on democracy itself (Fuszara, 1993; Kramer, 2004, 2006; Zielińska, 2000). 'What was really at stake was the extent of power to be held in Poland by a single, deeply undemocratic institution – the Catholic Church' (Graff, 2002: 19–20; Kramer, 2005).

The myth of the 'Polish Mother' ('Matka Polka') is an example of a traditionalist nationalist discourse that re-emerged in several countries, especially those dominated by the Catholic or Orthodox Church (Chołuj, 2003; Einhorn, 1993; Kramer, 2005). This myth sees women as holding a strong position within the family, a position, however, that derives from and is consonant with naturalized notions of masculinity and femininity and gender hierarchy (Heinen, 1995; Heinen and Portet, 2002: 145; Nowakowska and Piwnik, 2000: 105–6). This myth of the 'Polish Mother' was subsequently buttressed by the Pro-Family Policy adopted by the Polish government in 1998. This policy follows the Vatican's Family Rights Charter. It defines the family as based on 'natural' relationships that justify its 'inalienable rights' as a social unit. This policy was used to justify government withdrawal of subsidies for all contraceptives other than about four of the few oral contraceptives available (Lohmann and Seibert, 2003: 82; Nowakowska and Piwnik, 2000: 139, 141). In a more general sense, policies that narrow the scope of reproductive rights to reproductive policies inscribed within a discourse of family values seriously limit the space to develop individually understood identities and hence the possibility to exercise citizenship rights based on gender equality.

Reproductive rights encompass a whole range of issues, including the right to reproductive health, to sex education, access to contraception and abortion, maternity care, maternity and parental leave provisions, and childcare facilities. As such they are located at the centre of social policy regimes and form an important element structuring state–market relations as well as relations between the state, the household and the individual. Yet most of the related legislative and social policy decisions are taken – in Central and Eastern Europe just as in Western Europe – by male-dominated legislatures that presume to define and to decide for women what is best for their welfare, and/or will guarantee the welfare and future of the national body. The way in which these issues are addressed impacts directly on women's ability to act with sovereignty within the family, to access the market, and to influence the public sphere of politics. Reproductive politics is therefore a key indicator of both gender relations and women's citizenship status.

Sexuality has rarely been included in considerations of reproductive rights, nor in discussions of citizenship rights. I would argue that the question of sexual orientation, and in particular of tolerance for alternative sexual identities is perhaps a test case for the extent to which the individualism enshrined in liberal democratic theory has become a reality. Here the post-1989 record in the region is varied. While homosexuality was decriminalized in Russia in 1993, the situation in countries heavily dominated by the Catholic or the Orthodox Church is quite different. There, non-procreative sexual activity is publicly condemned. Former Yugoslavia presents clear illustrations of this: When the first Gay Pride parades took place in 2001 and 2002, the event went off without incident in Slovenia, but homophobic violence erupted in Croatia and Serbia, with activists and their supporters being severely beaten in Belgrade. However, a large police presence ensured that there were no assaults against Zagreb Pride 2003.

In Poland in July 2000, ahead of the October presidential elections, presidential candidate Lech Wałęsa used the issue of national reproduction to play the homophobia card. At a political rally he said: 'I believe those people need medical treatment – imagine if all people were like that – we wouldn't have any descendants' (http://www.ilga.org/Information/Legal_survey/Europe/world_legal_survey_europe.htm, accessed March 2002). Wałęsa's speech deliberately tapped into legitimate policy concerns about the falling birthrate. His speech also provided an example of how issues of sexuality are subordinated to concerns about the survival of the nation in several countries in the region. When the Polish Sejm gave preliminary approval in November 2004 to a bill giving partnership rights to lesbian and gay couples, Father Jerzy Koch, spokesperson for the Polish Episcopate, claimed it would 'bring irreparable social damage for marriage, the family and the upbringing of children' (Rothschild, 2005: 157). The Network of East–West Women reported in July 2005 that the Mayor of Warsaw had refused to issue a permit for the city's June Gay Pride parade. A week after an improvised Pride parade did nonetheless take place, the Mayor issued a permit for a so-called 'normality parade' (http://www.neww.org.pl/en.php/news/news/1.html?&nw=1380&re=3, 15 July 2005; accessed 4 September 2005). In the wake of this anti-gay demonstration, there has been a marked increase in harassment and physical abuse of lesbian, gay, bisexual and transgender (LGBT) people in Poland, including two people being shot and wounded in front of an LGBT club in Katowice. In a response to the Polish government's 2004 report, the UN Human Rights Committee singled out discrimination on the basis of sexual orientation as a key issue for concern. It also identified the lack of access to legal abortion, and restrictions on the availability of sex education, contraception and family planning services as hindering 'the ability of women in Poland to fully exercise their civil and political rights (Rothschild, 2005: 158–9).[3]

Concerns with the reproduction of the nation and (heterosexual) masculinity as its guarantor can be coercive to both women and men. On the one hand, hidden agendas of class and ethnicity underpin assertions of the right to control which – and how many – babies women produce, and with which men (Yuval-Davis, 1996). Women tread a precarious tightrope between adulation as 'mothers-of-the-nation' (in the metaphor of nation as extended family) and potential traitor-of-the-nation if they either fail to have children or, worse still, procreate with the 'wrong' men, men of the Other or enemy nation (Nagel, 1998: 259; Yuval-Davis, 1996, 1997a). They are thus seen as 'always suspect (potentially disloyal)' (Mostov, 2000: 98). Alongside this, the idea of male 'warrior-heroes' defending national identity stigmatizes both non-heterosexual men and those who resist this vision of militarized masculinity, casting the latter as 'deviant', or as the 'enemy within'. During the military conflicts of the early 1990s in former Yugoslavia, men who opposed the exclusionary 'ethno-nationalisms' that 'legitimized' them were denied the status of 'real' Serbs, Croats, or Bosniacs, and/or denounced as homosexuals (Bracewell, 1996; Korać, 1996; Mežnarić, 1994; Morokvašić, 1998; Mostov, 2000; Slapšak, 1997; Žarkov, 1995: 112). Similarly, men of the enemy ethnicity were derided as 'fairies' (Ugrešić, 1998a: 118). Within this militarized context, 'violence-oriented masculinity' became the only way for men to claim their national identity (Korać, 1996: 137). The symbolic feminization of the 'motherland' requires militarized masculinity to defend 'her' (Mayer, 2000: 11).

The case of abortion

Why do reproductive rights, and specifically the question of access to abortion, raise the political temperature to such a degree? At a time of political change, when one belief system, however despised, is swept from the table, there arises a vacuum, a need to re-define national identity and purpose. With the end of Soviet power and the demise of what had once been a liberatory ideology with supra-national aspirations, the point of identification and focus of commitment became the nation. George Mosse's (1985: 23) early insight that women provide 'the backdrop against which men determine[d] the fate of the nation' has historically often been translated into a perception that women's sexuality must be controlled in the name of national integrity and continuity. Thus it is within the discourse of nationalism, rather than that of democracy, that the issue of reproduction becomes redefined as a public rather than a private matter.

This section considers the issue of access to abortion as a strong indicator of reproductive rights, and hence as a barometer of citizenship status. It focuses specifically on differing approaches in Poland, Romania and Croatia.

A UNICEF survey published in 1999 claimed that women in the region, and – most worryingly – especially young women 'have relatively little knowledge of reproductive health issues'. Further, 'low awareness and inadequate access means use of contraception at first intercourse is low' (UNICEF, 1999: 65–6). Low levels of contraceptive use are especially true of Poland. Surveys show that almost half of Poles of reproductive age use no contraceptive method of any kind, about 25 per cent use the interruption method, and only a tiny minority use IUDs or oral contraceptives (Lohmann and Seibert, 2003: 84; Zielińska, 2000: 43, 49, note 52).

Nevertheless, use of contraceptives has increased across the region during the transformation period. Poland and Lithuania are two exceptions to this trend. There, contraceptive use may have dropped by half in the period from 1992 to 1995 (UNICEF, 1999: 65–6). By contrast, statistics from the Czech Republic suggest contraceptive use is equated with the decision not to have further children, with 75 per cent of couples with two or three children using contraception, but only 29 per cent of couples without children (Goldberg *et al.*, 1994: 34, cited in Wolchik, 2000: 69). A 1995 Slovakian study reports 87 per cent of women and 84 per cent of men agreeing with contraceptive use as a responsible part of family planning (Wolchik, 2000: 69–70).

Abortion rates in many countries remain very high relative to those in Western Europe. In Eastern Europe (but neither Central Europe nor Central Asia) the number of abortions exceeded the number of live births in 1997. This compares with an average of 20 abortions per 100 live births across EU member countries in 1994 (UNICEF, 1999: 63). There is considerable variation across the region. A UNICEF study in 1997 cites a rate of 63 abortions per 100 live births in the Czech Republic, 47 per 100 in Slovakia, and 90 in Hungary (UNICEF, 1999: 63). The Polish government prides itself on the low rate of abortion – a total of 138 legal abortions in 2001 – resulting from the draconian abortion law of 1993 (very slightly liberalized in 1997, but still failing to provide for abortion for social reasons). However, the Polish Federation for Women and Family Planning claims that this number fails to take account of the 80,000 to 200,000 abortions that are mainly obtained in private clinics or abroad with the help of openly operating 'gynaecological travel agencies' (Heinen and Portet, 2002: 156; Lohmann and Seibert, 2003: 81–2).

Other data claims that the rate of abortion per 100 live births in the Czech Republic fell from 85 in 1989 to 50 in 1995. According to the Czech Statistical Office, the main explanatory variable in the dramatic drop in abortions was increased contraceptive usage (Wolchik, 2000: 67–8). In Bulgaria, a new abortion law adopted in 1990 was more liberal than its predecessor in that women no longer required their husband's consent in deciding to have a termination. Yet the rate of abortion has remained very high, in 1995 considerably outstripping the number of live births (Daskalova, 2000: 345–6, note 37). Russia continues to suffer from an extreme lack of contraceptive availability, so that abortion is still used as the main form of contraception. It is the claim of UNICEF that there were two abortions for every live birth in Russia in 1997, and extremely high rates of 135, 152, and 166 per 100 live births for Ukraine, Estonia and Belarus respectively (UNICEF, 1999: 118, table 2.9).

Romania presents a somewhat exceptional case. The Ceauşescu regime defined population growth as the primary goal for the nation. From October 1966, abortion was legal only for women over 45 or women who already had four children (Kligman, 1998). Ceauşescu declared the foetus to be 'the socialist property of the whole society' (cited by Băban, 2000: 227). One of the first acts of the first post-Ceauşescu provisional government was to legalize abortion, which became available on demand (albeit at a prohibitive price) during the first trimester. Abortion thus appeared to many Romanian women as 'a "gift" of democracy' (Băban, 2000: 233), and 'as a sign of liberation' (Roman, 2001: 57). Abortion rates soared. This occurred in a context where the average salary decreased 52 per cent between 1989 and 1994. By 1994, 90 per cent of families with three children and 58 per cent of families with two children lived below the poverty line, and there had been drastic cuts in state benefits for families and children. However, by 1995, according to Ministry of Health figures, the rate of abortion had dropped to 212 per 100 live births. Adriana Băban questions these figures, as they do not include abortions performed in private medical practices. She considers the ratio to be nearer 3: 1; in either case, the rate is even higher than in Russia (Băban, 2000: 233–4). According to UNICEF, the Romanian rate had dropped considerably by 1997, to 147 abortions per 100 live births (UNICEF, 1999). UNDP reports a further drop to a rate of 114 abortions per 100 live births for 1998, compared with 315 in 1990. Nevertheless, despite the fall in the abortion rate, abortion remained the main form of contraception in Romania (UNDP, 2000: 9).

At the beginning of the 1990s in Croatia, 89.7 per cent of the population declared themselves to be Catholic, a symptom of the resurgence of traditional values and religious institutions in the vacuum left by the 'death' of socialist ideology along with the demise of state socialist regimes (Rittossa, 2005). This ranked Croatia with Poland, Spain, Northern Ireland and Italy as one of five countries in Europe where the influence of the Catholic Church is most dominant. One consequence has been a series of attempts (most seriously in 1995 and 1996) on the part of both religious and political leaders to revoke the existing legislation governing abortion. The 1978 Abortion Law provides for legal access to abortion within the first ten weeks of pregnancy on the woman's decision alone. Due to pressure from the Catholic Church and pro-life politicians in the nationalist ruling coalition, a form of 'conscientious objection' was introduced, allowing doctors to refuse to perform abortions.[4] Later terminations are conditional on the approval of a medical commission (two doctors, one of whom must be a gynaecologist, plus a social worker or hospital nurse). The commission's judgement must relate to one of three conditions: medical (compelling threat to the mother's health), eugenic, or legal and moral (relating to cases where the pregnancy is the result of rape or incest) (Rittossa, 2005). Interestingly, these 'indications' reflect those in force in the German abortion law, but lack that law's inclusion of a social clause.

Banning access to abortion often arises from nationalist perceptions of a threat to the demographic survival of the nation. The nationalist Croatian government of Franjo Tudjman first threatened to outlaw abortion in 1992. In 1996 it introduced the National Programme for Demographic Renewal which defined life as beginning at the moment of insemination. The Programme eulogized motherhood and women's duty to educate their children in the ways of the nation as 'the highest profession in the Republic'. Tax policies promised to discriminate against 'non-womanhood' (meaning non-motherhood). Femininity was here explicitly equated with maternity, as is often implicit in nationalist discourse. The right to abortion was ultimately sustained, but the National Programme for Demographic Development still warned of the need to stem the 'national haemorrhage' (Kešić, 2004: 78; Mostov, 2000: 99). Croatian women were exhorted to 'give birth to at least four new Croats' in response (Kešić, 2004: 65). Tudjman is no longer in power, but his party, the HDZ (Hrvatska Demokratska Zajednica – Croatian Democratic Union), which ruled from 1990–99, was returned to power in November 2003. Its new president and Prime Minister, Ivo Sanader, launched a new image as a moderate conservative government committed to Croatia's reintegration into Europe (www.babe.hr, accessed 19 May 2005, transl. Jelena Đorđević).

The Croatian case manifests some similarities with Italian policy. In both cases, strongly Catholic countries are prepared to hold in tension two diverging sentiments: one the Catholic belief in the inviolable right to life from conception, and the other respecting the human rights of the mother, and therefore, as specified in the CEDAW provision, a woman's right to determine the number and timing of children she bears. This holding together of apparently contradictory views is reflected in three public opinion surveys conducted in Croatia in 1998, in 2004, and in 2005 (Rittossa, 2005).

The results vary according to level of education and the rural–urban divide, yet they all reveal similar findings. A majority of respondents – 80.6 per cent in the 1998 survey – still viewed abortion as equivalent to the taking of human life. The 2005 survey shows a progressive decrease in the strength of this view amongst university students with each year of further study.[5] Simultaneously, however, all three surveys show strong support for the view that women have the right to make the decision about termination of pregnancy on the basis of their own moral judgement. In 1998, 64.4 per cent supported this view. The 2004 study of 18–24 year olds was conducted by the Centre for Market Research. It revealed significant differences according to education: of the total 65 per cent in favour, 76 per cent of respondents with tertiary education but only 34 per cent of those who had not completed elementary school supported women's right to choose. The 2005 survey results confirmed a sharp increase in support for a woman's right to determine on a termination.[6]

A level of irreconcilable contradiction appears to exist in Croatian public opinion regarding the competing claims of the right-to-life argument and support for women's right to decide. Contradictions notwithstanding, the findings of all three studies suggest unvaryingly overwhelming support for the right to legal abortion. Time will tell how serious the renewed threats to overturn the legislation permitting this prove to be. It is perhaps telling that despite strong and growing support for access to legal abortion, Prime Minister Ivo Sanader in March 2004 affirmed his support for his government's belief in the sanctity of life 'from the moment of insemination'. In early 2005 deputy prime minister Jadranka Kosor provoked a strong reaction from the Croatian Women's Network when, in standing for president, she claimed that if elected she would call for a referendum on the issue of abortion.

In Poland, abortion was legal under legislation passed by the state socialist regime in 1954. Protracted contention around this issue after 1989 culminated in the new law, promulgated in March 1993, which criminalized abortion. The few exceptions granted were cases of severe foetal damage, serious risk to the life or health of the woman, or where the pregnancy was the result of rape. Not only did this law prioritize the foetus over the woman by declaring that the life of the unborn should be protected from the moment of conception. It also introduced draconian punishment – two years' imprisonment – for anyone who 'causes the death of the conceived child' (Art. 149a of the Penal Code, cited by Zielińska, 2000: 31). A 1996 Bill introducing social factors as grounds for legal abortion was ruled unconstitutional in 1997 as a result of the influence of the Catholic Church which has also repeatedly quashed calls for a referendum on the issue.

Public opinion in Poland stands in clear contrast to the dominant political discourse reflected in the law. A series of opinion polls up to 1996, and the earlier 1992–94 Polish General Social Survey make clear that a majority of Poles favour liberal abortion policies. Although opinion poll data should be treated with caution, this gap demonstrates that 'politicians active in the abortion debate are clearly not listening to the voters' will' (Kramer, 2004, 2006; Zielińska, 2000: 41). A report by the Polish Women's Rights Centre – sponsored by the Ford Foundation and UNDP – goes further, declaring that 'limited access to family planning, including the right to terminate an unwanted pregnancy, violates basic human rights' (Nowakowska and Korzeniewska, 2000: 219). Nor has EU accession improved matters. Indeed during accession negotiations, Polish leaders sought assurances that they could continue to regulate what they called 'moral issues' without interference from the European Union (Rothschild, 2005: 161). Wanda Nowicka, executive director of the Polish Federation for Women and Family Planning, founded in 1992 in response to the threat to criminalize abortion, said in an interview conducted in 2000 that such restrictions on women's reproductive rights were 'an unexpected side effect of regaining democracy' (Nowicka, 2000, cited in Rothschild, 2005: 148).

The restrictive abortion law in Poland has not significantly lessened the number of abortions. Nor has it led to increased availability of and education about family planning methods, despite their being provided for in the law (UNICEF, 1999: 64). This demonstrates that the real motivation of the Polish politicians who introduced the anti-abortion law had less to do with limiting access to abortion than with the process of democratization itself. Eleonora Zielińska has argued that it helped to shape the models of democracy and the state being established in Poland (Zielińska, 2000: 44, 52). Anne-Marie Kramer demonstrates through an analysis of two newspapers the way that the abortion issue was instrumentalized in the name of the nation. Although the newspapers represented opposite strands of the political spectrum, both related abortion to the future survival of the Polish nation, in part by portraying abortion liberalization as a potential repeat of the Holocaust (Kramer, 2005: 134–6).[7] Although gender was notably absent from both depictions of abortion, both depended on a construction of Polish womanhood as a return to the traditional 'Polish mother' who sacrifices herself to the well-being of the family and the nation. Any alternative constructions of women's identity as feminists or lesbians are portrayed as 'an internal enemy and threat to national unity, and even the existence of the nation' (Kramer, 2005: 142; see also Rothschild, 2005). Restrictive reproductive politics appear here not simply as an outcome of a traditional gender regime, but as a key element shaping – and delimiting – democracy and politics (Gal, 1994: 258; Gal and Kligman, 2000a: 10, 30). As Kramer puts it: 'post-communist transformation is being effected in part through the eradication of the gender equality project in a way that impacts on women's claims to equal citizenship rights' (Kramer, 2005: 142). Thus the handling of abortion provides a clear example of gender as both cause and effect in the transformation process, both structuring principle and outcome.

Violence against women

If lack of access to abortion can be seen as a violation of human rights, so too does violence against women transgress their right to bodily integrity and protection from violence/well-being (UN CEDAW, 1979). A by now well-established finding shows that most violence against women occurs within the private sphere, with the perpetrator usually being a relative or 'friend' of the woman. Even in the state socialist period, all was not well with the socialist family (just as not all is – or was – well with the Western European family). Divorce levels during that period were extremely high across the region, with the exception of Poland. In the great majority of cases, the divorce proceedings were initiated by women (Einhorn, 1993). However, there was at the time a lack of data on domestic violence. Crude interpretations of Marxist theory created the official assumption that the elimination of private property would automatically wipe out all 'crimes against the person'. Thus violence against women officially ceased to exist under state socialist regimes and hence was not publicly documented. This does not, of course, mean that it did not occur; rather it was defined out of existence by gender-blind official rhetoric and public policy (Haney, 2002: 74–5; True, 2003a: 152).

Today, both awareness of the issues surrounding violence against women, and measures to deal with it, have increased dramatically in the region. In the years since the fall of the Berlin Wall, multiple transformations in the region have led to huge increases in material insecurity and social inequalities. The structural changes inherent in the economic shift from a centrally planned economy with social guarantees, to a market-based economy involving high levels of individual risk, were bound to produce dislocation in the family and shifts in the balance of power within it. Inevitably, unemployment, social insecurity and anxiety mean changes that are expressed in potentially more conflictual processes of negotiation around gender roles in the family. A rise in the level of domestic violence is not too surprising an outcome, since violence in private is often the expression of a sense of impotence and inability to alter outcomes in the larger context of the public sphere.

A UNICEF study completed in 1999 claims enormous increases in crimes of violence in general and domestic violence in particular in the region in the ten years to 1999 (UNICEF, 1999: 80–4). As in the West, there is always a question about whether documented increases reflect actual increases or simply public acknowledgement and hence increased reporting levels. Domestic violence simply did not feature in official statistics during the state socialist period. Nor was it publicly recognized as a social problem, despite the fact that alcoholism – often linked with domestic violence – *was* acknowledged as a serious issue in several countries in the region. This may mean that to some extent an existing problem has simply become visible in the post-1989 period.

Increased reporting does not in itself negate the probability of an actual rise in the incidence of domestic violence in the wake of the increased levels of unemployment, poverty and social inequality triggered by marketization (Haney, 2002: 211, 221; Szalay, 1996). It can also be seen as reflecting the resurgence of traditional attitudes, summed up in the Romanian dictum that 'beating comes from Heaven' (Roman, 2001: 58; see also Sperling, 2000: 182 on Russia). A 1997 survey documented the level of domestic violence reported by pregnant women in specific districts in three countries: Avon (England), Yaroslavl (Russia) and Brno and Znojmo (Czech Republic). This survey showed remarkably similar levels of emotional cruelty across the three countries, yet uniformly high but widely divergent levels of physical abuse. Almost one in 10 women in the Czech survey reported physical abuse, one in 25 in the Russian case, as compared with one in 50 in the UK case (UNICEF, 1999: 82, figure 5.4).

Of course one should approach statistical data of this kind with caution. However, the findings cited in this study are echoed in individual country studies by international human rights advocacy organizations and local women's NGOs, specifically the SOS helplines established in several countries in the region.[8] In Hungary, both police and welfare authorities are inclined not to treat domestic violence incidents as matters for public concern, reflecting a general shift towards privatization of responsibility for individual welfare (Haney, 2002: 211). It has also been suggested that strategies born of Western feminist insistence on forcing private violence out into the public arena for scrutiny and jurisdiction may be inappropriate in the context of deep mistrust of state agencies due to the 40-year experience of an all-intrusive state (True, 2003a: 153).[9] This view seems to pit a human rights approach characteristic of CEDAW against a cultural relativist view propagating a stance of non-interference.

Considering the issue of violence against women in the wider context of nationalist conflict, it is important to remember both that 'nationalism ... can grease the wheels of militarization', and that 'militarization itself, like nationalist identity, is gendered' (Enloe, 1993: 229, 245). Indeed nationalism is 'radically constitutive of people's identities, through social contests that are frequently violent and always gendered' (McClintock, 1995: 353). Gender is key to understanding the war in former Yugoslavia. The novelist Dubravka Ugrešić sees it as 'a masculine war. In the war, women are post-boxes used to send messages to those other men, *the enemy*. And *enemies* who were their *brothers* until a short time before, at that'. Ugrešić refers to a 1991 television report of a ceremony in which the President of Croatia handed out medals to the widows and mothers of '*brave Croatian knights* who had *laid down their lives on the altar of the homeland*' portrayed in patriotic poetry as 'the tormented mother, the holy mother, the Virgin Mother, whom "the murderers" (foreign men!) have dishonoured ...' (Ugrešić, 1998a: 119, 121–2; emphasis in original; on media representations of the war see also Lukić, 2000; Žarkov, 1997).

Rape in war can be understood as the ultimate expression of the link between nationalism and militarism. The case of former Yugoslavia is but one among many recent and historical examples, including Germany and Korea during the Second World War, or more recently Rwanda. A much discussed case is that of the rapes in Bosnia in the early 1990s (Cockburn, 1998; Hague, 1997; Hansen, 2001; Lentin, 1999; Mežnarić, 1994; Morokvašić, 1998; Mostov, 2000; Žarkov, 1995). In the subsequent partially successful international lobbying to get mass rape in war registered as a crime against humanity (Copelon, 1994; Hansen, 2001: 56, 69), debate arose on whether to categorize the mass rapes (and enforced pregnancies) as genocide or gendercide (Lentin, 1999; Lindsey, 2002). During the war, feminists in Yugoslavia were divided in their interpretation of the rapes according to whether they saw rape victims targeted as primarily representing their ('enemy') ethnicity or their gender. Those who supported the former view transferred their allegiance to the ethnic-nationalist cause, whilst those who favoured the latter interpretation continued as members of the small feminist anti-war activist groups (Lindsey, 2002). However, the analysis of mass war rapes is more complex than this binary would suggest. Contempt for women epitomized in rape is also both reflective and productive of a culture of domestic violence. Belgrade's SOS Hotline for Women and Children Victims of Violence noted huge increases in the level of reported rapes and domestic violence perpetrated during and after the military conflict in former Yugoslavia. Women in Black have also made explicit the connections between domestic abuse and military violence (Cockburn, 1998: 171). Maja Korać cites the 'post-TV News violence syndrome' in which domestic abuse often followed directly upon media representations of the 'enemy' ethnic group (Korać, 1996: 138) The Urgent Action Fund for Women's Human Rights claims that the cessation of hostilities brings with it an increase in the level of violence against women (Barry, 2005: 42).

Rape in war is about power, not about sex. It is the means to achieve other aims: to destroy the culture, indeed to eradicate the very identity of, the 'enemy' Other (Hansen, 2001: 60; Salecl 1994: 217). In patriarchal gender regimes of the kind that characterize fundamentalist nationalist groups, women are still regarded as their husband's property. Raping the female representatives of another group thus violates not only that group's cultural identity, but also their property. It symbolizes rape of the body of that community, polluting the seed and hence disrupting the ethnic integrity and cultural continuity of the enemy nation (Seifert, 1996: 39–40). Simultaneously, however, it remains true that 'if the aim of the war is to destroy the fantasy structure of the whole population; the aim of the rape, as is the aim of any other form of torture, is to shatter the fantasy structure of the individual' (Salecl, 1994: 218). Understanding rape purely in terms of a nationalist militarist strategy can risk erasing the individuals suffering the act (Morokvašić, 1998: 81). It is therefore important to recognize the dialectical relationship between symbolic rape of the nation and material rape of a woman. This relationship makes it crystal clear that women are raped in both capacities: as both 'female Other' and 'ethnic Other' (Žarkov 1995: 115). War rape must therefore be understood as both military strategy, a 'political act' and as personal violation (Mežnarić, 1994: 87). Rape in war is a direct expression of the intersections of gender, sexuality and militarism in militant nationalisms, a bodily expression of gendered power relations instrumentalized by nationalism.

Conclusion

This chapter has analysed a range of issues lying at the intersection of the public and the private in order to examine the nature and the effectiveness of the democratization process in the region. Its findings, while mixed, are not entirely positive for the future of democracy, since they reveal the emergence of deeply gendered discursive structures. The public–private divide, so challenged in the West that it has been declared irrelevant by some scholars, has in effect been reinforced, at least discursively. Cause for hope lies in the fact that this discursive re-inscription is at odds with the reality of most people's lives. Women have not followed calls for a 'return' to the home. They continue to work in the public sphere of the labour market – out of economic necessity – but this involvement gives them at least some degree of economic independence and does have some effect on the division of domestic labour, at least in some countries. The falling birthrate has been shown as a trend that began before the fall of state socialism, and parallels similar trends in Western Europe. Women have organized against violence against women, and against the kinds of exclusionary nationalist discourses that justify both essentialist gender discourse and the practice of rape as a weapon of war.

The extent and seriousness of violence against women has been acknowledged by international agencies. They view it not merely, or often not even, as a problem of gender justice but rather as a problem that hinders development. Amnesty International has joined the UN in making the elimination of violence against women a priority campaign for its activities worldwide (see Amnesty website). Whilst it is imperative not to under-estimate the gravity and urgency of overcoming violence against women, nevertheless, the way it has been placed centre stage by international agencies as *the* priority campaign can potentially elide broader concerns with reproductive rights, gender equality and the empowerment of women as political actors.

As long as 'the motherland is female, but the state and its citizens-warriors are male' (Peterson, 1994: 80), effective (political, state) power will remain defined in terms of norms of masculinity and male culture.[10] This raises not just the question of the effect of elevating nationalist discourses to state practice. More substantively in terms of our enquiry into the gendered nature of citizenship, it highlights a further problem. In stigmatizing women both within and outside the nation as Other, the essentialist discourses and exclusionary practices of nationalism effectively impede women's access to full political equality (Kandiyoti, 1991: 435; Kešić, 2004: 80; Korać, 1999: 197–8; McClintock, 1997: 89–90;

Mayer, 2000: 19; Werbner and Yuval-Davis, 1999: 1, 28). What discourses and strategies would more effectively empower women as political subjects? I argue that for all its flaws, the language of citizenship is better equipped to do this than the language of human rights.[11] Human rights discourse relies on a liberal and legalistic conception of wrongs perpetrated against individuals. Yet individuals themselves are normatively conceived in liberal democratic discourse as male. The human rights approach is less amenable than the language of citizenship to an understanding of how gendered discourses such as those of nationalism systemically cause discrimination. There are also severe limitations in relying on a human rights approach when policies formulated at an international level (UN, EU) require the nation state as the locus of enforcement (Werbner and Yuval-Davis, 1999: 20–1).[12]

The fact that feminist political struggle at the national level can achieve a loosening of nationalist strictures has been demonstrated in Croatia. Under the HDZ government of Franjo Tudjman during the transition from a multiethnic federation to an ethnically based nation state, women's bodies became symbolic and later actual battlefields (Nikolić-Ristanović, 1998: 235). During this period, women virtually disappeared from public life, accounting for only 5.4 per cent of the members of Croatia's first independent parliament. Yet in the elections of 2000, after concentrated lobbying by women's organizations, women won 21 per cent of the seats (Kešić, 2004: 79–80).

This chapter has demonstrated that at the intersection of the public and the private, the transformation process has been intrinsically gendered. It has also shown that this implies a form of democracy in many of the countries in the region that severely limits or indeed curtails women's citizenship rights. Yet there are hopeful signs in women's refusal of a traditionalist patriarchal discourse, in their continued labour force participation (discussed in Chapter 7), and in their political mobilization (discussed in Chapters 3 and 4).

6
Femininities and Masculinities
Gender Re-presented

Introduction

> Eastern Europe was a different world from the West. If nothing else, ... she confirmed the *Westerner*'s conviction that he lived in a better world. Eastern Europe was the dark reverse side, the alter ego, a world which Western Europe could have been like, but, fortunately, was not. And that is why the *Westerner* loved her. He loved her modest beauty, her poverty, her melancholy and her suffering, her ... *otherness*. ... The *Westerner* came to Eastern Europe, she could not go to him, and that was freedom too, freedom from reciprocity. ... Eastern Europe was his secret, a mistress content with little. At home he had a faithful wife, order and work. Like every mistress, Eastern Europe only strengthened his marriage.
>
> Ugrešić, 1998a: 240–1, 1998b: 300–1; emphases in original

In this text, the novelist Dubravka Ugrešić recasts the East–West dialogue as fairy tale, or modern myth. The relationship between Eastern and Western Europe is portrayed as a love affair gone stale. Ugrešić deploys recently 're-discovered' stereotypes of femininity and masculinity in her ironic version of the age-old tale. The 'real' possibility of marriage – with the fall of the Wall as Cold War divide – cools the passion, since with the possibility of official legitimation, the liaison has lost the allure of the illicit. What is worse is that gentle, feminine Eastern Europe is finding her voice, even making demands. 'Things have changed. Grey, silent Eastern Europe has begun to speak, to cross frontiers, and, hey, she doesn't seem to need the *Westerner* any more. He feels disappointed, no, not only because of the loss of an intimate territory. ... His former mistress is increasingly like his own wife!' (Ugrešić, 1998a: 241,1998b: 301).

In this version of post-Cold War East–West relations, the romance has gone out of the fairy tale. Disillusion and a certain malaise creep in. 'Cinderella of fairy-tale fantasy and dreams is back – whether to stay is not yet clear' (Einhorn, 1993: 216). Reinvented stereotypes of femininity and masculinity have been located – in some countries more than others – within a repackaged set of gender relations as hierarchical patriarchal family relations. The double or triple role of worker-mother-citizen prescribed by state socialist ideology has given way to discourses praising femininity as maternity, woman-as-nation, or youth and beauty as the route to individualist career success. Perhaps one could postulate this as a greater choice of roles than those available in the past? Certainly, the 'new' gender imaginings open up (the possibility of) discourses around identity in terms of sexuality in a way precluded by the asexual roles of state socialist rhetoric and imagery. What they do not include, however, is any kind of deconstruction of gendered discourses, gendered imagery, or gendered power relations. Nor are any forms of identity not conforming to hegemonic heterosexuality necessarily more tolerated in the new discursive landscape. Lesbian sexuality remains invisible in the media in a landscape of ritual homophobia in Serbian political discourse (Mršević, 2001). In Hungary, most politicians try to avoid taking a stand on issues of sexual preference, relegating them to the private sphere, yet homophobia is rife in the media, 'connected to sexist, nationalist and xenophobic discourses' (Riszovannij, 2001: 255, 260).

However despised state socialist ideology was, the vacuum left by its demise necessitates a re-casting of identities and motivations at the individual as well as the state level. Media imagery and official rhetoric during the state socialist period had cast the ideal female citizen as sacrificing her needs and individual aspirations to the common good in the guise (in practice distorted) of an egalitarian and socially just society. This woman appeared in literature and the media as a kind of Superwoman, uniting in her person a trilogy of socially prescribed roles: exemplary worker, model mother, and socially committed citizen. To the chagrin of most real women, Superwoman as she appeared in the women's magazines of the state socialist period not only 'mastered' her three roles with ease – she appeared in photos to be still smiling! (Einhorn, 1993: 240). Such images induced feelings of inadequacy and guilt in individual women, who failed to understand that their inability to live up to the ideal was not due to their individual failings. Rather, they were programmed to fail by this very Superwoman construct.

Natalya Baranskaya's novella *A Week Like any Other* eloquently describes this guilt-inducing role conflict in the Russian context, while Irmtraud Morgner's *Tightrope* becomes a grim morality tale about the impossibility of fulfilling these multiple demands (Baranskaya, 1989; Morgner, 1974, 1984, both cited in Einhorn, 1993: 52–3).

Even images of Superwoman as successful career woman highlighted her essential femininity as well as her domesticity and subservience to her husband and children. Often working women were depicted in attitudes of subordination, gazing up at male superiors who were instructing them. Thus any imagined threat to traditional gendered power relations posed by women as men's equal in the world of work was played down in the media. Female success in a labour market officially governed by an ideology of gender equality was both softened by a visual emphasis on beauty and femininity and undermined by the representation of powerful men dominating their working relationships (Dölling, 1993b: 171–2). These readings of media images during the late state socialist period preview a certain continuity beneath the apparent rupture between the media representations of the state socialist period and those of the new consumerist market media landscape. Irene Dölling goes so far as to claim a 'fatal resemblance' between the apparently so different images purveyed by state socialist and capitalist media (Dölling, 1993b: 169).

Media images and market realities

During the transformation (and even earlier in many countries) Superwoman faded away. The idealized and homogenized female socialist subject gave way to images of individual women and men apparently able to fashion their identity and their self-image within the discourses of liberal democracy and the free market. The de-politicization and re-individuation of role models was, understandably, welcomed. Replacement of the socialist woman worker's overalls by the more varied offerings of the fashion and cosmetics industry not only seemed, but actually was attractive to most women. Nor should it come as a surprise that the re-entry of sexualized and even pornographic images of women was in some quarters welcomed as a positive reassertion of femininity and individual choice after the de-sexualized imagery of state socialist iconography.

Indeed the return of masculinity and femininity in images of self-actualizing individuals represented liberation from a hated ideology of collectivism and sameness and hence fulfilled desires generated by a kind of oppositional discourse of repressed individualism and difference. Libora Oates-Indruchová argues that this 'resistant discourse' from the past coincided neatly with the 'subjecting power of patriarchal discourse' that in itself stemmed partly from pre-socialist traditionalist narratives that re-emerged after 1989 (Oates-Indruchová, 2001: 120–2). As the previous chapter makes clear, this newly emergent form of pre-socialist rhetoric espouses a traditional gender hierarchy of 'natural', essentialist masculine and feminine attributes and roles. In combination with the former oppositional discourse's propensity to idealize individualist solutions, it produced a somewhat uncritical readiness to consume Western-style product promotion via images of dominant masculinity and compliant femininity. Femininity also appears here in the guise of female sexuality ever available for male gratification. Sexually explicit imagery and 'the marketing of gender stereotypes' can be read in this context as affirming 'a new order of individualism, sexual identity and gender difference' (True, 2003a: 116). The integration of Central and Eastern Europe into a global market order is not simply about economic restructuring or the satisfaction of material needs via the market. Rather 'it also means assimilating to a new ideological and symbolic system suffused by new gender and class distinctions' (True, 2003a: 105). Attaining distinction and individual profile within this new system requires cultural capital in the form of feminine assets as much as – or even more than – economic capital embodied in educational qualifications or professional skills and experience (Bourdieu, 1984).

Postmodern theorists have postulated discourse as constitutive of identities (Hall, 1997; Woodward, 1997). Yet the disciplining power of identity-forming discourses and images is often masked (Foucault, 1979). The post-socialist marketplace provides a perfect example of how this works. Capitalist discourse encourages the acquisition of goods based on manufactured needs. Media advertisements suggest subliminally that the very act of acquisition brings with it aspired-to lifestyles and an elevated class position. The landscape of transformation is conducive to such shifts in aspirations precisely because of the total rejection of the ideological constraints of state socialist rhetoric by most potential consumers. Central and Eastern Europe present transnational corporations with a kind of 'virgin territory' open to conquest. Within this new Wild East of capitalism, unrestrained consumerism appears as the perfect antidote to the prescriptive ideology and restrictive shortage economy of the past.

In the new markets of Central and Eastern Europe, consumerism based on gendered subjectivities has been filtered through two other scripts that co-existed in people's consciousness during the transformation: the hated past ideology of collective labour and egalitarianism, and the discursive rejection of its implied suppression of gender – and class – differences. In this sense, consumerist Western-style advertising and media images were able to flourish on fertile ground. This chapter explores the ways this situation nurtured and encouraged the re-presentation of images of femininity and masculinity in the first 15 years of the transformation.

On the face of it, formerly suffering worker-mothers now ostensibly had choices. They could follow conservative rhetoric – whether it emanated from politicians anxious to slim down the workforce, from the Catholic Church, or from nationalists – in accepting their unemployment graciously and donning the role of virtuous, self-sacrificing mother-of-the-nation. Or they could decide to make their way in the marketplace and strive to follow the path of successful career woman. One version of this variant was the only slightly ironic portrayal of the prostitute as the forerunner of the successful female entrepreneur. In the words of Larissa Lisyutkina: 'the prostitute, the lone entrepreneur breaking taboos is the pioneer of the market economy, from which is supposed to come universal salvation'. Lisyutkina elaborates further on this idea: 'Without skipping a beat, the image of the woman worker was overthrown by the ideal of the woman as prostitute or beauty queen. ... In present-day Russia women ... have been demoted from "Mother Russia" to "Miss Russia" ' (Lisyutkina, 1993: 275, 284–5). A combination of the two roles in the attempt to have a career *and* a family, already problematic in the state socialist past, became even more difficult in the climate of shrinking labour markets and social welfare cutbacks.

Images of femininity and masculinity purveyed in the media since the beginning of the transformation process appear at first sight to differ markedly from those that preceded it. Yet they are no less prone to idealization and stereotype. Discourses and images contribute to identity formation; they shape the space available for the constitution of individual lifestyles and aspirations. If the idealized socialist citizen of the past appeared as an exhausted and de-feminized worker-mother, sacrificing her own needs and self-expression to the collective good, the woman who has taken her place may appear individualized, but in fact conforms to 'new' stereotypes of youth and beauty within a consumerist landscape constitutive of ideal womanhood. And it is womanhood rather than male identity that is the target of most media discourse. Mira Marody and Anna Giza-Połeszczuk comment on the gender 'asymmetry' whereby 'women, far more than men, have been targets of public debate concerning gender role identification'. They also point out, however, that symbolic re-presentations of gender identities both constitute, and are constituted by, the material realities of social and economic conditions within which gender relations occur (Marody and Giza-Połeszczuk, 2000: 152).

Superwoman teetering on a tightrope

Several analysts within the region argue that images of masculinity and especially femininity began to shift long before the systemic changes. Dimitrina Petrova maintains that Woman on a Tractor, the asexual worker-heroine of the 1950s, was displaced in the early 1980s by Woman Secretary. Woman Tractor-Driver gave priority to her work, in other words to the realm of production in the public sphere of the labour market, as consonant with state socialist priorities. She exemplified the triple burden: Superwoman as mother and wife, diligent worker and politically committed activist. 'Woman on a Tractor featured as an object to be photographed for the newspaper, and also as a figure on the platform at meetings and party congresses' (Petrova, 1997: 185). As early as the late 1960s and the 1970s, women began to complain that they could not live up to Woman on a Tractor's example, arguing that it was 'impossible to "carry three watermelons under one arm" ' (Petrova, 1997: 186).

Thus entered from off-stage: Woman Secretary. Woman Secretary's dreams centred on romance followed by motherhood in a private sphere encircled by a halo: 'Happiness, Woman Secretary thought, consisted of children's laughter and men's love. *Alternatively*, it could mean professional success' (Petrova, 1997: 187; emphasis added). The choice between career *or* motherhood, long dominant for women in Western Europe, had begun to catch up with women in Eastern Europe, it seems, even before the corpse of the egalitarian socialist dream had gone cold. Nevertheless, argues Petrova, Woman Secretary still hoped in the 1980s to have her cake and eat it too; in other words, she wanted it all in terms of privatized fulfilment, but not at the cost of her job. Petrova and others attribute this early image shift to a variety of factors. In particular, the state socialist regimes were in a panic about social problems (which they conveniently attributed to women's labour market employment and consequent absence from the home), and about the falling birthrate. The generous maternity and childcare leave policies of the 1970s – dubbed 'Mommy politics' by Myra Marx Ferree – are often interpreted as the policy response to such fears, as are magazine images from that time onwards showing women as model mothers rather than as vanguard workers (Ferree, 1993).

Stories written by women in eastern Germany from the mid-1970s onwards attest to the unbridgeable gap between official rhetoric about women's 'emancipation', and their everyday reality. Writers owned up in public to the fact that the three roles of worker, mother and committed political activist were actually irreconcilable. This revelation was given simultaneously poignant and darkly ironic expression in Charlotte Worgitzky's 1978 story *Farewell to a Career* (see Einhorn, 1993: 241–2). An ultra-successful female school director, mother of four and city councillor (all that in the person of one woman) confesses publicly that she owes her success to a secret pact – with an angel, no less (also female, naturally). She loses her job and is sent to a psychiatrist. The heroine of Irmtraud Morgner's 1974 story *The Tightrope* (Morgner, 1974/1984) is less fortunate. Dr Vera Hill walks to work by tightrope, high above the town, saving precious time in order successfully to combine her roles as nuclear physicist and single parent. Yet the magic proves insufficiently strong to withstand both the townsfolks' superstition and moral harangues from her hypocritical, sexually exploitative boss. One fine morning, she loses her footing, and her body is discovered in front of the local library (see Einhorn, 1993: 52–3). As the story's title implies, reconciling the two or even three roles required of women in state socialist rhetoric involved a precarious balancing act that could easily cost you your life (on the tightrope image, see also du Plessix Gray, 1991). The truth was out: becoming Superwoman was impossible without the help of magic, or divine intervention: both of these were means that were utterly incompatible with so-called scientific socialism.

The recognition that becoming Superwoman was impossible initiated the shift in ideal types. As early as the 1970s, and certainly by the early 1980s Woman Secretary 'looked down upon her mother with terror'. Where Woman on a Tractor 'wore overalls, had weathered hands and used no make-up', Woman Secretary 'was educated, worked in an office next door to the Director and carried nail polish in her purse' (Petrova, 1997: 183, 186). Constructing Woman Secretary as the foil to Woman Tractor Driver is interesting for several reasons. Not only does it expose the early re-inscription of essentialist gender roles. It also implies that by the 1980s, class distinctions had become salient again. Ideas of 'correct' or desirable gender roles thus reflect and construct the abandonment of state socialism's egalitarian ideal in terms of both gender and class. Even official women's publications began to portray 'emancipation' as a dubious goal and 'the "equal" woman was pictured as a self-mutilated creature, one who, to her sorrow, had deprived herself of her own femininity' (Petrova, 1997: 188). The shift in the portrayal of gender thus simultaneously expresses systemic critique and a discursive move away from the espousal of state socialist notions of (class and gender) equality.

Dimitrina Petrova interprets 'this ideological swing from the socialist promise to a conservative anti-feminism in the late 1970s, as part of the developing legitimacy crisis of Soviet-type systems, [which] prepared the general preconditions for the boom in right-wing value orientations that we have been witnessing since 1989' (Petrova, 1997: 188). It is also possible to view this shift as an official re-thinking of the earlier focus on the working class, exemplified in the heroic worker figures of early state socialist iconography (Waters, 1991: 238–40). The earlier iconography is still present in two statues that have survived the transformation (unlike most street names) on a central (East) Berlin square. These two larger than life-size stone figures portray a male industrial worker and a female agricultural worker. Could it be that what we actually see in the transition from 'Woman on a Tractor' to 'Woman Secretary' represents slippage in the centrality of the working class for state socialist rhetoric? In this way the rediscovery of masculinity and femininity and consequent prescription of gender-'appropriate' roles not only reveals class as well as gender shifts. It also previews the macro-economic shift from an economy dependent on heavy industry and agriculture to the more service-oriented post-industrial economy accompanying marketization.

Glamour puss sweeps the market

We have discussed the gap between official rhetoric and most women's reality in state socialist media images and literary representations of Superwoman. Similar gaps exist for most women between the glamour of current media imagery and the struggle to survive the exigencies of the new market landscape. Valerie Sperling remarks on the disjuncture between images of women as happy domestic servants or as sex objects, playing 'very restricted roles in the public sphere' and the reality of female street vendors 'striving to keep their families afloat during an extremely unstable period' in Russia (Sperling, 2000: 185).

A study of images of femininity in Polish magazines from 1974 and 1994 highlights the idea that such gaps are system-specific. This study is particularly interesting for consideration here, given that it analyses two of the same Polish magazines I had examined earlier (Einhorn, 1993: 245–50). The magazines in question are *Kobieta i Życie* (*Woman and Life*) and *Twoj Stil* (*Your Style*). *Kobieta i Życie* has been in existence since the 1960s and targets middle-class and urban working-class women, while *Twoj Stil* is a post-1989 publication targeting affluent career women. The content analysis of issues from 1974 and 1994 enables very direct comparisons to be drawn between the contrasting images of masculinity and femininity propagated in the two eras. Superwoman appears in 1974 as the 'idealized woman' of state socialism, 'above all, a social being', who is 'nearly devoid of any feminine or even individual features'. At that time, 'the state-controlled mass media provided little in the way of an idealized image of masculinity'. Twenty years later, the contrast is striking. Images of femininity in Poland in 1994 are divided between that of the homemaker, in the older magazine, and that of 'successful professionals who are active, glamorous, and dedicated to their careers' in the newer one. This binary echoes social reality more accurately than some 'magazine stories [which] portray women who successfully do it all', for 'it [is] almost impossible for women in Poland to combine career and family' (Marody and Giza-Połeszczuk, 2000: 158, 166–7).

Mira Marody and Anna Giza-Połeszczuk assert that these new images possess positive potential in their suggestion of individuality and self-expression as replacements for the earlier model of self-sacrifice in the name of others (the family or the building of state socialism). However, they also note that the individuality in question is almost exclusively expressed in terms of beauty and attractiveness to men (Marody and Giza-Połeszczuk, 2000: 168). Thus these new media images of femininity can also be undermining in terms of gender relations. 'Coming after years of what may be called the "a-sexualization" of communist era images of women as workers and mothers, the new emphasis on sexual attractiveness undermines women's position in relation to men. ... Instead of sacrificing themselves to serve the needs of family and society, ... women should now subordinate themselves to male desires and standards of beauty' (Marody and Giza-Połeszczuk, 2000: 170; see also Petkova and Griffin, 1998: 438–9).

In line with this development in Poland, there has been 'a real explosion of beauty/fashion magazines' in Bulgaria after 1989. There too 'the message conveyed is that beauty is the most valuable woman's "asset" and that every woman should try to make herself sexually attractive to men'. The essentialism inherent in this definition of femininity reproduces Western media imagery depicting women as sexualized 'objects' of the 'male gaze'. Such ideals of femininity are deployed to stimulate desire and 'needs' within the new consumerist, advertising-led culture. This cultural code in turn disciplines and limits women's freedom of choice in relation to the development of their individual potential. In Romania too, the media purvey the hitherto unfamiliar element of glamour as an essential ingredient in the newly proclaimed form of femininity as consumerism (Nicolaescu, 2001a). None of this should be too surprising, given the fact that even national magazine titles are now either franchises of, or competing with the dominant Western glossies such as *Cosmopolitan*. Katarzyna Więckowska argues that 'women's magazines participate in the management of social desire by regulating female desire'. In relation to Poland she therefore sees magazines as 'texts monitoring and producing models of female behaviour', highlighting the magazines' 'practices of surveillance and control'. In her view, therefore, women's magazines in the new market-driven landscape fulfil a control function designed to produce conformity rather than a proliferation of possible female images or role models (Więckowska, 2001: 241).

Jacqui True's analysis of the remarkable successes of *Cosmopolitan* and the pulp fiction *Harlequin* romances in the Czech Republic offers a counter-interpretation. She suggests that far from constraining women's identity formation, they provide a democratizing forum for a discussion of gender issues that 'empowers women as much as it subjects them to new forms of discipline' (True, 2003a: 106). A Romanian study of Western popular culture products draws similar conclusions. Madalina Nicolaescu identifies a paradox whereby consumer culture can be seen to be 'empowering and othering women at the same time' (Nicolaescu, 2001b: 135). A Survey of Bulgarian students appears to echo these views. In what Kornelia Slavova dubs 'the newly-born strange alliance between postcommunism and postfeminism', magazines such as *Elle* and *Cosmopolitan* both promote consumerism and escapism, yet also counteract the 'mythic femininity' and 'sacrificial logic' of earlier dominant role models by 'stressing narcissism, career development, self-sufficiency and entrepreneurial initiative' (Slavova, 2006: 6).

True contends that both transnational corporations have felt it necessary to modify their message in acknowledgement of the more demanding local reader market and the material difficulties of their transitional situation. Hence the Czech versions of *Harlequin* no longer feature the 'damsel in distress or pathetic female victim', but rather 'feisty career-women ... balancing multiple roles as decisionmakers, workers, lovers, and parents'. Although these independent Czech career women fall in love, implausibly, with American Indians or cowboys, these men are far from macho: rather they appear as sensitive, caring and even vulnerable 'beings who are incomplete without a woman'. The happy ending does not involve the heroine giving up her career ambitions, no: it features a 'mutually beneficial resolution'. Although the author of this study describes the (illicit) reading of pulp fiction during state socialism as offering 'the fantasy and hope of a new and better life', she seems in a puzzling manner to have abandoned this acknowledgement of the fantasy element in her wish to put a favourable gloss on what she concedes is a lowering of cultural and intellectual tastes thanks to the entry of market relations in the form of pulp fiction into the Czech Republic (True, 2003a: 115, 119–20).[1]

The story of (True, 2003: 122–9) the *Cosmopolitan* franchise in the Czech Republic is interesting. It appears that the local editor has been given considerable leeway, despite the parent company's editorial policy being frankly geared to shaping women's identities in terms of ever-new consumerist 'needs'. In addition to the usual columns featuring 'fulfilment through makeup, diets, and the possession of luxury commodities', not to speak of advice on catching and keeping your man, Czech women can read regular features on sexual harassment and other instances of labour market discrimination, women's political participation and issues such as trafficking.

In an unconscious reference to Woman on a Tractor, an editorial from 1998 on the use of female bodies to sell commodities is entitled 'Breasts between Tractors' (True, 2003a: 124). Nevertheless, as True herself concedes, *Cosmopolitan* is two-faced here: making concessions to the gender realities of its readers' everyday lives while simultaneously offering obeisance to market requirements promoting stereotypical femininity to sell commodities. Her assertion, therefore, that the Czech incarnations of *Harlequin* and *Cosmopolitan* can be regarded as 'nascent examples' of what Nancy Fraser terms 'counter publics' 'constituted mainly of women who have few avenues for voice in their transitional society dominated by male elites', seems to me optimistic. The idea that *Cosmopolitan* constitutes, beyond that, an effective medium for a feminist message is at the very least contested. Even more debatable is the conclusion that the mixed content results from the 'ingenious, even refreshing agency' of local groups 'in transforming the content of patriarchal cultural exports or neoliberal economic models' (True, 2003a: 125–6, 128–9). I would venture that this pays tribute rather to the instrumental inventiveness of individual editors seizing the opportunity to make their products palatable to the local market.

Kornelia Slavova too points to open discussion in the Bulgarian franchises of Western glossies of formerly taboo subjects such as sexuality, articles offering guidance in the previously unknown skills of compiling a cv or attending job interviews, and encouragement of 'new values such as self-esteem, self-help and liberal individualism'. The result, she claims, is that 'Cosmo girl' does offer 'alternative figurations of subjectivity for postcommunist women – especially the young generation (even if they are within the realm of fantasy' (Slavova, 2006: 6–7).

Despite a certain level of scepticism about the real plurality or actual uniformity of the potential identities purveyed through consumer discourse and celebrity culture, it is nevertheless important to acknowledge the weight of evidence from these studies conducted in the Czech Republic, Bulgaria and Romania. This evidence suggests that Western media images of femininity and subjectivity are in fact double-edged, with some positive potential for young women turned off by state socialist's Superwoman yet unlikely to be inspired by feminist theoretical critiques.

The binary along which consumerist media images of femininity appear varies somewhat from country to country. Tatiana Zhurzhenko identifies two available female identities in Ukraine: the housewife, and the businesswoman. She points out that the initial attractiveness of a 'housewife identity' to women themselves does not simply reflect the revival of patriarchal cultural values. Rather, it can be seen as 'an entirely understandable reaction' to the limited images of femininity available during the state socialist period, and as 'a protest against the imposed official ideology' of an egalitarian identity (Zhurzhenko, 2001a: 40). More common perhaps than the binary suggested by Zhurzhenko is the binary housewife–commodified sex object. Denise Roman describes how the Romanian media pits woman-as-mother-of-the-nation (paradoxically construed as either a backward, pre-modern peasant woman, or as romanticized 'pristine fairy', *Ileana Cosinzeana*') against the modern, emancipated woman (as strip-tease performer) (Roman, 2001: 60). She claims that newspapers profile women in domestic terms, and demonize strong women in business or politics (Roman, 2001: 61).

In stark contrast to the lack of explicitly sexual imagery during the state socialist period, current media images in Central and Eastern Europe are often highly sexualized as well as gendered in order to sell products. As in Western media, the subliminal suggestion is that buying the product is – for women – tantamount to achieving ideal feminine status, or 'buying' the glamorous lifestyle. For men, it suggests the ability to acquire – and consume – the woman portrayed in the advertisement. A study evaluating the influence of international assistance in the creation of independent mass media in the Czech and Slovak Republics notes that 'there is a need to mitigate the corrosive effects of the commercial media in an environment where a democratic public sphere is still nascent'. The study concludes that in these two countries, 'the goal of market success is often in conflict with the goal of promoting a well-informed citizenry' (Ballentine, 2002: 120). The focus on commercial media reflects the dominance of the Washington Consensus within the

US-based agencies offering assistance. This in turn both reflects and constitutes the pre-eminence of marketization over democratization. What is needed, the study argues, is to develop public service media, as stressed by European-based assistance agencies (Ballentine, 2002: 120).

Stereotypical images of femininity and masculinity in the media of the new market economies reflect (and in turn produce) a market in which job advertisements continue to be blatantly discriminatory in their specifications of standards of appearance and attractiveness as the 'qualifications' required of (especially young) women in the marketplace (Petkova and Griffin, 1998: 4–38; Sperling, 2000). Mira Marody and Anna Giza-Połeszczuk point to the perils of such imagery for gender relations. 'Because a woman's worth is now determined by her desirability to men, the new ideal of femininity reinforces male dominance'. They conclude that the disparity between media images and everyday social practices is even greater in the transformation period than it was during state socialism. Paradoxically, it seems that the purveyors of Western-style images of femininity may have misjudged their market, at least at the time of the Polish study in the late 1990s. Most women surveyed in Marody and Giza-Połesczuk's study neither identified with nor aspired to the new ideal of femininity. On the contrary, it seems, 'for many women, this emerging model of femininity only undermines their efforts towards self-recognition' (Marody and Giza-Połeszczuk, 2000: 168, 170, 174).

However, Krassimira Daskalova puts forward the opposite argument. She asserts that, perhaps understandably after years of imposed homogeneity, women do in fact 'choose' to aspire to this media-led model of femininity. Of course there is some ambivalence implied as to what 'choice' means in the context of being bombarded by the media. Foucault points out how systems of domination and subordination function without needing to resort to overt tools of suppression (Foucault, 1979). In 'choosing' to conform to the media images they are subjected to within a consumerist landscape, women become complicit in their own subjugation (Daskalova, 2001: 249).

Gender and national identity

In Ukraine, the revival of femininity as domesticity was additionally buttressed by the ancient myth of *Berehynia*, (the pagan goddess/ guardian of the home hearth). This metaphorical figure has been revived as mother of the nation. Here the imagery of femininity deploys myth and cultural traditions in order to validate domesticated womanhood rather than sexualized beauty as the preferred image out of the binary typology offered by consumerist media images of femininity. The reference to *Berehynia* attempts to identify women's empowerment with a housewife/homemaker identity by representing women as contributing to the re-establishment of national independence after the end of Soviet domination (Zhurzhenko, 2001a: 40). This metaphor has even been embraced by some women's movements in Ukraine. Marian Rubchak cites Kateryna Motrych, a Ukrainian writer who has appropriated the myth, writing in 1992: 'Woman-mother is the salvation of our nation ... hence we must return to ... Berehynia ... [and to] her sacred mission, that of mother of the nation'. Ukraine's male-dominated political leaders instrumentalize the myth of *Berehynia* as mother-of-the-nation for the purposes of their own political legitimation (Rubchak, 2001: 151–3).

A similar binary also operates in Belarus. Here too, femininity as seductive beauty is overshadowed by femininity as maternity and woman as 'the homeland personified'. The discourse of national revival relies on a traditionally hierarchical gender regime, privileging men as political subjects while confining women to their reproductive roles. Even more striking is the way in which discourses of masculinity and femininity are deployed in debates around the issue of where Belarus will position itself geo-politically. Historically, Belarus has always faced in two directions, westwards to Europe, and eastwards to Russia. Currently, the struggle between these two *political* impulses is defined and naturalized in terms of gender. A struggle that is generally presented as one between democracy and authoritarianism, between a return to Europe and a return to Russia turns out, in Elena Gapova's view, to be a struggle of one masculinity against another. Both positions exclude women; both depend on discriminatory discourses (Gapova, 1998).

Deploying gendered discourses in the cause of reconstituting the nation can have serious implications for the men and women of these re-emerging national entities. This has especially grave consequences in situations of conflict such as those in the early 1990s in former Yugoslavia. While women were constructed as the embodiment of the nation, so men were seen as its citizen-warriors (Peterson, 1994, 1996). Refusal of militarized identities and rejection of the conflict itself had serious effects on men's claim to masculinity. Any man who dared express opposition to the war was reviled as effeminate, labelled as gay and hence deviant, or as weak and cowardly traitor. The hypothesized link between militarized masculinity and national identity are made clear by newspaper articles in 1991 and 1992 (i.e. early in the war) classing both homosexuals and opponents of the war as 'bad' or 'poor quality'

Serbs, in other words as deficient men, deemed unworthy of defending the nation or incapable of reproducing it (Bracewell, 1996: 32; Enloe, 1998: 52–4; Mostov, 2000; Peterson, 1996: 4).

The use of idealized images of femininity and masculinity to legitimize new (ethno-) nationalisms operated very strongly in the context of the disintegration of Yugoslavia and the ensuing conflicts. Žarana Papić noted that 'in times of crisis and social transformation, the deconstruction of the previous gender order is one of the most fundamental factors of change, and an effective instrument of the global restructuration of power' (Papić, 2002: 127–8). Power was restructured in the ethno-nationalist discourses of the early 1990s along the lines of a patriarchal gender hierarchy (Korać, 1996: 136). A study of both official state-sponsored and independent newspaper reporting of events in 1990 and 1991 in Serbia corroborates these findings. Naturalized gender images were used by the media to legitimize Serbian government policies, fomenting the climate of ethnic hatred that fuelled the war. Within this gender code, men were represented within a 'logic of heroic militarism', based upon 'ideals of masculine bravery and worthy death' in defence of women portrayed as 'mythic *mothers*' of the nation (Lukić, 2000: 404, 410; emphasis in original). In this scenario, men – and war itself – are eroticized, in a process that denies internal differences in the name of demonizing the (homogenized) ethnic or national Other. Yet women continue to occupy an ambivalent position in relation to the nation. On the one hand, they (literally) embody the homeland, such that 'women's bodies actually become boundaries of the nation'; on the other, they remain suspect precisely on grounds of their sexuality. They are portrayed as potential traitors to the nation, even in cases where they are the victims of sexual advances – or rape – by the Other nation's men. Women are thus both literal and symbolic 'potential suspects in border transgressions'. Julie Mostov points out that 'this eroticizing of social relations within the embrace of the nation serves an important depoliticizing function in ethnocratic state-building strategies' (Mostov, 2000: 90, 92, 98, 101).

Dubravka Ugrešić reflects on the essentialist gender identities manipulated in nationalist discourse for the purpose of war in her bitterly ironic essay *Because We're Just Boys*:

> Yugo-man, the male inhabitant of the former Yugoslavia, hardly exists in the singular. He is rarely an isolated instance, a person, an individual, he is most frequently a group of men. ... The male group is his natural habitat. ... And that's why contemporary supporters of

masculinism, in their search for a lost male identity, need not travel to New Guinea. Tried and tested male identity is here, right in front of them.

In the Yugo-male mindset one of the most important places belongs, of course, to woman. The 'image' of woman has not been tarnished by either the political changes brought by the Second World War ..., or almost fifty years of socialism ..., or the dominance of women in some fields ..., or their presence in public life ..., or the phenomenon of feminism, or the so-called democratic changes, or even the new war. In this male mindset woman has the fixed, unchanging status of an inferior being. (Ugrešić, 1998a: 114)

Žarana Papić elaborates the ways in which 'the structural connection between ethnic and gender violence is most clearly seen in the case of former Yugoslavia. ... Furthermore, ethnic nationalism, or, more precisely, *ethno-fascist nationalism*, is based on a specific gender identity/ difference politics in which women are simultaneously mythologized as the nation's deepest "essence", and instrumentalized in their "natural" difference – as the nation's life/birth saver/producer.' She therefore insists that the wars in former Yugoslavia should be seen, not as the expression of ancient ethnic hostilities, but 'as a contemporary phenomenon of violent, post-communist strategies of re-distribution of ethnic/gender power by defining new ethnic and sub-ethnic borders *between men*' (Papić, 2002: 128; emphasis in original). In this section, I have quoted women from the region at length, as I feel there is little to add to their trenchant observations.

Hegemonic femininity: a conclusion

The media examples and discourses discussed in the previous sections support the earlier argument that there are (uncomfortable) continuities as well as ruptures evident in the emerging gender regime of the transformation period (Einhorn, 1993). Much has been made of how the advent of the market was welcomed precisely on the grounds that it would enable individuation and self-expression in contrast to the homogeneity of prescriptive socialist definitions of womanhood. Yet for all the apparent diversity of the new women's magazines, Katarzyna Więckowska comments on their 'cultural production of sameness, ... of a universal character of womanliness. ... In the discourse of women's magazines, "woman" exists as a definable category, a fixed entity with some essential needs that the magazines purport to satisfy' (Więckowska, 2001: 241).

Media discourses play a part in constituting identities. The production of sameness as opposed to diversity in images of femininity goes against the hope that the new market brings the freedom to construct heterogeneous identities. Consumerist media imagery exerts pressure to conform, and favours the construction of homogeneous feminine identities. A study on fashion points to 'models' hegemonic beauty as a mechanism defining and regulating the normative standards for acceptable identity'. It identifies a social discourse that links 'beauty with socioeconomic power and high self-esteem' (Soley-Beltran, 2004: 319, 323). Such discourses with their suggestion of attaining economic independence through the performance of ideal femininity are understandably attractive to young women in Central and Eastern Europe, for whom 'this discourse on the "New Cinderellas" presents modelling as a valid opportunity to escape poverty' (Soley-Beltran, 2004: 319).[2] The message – and the pressures to conform – may be subliminal and far less visible than those inherent in the iconography of state socialist ideology. Nevertheless, they together impose very real limits on what conceptualizations of self-image and identity are available.

Continuities as opposed to rupture between the ideology-laden past and the 'free' media of the present can also be observed in filmic representations of femininity and masculinity. An analysis of Russian cinema describes how independent female protagonists are either neutralized or punished (Attwood, 1993, 1999). This is reminiscent of early post-Second World War Hollywood movies, but also of the fate of Superwoman in her precarious tightrope act. According to Elżbieta Ostrowska, it was also true of early post-war Polish films (Ostrowska, 1996). However, the difference in the present might be that ideals – and hence images – of femininity and masculinity are ever more distanced from each other in contrast to the past gender-neutral image of the Soviet citizen. In the process, masculinity and femininity are drifting further apart, reflecting a widening gender gap with potentially negative implications for gender equality and for gender relations more generally.

The punishment of independent females is suggestive of the virgin–whore binary. In this tradition, representations of women as the 'Polish Mother' over a period of 200 years have been astonishingly stable, since they constituted a central plank in the discourse of the nation after Poland's partition by Prussia, Russia and Austria in 1792 (Ostrowska, 1998). The poem *To the Polish Mother (Do Matki Polki)* by Adam Mickiewicz enshrines the ideal of women putting their femininity – equated with maternity – in the service of the nation. This ideal was originally based on the Marian cult that originated from the coronation of the Holy Mother Mary as Queen of Poland in 1656. Like the Virgin Mary with her son Jesus, the 'Polish mother' was enjoined – in Mickiewicz's poem and nationalist discourse more generally – to raise sons to fight in the nation's lost battles and hence to prepare them for personal martyrdom in the name of the nation. This cast her practically as the executioner of her own child. It was therefore unnecessary to invent a parallel symbolic signifier for men, since they were able to prove themselves in reality as knights, as patriots, and as heroes, fighting or fallen in defence of the lost nation's honour. The 'Polish Mother' meanwhile had the duty to stay at home with her many children, bodily occupying the yet-to-be-liberated territory of the nation (Chołuj, 2003: 207–9).

This image of suffering womanhood as signifier of the motherland enslaved has long historical antecedents. In this trope, especially in Romantic nationalist Polish poetry, drama and painting, the female figure is inevitably both pure and perfect, but also, as a consequence, unable to develop her own identity. 'Needless to say, this idealization of woman makes her a perfect but totally one-dimensional figure. … deprived of the right to make a choice, to be herself' (Ostrowska, 1998: 423). This symbolic construction offers a clear parallel with the figure of Mary, mother of Jesus, and hence connects with Catholic Church discourses that construct femininity as synonymous with maternity, as well as virginity and purity. Despite its ostensibly diametrically opposed discursive framework, post-Second World War state socialism, like nineteenth-century Polish nationalism, deployed the self-same image of suffering womanhood. In early socialist realist films (as in early socialist realist novels, see Einhorn, 1993), the female figure is the positive heroine, this time around defending Communism rather than Polish national identity from attack by cynical male individualists and/or saboteurs. As such she has an educative effect on shirking or insufficiently motivated male figures (Ostrowska, 1998).

It is perhaps even more surprising that the 'Polish Mother' outlived the simplistic early expressions of socialist realist aesthetics, surviving to make an appearance in later politically critical films which purported to deconstruct socialist realist falsity. Andrzej Wajda's two acclaimed films *Man of Marble* (1977) and *Man of Iron* (1981) are united by the figure of Agnieszka, the central female character. In the first of the two films she is rescued from the masculinizing effects of supposed liberation through work. In the second film, she embodies simplicity and purity as wife and mother, symbolizing the national struggle – in this case against Communist oppression as opposed to resisting the external invaders of nineteenth-century Romantic nationalism. In relation to *Matka Krolow* (*Mother of the Kings*), made by Janusz Zaorski in 1982, Ostrowska comments that acceptance of the role of the morally superior, suffering 'Polish Mother' 'inevitably excludes an individual from full participation in historic specificity and renders her as sublime yet entrapped myth' (Ostrowska, 1998: 425–6, 428, 430–1; see also Heinen, 1995: 104).

Elżbieta Ostrowska's view is that women's actual moral status within the Polish family as based on this idealized image masked 'a strengthening of traditional patriarchal structures through this set of female obligations to the motherland'. Thus, despite the apparent power conferred by the role of 'Polish Mother', 'these representations and practices ... were nevertheless a fiercely constraining model for Polish femininity'. Her hope is that although 'western models of femininity increasingly colonise' the potentially empty space of the sign, feminist alternatives may eventually provide a counterweight (Ostrowska, 1998: 435). Not surprisingly, the new Polish women's movements explicitly distance themselves from the 'Polish Mother' tradition (Chołuj, 2003: 217). Mira Marody and Anna Giza-Połeszczuk see hope in the disjuncture between the clarity of magazine images of femininity and masculinity, and the 'inconsistent and contradictory' level of internalized social norms, as revealed in sociological survey data (Marody and Giza-Połeszczuk, 2000: 172).

Clearly, the process of identity formation – like the transformation process itself – is still in flux. However, emerging trends seem worthy of more detailed attention. One concerns the binary nature of images of femininity purveyed by women's magazines in the new consumer-oriented market. This binary sets sexualized (wild, free, above all youthful) femininity (which can incorporate the capacity to have a career as well as catching your man, *Cosmopolitan*-style) against the domesticated but caring identity of the housewife/mother. Both contain uncomfortable echoes of the past with their suggestion that women's self-determination is being sacrificed to male needs and desires. Nor is either image consonant with ideals of gender equality. Rather, the images of masculinity and femininity re-presented – or re-packaged – in the newly developing consumer societies of Eastern and Central Europe seem remarkably reminiscent of a traditional gender contract, except for its setting within a consumerist landscape. This aspect is even more starkly evident when idealized notions of femininity and masculinity are manipulated in the name of the re-constituted nation.

In effect, the ideal woman within consumer culture turns out to be uncomfortably closely related to her socialist sister. What unites them is not new-found independence and the capacity for self-determination. No, their bond is self-denial and self-sacrifice. The difference lies merely in the reason for such abandonment of self, not to speak of the abandonment of rights or potential. Where Superwoman set out to serve the family, society and the state in the cause of a glorious future, the new images of femininity appear in binary form: abdication from self-development in the name of the family (the wholesome homemaker) (Zhurzhenko, 2001a: 48) or the nation (Kramer, 2005: 139), or in the quest to please men (the glamour puss and/or sex kitten) (Daskalova, 2001: 249). In Romania, the notion of female self-sacrifice within this new media context transcends all earlier incarnations: including both the pre-Communist, traditional peasant type of femininity symbolized by the Virgin Mary – and the proletarian woman of communist iconography, representing the New Socialist Being (Harsanyi, 1993: 40; Roman, 2001: 56). Whereas masculinity was conspicuous by its absence from the media in state socialist days while Superwoman reigned supreme, there has been a 'male comeback' in the current era. In the new media landscape, delicate feminine models are partnered by advertisements featuring strong, dominant men (Marody and Giza-Połeszczuk, 2000: 170; Oates-Indruchová, 2001). The aspirations being nurtured here are neither personal career development nor social service in the name of political commitment, but purely the need to ensnare one's man and live happily – or dangerously – ever after. Truly the age of the fairy tale has returned. Yet the chances of happy endings are becoming more scarce.

What is clear is that discourses and images of femininity and masculinity have material repercussions for real men and women. Consumer capitalism not only propagates a free market and promotes a taste for conspicuous consumption. In the course of apparently supporting individual self-realization and the fulfilment of individual material aspirations it is also instrumental in (re-)constituting gender – and class – relations within these increasingly unequal societies. Simplistic binaries or homogenized images of acceptable femininity belie the rhetoric of choice, limiting the identities available within a consumerist landscape. As such, they are not conducive to the development of independent political agency or even voice, nor to fostering social relations characterized by gender equality.

7
Labour Market Access
Persistent Patterns of Inequality

Introduction

> ... now all I hear is that everyone is supposed to be an entrepreneur. Well, I'm not cut out for that. Even if I had the capital, I'm not like that, not so brave, and wily, and convoluted. Some people are born to work, not everyone can be an entrepreneur. And this new system, it humiliates and ruins those who work.
>
> Woman cannery worker in the town of Karikás in Hungary, Kovács and Váradi, 2000: 193

> I will learn what is necessary today – computer technology, bookkeeping. It does not really matter what I do. I just do not want to sit at home. I enjoy it [the retraining] but I know that I haven't got a chance of getting a job again. ... Because of my age they didn't even want to let me do retraining. But I knew there wasn't a law anywhere that bans a woman over 50 years of age from doing a retraining course. I knew that, but the Labour Office tried to stop me anyway.
>
> Former section leader of a clothing firm in Cottbus, East Germany, 53 years old, Alsop, 2000: 160

Understanding the impact of transformation on the labour market in Central and Eastern Europe is crucially important. This is because the transformation process itself has been dominated by a type of neo-liberal agenda that privileges the market over the state – and hence marketization over democratization. Such a hierarchy of priorities clearly affects the understanding of citizenship that prevails in the region. Currently, despite discursive attribution of importance to the democratization process and the accompanying role of civil society, in fact it is economic restructuring that has taken centre stage. Within this conception of the market as sole regulator of society, the state (and hence also the polity) takes a back seat. The citizen in this scenario is the economic actor with the power to exchange contracts in the marketplace. A secondary but nonetheless crucially important role within a form of market capitalism dedicated to promoting consumerism of a type that was clearly absent from the previous shortage economies, is that of the citizen as consumer (Heinen and Portet, 2002: 149).

Labour market studies have long acknowledged gender as a key variable. It therefore provides a crucial indicator of the risks and benefits associated with economic restructuring in Central and Eastern Europe. Labour market relations have radically altered in the process, often to women's disadvantage (Steinhilber, 2001: 211). Analysis of the politics of the family and reproductive rights in Chapter 5 showed how the empirical data often contradicted the dominant discourse. There was evidence that discursive endorsement of a 'return home' to a traditional gender model had not been wholeheartedly embraced by women themselves (Nickel, 2000: 109; see also Nickel, 2002). On the contrary, despite the gender-unequal distribution of the high unemployment that accompanied economic restructuring, women's desire to remain economically active has remained remarkably constant.

This chapter pursues these contradictory trends. On the one hand, qualitative data attests to the significance of their identity as workers to women's sense of self. On the other, quantitative data documents the structural constraints on the exercise of this identity, certainly in terms of equality of access to the marketplace, and also in terms of gender equality within it. Labour market participation persists as a central element in women's self-understanding, despite the fact that this activity was in the past often experienced as an obligation rather than a free choice. The historical irony here is that the neo-liberal market model, predicated as it is on the individual, is intrinsically gendered in ways that often mitigate against women's exercise of the choice to be a worker.

Gendered labour market relations persist in aspects that remained unreconstructed during the state socialist period (as in West European labour markets). These include occupational segregation and the gender wage gap. Additional barriers such as discriminatory hiring practices have been introduced as by-products of the twin processes of marketization and privatization. Gendered and discriminatory practices in the labour market mean increased inequalities, not only between men and women, but also between women and women (Bast-Haider, 1995;

Schenk, 2001: 228). This is particularly true in Hungary, for example, where highly educated (often childless) upper middle-class women have successfully retained their positions in the labour market, while poor (and especially ethnic minority Roma) women are socially excluded along lines of gender, ethnicity and class. They have been impoverished through welfare benefits that provide only for subsistence-level living (Fodor, 2005; Steinhilber, 2006; Szalai, 2005).

In my earlier book I argued that it was 'as yet unclear what the future patterns and levels of female employment will be. Whether economic restructuring could ultimately favour women's employment opportunities remains to be seen'. This raised the question: 'Is there a middle way between the *duty* to be a worker [characteristic of state socialist ideology and practice], and the *right* to be unemployed, sanctified in motherhood [the trend in the early years after 1989]? And where in these "oughts" is the autonomous choice of women themselves?' (Einhorn, 1993: 139; emphasis added). Autonomous choices can only be made within the parameters of discursive models and social policies that facilitate or hinder them. Yet in the Czech Republic, for example, while a dual-earner family is materially necessary, there has been no shift in the traditional gender regime within the family. Thus women continue to fulfil a dual role as worker and mother, but within a social policy regime that favours only one of the two: motherhood (Čermáková *et al.*, 2000: 130).

There has been much discussion, not least from analysts within the region, about how to interpret data on employment and unemployment. Some argue that the drastic immediate unemployment levels and other adverse effects of the economic transformation process have eased somewhat, especially in some Central European countries, as opposed to those further to the East or in the CIS region. Still others insist that although women's labour market position has deteriorated, the deterioration is less acute than suggested by early data. It is also less grave relative to men's position than first expected (Fodor, 2005). Furthermore, there are intra-country differences, for example between the Czech Republic, Hungary and Poland, due to the pace and nature of economic restructuring and the differing social policy models adopted (Fodor, 2005; Steinhilber, 2006).

Nevertheless, it must be said that many of the gender-specific disadvantages of changes in the labour market identified in my earlier book persist. It seems that choice exists only in the negative – especially for younger women – as a choice *between* paid employment *or* motherhood. The nature of economic restructuring and social policy shifts have replaced the dual role by an either-or situation, scarcely indicative of autonomous individual preference (Begenau and Helfferich, 1997; Einhorn, 1993, 1997; Lohmann and Seibert, 2003: 84; Macková, 2000: 98). In the past there were undoubtedly negative aspects to women's labour force participation. It expressed the obligation rather than the right to work; it resulted in a dual or triple burden for women; it altered little in the gendered division of domestic labour. Nevertheless, it did render obsolete the necessity to choose *between* a career and motherhood.

The case of East Germany is still a touchstone for the impact of the transformation process on the labour market. This is because the eastern part of Germany was instantly (rather than gradually) absorbed into an already extant market economy. In the process, East German workers were confronted not just with a totally new economic system underpinned by a different social policy model, but also with the effects of growing recession in the West. It is important to bear in mind that transformation involved a dual process, in the course of which Western *and* Eastern European economies have undergone both restructuring (macro-economic shifts from an industrial to a post-industrial economy) and recessionary pressures resulting in crumbling welfare state edifices. German unification incorporated East Germany into a West German economy that was increasingly in dire straits, and not solely as a result of German unification. By 2003, high and rising levels of unemployment looked like a semi-permanent feature of the German economy and constituted the major issue in the 2002 and 2005 Federal German elections. Economic crisis signified radical reorganization of both the economy and the social welfare regime. Both processes imply 'a reordering of gender relations' (Dölling, 2001: 57). It is within this context that we need to understand the disproportionate share of the burden of economic restructuring borne by East German women.

Clearly the particular manifestations of restructuring differ from country to country. Nevertheless, it is important to acknowledge the commonalities arising from three supra-regional processes that have contributed to high unemployment and the loss of social (welfare) services. The first of these is economic globalization, which placed Central and East European workers and industries for the first time within a situation of competing in the global market. The impact on heavily feminized industries in the region such as textiles and clothing were immediate, with the loss of earlier heavily subsidized trade with and the guaranteed market of the former Soviet Union, and the 'gained' competition with cheaper female labour in East and Southeast Asia. Globalization also tends to produce insecurity of employment and unprotected working conditions for both men and women (Knothe, 2005; UN, 1995). The second explanatory variable arises from the recessionary trends affecting Western as well as Eastern European economies, facilitating the introduction of neo-liberal regimes with their agenda of state retrenchment. A third is the impact of EU regulatory policies, especially for the first group of new member states.[1] Analysing the cumulative impact of globalization, economic recession, and the pressures to conform to EU labour standards is beyond the scope of this study. Nevertheless, these forces should be borne in mind as the wider context within which the economic transformation in Central and Eastern Europe has been occurring (Ruminska-Zimny, 1999).

A survey paper for the International Labour Organization (ILO) observed that there was a need – beyond single-country studies – for both more detailed and disaggregated data on an industry or sectoral basis, and more comparative studies (Einhorn, 1997). The latter are still lacking, but what has emerged is a range of detailed micro-level studies using gender as the key variable in analyses of single regions or economic sectors.[2] These studies take into account a range of variables such as education and qualifications, age and mobility. Their findings appear to indicate that gender is still the most compelling explanatory variable in relation to unequal access to the labour market, occupational segregation and the gender pay gap. This situation pertains not just to Central and Eastern European countries, but to continuing trends in Western Europe (Rubery *et al.*, 1999; Ruminska-Zimny, 2002).[3]

Subsequent sections of this chapter explore ongoing gender-based disadvantage in the economic transformation process. The first section considers whether economic restructuring has produced systematic male bias. The second section presents the ways in which the emerging labour markets are gendered. This is followed by discussion of persistent patterns of occupational segregation and presentation of qualitative data reflecting women's experiences of economic transformation. The final section investigates the impact of altered social policy models on access to and discrimination within the labour market.

Male bias in economic restructuring?

In a discussion on the relationship between economic citizenship and social rights or entitlements, Jane Lewis has stressed their interconnection. This derives from the fact that 'in European welfare states, the work/welfare relationship has always been central to the development of social policies' (Lewis, 2003: 176). This nexus was even more powerful in shaping entitlements during the state socialist period. It was the norm in most countries in the region for all adults, including women, to work full-time, and social benefits were dependent on this labour force participation. The economic transformation process has substantially weakened this nexus, in that women have been displaced from the labour market on a massive scale, social welfare has shifted from universalist to residual models, and social policy regimes have moved toward a male-breadwinner model.

The very idea that it is normal for all (or even most) women to work outside the home has been explicitly challenged in many quarters, both as economically unrealistic and as contravening the 'natural' social order (Marksová-Tominová, 2003: 30; Sperling, 2000: 179). When Václav Klaus was Czech Finance Minister in 1990, he cited the 'overemployment' of women in announcing state-supported inducements for women to stay at home. Neatly integrating economic interests with traditional gender expectations, he expounded how sending women home would save money 'because when women work they need state-supported care' (Klaus, 1990, cited in True, 2003a: 59; see also Šiklová, cited in Rosen, 1990: 12). This chapter explores the extent to which the economic restructuring process is gendered, manifesting a 'male bias' similar to that which Diane Elson earlier identified in IMF- and World Bank-dominated structural adjustment policies (Elson, 1991/1995). Gender is a key element shaping the transformation process. This in turn reshapes gender relations in the labour market (True, 2003a: 75).

Economic transformation in Central and Eastern Europe involves a dual process: on the one hand marketization (conceived as synonymous with privatization), on the other a simultaneous process of structural adjustment. The latter involves a major macro-economic shift from industrial to post-industrial economies, a process that has also taken place, albeit at a more gradual pace, in West European economies. Much standard economic analysis suggests a bonus effect for female employment in the ensuing expansion of consumer goods production and information technology, plus enhancement of the service sector, all of these sectors of the economy having been female-dominated during the state socialist period. The expansion of the service sector began in 1993 in the region. By 1999 it accounted for the largest share of total employment in all countries of the region except Romania (Steinhilber, 2001: 207–8, citing European Commission findings from 1999).

However, this optimistic prognosis of a bonus effect for female employment has not been borne out. On the contrary, there has been a marked displacement of female by male labour in the very sectors whose expansion had been predicted to favour women's employment. While the (public sector) caring professions have remained female-dominated, banking and trade in the private sector have not. Here too gender is demonstrably the variable that accounts for the relative displacement of women by men, especially from managerial posts (Steinhilber, 2001: 203). Sectors such as banking, finance and insurance were marginal in command economies, but are central to market-based systems. The newly established importance of these branches has in turn meant both status enhancement and higher pay levels. Both aspects have resulted in a 'clear tendency for the well paid jobs in banking, trade and tourism to become male-dominated, while badly paid unskilled jobs in smaller enterprises are female-dominated' (Steinhilber, 2001: 208). This appears to reinforce the somewhat pessimistic conclusion drawn by UNICEF in 1999 that 'women's economic futures are more closely tied to the shrinking rather than to the growing sectors in transition economies' (UNICEF, 1999).

This trend is replicated in country-based studies. In eastern Germany, jobs have been re-classifed during the period of economic reconstruction in ways that have overwhelmingly benefited male workers. While men have moved into some traditionally female areas of employment, the converse has not been true. A study by the Federal German Labour Ministry's Institute for Labour Market Research in 1993 confirmed that all economic branches recorded a relative increase across the board in male employment and a corresponding decrease in female employment (Federal Labour Market study, cited in Alsop, 2000: 96). In Poland too the number of men employed in jobs previously defined as 'women's work' (in retail and trade, health and education) increased, without a corresponding shift of female employment to other sectors (Heinen, 1995: 93).

Studies on the Czech Republic, Hungary, Slovakia and Poland confirm this trend. Previously female-dominated sectors and occupations are becoming more mixed (Steinhilber, 2001: 203, referring to studies by Paukert, 1995 and Knothe, 1999). Where new employment opportunities arise, these benefit men and thus disadvantage women. The pattern of gendered segregation by economic sector during the state socialist period has persisted. Case studies of the retail sector suggest that while routine service and administrative jobs were rationalized, thus shedding female labour, higher managerial posts became dominated by men (Pollert, 1999: 209).

The narrow range of retraining options on offer presents a further constraint on gender equality in the labour market. A study of workers displaced from the former textile and clothing industry in Cottbus, a town in Brandenburg, East Germany, confirms this. One worker notes that 'almost everyone learns office and business skills'. Another complains that 'I would rather not work in an office. I am more of a practical person. ... At the time nothing else was on offer.' And a third remarks that 'not everyone can work in an office or in trade'. Many of the interviews conducted in this study make clear the de-skilling process involved in retraining former qualified engineers and section supervisors as office workers (Alsop, 2000: 166–7). A study of unemployed women workers in Łódź in Poland underlines both the de-skilling process and the gendered ageism operating in the new market system. A 38-year old skilled technician says: 'Go in for computer training? I don't know if that would be very much use. When I looked for work in my sector, I was told no, that at my age it was no longer possible' (Heinen, 1995: 102).

Gender-unequal access to the labour market

A study for the International Labour Organization (ILO) in 2001 used European Commission figures from 1999 to show that in the economic restructuring process almost 7 million jobs were lost in the region between 1989 and 1997 (Steinhilber, 2001). According to UNICEF, slightly more than half of these jobs were held by women. UNICEF calculates that this represents the disappearance of every third job for women (UNICEF, 1999). Labour force participation rates fell in all countries in the region during the 1990s. However, women's labour force participation declined more than men's. In Bulgaria, overall employment has dropped by 28.2 per cent since 1990, but women's employment rate fell particularly sharply, from 87.6 per cent in 1989, to 48.2 per cent in 1993 and 37 per cent in 2001, representing the lowest rate amongst the then EU candidate countries (Marinova *et al.*, 2003: 13).

The ILO study referred to above documents the cases of Slovakia (women's participation rate down by 13.4 per cent), Latvia (down by 11 per cent), Czech Republic (down by 10.4 per cent), Hungary (down by 10.1 per cent), and Estonia (down by 9.9 per cent). It also points out that the decline in women's labour force participation throughout Central and Eastern Europe runs completely counter to trends in the rest of the world and especially in Western Europe, where women's employment rates continue to increase (Steinhilber, 2001: 201, 203).[4]

Data from 2003 demonstrate a sizeable gender gap of 10–15 per cent in labour force participation rates in Bulgaria, Poland, Hungary and Croatia (Knothe, 2005: table 1). In Croatia, Bulgaria and Poland, more than 50 per cent – in Hungary, just under 50 per cent – of women had no direct relationship to the formal labour market. This in turn affected their entitlements to social security, often leaving them dependent on family rather than state support (Knothe, 2005). The 2003 data suggests that contrary to the earlier years, unemployment is no longer totally female-dominated, but rather evenly shared between men and women across the region (Knothe, 2005: tables 4, 5). However, women are still over-represented among the long-term unemployed, and in some countries, a higher percentage of unemployed women than men fail to receive unemployment benefits (Knothe, 2005: table 6). Women clearly dominate in data reflecting labour market inactivity rates across the region, with a gender gap of 8–15 per cent (Knothe, 2005: table 7). The Karat Coalition of NGOs from the region in 2005 lobbied both the UN and national governments in the region to 'thoroughly investigate the impact of privatization and other elements of neoliberal economy on the dramatic decrease in the activity rate of women in CEE/CIS region' (Karat, 2005a).

Added to the gender gap in labour force participation, the effects of direct and indirect discrimination in employment, plus the impact of flexibilization make clear that the negative effects of economic transformation and restructuring in the region continue to be borne disproportionately by women. It is possible to argue that the process of economic restructuring is intrinsically and fundamentally gendered in form and impact. This makes it all the more astonishing that the vast majority of analyses of macro-economic changes in the region ignore gender as a variable. They concentrate on other indicators such as country-specific variations. Yet many of these are not specific to the transformation process, but already existed before the establishment of state socialist regimes after the Second World War (Einhorn, 1993; Pollert, 1999: 21–2).

Early data showed that unemployment grew very fast across the entire region in the early 1990s, but began to fall in several countries from 1993–94. Although the unemployment rate for women has fallen in most countries from 1995 on, this may actually reflect discouragement, in other words women experiencing such difficulty in finding re-employment that they withdraw altogether from the formal labour market and do not therefore appear in unemployment statistics (Karat, 2005a). It is noteworthy by contrast that in the first months of 1999, seven countries (Croatia, Czech Republic, Latvia, Lithuania, Romania, Slovakia and Yugoslavia) reported their highest unemployment rates since the beginning of the transformation process (Steinhilber, 2001: 205).

Up until very recently, unemployment in most countries in the region certainly continued to be skewed by gender. A study by Czech sociologists in 2000 noted that 'unemployment, like employment, is [gender] segregated' (Čermáková et al., 2000: 122). The total unemployment level was initially very low in the Czech Republic compared with other countries in the region, but rose steeply after 1997, with women's unemployment rate of 10.7 per cent since 1999 considerably higher than the rate for men of between 6 and 7 per cent (Marksová-Tominová, 2003: 37, 40). The most notable exception to the rule is Hungary. While in the Czech Republic in the initial restructuring period the female-dominated service sector lost more jobs than the still protected industrial sector, the opposite was true for Hungary, where inefficient heavy industries were targeted in the first round of privatization with a consequent heavy loss of male blue-collar jobs (Fodor, 2003: 159–60; True, 2003a: 81). Figures for 1998 showed women's rate of unemployment as higher than men's in all countries of the region barring Estonia, Hungary, Lithuania and Romania (Steinhilber, 2001: 206, fig. 2; see also Alsop, 2000: 89, fig. 5.3; Kotowska, 1995: 81, table 2; Lokar, 2000: 18, table 4; Nesporova, 2003: 5; Pollert, 1999: 78, table 4.5).[5]

The situation in Poland is particularly shocking, with women's unemployment rate 20.6 per cent higher than men's. This is seen by Polish analysts as the main problem hindering Polish women's ability to complete on an equal basis with men in the labour market and preventing them attaining economic independence (Lohmann and Seibert, 2003: 10). Nor does their considerable educational capital protect women from unemployment. This is surprising in the context of a shift to a post-industrial economy with its need for workers with higher qualifications and skills. Despite women's increasing share of tertiary education in Poland, 'it would seem that a degree protects men from unemployment more than it protects women' (Fuszara, 2000: 269, 283; Marinova et al., 2003: 55).[6]

Women were until very recently also more likely than men to fall into long-term unemployment.[7] What is sometimes termed hidden unemployment covers women's permanent or temporary withdrawal from the labour force, for example through extended child-care leave. Paradoxically, there is simultaneous evidence of women failing to take the childcare leave legally available to them for fear of its deleterious effect on their ability to return to their job (UNICEF, 1993: 61, cited in Kotowska, 1995: 82; Macková, 2000: 93; Pollert, 1999: 78–9). Another reason for 'hidden' female unemployment is to be found in the probable – though difficult to document – preponderance of women in the growing 'grey' or informal economy, for instance in home-based work, work for which they have no formal contract, or in the 'thriving sex market' encompassing both prostitution and trafficking which has sprung from the fertile ground of high unemployment, increasing socio-economic inequalities, and processes of immiseration (Steinhilber, 2001: 203; True, 2003a: 75, 93–8; cf. also Agustín, 2005; Anderson and Davidson, 2004; Bruno, 1997: 59; Buchowska, 2000; Davidson, 2003; Kligman and Limoncelli, 2005; Kobelyanska, 2000).

Young people as a whole have been badly affected by economic restructuring. The International Labour Organization's statistical yearbook for 1999 shows young women bearing a higher share of unemployment than their male counterparts in Bulgaria, Croatia, Czech Republic and Poland (ILO, 1999, cited in Steinhilber, 2001: 207). In Poland, people under 25 accounted for 36 per cent, and people under 35 a staggering 64 per cent of the total unemployed in figures from December 1993. And women in Poland had at that time a far higher unemployment rate than men in precisely these age groups of 15–34, as well as in the age group 45–54 (Kotowska, 1995: table 3: 82, 84). By 2002, the unemployment rate for women under 25 in Poland had reached 37.8 per cent (Lohmann and Seibert, 2003: 32).

As a direct consequence, parenthood is emerging as a distinct disadvantage in the search for jobs, at least for women, although not for men. Young women are considered either as a potential risk, since they may have children and make use of maternity leave and/or still extant childcare leave policies, or as 'unreliable', accused of having a higher absentee rate because of their family responsibilities (Čermáková *et al.*, 2000: 131; Marinova *et al.*, 2003: 59). Citing labour force surveys conducted in Poland during the 1990s, UNICEF cites as the 'main determinant' in women's greater difficulty in finding work their greater responsibility for childcare. Marriage status was 'not a factor for unemployed men in finding work, but was a serious handicap for unemployed women' (UNICEF, 1999: 29; see also Becker, 1998: 346; Heinen, 1995: 93 and Knothe, 2005: 12).

Qualitative evidence from Poland suggests that young women are sometimes asked by potential employers to give a written undertaking that they do not intend to have children within a given time period. Others feel that their only chance of finding a new job, even one for which they have been specifically re-trained, lies in a decision never to have children. Most complaints laid with the Polish National Labour Inspectorate concern employer demands for non-pregnancy certificates or women being fired during pregnancy or childcare leave

(Heinen, 1995: 94, 102; Malicka, 2000: 17; Nowakowska and Swedrowska, 2000: 57). Thus the age-old choice between having a career *or* having children, formerly regarded by women in the region as a relic of the past, has re-emerged as a market force shaping or distorting women's life plans. The Polish Women's Rights Centre points out that 'neither the law, nor social policy expects a man to reconcile his professional life with family obligations. In practice, women have two jobs under the law, in the workplace and at home'. The Centre's study identifies the ostensible gender-neutrality of the market as responsible for this situation. Its authors comment further that 'in this context, it is not difficult to understand why some women are tired of "equal treatment", as it is a burden that only they have to carry on their shoulders' (Nowakowska and Swedrowska, 2000: 53; see also Becker, 1998: 346; Hornig, 1995: 184).

Apart from young women, the age cohort most vulnerable to long-term unemployment are women over 45 (ILO, 1999; Lohmann and Seibert, 2003: 51; Marinova *et al.*, 2003). In a double discrimination based on both age and gender, they constituted over half of the long-term unemployed in the east German state of Brandenburg in 1997 (Bundesanstalt für Arbeit, 1994: 57, cited in Alsop, 2000: 90). An east German woman was told in 1991 that aged 49, she was 'too old' to be 'worth' re-training, since she would never find another job (Einhorn, 1993: 138). Since then, it appears that at least in some countries, age discrimination sets in even earlier. Job advertisements in Polish newspapers in 2003 specified an age limit of 35 for women and 45 for men (Lohmann and Seibert, 2003: 55). Gender-differentiated age barriers stand in stark contrast to actual demographic shifts. There has been a sharp drop in life expectancy throughout the region in the period since 1989, and it is especially marked for men (Bridger, 2000a: 46; Watson, 1995). This makes a nonsense of 'age limits' that disadvantage women, making clear that the key variable responsible for discrimination here is gender, and not age.

Hidden unemployment and informal sector employment both mask even higher rates of female unemployment than are evident from available unemployment data. In East Germany after German unification there has been a 'general "de-feminization" of waged labour', intensified by a re-segregation of the labour force in favour of male labour (Alsop, 2000: 94). Those women lucky enough to remain in work suffer high levels of discrimination and harassment at work. This is documented in reports by the Lithuanian equal opportunities ombudsman and by UNIFEM (both cited in Steinhilber, 2001: 209). Such discrimination occurs in hiring and firing practices, in the payment of wages and benefits, and in sexual harassment at the workplace, especially in the private sector.[8]

Once unemployed, women face greater difficulty than men in finding new jobs (Alsop, 2000; Knothe, 2005; Lokar, 2000; Steinhilber, 2001: 206–7; UNICEF, 1999). This trend, which I had identified in the early post-1989 period, appears to be unchanged, as do the reasons for it (Einhorn, 1993). The protective legislation still in place in Poland among other countries actually acts as a barrier to re-employment, since it allows managers to regard women as 'unreliable' employees (Fong and Paul, 1993; Nowakowska and Swedrowska, 2000: 45–6; Steinhilber, 2001: 207). Thus the dual role as worker *and* mother which was to some extent eased by state socialist provision, for example through generous maternity leave allowances, now forms the basis for gender-based discrimination in the labour market.

Discriminatory hiring practices are widespread. Managers in many countries in the region openly state their preferences for male workers.[9] Equal opportunities and sex discrimination legislation does now exist in most countries, but it is often not implemented.[10] For example, discriminatory, gender-specific job advertisements were not explicitly banned by law in Poland during the 1990s, and many advertisements specify the gender and physical attributes of the applicants being sought (Fuszara, 2000; Heinen and Portet, 2002: 151). In the Czech Republic, the gender-neutral advertising practices required of foreign firms in their home countries are cheerfully jettisoned in the 'virgin territory' of this new capitalist marketplace (True, 2003a: 87–8). Even where equal opportunities or anti-discriminatory legislation is in place, it tends to be disregarded by employers. Nor are women always aware of their rights. In many cases the mechanisms for asserting employment rights via legal claims are lacking. Women's level of organization and voice within trade unions in the region is also relatively weak. A report published by the International Confederation of Trade Unions (ICFTU) is tellingly entitled *The Male Face of Trade Unions in Central and Eastern Europe: The Secret of Invisible Women* (Petrović, 2002; see also Steinhilber, 2001: 209).

Marketization and occupational segregation

Marketization has been seen across the region as synonymous with privatization, with costly effects. A comparative case study of Czech, US and British-owned department stores located in the Czech Republic decries as empty myth the idea that privatization is a necessary prerequisite for market transition. Marketing and management skills inherited from the past could have provided the preconditions for publicly owned stores becoming profitable, market-oriented enterprises. Instead, 'ownership became a quagmire of corruption and asset stripping' (Pollert, 1999: 217). This finding can be generalized for other economic sectors.

The extent and impact of occupational segregation in the early to mid-1990s are confirmed for the late 1990s by an ILO study (Einhorn, 1993, 1997; Steinhilber, 2001: 207–8). As I had established earlier, occupational segregation – both horizontal and vertical – was widespread during the state socialist period. Mining, metallurgy, chemicals, machine-building, construction and transport were overwhelmingly male-dominated sectors of the economy (apart from their large clerical, administrative and research sections), while light industry, communications and services remained female-dominated. A number of studies document the ways in which this gender-based segregation of the labour force has been, if anything, exacerbated in the course of the transformation process (van Hoven-Iganski, 2000: 139; Koncz, 2000; Mackova, 2000: 89; Nickel, 2002; UNICEF, 1999). In the Czech Republic the number of women's jobs in the female-dominated textile industry was halved between 1990 and 1995, in order to 'save men's jobs' (True, 2003a: 81).

National statistics from Slovakia show that in 1990, women comprised 82 per cent of the labour force in the textile and clothing industry, 78 per cent in health and social care, 75 per cent in education, 72 per cent in banking and insurance, 66 per cent in hotels, restaurants and retail, and 62 per cent in food manufacturing. Ten years on, in the second quarter of 2000, several sectors, especially those in the caring professions, had been further feminized. Women's share of employment in education rose from 75 per cent to 86 per cent, in health and social care from 78 per cent to 85 per cent, and in food manufacturing from 62 per cent to 78 per cent. Conversely, in those sectors whose importance – and hence wage levels – had been enhanced by the transition to a market economy, there was a relative displacement of female labour. In privatized hotels and restaurants the female share dropped from 66 per cent to 58 per cent, and in banking and insurance from 72 per cent to 62 per cent (Macková, 2000: 89–90). These data demonstrate that the high educational levels and professional qualifications of women in previously female-dominated sectors such as banking and insurance – presumed by some analysts to constitute advantageous intellectual capital in the transformation process – did not in practice help them to maintain their share of employment in the most desirable branches of the service sector (Fodor, 1997; Fong and Paul, 1993). Even in the Czech

Republic, which was quick to establish a flourishing service sector due to tourism and rapid privatization of small retail outlets, 'contrary to institutionalist predictions' women have failed to maintain their comparative advantage in the sector (True, 2003a: 82).

However, the picture is complex, documenting gains as well as losses, opportunities as well as gendered risks. One study describes the new market economy of the Czech Republic in the 1990s as 'a voracious, hyper-masculine, Czech brand of capitalism'. Yet the same study asserts that feminist accounts of the transformation – at least in its early stages – over-emphasized the extent to which it negatively affected women, partly because of a focus on women, rather than on gender relations (True, 2003a: 24–5, 75–6). An East German study similarly rejects as simplistic the dichotomy suggested in earlier studies that portrayed women as the 'losers' of German unification. It also argues that the binary of losers and winners casts women as 'the lucky or unlucky victims of a structural process over which they have no influence' (Nickel, 2000: 108; see also Becker, 1998: 348; Young, 1999). Women's share of employment in the retail trade in East Germany fell dramatically in the first half of the 1990s. The drop was all the more marked when one takes into consideration a growth in the overall numbers employed in this branch in the same period. Yet by the late 1990s, whilst the overall number of jobs in the branch had declined, women held almost 75 per cent of them. Nevertheless, women were being edged out of 'slimmed down' corporate hierarchies by West German male managers. By contrast women had held two thirds of GDR managerial posts in retail in 1988. While the service sector in eastern Germany had been almost exclusively female (90 per cent) prior to 1989 and was still 70 per cent female in 1995/96, this displacement of women by men was dubbed 'the new genderization' (Nickel, 2000: 112).[11]

These findings on the displacement of female by male labour, especially at managerial level, are borne out by two sectoral studies from eastern Germany, one on banking, finance and insurance, and the other on the German railways. The gender-specific occupational segregation of the East German labour force prior to 1989 gave women in banking and insurance a fighting chance of maintaining their employment levels after German unification. Initially, they benefited from a hiring boom in this expanding sector, followed by a corporate 'training offensive' designed to bring women's existing qualifications into line with the requirements of the service sector under market conditions. It therefore appeared at first that women might be at an advantage in this tertiary sector of the East German economy (Nickel, 2000: 113; Peinl, 2001).

This hope appears at first sight to have been borne out by the fact that women still constitute a higher percentage of branch managers and team heads in eastern than in Western Germany. However, this positive statistic is counteracted by several trends. The financial sector in eastern Germany has gained increased economic importance and hence social prestige as a result of its incorporation into the Federal German market economy. This has been reflected not only in a greater number of training applications by men, but in personnel policies that favour male applicants during selection procedures. As in the retail trade, women have lost their comparative advantage at managerial level to men, especially in lower and middle level management. New job requirements, especially in terms of mobility and commitment to long working hours, tend to discriminate against women.

A post-unification study of savings banks in Eastern Germany suggested that two factors disadvantaged the East German women workers who had formed 90 per cent of the workforce in this branch prior to 1989. The first was the import of a Western structural model that favoured male managers. The second was a mismatch between the training and skills of existing workers and the exigencies of the banking and finance sector under the new market conditions. As a result, East German women workers and especially those at management level found themselves doubly in competition for their jobs: first from West German men, second from West German women (Maier, 1993; Nickel, 1993, 2000: 114).

In the Czech Republic too, women's share of employment in banking and financial services has decreased from 80 per cent in 1988 to 65 per cent in 2000, while average salaries in this sector increased by a factor of seven between 1990 and 1998 (True, 2003a: 82). Nevertheless more recent trends, observable for example in the hiring practices of Western banks, have the potential to favour qualities often associated with women, such as non-hierarchical ways of working, conflict resolution capacities, and 'a friendly manner with clients' (Nickel, 2000: 113–15).

Restructuring the eastern German railway system before and after its final merger with West German railways in 1994 resulted in the loss of over a third of jobs. Women bore a disproportionate share of these losses and their share of the workforce fell from 32 to 26 per cent. Both the banking and the railway service sector studies show that, 'gender is a feature that without any doubt still exercises a crucial "usherette" function, allocating people places in the increasingly bitter battle over the distribution of labour, and more especially the battle over income and positions (of leadership)'. At the same time, however, these studies indicate hugely expanding differentiation and hierarchies among women themselves (Nickel, 2000: 121).

Overall, both these studies confirm the growing exclusion of East German women from paid employment noted earlier. Nevertheless, changes in organizational strategies and labour requirements within the service sector mean 'that opportunities arise here for redefining the gender division of labour, with some equalisation of career prospects for men and women ... besides, it is becoming harder to draw a boundary between male and female domains, which has hitherto been the decisive segregation mechanism in implementing integrated strategies' (Goldmann, 1997: 157, cited in Nickel, 2000: 120–1). The jury is therefore out on whether there is hope for a more gender equitable future in the service sector (Nickel, 2000: 118, 121).

The gender wage gap both characterizes and perpetuates gender-based segregation in the labour market. Women in Central and Eastern Europe earn on average 70 to 80 per cent as much as men. This level is no worse; indeed, in many cases it is better than the gap operating in most 'old' European Union member states (Allen and Sanders, 2002; Karat, 2005a; Marinova et al., 2003: 64). In the Czech Republic, it is notable that the gap persists despite the fact that women generally have similar or better education and qualifications than men (Marksová-Tominová, 2003: 43). Indeed throughout the industrialized world the gender wage gap is both consistent and persistent, with women earning only 60 to 73 per cent as much as men in many countries. However, it remains disappointing when considered in the context of the longer history of equal pay policies promulgated by state socialist regimes in the region. A UNICEF study documents that gender is the decisive variable here, since it has been demonstrated (for many countries, not only in this region) that women's wages in female-dominated occupations is lower than men's even when other variables such as educational qualifications, skills, or experience are taken into account (UNICEF, 1999: 36; for Western Europe see also Allen and Sanders, 2002: 63 and Rubery, Smith and Fagan, 1999).

There has been considerable improvement in the years since the transformation process began, at least in Central if not in Eastern Europe, but the gender wage gap – as in Western Europe – still falls far short of pay parity.[12] One factor that exacerbates the trend is the predominance of women in the public sector, which offers lower wages than the male-dominated private sector, and even lower than those offered by foreign firms. In the Czech Republic, average wages paid by foreign firms are 50 per cent higher than those in the public sector. The wage differential between managers and workers is also greater in foreign firms, disproportionately affecting women who are under-represented at the top level of management (True, 2003a: 85–6). Indeed further eastwards the wage gap has widened in the past decade.[13] While one may be sceptical of statistical data that purports to measure this so precisely, nevertheless the persistence of the gender wage gap is clear. So too are the diverging trends within Central and Eastern Europe, leading to a two-tier economic system of EU members and non-members. The further East one travels, the worse economic conditions in general are, and the more extreme the level of gender discrimination. Economically speaking, this is like simply shifting the Cold War East–West divide further eastwards after the first two rounds of enlargement (comprising eight countries in 2004 and a further two – Bulgaria and Romania – in 2007). This fear is expressed by the Karat Coalition, a network of lobbying NGOs from the region, in their reaction to the European Union's proposed new financial instruments to govern the further enlargement process. Not only is gender notable by its absence from these documents. They also describe an implied three-tier status within Europe, comprising candidate countries (Croatia and Turkey), potential candidate countries (Albania, Bosnia and Herzegovina, Serbia and Montenegro, Macedonia), and so-called neighbouring countries, who are presumed to aspire to become European Union members, but who have little hope of accession in the near future (Belarus, Ukraine, Moldova, Georgia, Armenia, Azerbaijan) (Karat Coalition Press Release, 2005c; Lohmann, 2005).

A remark about Russia that could apply to the region as a whole is that 'entrepreneurship and small and medium enterprise formation have become key words and all-favourite policy recommendations in the transition process to the market' (Bruno, 1997: 56). There has been much speculation by economic analysts as to why women have been 'left behind' in this process of privatization. They are under-represented in the private sector both as employees and as entrepreneurs. 'Women have created fewer businesses than men, own smaller businesses, employ less people' than men, and 'in large private companies, women are strongly under-represented in the higher echelons of decision-making' (Steinhilber, 2001: 208–9). Jacqui True goes so far as to speak of a 'female public sector, male private sector' (True, 2003a: 80).

Whether it can be interpreted as cause or effect, the public sector has become increasingly feminized during the 1990s. In the Czech Republic, men made up 84 per cent of employees in the newly emerging private sector in 1990, and 61 per cent in 1998, a considerable fall, but still a clear predominance. They accounted for 75 per cent of all entrepreneurs and employers in the late 1990s. Women's share of public sector employment increased from 46 per cent in 1990 to 60 per cent in 1998 with more than 75 per cent share of education and health (True, 2003a: 80–1). In Slovakia, a Confederation of Trade Unions study published in 1999 showed that whilst women constituted 44.5 per cent of the workforce in the public sector in 1990, by early 1999 their share had risen to almost 65 per cent (Macková, 2000: 89).

An International Labour Organization study of four Central European countries in 1995 argued that women's continuing or even increased predominance in public sector employment should not be attributed to women being somehow less prepared to take risks than men. Rather there were structural reasons for this over-representation. The spheres of public administration, health care, social services and education – all of them highly feminized sectors in which women account for about 75 per cent of all employees – happen to be the economic sectors that are less interesting to private capital and hence have remained in state control. Additional factors include the gender-biased hiring practices of private firms and women's relative lack of time for the retraining often required by the private sector (Paukert, 1995).

A report to the UN Commission on the Status of Women (CSW) in New York in March 2000 by Karat, a network of advocacy NGOs in the region, urged that 'special attention' be given to 'the possibilities of self-employment' for women. It recommended 'micro-credit projects with a special focus on women's self-reliance as a key to people-centered, sustainable development' (Bijelić, 2001). I have argued earlier that the much-vaunted role of entrepreneur could only ever represent a solution for a minority, not for the mass of unemployed women (Einhorn, 1993). It requires a level of skills and initiative which the work experience of many unemployed women has simply not equipped them for, not to speak of their lack of financial capital and access to 'old boy' information networks. A more probable outcome already sees women over-represented in the growing informal and unregulated sector. Nevertheless, Russian women are resorting to becoming businesswomen not merely as a survival strategy. Rather, they appear to be playing on notions of gender difference in a conviction that women have the potential to transform private entrepreneurship into a social mission, espousing a 'set of values ... which could improve not only the economic sphere but the very identity crisis of the Russian nation' (Bruno, 1997: 64–5). Despite the hurdles encountered by Russian women wishing to set up in business, and despite their relative invisibility as entrepreneurs, they are trying to invent a new kind of entrepreneurship that distinguishes itself 'both from the Soviet experience and from Western cultures of market relations'. Women entrepreneurs seem to approach business in a different way and offer modes of operating that could transform business relations (Bruno, 1997: 72-3).

The re-institution of private ownership of land has also had gendered effects, particularly in terms of shifts in the public–private divide, and the establishment of the family as both patriarchal gender hierarchy and economic institution. In Bulgaria, private property rights have restored the economic function of the family in small firms and family farms. Analysts fear that this could lead to changes in family roles that would be disadvantageous to women (Kostova, 1994: 95). It involves reverting to traditional family farms which men own while women 'work the land as unpaid workers' (Steinhilber, 2001: 208; cf. also Bridger, 1996 and 2000a: 49). Clearly the division between (male) ownership and (female) labour on family farms must have repercussions in terms of gender relations. A likely outcome for rural women in the new Russia is that they have 'little choice but to sacrifice themselves for their family's survival' (Bridger, 1996: 253).

Experiencing unemployment

Paradoxically, levels of female labour market participation have remained high, despite the disproportionate female share of unemployment and the overall loss of jobs. In other words, while the revival of traditionalist and nationalist discourses would displace women from the public sphere of the market, relegating them exclusively to the domestic sphere, with an attendant danger of social exclusion and marginalization women's behaviour in practice contradicts these prescriptive notions. This demonstrates that the notion of women's 'return home' was, as Jiřina Šiklová claimed ten years ago for the Czech Republic, 'unrealistic' in a country where most men do not earn anything like a breadwinner salary and where women have obtained education, professional skills and higher status based on their labour force activity for at least two generations (Šiklová, 1993: 78). In Hungary too 'the generation of women who grew up between 1945 and 1990 with the expectation of a full-time, life-long career still express pride in their work and in their participation in the labor force, as do their daughters who saw their mothers go to work every day' (Fodor, 2003: 159). In East Germany, a 1997 survey showed 74 per cent of women wishing to retain their identity as workers (Young, 1999: 224).

Women have therefore failed to internalize discursive constructions of them as housewives supported by a male breadwinner (Becker, 1998: 319; Hornig, 1996: 184; van Hoven-Iganski, 2000: 147; Nickel, 2002; Steinhilber, 2001: 204). Traditionalist rhetoric also failed in Slovakia, despite exhortations to women – endorsed by figures of authority like Emilia Kováčová, the wife of the former Slovak president – to devote their lives to their 'primary role – childrearing' as 'the only guarantee for the future of the country'. Economic pressures requiring a second family income and the high level of social capital attained by Slovak women during the state socialist period have combined to maintain high rates of female employment, with women forming up to 45 per cent of the total labour force throughout the 1990s (Bitušiková, 2005b: 5).

An earlier survey conducted for the ILO in 1995 already documented persistent labour market attachment on the part of women workers in the Czech Republic. While 28 per cent of married women said they would like to stay at home if their husbands earned enough for them to do so, a substantial 40 per cent voiced explicitly their wish to continue working even if this were not financially necessary. And in Poland, young people of both sexes regarded women's employment outside the home as the norm (Paukert, 1995: 7; see also Čermáková et al., 2000: 69). This data established early and beyond doubt that the overwhelming loss of women's jobs during the transformation process can not be read as evidence of 'voluntary' withdrawal from the market.

Nor has the suggestion that women in the region might adopt the West European model of part-time work as the preferred modality facilitating the harmonization of family and career been borne out. In the Czech Republic, 92 per cent of working women work full-time (42.5 hours per week, a longer working week than in most European Union countries; Čermáková et al., 2000: 21).[14] In Hungary, women's employment dropped massively in the decade after 1989. National statistics showed only 61 per cent of Hungarian women as employed in 1995. Yet a survey of Hungarian women in the same year gave clear expression to contradictions arising from the conflict between women's need to work for the economic survival of the family and their idealized aspirations of moving to part-time work. Two-thirds of female respondents thought that women *should* work outside the home, but of these, 60 per cent felt women *should not* work full-time. Yet in the same survey, only 10 per cent of women actively employed at the time expressed a willingness to move from full-time to part-time employment (Kovács and Váradi, 2000: 179).

Qualitative interviews conducted during the 1990s across the region show that persistent employment aspirations can not be reduced to a question of economic necessity. Rather, they can at least in part be attributed, as I have argued earlier, to the sense of identity and self-worth gained from the social context of work (Einhorn, 1993). Unemployment leads to a loss of social contacts, intensifying a loss of self-esteem. A woman in her forties who had been a supervisor and qualified engineer in the textile and clothing industry in Cottbus, East Germany was interviewed after she had been made redundant and then completed a 13-month computer-based retraining course. She stressed her wish to work with others. 'For me, the contact with people is very important. Of course income as well, but the crucial factor is working with people. [...] The collective was like my family' (Alsop, 2000: 168–9; see also Becker, 1998: 345; Heinen, 1995: 98–9 and van Hoven-Iganski, 2000: 139, 144). A Hungarian study of women industrial workers in the town of Karikás found that despite the alienating, exploitative and physically hard nature of their work, women in a cannery experienced the factory 'as a kind of surrogate family'. They felt that the social value of their work was affirmed. The high level of redundancies following the factory's privatization eroded this sense of 'family' solidarity, giving way to a situation where 'we are afraid of each other'. Women workers experienced 'the cultural devaluation of labour itself, both for its own sake and as a guarantee of a livelihood' (Kovács and Váradi, 2000: 192–3).

Life history interviews suggest that for East German women of the generation who were around 25–30 in 1989, labour market participation is such an integral element of their identity and biography that 'unemployment constitutes a threat not only to women's material circumstances, but also to their psychological wellbeing'. The risk of unemployment for women in this age cohort in East Germany was 3.7 times higher in 1995 than for men of the same age. In this way, structural change actually affects women's self-image and forces them to rethink – and actively restructure – their biographies (Becker, 1998: 310, 346–8).

Personal testimonies from a range of countries contrast the sense of social cohesion and solidarity at the workplace experienced (at least in retrospect) in the past, with new workplace hierarchies, increased insecurity of employment and a resultant rise in competitiveness and aggression at work. Seamstresses in an East German clothing factory subjected to Western piecework rates literally fought over access to sufficient pieces to fulfill the company's production norms (Bast-Haider, 1995: 58; van Hoven-Iganski, 2000: 145). Another factor integral to the economic restructuring process is de-skilling (Einhorn, 1993; van Hoven-Iganski, 2000: 145). Deskilling affects women still in work as well as those who – once unemployed – find themselves unable to find another job due to now anachronistic skills and qualifications acquired under a different economic regime (Bast-Haider, 1995: 55, 59).

A qualitative study of women workers in Warsaw and Łódź corroborates both the persistent desire to work outside the home and the reasons already proffered for it. Such labour market attachment stands in direct contrast to the tendency whereby women – especially young women – expressed a wish in the late 1980s and early 1990s to exercise the 'choice' to stay at home with the children (Einhorn, 1993; Heinen, 1995: 90, 95–6). East and West German data show a marked difference in this respect. During 1996, 53.9 per cent of married mothers with children under 3 in the East, but only 39.3 per cent of the equivalent group in the West were employed outside the home. The discrepancy was even more marked among mothers with children aged 3–6 (i.e. pre-school children; children in Germany go to school only at age 7), of whom 71.2 per cent were employed in the East compared with 45.9 per cent in the West. This data demonstrates that working women in Eastern Germany remained attached to earlier role models in their desire to combine work and motherhood roles, resisting a transition to the West German male-breadwinner model. However, in the eastern state of Mecklenburg-Westpommerania, there were signs that this labour market attachment was breaking down in the next generation. The difficulties that young female school-leavers faced in finding employment or apprenticeships was having a knock-on effect in that schoolgirls were expressing the desire to become full-time housewives and mothers (van Hoven-Iganski, 2000: 148).

The impact of social policy changes

The nature and pace of economic restructuring has varied between countries. So also has the choice of social policy regime. Nevertheless, it is possible to identify a general trend away from universalist to residualist models of social welfare and the widespread assumption of a male-breadwinner family model (Steinhilber, 2006; Szalai, 2005).

The evolution of different types of welfare regime in Hungary suggests there are lessons to be learned by the West from the experience of the East. Successive welfare regimes in Hungary were predicated upon, and shaped the formation of different gender identities. The early state socialist approach to welfare acknowledged and fostered an array of possible identities for women – as workers, mothers, spouses and family members. By contrast, 'the late socialist state constituted women primarily as mothers and secondarily as workers'. More seriously for the formation of gender identities, the post-1989 welfare regime has 'collapsed all identities into one – the materially deprived' (Haney, 2002: 241, 244). This residualist approach individualizes the problem of welfare, reducing both the sense of entitlement and the possibility of making claims on the state. This renders women who fall into poverty dependent on family support networks or the market. Lynne Haney argues that the progressive reduction in the identities on which it is possible to base claims excludes many women and limits the space to act as subjects in their own right. A system of positive entitlement to welfare on the basis of social contributions becomes degraded into stigmatization of those individuals seeking assistance. This development not only offers insights into the workings of a type of welfare liberalism that currently prevails in many Western countries; it also constitutes a powerful indictment of what Haney calls the 'material reductionism' of welfare that acts to disempower its clients (Haney, 2002: 246–8).

One social variable which has decisively influenced women's ability to access the marketplace on an equal footing with men is the availability and affordability of childcare facilities. We have already seen how other policy measures such as extended maternity or parental leave can produce mixed results in terms of gender equality (Marinova *et al.*, 2003: 71; Marksová-Tominová, 2003: 57). Chapter 5 has already referred to the significant losses in childcare right across the region.[15] In Poland, the decision to devolve financial responsibility for childcare centres from the central state budget to local governments has meant both diminished availability and higher costs to families (Kotowska, 1995: 85). A vicious circle ensues: the ability for young mothers to take up a new job necessitates having childcare in place. Yet being made redundant will often have lost them the entitlement to a previously held place. Privatization of childcare and massively increased childcare fees both exacerbate the problem (Daskalova, 2000: 347; Einhorn, 1993, 1997; Knothe, 2005: 14; Maier, 1993; Pine, 1994; Szabó, 2003).[16]

Another variable influencing women's ability to exercise choice in relation to labour force involvement derives from altered maternity, family and childcare benefits. In Hungary and Bulgaria, parental leave and other related benefits have been curtailed during the restructuring process in direct response to 'pressure', or even 'requirements and suggestions' from the World Bank and the IMF (Daskalova, 2000; Goven, 2000: 290). Social welfare retrenchment in Bulgaria and other post-socialist countries has 'effectively dissuaded women from having children' (Daskalova, 2000: 346–7). Despite the formal availability of parental rather than maternity leave in the Czech Republic, the persistence of conservative attitudes means that fathers avoid taking it (Ćermáková et al., 2000: 88; on Romania see also Gheaus, 2001: 187).

Pension reform in the region also impacts on women's ability to become – and to remain – independent economic agents without falling into poverty. A study conducted for the ILO on pension reforms in three Central European countries [Poland, Hungary and Czech Republic] notes that gender equality has not been a factor driving pension reform. This has led to some unforeseen disadvantages for women. While the reforms in each of the three countries have assumed the formal equality of men and women, existing inequalities in the wider social and economic environment mean that such formal equality can actually mask gender-based disadvantages. In all three countries the reforms are strongly based on individually accumulated pension rights and simultaneously seek to establish closer linkage between individual pension contributions and the resulting benefits (Steinhilber, 2002b: 15). As in Western European countries, this individualized approach disadvantages women for a variety of reasons, enumerated below.

First, the gender wage gap, coupled with occupational segregation, means that women's pension contributions will, over their working life, be lower than men's. Second, societal expectations of women's primary responsibility for unpaid caring functions are reinforced by the empirical fact that it is overwhelmingly women who take childcare leave, even when it is titled as parental leave. This results in longer career breaks in women's employment histories, which in turn contribute to a lower level of accumulated pension contributions. These two factors – lower wages and a discontinuous career pattern – together result in lower pension contributions on the part of women. They are further exacerbated by a third factor, namely that throughout the region, women's retirement age is still officially five years earlier than men's, making for a shorter total period of pensionable employment than men. In pension schemes linking pension benefits to individual contributions therefore, the gender wage gap, lack of continuity in employment and shorter working life are bound to translate cumulatively into a yawning gender pension gap. The fact that women have on average six years longer life expectancy than men in the region heightens the likelihood of the feminization of poverty in older age (Ćermáková et al., 2000: 57; Daskalova, 2000; Steinhilber, 2002b; UNDP, 2000: 41, figure 5; Watson, 1995). To a considerable degree, then, pension reforms both reflect and in turn perpetuate the gendered inequalities of the societies within which they are promulgated.

Conclusion

Despite the currently gender-skewed labour market, several analysts are hopeful that future developments may prove positive in terms of gender equality in the labour market (Fodor, 2005; Nickel, 2000; True, 2003a). Nevertheless the impact of economic globalization means an increase in insecure employment conditions for both women and men (UN, 1995). Hildegard Maria Nickel poses the question as to whether global market pressures and economic restructuring are producing gender equalization within a general worsening of labour market conditions: 'Have structural changes perhaps been leading to a feminization of male employment (with low incomes, precarious jobs, pseudo-self-employment, and so on), to an equalization downwards, democratizing the gender pact only in the sense that a man's working life is now more like a woman's?' (Nickel, 2000: 111).

In her sober – and in large part not gender-differentiated – study of economic transformation of the region, Anna Pollert points to rising poverty, increasing income inequalities, a drop in the birth rate across the region, and deterioration in diet and health resulting in rising rates of infant and adult mortality especially among men, alongside increased morbidity among women (Pollert, 1999; see also Watson, 1995). Pollert's conclusion is damning. She asserts that 'there is little to show, after ten years, that the transition agenda has been a success either in human or economic terms'. She cites an earlier study that fundamentally critiques the purely market-oriented neo-liberal model adopted across the region. Pollert also refers to Gowan (1995) who argues that the way the economies in the region have been inserted into the global capitalist system, especially in relation to the European Union 'have created a harmful dependency relationship for the transforming economies, with the market's "invisible hand", actually creating the space for the highly political "visible hands" of Western states and capitalist interests to shape the position of the post-communist states in the global economy' (Gowan, 1995, cited by Pollert, 1999: 80).

There is a need to develop alternative models. Genuine gender equity in employment in Central and Eastern Europe necessitates a package of what a World Bank study published in 1992 called 'proactive measures'. These would combine equal opportunities legislation with social provisions that underwrite the capacity to exercise the equal right to work. Such provisions would include publicly provided, affordable childcare facilities, appropriate retraining programmes and affirmative action schemes for women's career enhancement and promotion. This early

World Bank study had already pointed to the ways that gender bias was distorting the transformation process itself (Fong and Paul, 1992, 1993). In a similar vein, an early OECD study argued for a macro-level approach that harmonizes economic and social policy in order 'not only to counteract discrimination against women but also to more efficiently utilize human resources' (OECD, 1991, cited by Kotowska, 1995: 87–8; see also Pollert, 1999: 80). I would concur with these analyses. Gender equity in the labour market is not only a laudable end in itself and a precondition for social justice more generally; it is in fact necessary to the harmonization of an efficient economy.

8
Citizenship in an Enlarging Europe
Towards Gender Equity?

Introduction

In choosing to focus this book on the concept of citizenship, it has been important to bear in mind that the very concept is a construct of liberal democratic theory and hence problematic. Many feminist political theorists have pointed out that the liberal democratic theory of citizenship, while ostensibly based on universal principles and hence gender-neutral, has always been in practice mediated by gender, class and 'race', with women of all groups historically and currently excluded from full political agency (Lister, 1993: 3; Vogel, 1991). Anne Phillips notes that the end of state socialism proved to be not 'the end of history', but 'only a preamble to renewed discussion of the forms and principles of democracy' (Phillips, 1999: 4).

It is to this discussion that the present volume makes a contribution. The analysis of transformation processes in Central and Eastern Europe offered here suggests that if a test of democracy is gender equitable citizenship, then the democratization process in Central and Eastern Europe must be regarded as incomplete. Moreover, I have argued that the concept of citizenship has itself been impoverished by the currently dominant neo-liberal paradigm with its exclusive focus on the market and hence (economic) citizenship. This is construed as a combination of the ability to exchange contracts in the market place, access to which is unequal, with gender structuring that inequality, and consumerism, mediated by dominant images of masculinity, femininity and heteronormativity. Nevertheless, I follow other feminist political theorists in believing that the concept and practice of citizenship offers the best conceptual and political tool for thinking about – and working towards – societies characterized by social justice in general and gender justice in particular. Analysing the transformation process in Central and Eastern Europe – and the influence of European Union enlargement on that process – from the perspective of gender illuminates some problems associated with a citizenship perspective. In this way the analysis of historically, culturally and regionally specific transformation offered in these pages produces insights that facilitate refinement of the concept of citizenship itself.

This final chapter fulfils a dual function. First, it revisits and summarizes some of the main theoretical arguments of the book, particularly those pertaining to the question of what discursive and institutional frames are most conducive to the achievement of gender equitable societies. Second, it contributes to debates about citizenship and the bases on which it could become gender equitable. Each of these two aspects is considered in two sections of this chapter. The first section briefly reviews strategies with a civil society focus and the associated language of empowerment. This is followed by reconsideration of the most relevant institutional framework for the realization of gender justice. The third and most substantive section discusses whether discourses of agency or capabilities, rights or entitlements provide the most useful basis for theorising citizenship focused on the goal of gender (and social) justice. The final section revisits debates about approaches based on equality or on difference before returning to the potential for enacting new forms of politics that transcend national, ethnic, class, religious and even regional divides.

Civil society and the language of empowerment

The privileging of civil society initiatives in East Central Europe is consonant with a global trend.[1] Civil society discourses construct the associational activities occurring in this space as both vibrant evidence of, and an essential ingredient in, functioning democracies.[2] Indeed, proponents of civil society as an enabling and politically empowering space sometimes reject the notion of citizenship as conferring a merely formal political status, or as excluding both 'outsiders' (such as migrants) and discriminated minority groups (such as Roma, gays, or lesbians) from membership of the polity (Lister, 1997: 65). Some theorists have tended to see 'empowerment' as a concept more applicable to women's activities, validating and incorporating women's experiences in a politics of 'power to', or 'power from within' rather than 'power over' others. The idea of empowerment has been applied particularly in the context of development. A feminist model of power would draw on Foucauldian ideas about power as relational. It would also 'incorporate a gender analysis of power relations that includes an understanding of how "internalized oppression" places internal barriers to women's exercise of power, thereby contributing to the maintenance of inequality between men and women'. Jo Rowlands maintains further that the empowerment discourse is supported by Maxine Molyneux's early theoretical contribution distinguishing between women's practical and strategic gender interests (Rowlands, 1998: 13–14, 16; Molyneux, 1985, 1988/1998/2001).

There are, however, several problems with an empowerment approach. First, it completely elides the realms of mainstream politics and the state, devolving not only power, but more importantly responsibility, to individual or grassroots societal level. Nira Yuval-Davis describes the discourse of 'empowerment' as part of a 'populist ideology which assumes "the people" and "the grassroots" to be the origin of all that is good and authentic'. In her view the weakness is to be found in the way that this discourse 'firmly situates the individual inside a more or less egalitarian and homogenous grouping which is "the community" '. As such, it can not exclude the possibility of 'power over'. In other words, it fails to take into account inequalities of power based on gender or indeed on other markers of difference such as class, ethnicity or sexuality (Yuval-Davis, 1998: 173–4). Rowlands herself concedes the possibility that 'one person's "empowerment" process may be another person's "disempowerment" ' (Rowlands, 1998: 24).

Furthermore, the space of civil society is itself predicated upon the public–private divide which feminist scholars regard as reinforcing gendered inequalities of power. As we have seen in Chapter 4, it is therefore far from constituting a (gender-)neutral space. Rather 'civil society is a deeply fraught space with hidden and explicit dangers that lurk there in the garb of national, religious, and ethnic identities as fashioned by male-directed movements of various kinds' (Rai, 1996: 17). There is thus no basis for assuming that 'civil society' will be more open, and responsive to, women's political claims than existing state institutions. 'Both spaces – of informal and formalized networks of power – are imbued with masculinist discourses; neither is "uncoerced", however different the forms and mechanisms of coercion' (Rai, 1996: 18). Some Western feminist analyses argue that civil society independence of state influence is often 'illusory' (Yuval-Davis, 1998: 178). In practice, it is indeed more often insecure support ('soft money') from national or international agencies rather than state institutions on which NGOs in Central and Eastern Europe are dependent. This can constrain their capacity for independent action, as was documented in Chapter 4.

My argument follows these critiques in noting (gendered) imbalances of power *within* civil society. My particular contribution to this discussion lies in formulating two potential pitfalls of an exclusive focus on empowerment through civil society activism. Both of these drawbacks to placing all hopes for women's 'empowerment' on this discursive – and political – space are magnified in practice by the common equation of civil society with NGOs. I have identified the de-politicization inherent in civil society activism as service provision. This constitutes what I call the civil society 'trap'. Second, I have questioned whether civil society involvement automatically guarantees access to the legislative and policy-making power of the state: this pitfall I have named the civil society 'gap'.

Chapter 4 identified the hazards of limiting the definition of civil society associations to NGOs. The way that this has come about is through financial dependency within a framework of project-related funding. The outcome of this is that both state and international donor agency funding is channelled to and through NGOs. It is NGOs that have the capacity, in terms of both the personnel and the requisite skills, to traverse the difficult terrain of funding applications. While there is indubitably an element of empowerment that results from the learning processes involved, and from the expertise and professionalization that follow, this has resulted in what Sabine Lang has called the 'NGOization of feminism' (Lang, 1997). By this she meant that donor dependency has transformed NGO activism into a career track for a small number of women, narrowed the goals set by civil society organizations, and depoliticized their aims in making them acceptable to donors. There has been much discussion of this phenomenon since Lang's article. Several analysts assert that international networking and international funding can be a process with two-way learning benefits (Sperling et al., 2001), or indeed that professionalization is precisely what NGOs in the region need (Lohmann, personal communication 2005). Nevertheless, there is ongoing concern that activist goals may become distorted or even lost as a result of donor dependence. Small, more radical grassroots (especially feminist) groups with a socially transformative agenda may become marginalized altogether because they are either unwilling or unable to conform to the exigencies of funding applications, and because their political aims do not fit the more conservative – or simply more bland – agendas of the European Union, the United Nations or even independent donor agencies (Hašková, 2005).

The civil society 'trap' characterises the activities of those women's groups that are not motivated by strategic gender interests. Rather, they are stopping the 'gap' left by state retrenchment and the ensuing loss of public welfare provision. The activities of many such groups could be considered as fulfilling practical gender interests through an agenda of poverty alleviation or simple damage limitation, working to mitigate the brunt of new economic and social inequalities and (the feminization of) poverty. The neo-liberal model adopted in Central and Eastern Europe paints state intervention as universally negative, thus devolving social responsibilities to the smallest social units, notably the family. Neo-liberal discourse stresses individual rather than social responsibility for welfare, well-being and social reproduction more generally. In this context, what Margaret Thatcher once called 'care in the community' is often a euphemism for the unpaid (and largely invisible) labour of women who thus shoulder the social costs of reproduction. Such commitment to the powerless at the local level – while both necessary and worthy in itself – potentially limits women's capacity to act as political subjects at the state level (Randall, 1998: 195).

The civil society 'gap' describes the lack of mechanisms for the translation of grassroots initiatives into legislation and public policy. Despite the requirement in EU legislation for the national women's machineries to engage with 'social partners', this idea of a two-way process of communication and mutual influence remains very poorly developed. Most countries lack institutionalized means of communication between NGOs and social movements on the one hand, and political power structures and state agencies on the other. In this context, it is easy for civil society initiatives to be 'lost' in transmission. This problem is exemplified in a report on NGOs in four Eastern European countries by the lobbying network Karat Coalition. The report identifies as 'the main obstacle' 'the unresponsiveness and unwillingness of the administration to engage in a dialogue with civil society'. As a result, 'NGOs are kept outside mainstream policy formation' (Barendt, 2002).

Which institutional framework?

The danger in Central and Eastern Europe is that the state could use the existence of civil society associations as a fig leaf, in other words as proof of democracy in practice, thereby exonerating itself from addressing issues of democratization, gender justice, or even the social needs dealt with by such groups. An alternative view suggests that the resonance of civil society discourse implies that the links between the global and the local can operate without, and can even benefit from, by passing the national state altogether. Ruth Lister mentions the growing impact of social movements and international NGOs on conceptions of a global civil society. She feels that the UN summits of the 1990s suggest movement towards the development of a notion of global citizenship (Lister, 1997: 62, 64; see also Mackie, 2001).

Indeed the nation state, as discussed in Chapter 2, is often perceived as losing autonomy or even legitimacy in the face of powerful supra-regional governments such as the European Union, international agencies such as the IMF or the World Bank, or the global movement of capital (Fraser, 2005). There is a need for caution in interpreting this threat, since it is possible to under-estimate 'the continued power of the nation-state to delineate and control the boundaries of exclusion'. In a best-case scenario, 'international human rights law, enforced by more effective institutions of global governance, could subject nation-states' exclusionary powers to an internationally agreed set of principles including that of non-discrimination' (Lister, 1997: 65). In the meantime, however, nation states retain an array of powers directly impinging on the daily lives of their inhabitants. State institutions still arbitrate over entry and right of residence, retain the power to confer citizenship, provide education and welfare, promulgate legislation and monitor implementation of laws governing reproductive rights and violence against women, and control – at least to an extent – working conditions (UN, 1995; Waylen, 1998: 7). The point here is that the nation state remains the source of legislation, the instigator of social welfare regimes, and the monitor of labour market conditions; in short it is the nation state that retains the power of inclusion and exclusion (Somers, 2005: 13). All of these forms of state power both reflect and create regime-specific forms of gendered power relations. Nonetheless, the nation state is still more accessible and accountable to citizens than transnational organizations such as the ILO or the UN or supra-national political instances such as the European Union, the European Court of Justice, or the European Court of Human Rights (Nussbaum, 2000: 105).

Feminist critiques of the 1980s suggested that the state was merely oppressive, its monolithic structures effectively hindering women's agency (Waylen, 1998). This view was also, understandably, prevalent in the immediate aftermath of state socialism. Júlia Szalai posed very early the crucial question: 'whose state?' arguing that 'there is a strong and broad opposition in our countries to everything that has the slightest flavour of "statism". It is a long process to get rid of the idea and practice of the totalitarian state and to define a state that is "ours", that is created and controlled by the democratic processes of civil society' (Szalai, 1990: 34–5). This position has largely prevailed in the region, while feminist discussion in the West and the South during the 1990s took a different tack. Under the influence of post-structuralist theory, the state itself was deconstructed. It began to be seen, not as a unitary or monolithic structure, but as a dynamic arena for the contestation of issues, and as such, not static, but rather as a set of discourses and practices subject to change and contestation.[3] Rosemary Pringle and Sophie Watson argue that ' "the state" as a category should not be abandoned', but that there is a need for 'recognition that, far from being a unified structure, it is a by-product of political struggles' (Pringle and Watson, 1992: 67). Georgina Waylen concludes from this that 'if the state is not a homogeneous entity but a collection of institutions and contested power relations, it is far better to see it as a site of struggle' (Waylen, 1998: 7).

In parts of Central and Eastern Europe, and in Russia, there are some signs that strong reactions to earlier political control and disempowerment by state socialist regimes may be giving way to a greater readiness to engage with the state. This is prompted by recognition that the social rights once granted from above are indeed rights that need defending. 'The division between social movement groups intent on retaining "autonomy" and those hoping to influence the state does not seem terribly salient in mid-1990s Russia'. Most women interviewees from 50 women's organizations 'expressed a desire to influence state policies on their issues' (Sperling, 1998: 163). In Bulgaria too, women show a propensity to resort to petitions to state bureaucracies or the National Assembly rather than attempting to mobilize support in the form of broad public campaigns (Daskalova, 2000: 362). These case study findings show a rekindling of belief in social rights and the state's co-responsibility for social justice. They suggest a nascent determination to launch claims on the state, rather than reliance on the grassroots and devolved responsibility for welfare provision. As such, they may presage moves to overcome the civil society 'trap'.

Karat Coalition, the powerful research and advocacy movement of NGOs in Central and Eastern Europe has warned of the negative consequences in the region of state retrenchment in favour of social regulation by market forces. Their spokesperson Regina Barendt argues that 'the only way to break down patriarchal gender power relations is through aggressive state intervention' (Barendt, 2002: 2). Yet she is equally wary of a narrow reliance on labour market regulation, as was the case during state socialism. This merely led to increased gender discrimination in the workforce while leaving gendered power relations in the private sphere intact. Here the European Union might learn much from the experience accumulated in the region during the state socialist years.

While stressing the need for state intervention, Karat supports the idea that only pressure from below can guarantee and maintain this. In its 2000 statement to the UN General Assembly, Karat demanded that national equal opportunities machineries should be located at ministerial level to give them maximum leverage on the government. At the same time, Karat stressed that 'it should become a normal and accepted practice for government bodies to work with and consult with women's NGOs' (Karat, 2001).

Karat's position echoes views about the necessity for grassroots pressure from autonomous women's movements as well as engagement with state institutions and the promotion of women to positions of political power (Einhorn, 1993; see also Randall, 1998: 200). This insight is particularly acute for countries undergoing systemic transformation in Latin America, China and Russia (Craske, 1998; Howell, 1998; Sperling, 1998). In other words, such a strategy is not necessarily region-specific. Rather it derives more generally from the experience of marketization and economic restructuring within the terms of the neo-liberal paradigm. This means that 'for many feminists, that point is no longer at issue; the state *must* be engaged and the question now is what are the most effective strategies for empowering women in this engagement' (Randall, 1998: 202–3). An exclusive focus on empowerment through civil society involvement 'has tended to marginalise discussion and analysis of other political phenomena which are of at least as much significance both for what they have contributed to our thinking about institutional areas for advancing women's interests, and for what they have achieved in practice' (Molyneux, 2001: 140). It is therefore necessary to combine (and most importantly, to create linkages between) top-down institutional approaches and civil society activism. Both a vibrant civil society *and* gender-sensitive state institutions and equality legislation are necessary pre-requisites for overcoming gender inequalities and facilitating full and active citizenship for women.

Citizenship: agency or capabilities, rights or entitlements?

In her important book on citizenship, Ruth Lister defines active citizenship as 'both a *status*, carrying a set of rights including social and reproductive rights, and a *practice*, involving political participation broadly defined so as to include the kind of informal politics in which women are more likely to engage'. She postulates 'human agency' as the element capable of producing a 'critical synthesis' between the two classical traditions of citizenship theory: the participatory approach of civic republicanism: 'citizenship as participation' which 'represents an expression of human agency in the political arena' and rights-based liberal democratic theory: 'citizenship as rights' which 'enables people to act as agents'. Agency is only effective in instigating change, Lister argues, when mobilized as collective action (Lister, 1997: 34, 36–7, 40).

Persuasive as I find the concept of human agency posited here, I see a potential 'Catch 22' (or at least an internal contradiction) in Lister's argument. On the one hand, 'citizenship as participation represents an expression of human agency in the political arena, broadly defined; citizenship as rights enables people to act as agents'. On the other, human agency is only attained by the combination of civil and political with social and economic rights. Thus Lister sees a combination of formal (civil, political) rights and substantive (social and economic) rights as a 'prerequisite of human agency'. Yet she posits the exercise of human agency as the very tool required in order to achieve this combination. She herself concedes, however, that social rights only 'in theory', but by implication not always in practice, 'enable citizens to exercise their political and civil rights on equal terms and create the conditions for full social and political participation' (Lister, 1997: 34, 36, 41, 196). The sticking point here, in my view, is the lack of a mechanism to ensure the integration of civil and political with social and economic rights and thereby the exercise of 'human agency' that would signify full citizenship status.

What is required is for people to possess both the *resources* and the *capacity* that enable them actually to access, and to exercise their paper rights. This suggests that what is needed is a conceptual approach that encompasses the transformation of resources into active agency. Amartya Sen uses the fact that individuals vary in their ability to convert resources into functioning to argue for a capabilities approach. Martha Nussbaum distances herself from Sen's distinction between well-being and agency, arguing that the more useful distinction to make is one between capabilities and fully human functioning (the equivalent, perhaps, of Lister's 'human agency') (Nussbaum, 2000: 14; 2002: 56). Despite its many advantages, however, the theory of human capabilities is in my view weak when it comes to addressing both systemic inequities and issues of implementation. The following discussion sets out arguments underlying my preference for the language of entitlements, rather than that of agency, capabilities or rights, as better suited to the pursuit of gender equitable citizenship in societies characterized by social justice.

In practice, the fundamentally gendered nature and impact of the democratization and marketization processes in Central and Eastern

Europe has erected barriers that obstruct women's capacity to access the marketplace, the site of citizenship as economic agency in the neo-liberal paradigm. These barriers result precisely from the removal of earlier social rights through state retrenchment within this economy-led model of transformation, as well as from their discursive discrediting within both neo-liberal and traditionalist discourses. This neo-liberal ' "re-privatisation discourse" [is] increasingly framed in terms of a new definition of citizenship which denies that the citizen can claim universal social rights from the state' and in which 'the new common good is one which promotes efficiency and competition' (Brodie, 1994: 57).

The erosion of both political and social rights occurs in a context that privileges economic rights as the basis of citizenship. Precisely this context, dictated by the currently dominant neo-liberal paradigm, has dominated the transformation process in Central and Eastern Europe. Marketization, economic liberalization and privatization have taken precedence over democratization and concerns with either social justice or the starkly increased levels of social inequalities. This might suggest the need to return to the language of human rights, defined by the United Nations *Human Development Report 2000* as claims to 'a set of social arrangements – norms, institutions, laws, an enabling environment – that can best secure enjoyment of these rights' (UNDP, 2000: 73). The key word here would seem to be 'claims'; in other words, the mechanism for ensuring the establishment of 'an enabling environment' for institutional implementation facilitating individual enjoyment of human rights.

The United Nations Convention on the Elimination of Discrimination against Women (CEDAW) is a powerful instrument. Most countries in Central and Eastern Europe signed up to it prior to the dismantling of the state socialist regimes (Schoepp-Schilling, 2005). It has also been used to call individual countries to account for non-implementation of its provisions in the period since 1989. Nevertheless, I would argue, with others, that the language of human rights has several limitations. Even though human rights cover both so-called 'first-generation rights' (political and civil liberties) and so-called 'second-generation rights' (social and economic rights), in practice it is civil and political rights that predominate in the tradition of liberal democratic thought. Thus the language of rights appears mainly in the guise of 'violations' of human rights. Here we have a clear indication of the twin weaknesses of human rights discourse: it has historically focused primarily on negative liberty (the right to 'freedom from' individual attack or state interference); and its implementation depends on access to legal redress. An example is the right to enjoy bodily integrity free from violence or sexual harassment, a right crucial in establishing women's reproductive rights on the one hand and employment rights on the other. Yet as the case of rape – whether in marriage or in war – makes plain, the possibility of legal recourse is both beyond most women and far from effective. Human rights are endowed at individual level, but individuals are rarely in a position to seek redress, either from national courts or supra-national bodies such as the European Court of Human Rights or the International War Crimes Tribunal.

When it comes to defining human rights as rights *to*, as opposed to freedom *from*, there is very little agreement on what is included. In the past, state socialist regimes put great emphasis on economic and social rights, offering their citizens guaranteed employment, shelter, and highly subsidized food and public transport. Yet such provision masked the lack of political and civil liberties granted by these regimes. Notwithstanding criticisms of the quality of work, housing or public childcare facilities, however, the level of social and economic rights in these countries presented a marked contrast, during the Cold War era, to interpretations of human rights as solely political and civil rights in Western countries. Thus the USA used human rights discourse to accuse the Soviet Union – or more recently China – of violations in the area of civil and political rights: classically the right to freedom of association and free speech. This example illustrates how the application of human rights discourse is both relative and subject to political manipulation, and how consensus as to its substance has always been lacking.

Diane Elson argues powerfully for adopting a human rights framework on the grounds that 'equity objectives may be treated as optional, but respect for human rights is obligatory' in the current global context (Elson, 2002: 87). She points out that Articles 22 and 28 of the Universal Declaration of Human Rights go beyond an individual focus to demand the construction of an enabling environment for the realization of rights (Elson, 2002: 98). Yet in many countries in the South, as well as in Central and Eastern Europe, whilst women's human rights are enshrined constitutionally, and the CEDAW treaty has been ratified, this is a far cry from the realization of human rights, not to speak of their being enjoyed equally by both men and women. This applies as much to social and economic rights, as Chapters 5 and 7 have demonstrated, as to political rights, discussed in Chapter 3. As Martha Nussbaum points out, political rights on paper are truly given 'only if there are effective measures to make people truly capable of political exercise' (Nussbaum, 2002: 68). In her view this justifies the language of capabilities, encompassing the capacity to exercise paper rights in reality. This would include the use of 'temporary measures' or affirmative action such as quotas in order to create the conditions for women to enjoy equality of access to political rights (Phillips, 2002).

I will argue below, however, that the notion of capabilities, like the language of human rights, still elides the problem of how to guarantee either 'human agency' or 'fully human functioning', and indeed whose responsibility it is to do so. This is, in my view, where the concept of 'entitlements' has the edge. It overcomes the emphasis on individual responsibility present in both traditional liberal democratic theory and in neo-liberal discourse. It enables a focus on systemic discrimination, and thus reinstates the notion of social responsibility for the collective good as well as a commitment to social justice. It also provides the mechanism for linking individual or group claims to redress inequalities with the institutions capable of response, whether these be market or state instances. As a conceptual or theoretical framework it is therefore more effective than either the language of capabilities or human rights discourse. Finally it provides a single, inclusive discourse where Nussbaum sees the necessity to retain human rights discourse alongside the language of capabilities (Nussbaum, 2002: 70–1).

The concept of 'entitlements' has, however, been given a bad press not only by some feminist theorists, but by left political theorists and neo-liberal politicians alike. In neo-liberal discourse the concept of 'entitlements' has become tainted by association with the notion of 'welfare dependency'. Left radical critics too have rejected its seemingly passive connotations, suggesting an understanding of social citizenship rights as endowed by a paternalist welfare state. In other words, they feel it construes citizens – and particularly women – as the passive recipients of state policies, rather than as active political subjects (Lister, 1997: 18, 35). In the context of Central and Eastern Europe, Irene Dölling described in an early analysis the passivity engendered by the 'paternalist patriarchy' of state socialist regimes (Dölling, 1991). Krassimira Daskalova has claimed more recently that Bulgarian women's movements have shown what she calls a welfarist tendency since the transformation began. She opposes the notion of 'entitlements' as casting women as 'victims' of the process, as the passive 'beneficiaries' of state handouts. She therefore prefers a rights-based approach (Daskalova, 2000: 360).

Lister's notion of 'human agency' is certainly attractive, not least because it rests, on the face of it, on a more active and dynamic political subject than the citizen possessing entitlements. Yet constraints on the capability to *exercise* 'human agency' in a neo-liberal landscape suggest that the concept of entitlements is still relevant. Such a concept gives greater definition to the notion of citizenship as active agency. The

Towards Gender Equity? 183

language of entitlements exposes the interaction of legal, civil and political rights with property rights, economic rights and social rights (Einhorn, 2000a: 114). It thus renders transparent the links between states, markets and households, and between individual and social rights and responsibilities. In these ways, it acknowledges the dialectical interaction between individual agency and structural constraints. It opposes the de-linking of states and markets implied by neo-liberalism's focus on the market as sole regulator of society. Rather, it enables us to map the aggregate effect of both market forces and state interventions on social rights and individual (or group) capabilities.

Basing citizenship on entitlements reveals that social and economic rights can be successfully exercised in conjunction with civil and political rights only if underpinned by the relevant state legislation and public as well as private social/welfare provision. The state provides a focus for addressing claims whose fulfilment enhances active agency by facilitating the capability to exercise it. The language of entitlements construes the individual as belonging both to a wider society that acknowledges collective responsibility for its members, and to a polity that accepts a certain level of rights as being conducive to active citizenship. The language of entitlements thus conveys, in a way that neither the language of rights nor the language of capabilities necessitate, both the right to make claims, and state responsibility for facilitating their realization. In other words it implies the necessary interaction of individuals and civil society groups with the state as well as with the market in order to achieve full functioning as active citizens. It allocates both rights and duties equally to the state and individual citizens, in contradistinction to the neo-liberal agenda that devolves responsibility for well-being and quality of life to the individual.

This conceptualization of 'entitlements' has affinity with the entitlement-based 'capabilities' theory pioneered by Amartya Sen (Einhorn, 2000a: 113–14). Sen defines entitlements in a 'private ownership economy' as resting on two basic parameters: 'endowment' and 'exchange entitlement mapping'. The latter rests on 'the conditions governing the exchange of labour power (e.g. employment, wages and prices, and social security, if any)', since 'for most of humanity, virtually the only significant endowment is labour power' (Sen, 1990: 140–1, 1995: 267, 1999). Individuals thus possess certain levels of endowments and are involved in exchange through a 'network of entitlement relations' (Sen, 1981: 159). What Sen calls 'entitlement failure' occurs when an individual is unable to acquire the goods and services that would ensure their functioning at a basic human level. He characterizes poverty as 'a deprivation of basic capabilities' (Sen, 1999: 20).

Diane Elson points out how entitlements are also gendered. She gives the example of entitlement failure occurring because of 'male breadwinner bias', which means 'women are not entitled to resources in their own right, but only by virtue of their relationship to an adult male' (Elson, 2002: 103). This is related to Hana Papanek's work on entitlements, on which Sen built. Papanek emphasized the ways in which internalized perceptions of lesser entitlements within the family and society lead women themselves to perpetuate systems based on gender discrimination (Papanek, 1990: 173). Sen has argued that women's gainful employment increases the family's social entitlement in an absolute sense. This in turn results in an increase in women's status, and hence their relative entitlement share within the family (Sen, 1990: 144). Obviously Sen's theory derives from the Indian, and not the Central and East European experience. Nevertheless, it may have some relevance here, especially in Papanek's reference to the longevity of a 'culture of female sacrifice' which is mirrored in the cultures of many Central and East European countries (Papanek, 1990: 176).

Martha Nussbaum explicates Sen's theory of human capabilities as not merely encompassing people's satisfactions, nor the level of resources they can command, but rather 'what people are actually able to do and to be – in a way informed by an intuitive idea of a life that is worthy of the dignity of the human being' (Nussbaum, 2000: 5,12; 2002: 49, 1995). In other words, what is necessary here is the ability to exercise rights, founded both on capabilities as the basis for citizenship claims and on Sen's notion of 'well-being' or quality of life. The outcome, according to Nussbaum, should be what she calls 'truly human functioning' (Nussbaum, 2000: 13; 2002: 49).

Nussbaum uses the idea of capabilities (some of which have already been incorporated as United Nations Human Development indicators) to speak of a 'threshold level of capabilities' as a list of demands that citizens have the right to demand of their governments, and below which quality of life or well-being is not guaranteed (Nussbaum, 2002: 49). She concedes the possibility that once what she calls a 'capability threshold' level has been attained, individual preferences might vary the way that different people choose to function. The need to allow for individual choice within a framework of liberal political liberties leads her to assert that 'capability, not functioning, is the appropriate political goal' (Nussbaum, 2000: 87–8; 2002: 64). It may be realistic, pragmatically, to thus scale down expectations from 'truly human functioning' to 'capability'. Yet it reveals a fundamental weakness in the idea of the 'threshold level'. This is the possibility that governments could restrict their efforts to achieving a basic minimum level of capability for their citizens, rather than addressing higher expectations about what constitutes 'well-being' or quality of life.

Nussbaum has recently claimed that her capabilities approach goes beyond Sen's in being grounded in 'the Marxian/Aristotelian idea of truly human functioning' (Nussbaum, 2000: 13). It also in her view better enables a feminist perspective and the incorporation of gender-based claims (Nussbaum, 2002: 48–9). She develops three different levels of capabilities: basic capabilities ('the innate equipment of individuals'); internal capabilities ('states of the person that are, so far as the person herself is concerned, sufficient conditions for the exercise of the requisite functions'); and 'combined capabilities, which may be defined as internal capabilities combined with suitable external conditions for the exercise of the function' (Nussbaum, 2002: 63–4). The notion of basic capabilities as 'innate equipment of individuals' has a distressingly essentialist ring to it. Moreover, Nussbaum's concept of 'combined capabilities' appears almost indistinguishable from the notion of entitlements. This elision of the two concepts is even more apparent when Nussbaum asserts that 'these necessary elements of truly human functioning ... can be regarded as the basis for a set of fundamental constitutional entitlements'. Further, in stressing the interdependence of the ten capabilities on her list, she argues 'that the goal of creating a minimally just society is not achieved when entitlements in any of these areas are not secured to citizens' (Nussbaum, 2002: 59–60, 62).

In distancing herself from Sen's distinction between mere well-being and agency, Nussbaum appears to be giving up on the notion of social equity in the name of an approach centred on the individual's capacity to make claims (Nussbaum, 2000: 12–14). The individualization of claims-making on the basis of a 'threshold level' of capabilities could appear to renounce the goal of active citizenship within a society committed to the goal of social justice. In fact, the central problem of Nussbaum's theory lies in the area of implementation, in other words in the realm of the political. Nussbaum's approach is useful as a gender-sensitive tool in its insistence on disaggregating the family, in so many societies the source of gender-based discrimination against women. 'What this approach is after is a society in which individuals are treated as each worthy of regard, and in which each has been put in a position to live really humanly' (Nussbaum, 2002: 59). The weakness lies in the opposite direction: not in instituting a set of constitutional principles based on the individual, which is how Nussbaum envisages her list of capabilities being implemented, but in the lack of a specified strategy to move from the individual back to the social, and from the elaboration of principle to adoption and implementation of a capabilities approach by nation states.

Despite an entire section dealing with it, Nussbaum is vague on the issue of implementation, both in getting the list of capabilities enshrined as constitutional principles (her stated aim), and – even if this were successful – in ensuring that such principles are actually realized in individuals' lives and capacities. She states that 'in order to be doing what they should for their citizens, states must first be concerned with all the capabilities, even when these seem not so useful for economic growth, or even for political functioning' (Nussbaum, 2000: 90). There is, however, no indication beyond vague exhortation as to how states are to be held to account to deliver on this, and by whom (other than the said citizens). 'Practical implementation must remain to a large extent the job of citizens in each nation' (Nussbaum, 2000: 105).

Given that women do not have equal citizenship status in most countries of the globe, a fact which itself constitutes a fundamental premise of Nussbaum's work, their potential to ensure implementation of the capabilities agenda must be viewed as severely limited. This is precisely where the language of entitlements has the edge, since it implies not just the need for pressure from citizens to ensure state acceptance of the principle of a capability threshold, but a level of obligation on the part of the state to deliver on its citizens' needs. The language of entitlements recognizes that the market can not deliver social and political, nor even fully equitable economic rights, but that what is needed is 'an enabling system of well-regulated and socially responsive markets *and* universal entitlements for all members of society, designed to avoid male breadwinner bias and commodification bias' (Elson, 2002: 105–7; emphasis added). In other words, unlike the individualized accounts of the rights or capabilities discourses, the language of entitlements encompasses both an acknowledgement of systemic inequalities and a recognition of the two-way and complex process of negotiation of power between states, markets and citizens. This makes it a powerful tool. The concept of 'entitlements' offers a means to address the need to provide all citizens within the gendered processes of transformation in Central and Eastern Europe with the resources *and* the capacity to exercise the political, social and economic rights of citizenship, exercising 'human agency' within participatory democratic political processes.

Identity, differences, and the capacity for joint political strategies

Chapters 5 and 6 described the ways in which nationalist discourses play on ideas of cultural, ethnic and especially gender differences to produce exclusionary narratives. These discourses have ultimately resulted in ethno-nationalist conflict in the name of a-historical and indefensible notions of ethnically homogeneous states. The fundamentally gendered symbolism of these discourses have very real material consequences for the gender identities people within ethnically defined national communities are able to assume.

This chapter sets out to elaborate possible ways to conceptualize a form of political strategy that encompasses gender justice, and social justice more generally. Such a strategy would need to transcend the politics of identity based on cultural differences in order to enable people to reach out and make politically strategic links across gender, ethnic, national and regional differences. It is first necessary to analyse the completely understandable, but potentially fatal attraction of the concept of difference after over forty years of experiencing the distorted applications of egalitarian principles. The 'socialist citizen' was conceptualized in gender-neutral, universal terms, but revealed itself as no less gendered in practice than his (sic) liberal democratic 'brother'. Socialist citizenship was universal only in the sense that apart from a tiny elite, neither men nor women could actually access, let alone exercise, much political power. Politics aside, both the public sphere of employment and the private sphere of the family were characterized by unequal relations of power along gendered demarcation lines. Within both the public and private realms, all citizens were disempowered, particularly in terms of civil and political rights. Gender inequalities tended to disappear within a notion of the personal 'us' versus the faceless 'them' of the state. The egalitarianism promulgated in official rhetoric was interpreted as colourless sameness involving the loss of individuality and sexuality. This history inevitably rendered palatable the reinvented categories of masculinity and femininity which script Western-style consumerism and assign men and women to gender-divided 'natural' spheres of influence that re-inscribe the public–private divide. This explains why the first outcome of the cultural and discursive shifts inherent in the transformation process was a celebration of (gender) difference.

Analysts within the region have also stressed the differences between and within individual countries, on the basis of their diverse history, culture and level of economic development. In other words, in addition to the 'rediscovery' of masculinity and femininity as inherent, essentialist traits, there has been an over-emphasis on cultural distinctiveness between countries and sub-regions in Central and Eastern Europe. Inevitably, the stress on cultural difference has also impeded East–West understanding. While it is necessary, and fruitful, to acknowledge and respect cultural differences, it can be politically self-defeating to elide commonalities in the process. Difference-based politics have the potential ultimately to render impossible political mobilization on grounds of gender, as many theorists have recognized (Lister, 1997; Phillips, 1993; Randall, 1998).

In practice, the gendered inequalities produced by ostensibly egalitarian state socialist ideology are matched by those induced by the individualist neo-liberal meta-narrative. No amount of discursive deconstruction can alter the fact that the neo-liberal agenda of democratization within market-driven policies of economic restructuring has a major impact on the potential for gender justice, in East and West, North and South. Inevitably, many aspects of the gendered transformation processes in Central and Eastern Europe are regionally specific, reflecting both the state socialist legacy, and the nature and pace of democratization and marketization in each country (Dawisha and Parrott, 1997, cited in Outhwaite and Ray, 2005: 115). Nevertheless, it is important to recognize that neo-liberalism as the over-arching discursive and policy context, is currently shared globally. Assertions that neo-liberalism has had its day, as argued in chapter 1, are still premature.

In this context, the utility of the concept of citizenship follows from its ability to transcend the binaries of equality versus difference, universalist principles versus the politics of identity. A number of feminist theorists have argued against abandoning universalism altogether, despite the fact that the disembodied, abstract individual citizen in classical political theory has been revealed in practice to be male (as well as white, heterosexual and able-bodied, as Ruth Lister points out). Lister makes a plea for rescuing what she calls 'a differentiated universalism' in order to construct a 'politics of solidarity in difference' (Lister, 1997: 66). Anne Phillips argues cogently that 'feminism cannot afford to situate itself *for* difference and *against* universality, for the impulse that takes us beyond our immediate and specific difference is a vital necessity in any radical transformation' (Phillips, 1993: 71; emphasis in original). The concept of citizenship allows for integration of the cultural politics of difference with the social politics of equality. Nancy Fraser argues for the necessity of such a synthesis on the grounds that 'justice today requires *both* redistribution and recognition' (Fraser, 1995: 69, 1997: 12, 1998: 431).

Western feminists need to acknowledge the cultural and historical contingency of their theories, which makes them potentially neither directly relevant nor applicable to the transformation process in Central and Eastern Europe, nor regarded as useful by feminists in the region. This acknowledgement is an important first step in the process of mutual understanding. Anne Phillips points out that 'equality may depend on greater respect for/recognition of difference'. Nevertheless, she argues that 'it has to be possible to be both different and equal' (Phillips, 2002: 119–20). Phillips makes this argument in a discussion of the relationship of multiculturalism to universalism and democracy. To me, it seems possible to apply the principle to the context of East–West feminist dialogue. Thus, pursuit of the means to achieve gender justice within specific societies can become a shared process Europe-wide, in a context where the cultural contingencies and specificities of the participants are recognized in a dialogue between equals.

The vibrant culture of women's NGOs in Central and Eastern Europe, the thriving Women's and Gender Studies programmes, and the regional networks such as the Karat Coalition or the electronic Women's Studies network all testify eloquently to the success of region-specific theorizing and activism. Given the powerful discursive hegemony of neo-liberalism and the influence of economic globalization, as well as the impact of European Union enlargement, the next step towards a coalition politics will be to expand on East–West networking, research and joint political campaigns. These extended initiatives could establish debating and campaigning fora on the basis of joint research findings.

Cynthia Cockburn documents moving examples of women working across ethnic, religious and nationalist divides, especially in conflict or post-conflict situations. She shows how women involved in projects in Bosnia, Israel, Northern Ireland and Cyprus acknowledge and respect their differences while maintaining a willingness to work through the pain suffered as a result of their respective positionings within nationalist conflicts. Without attempting to subsume, eliminate or resolve those differences, women in these projects have engaged in difficult dialogue to create strategic political alliances (Cockburn, 1998, 2000, 2004; Cockburn et al., 2001; Cockburn and Žarkov, 2002; see also Borić, 1997, Jacoby, 1999; Lukić, 2000 and Žarkov, 1995). Overcoming the potential political paralysis of an unproductive insistence on differences means, Nira Yuval-Davis asserts, that 'all forms of feminist (and other forms of democratic) politics should be viewed as a form of coalition politics in which the differences among women are recognized and given a voice, ... and [that] the boundaries of this coalition should be set not in terms of "who" we are but in terms of what we want to achieve' (Yuval-Davis, 1997a: 126).

Creating alliances across difference through dialogue enacts what Yuval-Davis has called 'transversal politics',[4] aiming *not* for homogeneity, but for an inclusive approach to the common problems inherent in gendered nationalisms (Yuval-Davis, 1997a: 125–32; see also Cockburn, 1998). She develops this idea further, seeing 'multi-layered' citizens acting together in an age of 'glocalization' that brings together the global and the local (Yuval-Davis, 1999). Careful listening and preparedness to learn from each others' disparate experiences in Central, Eastern and Western Europe is key. What is needed is 'to regard democratic polities as facilitating the negotiation of difference *in a common space* as opposed to being the site of *competition over space*' (Bhambra, 2005: 5; emphasis in original). Acknowledging and respecting diversity could become the creative ferment in creating new conceptualizations of citizenship and formulating new strategies for transforming each of our societies towards the shared goals of gender equity and social justice.

Notes

1 Democratization and Reinvented National Identity: Contradictory Trends?

1. For a study that integrates issues of trafficking and prostitution within the broader context of gender and migration, see Kofman, Phizacklea, Raghuram and Sales (2000), especially pp. 63–4, 94–5.
2. Interestingly, Tanya Renne wrote in 1997 that 'although the charge that some Western feminists try to colonize their Eastern sisters may be partially accurate, it is my experience that such an act is impossible' (Renne 1997: 9; see also Havelková, 1997).
3. Indeed the most gratifying feedback on *Cinderella Goes to Market: Citizenship, Gender and Women's Movements in East Central Europe* (1993) was the warm reception it received from women activists and scholars in Central and Eastern Europe.
4. Post-colonial writings, and work by women scholars of colour, and those from the South, have also sometimes regarded 'Western' feminism as an alien import redolent of American imperialism. For these kinds of critiques of Western feminism's perceived imperviousness to the contingent specificities of (post-) colonial, ethnic or racial discrimination, see Bhavnani, 1994/1997; Childers and hooks 1990, Collins 1990, Mohanty, 1984 and various reprints, and Mohanty 1998). Indeed it is striking that Eastern European feminists have often chosen to use the language of post-colonialism as the frame in which to couch their critiques of the 'colonialist gaze' (Bassnett, 1992) of Western and especially US feminists (Busheikin 1997; Havelková 1997; Kašić, 2004; Renne, 1997; Šiklová, 1993; Šmejkalová, 2001; Zherebkina, 2001).
5. There has been a wealth of publications on the intimate relationship of gender with the transformation process in Central and Eastern Europe since my seminal *Cinderella Goes to Market: Citizenship, Gender and Women's Movements in East Central Europe* (Einhorn, 1993). Many of them include work by – or indeed emanate from – scholars within the region. The first studies to appear were single-country studies that appeared either in edited volumes (Buckley, 1997; Corrin, 1992; Funk and Mueller, 1993; Gal and Kligman, 2000b; Jähnert *et al.*, 2001; Marsh, 1996; Rai *et al.*, 1992; Renne, 1997; Rueschemeyer, 1994/1998; Scott *et al.*, 1997; Women in Black, various years), or in special journal editions (*Feminist Review* 39, 1991; *Signs* 17(1) 1991; *Social Politics* 2(1) 1995; *Women's Studies International Forum* 19(1–2) 1996; *European Journal of Women's Studies* 5(3–4) 1998). Most single-authored monographs are more recent and constitute single country case studies (Alsop, 2000; Fodor, 2003; Haney, 2002; Reading, 1992; Sperling, 1999; True, 2003a; Young, 1999). Thus there is a lack of cross-cultural and comparative studies such as that offered in this monograph.

6. For an analysis of the wrecking impact on the economy of the IMF model in Hungary in the first half of the 1990s, see Nagy (2003). IMF policies *required* the cutting of public services. As Einhorn (1993) has argued, and Chapter 7 below emphasizes, this has a direct effect on women's ability to access the labour market on an equal basis with men. Nagy's study is referred to by Monbiot (2003). See also Chang (2002) for a powerful critique of the so-called Washington Consensus 'free-trade' model and its misguided minimization of the role of the state. See also Wade (1990) on this point.
7. It remains true that most mainstream studies of 'transition' are fundamentally flawed in their failure to address the gendered nature of the social, economic, and political transformations in Central and Eastern Europe. For examples of such titles, see Bönker, Müller and Pickel 2002; Bryant and Mokrzycki 1994; Burawoy and Verdery 1998; Gill 2003; Kaldor and Vejvoda 1999/2002; Offe and Bönker 1996; Schöpflin 2000 and White, Batt and Lewis 1993. This failure has to some extent been remedied by the publication of several edited volumes and journal special issues which have used gender as the perspective through which the processes of transformation are analysed. See Božinović *et al.*, 1998; Bridger and Pine, 1998; Buckley, 1997; Corrin, 1992, 1996; Funk and Mueller, 1993; Gal and Kligman, 2000a and 2000b; Jähnert *et al.*, 2001; Jaquette and Wolchik, 1998; Lazreg, 2000; Marsh, 1996; Moghadam, 1993; Posadskaya, 1994; Rai, Pilkington and Phizacklea, 1992; Renne, 1997; Rueschemeyer, 1994; Scott, Kaplan, and Keates, 1997. For journal special issues: cf. *Feminist Review* no. 39, 1991; *Signs* 17(1) 1991; *Women's Studies International Forum* 15(1) 1992, and 19(1–2) 1996; *Social Politics* 2(1) 1995; *European Journal of Women's Studies* 5(3–4) 1998. This list can not hope to be exhaustive, since there are several individual chapters or clusters of chapters dealing with the region in other edited volumes. For examples of single country-based monographs, see Alsop, 2000; Fodor, 2003; Haney, 2002; Harris, 2003; Reading, 1992; True, 2003a; Young, 1999.
8. The countries that became members in March 2004 as part of the first round of enlargement were: Czech Republic, Estonia, Hungary, Latvia, Lithuania, Poland, Slovakia and Slovenia.
9. Given that such non-compliance in no way delayed Poland's membership, there is a question mark over EU commitment to gender equality norms. On this, see Regulska, 2001 and Steinhilber, 2002a.

2 Issues of Governance: Contested Strategies for Gender Equity

1. It goes without saying that the transformation process has differed in pace, scope and nature within individual countries in the regions. Beyond individual country differences, the trends evident over the past 15 years vary within the region. Thus there are both notable inter-country differences and contrasting directions of development between the sub-regions of East Central Europe, Eastern and South-Eastern Europe and Central Asia. The process of European Union enlargement is contributing to widening the gaps between these regions in terms of political representation, as this chapter illustrates.

2. Some might argue that both of these strategies are top-down mechanisms; however, it could be argued that quotas are a mechanism women's movements in many countries have fought to have introduced. The argument in favour of the use of quotas is that whilst having more women politicians does not guarantee the introduction of gender-sensitive legislation or the implementation of gender equitable policies, nevertheless, achieving a 'critical mass' of women is a precondition for this to occur, since marginalized 'token' women have no possibility of altering the prevailing gendered hierarchies of power.
3. See Lovenduski, 2001: 743, 745, 752 on this in relation to the UK elections of 2001.
4. Women's political representation fell drastically in the first democratic elections from an average 30% to levels of 10% and below. Even more alarmingly (given the token nature of representation during the state socialist period), the level fell further in several countries in subsequent democratic elections. Thus in Albania, for example, women held 36% of parliamentary seats prior to 1989. Their share fell to 20% in 1991, but much more drastically, to 7% in the 1997 elections. There appears to be an East–East divide opening up, with Central European countries showing improvements in levels of female political participation in subsequent elections, while in Eastern and South-Eastern Europe and the Central Asian republics levels continue to fall. Moreover, in several countries where there has been improvement, it is only slight. In Ukraine, women held 4.2% of parliamentary seats in 1994, and 5.6% in 1998. In Hungary, the level rose from 7% in 1990 to 8.5% in 1998 (NWP/OSI, 2002: 11; UNICEF, 1999; in several cases, what has happened is that the East European level has fallen to one comparable with Western European countries).
5. For further work on the gender impact of EU enlargement, see Bretherton, 2001; Mazey, 2000; Regulska, 2001; Roth, 2002; Steinhilber, 2002a; Watson, 2000b.
6. Maria Stratigaki (2005: 167) notes that 'both "gender" and "mainstreaming" are conceptual terms that have evoked more confusion, misunderstanding and questions than any other terms used in EU equality policies. Until 1996, there was no clear definition in Community documents for the term "gender mainstreaming" '. On the lack of definitional clarity, see also Rees, 1998: 191–4, 2002: 65.
7. While positive discrimination permits enhancing the number of women candidates for political office through women-only short lists, quotas, or placing women top on party lists, positive action allows only the encouragement of women to put themselves forward for office, but no measures which could be seen as going against gender-neutral equal opportunity legislation. An example was the introduction in 1996 of women-only short lists for political candidacy in the UK, only to be overturned by an industrial tribunal on the grounds that it contravened the UK's Sex Discrimination legislation. Interestingly, Maria Stratigaki (2005) uses the term 'positive action' in contrast to equality-based gender mainstreaming approaches. Joni Lovenduski (2001: 751) describes how the equal opportunities approach in the Westminster electoral system – 'the change from positive discrimination (mandatory quotas of women) to positive action (voluntary quotas for women candidates' – led

to a fall in the number of female MPs between the 1997 and 2001 elections. In terms of difference-based, gender-specific policies, I would therefore argue that 'positive action' constitutes a diluted and much weaker form of action than 'positive discrimination'.
8. As of 2005, Magdalena Środa is the Plenipotentiary for the Equal Status of Women and Men in Poland.
9. See Chapter 3 for discussion of the substantial increase in the level of female parliamentarians following this election.

3 Gender in Mainstream Politics: Scaling the Structures

1. In the course of research for this chapter, I was struck by the relative paucity of studies analysing the realms of mainstream party politics and state-level governance, and in particular their gendered institutional structures. This area of investigation is conspicuous by its relative or absolute absence in several edited volumes dealing with transformation in the region (see for example Gal and Kligman, 2000a and 2000b; Jähnert et al., 2001; Lazreg, 2000; Scott et al., 1997). Typically, sections devoted, for example, to the analysis of 'women and the state', or 'arenas of political action' concentrate mainly on issues of civil society, feminism, nationalist discourses, and women's movements. Two recent research projects, both funded by the European Commission's Fifth Framework Programme, have begun the process of addressing this omission. The Birmingham University-based Network of European Women's Rights (2003–05) divided its work into four areas of study, one of these being political participation. The Queen's University Belfast-based project entitled 'Enlargement, Gender and Governance' (2002–05) focused more centrally on 'The Civic and Political Participation and Representation of Women in EU Candidate Countries', commissioning country reports from ten countries in the region. A further study funded by the US National Science Foundation considers the question of 'Constructing Supranational Political Spaces: The European Union, Eastern Enlargement and Women's Agency'.
2. Joni Lovenduski states that 'the figure set for critical mass of women is about 30% of the legislature' (2001: 744).
3. In the 1990 local elections, women gained 17% of seats in Hungary, 16.7% in the Czech Republic, and 10.4% in Poland. In the Polish and Czech cases, the levels of female political representation were higher at local than at national level. In addition, the levels increased between 1990 and 1994: in the Polish case, to 13%, in the Czech case to 17.9%, (Fuszara, 2000: 281; Graham and Regulska, 1997: 73; Kligman, 1996: 71, notes 12, 13; Wolchik, 1998: 168). In a continuing rise, 23% of municipal councillors (but only 5% of mayors) in Poland were women in 2001 (Chimiak, 2003: 17). The authors of a 2003 Czech study claim that on average women constitute 14% of members of district assemblies, and 16% of local municipal assembles, but that there were only 8% of mayors in the Czech Republic in 1997 (Křížková and Václavíková-Helšusová, 2003: 27–8). In the town of Karikás in Hungary, the level of female representation dropped from 22% of council seats prior to 1989 (13 out of a total 58), to only 3 women councillors elected of a total 23 in 1994 (approximately 11%) (Kovács and Váradi, 2000: 181).

4. See for example Bönker, Müller and Pickel, 2002; Bryant and Mokryzycki, 1994; Kaldor and Vejvoda, 1999/ 2002; Offe and Bönker, 1996 and White, Batt and Lewis, 1993.
5. Yet the high Inter-Parliamentary Union figures for 1995 cited by Fuszara (2000: 272, note 15) for the Netherlands (31.3%), Denmark (33%), Norway (39.4%), Sweden (40.4%), or by Rueschemeyer (2001), for Germany in 1998 (*c.* 33% women MPs) represent exceptions that highlight the rule.
6. In Hungary, the level of female political representation fell from 10% to 7% in the second democratic election of 1990; and in Lithuania, from 10% in 1990 to 7% in 1992. Yet these low figures still bettered the level at that time of 6.3% in Britain, the much vaunted 'mother of democracies', and 5.7% in France (Janova and Sineau, 1992: 117, table 1; Purvaneckiene, 2003. See also Gaber, 1997; Einhorn, 1993, 2000a; Fuszara, 1997; Mertus, 1998 and Petö, 1997).
7. Hanna Beate Schoepp-Schilling sounds a salutary note of warning here against the tendency to indulge in easy retrospective judgements about the 'false rhetoric' of state socialist commitment to women's 'emancipation'. In fact, as she points out, it was their genuine belief in formal legal equality that led these regimes to be among the first in the early 1980s to ratify the UN CEDAW Convention. She reminds us that it is only from today's vantage point that we can recognize the persistence of patriarchal gender regimes within state socialist social arrangements, particularly their failure to question gender-divided arrangements within the private sphere, and the persistence of gender stereotyping that inhibited women's political influence (Schoepp-Schilling, 2005).
8. Women in the Czech Republic held only 11% of seats in the Czech National Council in 1990, falling to 9.5% in 1992 and 1994. However, the level rose to 13.5% of seats in the Chamber of Deputies, and 11% of those elected to the Senate in June 1996. The figure for parliamentary representation rose again in 1998, to 15%, and reached 17% in 2002 (Rakušanová, 2003: 20, table 1). Yet these reasonably positive figures were somewhat counteracted by the fact that there has been a total of only five women Cabinet ministers in the Czech Republic between 1990 and 2002 (Rakušanová, 2003: 23–4). The percentage of women MPs in the Slovak National Council rose from 12% in 1990 to 15% in 1994, fell to 14% in 1998, and again reached 15% in 2002. The 2002 level improved further to 19% after several male MPs became Cabinet Ministers, ceding their parliamentary seats to the next candidate on the party list (Bitušiková, 2005b, table 2.1).

The first multi-party elections in Croatia in 1990 returned a miserable 4.5% women to the House of Representatives. This rose to 8.7% in 1995, and jumped to 22.5% in 2000 (the same level as the last state socialist assembly) (Borić and Jelavić, 2003). In Bulgaria, the percentage of women in Parliament fell from 21% in 1989 to 8.5% in 1990, rising to 14% in 1991, but falling to 11.2% by 1997. In 2001, it rose dramatically to 26%, less as the result of gender training for women politicians in the project 'Women Can Do It' run by Bulgarian women's NGOs, than as the result of the new political party entitled National Movement Simeon the Second, which elected 48 women MPs, 40% of whom represented this particular Parliamentary fraction (Daskalova, 2003: 10–12).

In Hungary, the level of female political representation rose from 7% in 1990 to 11% in 1994, but fell to 8% in 1998, and only climbed back to 9.1% in 2002 (Inter-Parliamentary Union, 2005). In Romania, the share of female deputies rose from 4% in 1992 to 7% in 1996, but the proportion of women in the Senate fell in the same period from 2% to 1%. Similarly, women's share of positions of leadership and senior office in the fields of public administration and the economy fell from 29% in 1996 to 24% in 1998 (Official Romanian statistics, cited in UNDP, 2000: 59, table 7.1, 63, figure 7.4). In Lithuania, 10% of politicians elected in 1990 were women. This percentage fell in the 1992 elections to 7%, but rose dramatically in the 1996 elections to 18%, only to fall back to 10.6% in 2000 (Purvaneckiene, 2003).
9. In the period 1980–89, the level of female political representation in Poland fell from 23% to 20%. In 1991, it fell by half, from 20% in 1989 to 10% in 1991, but rose again to 13% after 1993 (*Statistical Yearbook*, 1997, cited in Fuszara, 2000: 271,table 9.7; see also Siemieńska, 1998).
10. The percentage share of women politicians in the Sejm (Parliament) rose from 13% in 1997 to 20% in 2001. In the Senate, the percentage almost doubled, from 12% in 1997 to 23% in 2001. The political parties which introduced 30% quotas for their electoral lists were: Unia Pracy (UP – Labour Union), acting together with Sojusz Lewicy Demokratycznej (SLD – Democratic Left Alliance), and Unia Wolnosci (UW – Freedom Union). In the event, the Freedom Union did not get into parliament, having failed to gain sufficient votes to pass the electoral threshold (Renc-Roe, 2003: 17–18; Spurek, 2002: 11,18–21).
11. For the unique parity debate in France during the 1990s, see Duchen, 2000 and Lépinard, 2005.
12. In 1997 Bosnia-Herzegovina successfully deployed a strategy of combined pressure from a nation-wide network of NGOs, strong female politicians, and the support of international actors to enact the very first strong national-level quota rule in South Eastern Europe. This was replicated in Kosovo in 2001. In Serbia it was only possible to get a quota rule instituted for the 2002 local elections, again due to strong behind-the-scenes lobbying of party leaders by women politicians together with women's NGOs. The enactment of a quota rule for the 2002 elections in Macedonia was the result of a strong coalition between the Macedonian Women's Lobby (itself a group crossing mainstream political, institutional and NGO groups, and the media) and the leaders of the government's national machinery for gender equality. The authors of the project report point out that the quota alone might not have succeeded in raising the number of female politicians. In combination with cross-party lobbying to have women placed high on electoral lists and the respecting of the quota by the largest party in the winning coalition, Macedonia now has 18.33% female MPs (Lokar, 2003: 41,43). Where there was disunity between women politicians and civil society groups, proposals to introduce a quota rule failed in parliament. This was the case in Slovenia in 1996 and Croatia in 1999 (Lokar, 2003: 42). Nevertheless, a Coalition for Parity initiated by social democratic women in Slovenia in 2001 was successful in enacting a 40% quota for the European Parliamentary elections. The comparison with the level of 12.2% women politicians in the Slovenian Parliament in 2004 led the author to the rueful conclusion that quotas

have become acceptable for the European Parliament 'which does not have real political power', but not in the Slovenian Parliament 'where actual decisions are taken' (Lokar, 2005: 26). In Bulgaria in 2001, a second reading of the Electoral Law proposing a 40% quota failed by only 12 votes, despite the weakness of the coalition between women politicians and NGOs (Lokar, 2003: 42).

4 Civil Society or NGOs: Empowerment or Depoliticization?

1. This chapter is indebted to Einhorn and Sever (2003), and the expanded and updated version in Einhorn and Sever (2005).
2. Brigitte Young writes of 'the gendered opportunity structures of the different states in the former Eastern European countries and their impacts on the formation and development of the women's movements', structures which in her view can help us to understand 'the marginalization of women during the transition process' (Young, 1999: 226). In relation to South Africa and Uganda, Anne-Marie Goetz and Shirin Hassim emphasize that 'the nature of a political transition away from authoritarianism determines the way civil society groups can influence the political system that follows' (Goetz and Hassim, 2002: 325).
3. There has been much discussion in the social scientific literature on the relative advantages of the terms 'transition' or 'transformation' to describe the complex processes of democratization, economic restructuring, and profound social change occurring in the Central and Eastern Europe since 1989. In my view, the term 'transition' is fatally flawed, both logically and ideologically. It implies a single, known outcome, and additionally codes this outcome in advance as positive. This is not only premature and presumptions, but based on the ideological assumption that Central and Eastern Europe should become 'like' the West. It thus suggests a common understanding that democracy and capitalism are undisputed 'goods'. Such a 'transition' is not necessarily unproblematic, nor does it automatically signify progress.
    My own preference is for the term 'transformation' as both more open-ended and more ideologically neutral (Einhorn, 2000a). It also takes account of the historical, cultural, political and economic differences between individual countries and sub-regions that speak against the homogeneity of outcome suggested by the term 'transition'. 'Transition' homogenizes not only the state socialist regimes of the past, but also the capitalist regimes of past and present in the West. In its evocation of a shift from one known system to another, totally different one, it fails to acknowledge any element of continuity before and after 1989 in the region, or any commonalities between Western and Eastern Europe before 1989, especially with regard to gender inequalities. Moreover, as already pointed out in chapter 1, most 'transition' studies neglect the impact of gender as a variable in these processes of fundamental change.
4. Feminist political theory has deconstructed this vision of civil society space in a variety of ways, pointing out first that it is neither 'empty' space nor free

of gendered relations of power (Einhorn and Sever, 2003, 2005; Watson, 1997, 2001). Further, the private sphere of the family is of course not 'unregulated', but on the contrary directly structured and controlled by the material as well as ideological effects of state policies around marriage and reproduction, as well as social and welfare policies (Cannan, 1995, 1996; Lewis, 1993, 2003).
5. This group included, in the East German case, groups like 'Women for Peace' which were not directly religious, nor sponsored by religious institutions, but used – to an extent successfully – the political shelter, as well as the physical space, offered by the church in order to escape state intervention.
6. It is worth noting here that the homogenization of 'Western feminism' in this dialogue is itself misleading, since there were marked differences both within and between British and US feminisms, not to mention French or Italian feminisms (see for example Bono, 2000; Bono and Kemp, 1993; Bryson, 1999; Duchen, 1986, 1994; Du Plessis and Snitow, 1998; Randall, 2000; Roseneil, 1995, 2000; Rowbotham, 1989, 1997 and Segal, 1987, 1999). And since the 1980s, Western feminisms have themselves been continually modified in response first to critiques from non-white and Southern feminists (Collins, 1990; hooks, 1981; Mohanty, 1984/1991), and to postmodernist deconstructions of the category 'woman' (Butler, 1990; Nicholson, 1990 and Weedon, 1987).
7. Similar objections to 'this form of "feminist" globalizing' were earlier raised by feminists in the South (see for example Grewal and Kaplan, 1994: 17).
8. Edmondson, 1984 is an exceptionally early source on early Russian feminism. On Russia, see also Edmondson, 1996; Sperling, 1999; on Bulgaria: Daskalova, 1997; on the Czech Republic: Hašková, 2005; Havelková, 2000; Věšinová-Kalivodová and Šiklová, 2001: 341; on Poland: Chołuj, 2003; Fuszara, 1997; on Hungary: Acsády, 1997; Petö, 1997, 2002, 2003.
9. On the Belgrade Women's Studies Centre: Duhaček, 1998b; Litričin and Mlađenovic, 1997; on the Zagreb Women's Studies Centre: Kasić, 2001; on Poland: Bystydzienski, 2001: 507; Fuszara, 2001; on the Humboldt University in Berlin: Dölling, 2001; Nickel, 2001; Schäfgen, 2001; on the Czech Republic: Grünell, 1995; Věšinová-Kalivodová and Šiklová, 2001; on Romania: Roman, 2001: 59; on Lithuania and Latvia, Novikova, 2001. See also Einhorn and Sever, 2003, 2005.
10. Laura Grunberg says that her research shows 60 rather than 50 organizations actively involved in women's issues in Romania. However, she resists over-optimism in the face of this number (Grunberg, 2000: 311–12).
11. In her discussion of the links between local women's movements and global emancipatory objectives, Amrita Basu notes that 'the vitality of the women's movement does not lie primarily in the activities of large national organizations', but that 'small, local-level activist groups often provide the dynamism behind women's movements (Basu, 1995: 14).

5 Family, Nation and Reproductive Politics: Between the Private and the Public

1. The gendered impact of economic restructuring is discussed in Chapter 7.
2. On differing social policy models and their gender-specific impact on women's citizenship status, see Cannan, 1995, 1996; Esping-Andersen,

1990 and Lewis, 1992, 1993,1997; on the impact of a starkly different social policy model on East German women, see Chamberlayne, 1995: 32; van Hoven-Iganski, 2000: 146–7; Nickel, 2000: 120 and Rosenberg, 1991, 1993.
3. There has been no national compulsory sex education teaching in Polish schools since 1999 (Rothschild, 2005: 160).
4. A 1997 shadow report by Croatian women's organizations to CEDAW on the Status of Women in Croatia alleged that the same doctors were ready to perform abortions illegally outside working hours for a high fee (B.a.B.e., 1997).
5. Whilst 72% of first year students in the 2005 study saw abortion as the taking of life, 60% of second years, 54% of third years, and only 24% of fourth year students shared this position (Rittossa, 2005).
6. Amongst the 277 university students in the 2005 study conducted in the Faculty of Law at Rijeka University by Dalida Rittossa, support for a woman's right to decide was uniformly strong, varying from 73% among second year students, to 80% among third years and a striking 100% among fourth year students (Rittossa, 2005).
7. The newspapers were *Trybuna* (*Tribune*) closely linked with the post-communist ruling party alliance (SLD), the other *Gość Niedzielny (Sunday Visitor)* is a Catholic weekly.
8. On telephone hotlines in Romania, see Gheaus, 2001: 187; on Croatia, see Borić and Desnica, 1996; on Belgrade's SOS hotline, see Mlađenovic and Matijašević, 1996 and Mršević, 2000; on Hungary, see Szalay, 1996; for Poland, see Nowakowska and Jablonska, 2000; on Russia, see Khodyreva, 1996; on Ukraine, see Kobelyanska, 2000; for confirmation that violence against women is not confined to this region, but is a global problem, see Corrin, 1996.
9. While such a reaction is understandable, it has the unfortunate connotation that the expectation of certain inviolable human rights guaranteed in CEDAW might be jettisoned out of cultural relativist respect for the specificity of a particular historical conjuncture.
10. Cynthia Enloe has cautioned against simplistic assumptions that 'all the men are in the militias, all the women are victims' in nationalist conflicts. She rightly observes that some women in former Yugoslavia actively supported the ethno-nationalist wars, while some men fled conscription in Serbia (Enloe, 1998: 52–5, 2004).
11. See Guichon and Hellsten (2005) for a critique of human rights discourse. See Schoepp-Schilling (2005) for a counter-argument in relation to UN CEDAW as a more powerful instrument than originally envisaged in going beyond merely formal and legalistic conceptions of gender equality.
12. While the Optional Protocol to CEDAW enables ordinary individual women to claim their rights, this Protocol has been ratified by very few countries.

6 Femininities and Masculinities: Gender Re-presented

1. It is worth noting that Mills & Boon romances in the UK also involve the heroine in some form of career, which does not, however, prevent her experiencing both insecurity and nameless guilt, and longing for fulfilment in

marriage. Thus 'most Mills & Boon romances accept the subordination of women and support the status quo'. 'Fantasy, which might be thought to liberate ... is in the Mills & Boon romance usually only an imaginative projection of confining forms of reality' (Margolies, 1982–83: 11–13; see also Dixon, 1999).
2. This article's reference to the lure of fashion and modelling for the 'New Cinderellas' of Central and Eastern Europe echoes the title of my earlier book (Einhorn, 1993).

7 Labour Market Access: Persistent Patterns of Inequality

1. The first round of enlargement, implemented in 2004, integrated the Czech Republic, Estonia, Hungary, Latvia, Lithuania, Poland, Slovakia, and Slovenia. However, as a result of a European Commission decision in October 2002, it did not include – as originally envisaged – Bulgaria and Romania, both of whom will join in 2007 (Kulke, 2001; Regulska, 2001; Roth, 2002; Steinhilber, 2002b; UN, 1995).
2. For examples of such studies, see on East Germany: Alsop (2000: 164) on the textile and garment industry in the state of Brandenburg, with a case study of the city of Cottbus in which 9 out of every 10 textile workers lost their jobs following the transformation; Bast-Haider, 1995 on an East German clothing factory; Nickel, 2000, on banking, finance and insurance in East Germany; Nickel, 2000, and Peinl, 2001, on the German Railways; or, for Poland, Heinen, 1995 on women workers in Warsaw and Łódź; on the garment industry, Karat 2005d; for Hungary, Kiss, 2002.
3. 'Twelve months ago, in this column, we concluded that there was no explanation for the lack of senior women other than insitutionalised corporate sexism at the most senior levels. Nothing has changed to suggest we were wrong' (*The Guardian*, 5 August 2005: 21).
4. There are some exceptions: while the total labour force in the Czech Republic has declined, women's share of it has remained constant. Women made up 46 % of the labour force in 1988, and 44.8% in 2000 (True, 2003a: 78).
5. van Hoven-Iganski (2000: 141) points out that 75% of agricultural employees in eastern Germany were made redundant between 1989 and 1995, and that of all jobs lost in eastern Germany after German unification, 75% had been held by women. Romaniuk (1998: 45, table 3) suggests that 67% of those unemployed in Ukraine in 1997 were women (see also ILO, 1999).
6. In Poland, where, as Fuszara points out, women have a high level of education, Labour Force Survey data shows that the female rate of unemployment in 2000 was 18.1% as against the male rate of 14.2%. Expressed in percentage terms, women accounted for 54.8% of the unemployed in June 1995, but their share had risen to 61.2% by 1997. In 1998, the female share lessened somewhat, falling to 58.5% (Labour Force Survey Data from 1997, cited by Fuszara, 2000: 268–9; see also Heinen, 1995: 102; Nowakowska and Swedrowska, 2000: 66; and Pollert, 1999: 79). The Czech Republic had lower unemployment overall for the first decade of transformation, but the level is now rising. There too, the female rate in 2001 was 9.2% compared with the male rate of 8.1% (Ruminska-Zimny, 2002).

Notes   201

7. In Poland in 2001, 52% of unemployed women had been unemployed for more than a year, compared with only 36% of unemployed men. Expressed differently, in 1997, 72% of those who had been without a job for over 12 months were women (Nowakowska and Swedrowska, 2000: 42,66; see also Alsop, 2000: 90; OECD figures for 1993 and 1997, cited in: UNICEF, 1999, 29, fig. 2.9).
8. In a survey conducted by the Bulgarian National Public Opinion Centre in 2000, 74% of those interviewed saw sexual harassment and abuse at the workplace as the most serious problem faced by women (Bulgarian National Public Opinion Centre, 2000). A mini-survey of 30 women conducted in Poland in the 1990s showed that 18 of those interviewed had suffered harassment, with a substantial 7 reporting invitations to sex or attempted rape. Of the 18 who had been harassed, 11 said they had had to leave their jobs as a result. Most of the women felt helpless to combat sexual harassment at work. However, in one Warsaw legal case in the mid-1990s which may have set an important precedent, a victim was awarded substantial compensation (Fuszara, 2000: 270).
9. On manager preferences, see data from the Slovak Confederation of Trade Unions published in 1998. This states that as many as 88% of managers in private firms, and 52% of those in the public sector, openly admitted to preferential treatment of male job applicants. The same study notes that while women hold around 35% of managerial posts in Slovak firms, their share of managerial posts in foreign and international firms is lower (KOZ, 1998, cited in Macková, 2000: 90–92; the figures for the female share of management may be less positive than appears here, as they are not disaggregated into middle and top management). Čermáková *et al.*, document 'discriminatory practices of Czech and foreign companies, which prefer men in managerial and leading positions' (Čermáková *et al.*, 2000: 122; see also True, 2003a: 87). Jacqui True documents the acknowledgement by Czech managers 'that they used gender as a high criterion ... for making employees redundant' (True, 2003a: 81, citing Paukert, 1995). An opinion poll conducted by the Bulgarian National Public Opinion Centre in 2000 saw interviewees accept as 'natural' employer preference for women employees in sectors traditionally dominated by women such as education, culture, healthcare and services, with a corresponding preference for employing men in politics, manufacturing, technology, and finance (Bulgarian National Public Opinion Centre, 2000).
10. Most countries in the region have introduced equal opportunities legislation, as part of the process of alignment with EU legislation in the run-up to accession. In Poland, a draft Equal Status Act was laughed out of the Parliament in 2001 (see Chapter 2). In Bulgaria, a draft Equal Opportunities Act before the Parliament was scrapped at the end of 2001 after a new government came into power in mid-2001. It was replaced (and this is a trend also evident in Poland) by a more general anti-discrimination directive, encompassing all forms of discrimination.
11. According to the German Federal Statistics Office, women's share of jobs in the retail sector fell from 71.9% in 1991 to 64.2% in 1994 (Nickel, 2000: 113, note 24; 122; see also Alsop, 2000: 99–100).
12. In Britain, the gender pay gap is still 17% for full-time workers and 38% for part-timers, one of the biggest pay gaps in Europe. The gap in full-time pay

was 29% in 1976, prompting the Fawcett Society (which campaigns for gender equality in the UK) to predict that at the present rate of progress, pay equity will not be achieved for another 80 years (Curtis and Branigan, 2006; Hinsliff, 2006).
13. In the Czech Republic, women's wages were 66.1% of men's in 1987, but had risen to 81.3% in 1996; however, in 1997, women earned on average 73.4% as much as men, but actual earnings ranged between 65% and 82% of men's, depending on level of education. In Slovakia, women's earnings have risen from 66.1% of men's in 1987 to 78.2% in 1996. In Hungary the percentage of men's wages earned by women rose from 74.3% in 1986 to 78.1% in 1997. In Poland they rose from 73.7% in 1985 to 79% in 1996. Some examples of a widening gender gap are: Bulgaria, where women earned 74% of men's wages in 1990, but only 69.1% in 1997, Romania, where the relevant figures were 78.6% in 1994 and 76.2% in 1997, Estonia 79.8% in 1992, but only 72.6% in 1996, and Russia, where they fell from 70.9% in 1989 to 69.5% in 1996 (Čermáková et al., 2000: 27, table 1.1; ILO, 1999: 33, table 2.2).
14. An ILO study published by *The Economist* on 11 September 1999 claimed that in 1996, more than 80% of Czech women worked more than 40 hours per week, compared with 60% of women in the USA, 20% of women in Germany, and 10% of women in the Netherlands (ILO, 1999, cited by Čermáková et al., 2000: 21, note 12).
15. See Alsop, 2000: 113 on eastern Germany. In Poland in 1990, the number of nurseries for the under-3s decreased by 9%, in 1991 by 27%, and in 1992 by 21%, in relation to 1989. The number of kindergartens declined by 3%, 11% and 8% respectively (Kotowska, 1995: 85). In the Czech Republic, the number of kindergartens decreased by 14% during the 1990s, but this fall has been interpreted as due in part to the dramatic fall in the birthrate. However, by 2000 the number of nursery places on offer could accommodate only 5% of the children who would have attended in 1990 (Čermáková et al., 2000: 13; Marksová-Tominová, 2003: 61).
16. A 1999 UNICEF study shows that fees for private nurseries in Romania represented 65% of the average wage, hence the enrolment rate, not surprisingly, was 2% of children in the relevant age cohort. Fees for public kindergartens amounted to 25% of the average wage, but 79% of the minimum wage, and in private kindergartens to 81% of the average wage. Nevertheless, the enrolment rate was 63% of those children in the relevant age group (UNICEF, 1999: 56, table 3.5).

8 Citizenship in an Enlarging Europe: Towards Gender Equity?

1. In development discourse this idealization is recognizable in phrases stressing the importance of 'participation' and 'action from the grassroots', often eliding issues of power and social differentiation (Howell and Pearce, 2001: 28).
2. I find useful Ruth Lister's definition of civil society, itself taken from W. Adamson, 'Gramsci and the Politics of Civil Society', *Praxis International*, 7(3–4), 1987/1988: 320. Adamson sees civil society as 'the public space

between large-scale bureaucratic structures of state and economy on the one hand, and the private sphere of family, friendships, personality and intimacy on the other'. Lister adds the proviso that the public–private divide upon which this definition rests should be understood as permeable rather than fixed (Lister, 1997: 207, note 24).

3. Ernesto Laclau and Chantal Mouffe (1985) provide an early deconstruction of 'the state' as a non-unified entity. They see it as having many facets, so that political actors can be at the same time on the 'inside' and operating 'outside' of the state. 'The state' may also be operating together with what are officially seen as non-state actors, for example through indirect influence, funding and so on.

4. As Nira Yuval Davis acknowledges, the concept of 'transversal politics' was first developed by Italian feminist anti-war activists. However, she has developed it further in relation to the discourses of both nationalism and citizenship (Yuval-Davis, 1997a: 125–32), while Cynthia Cockburn has illustrated its applicability in projects designed to transcend the boundaries of national, ethnic or religious conflicts (Cockburn, 1998, 2000, 2004).

Bibliography

Acsády, Júdit (1999) 'Urges and Obstacles: Chances for Feminism in Eastern Europe', *Women's Studies International Forum*, 22 (4): 405–09.
Acsády, Júdit (1997) 'The Construction of Women's Case: Turn-of-the-Century Hungarian Feminism', in Tanya Renne (ed.) *Ana's Land: Sisterhood in Eastern Europe* (Boulder, CO: Westview Press), pp. 102–6.
Agustín, Laura (2005) 'Migrants in the Mistress's House: Other Voices in the "Trafficking" Debate', *Social Politics*, 12 (1): 96–117.
Allen, Jim and Sanders, Karin (2002) 'Gender Gap in Earnings at the Industry Level', *European Journal of Women's Studies*, 9 (2): 163–80.
Allen, Judith (1990) 'Does Feminism Need a Theory of "the State"?', in Sophie Watson (ed.) *Playing the State: Australian Feminist Interventions* (London and New York: Verso), pp. 21–38.
Alsop, Rachel (2000) *A Reversal of Fortunes? Women, Work and Change in East Germany* (New York and Oxford: Berghahn Books).
Alsop, Rachel and Hockey, Jenny (2001) 'Women's Reproductive Lives as a Symbolic Resource in Central and Eastern Europe', *European Journal of Women's Studies*, 8 (4): 454–71.
Alvarez, Sonia (1999) 'Advocating Feminism: The Latin American Feminist NGO "Boom" ', *International Feminist Journal of Politics*, 1 (2): 181–209.
Anderson, Benedict (1983; revised ed. 1991) *Imagined Communities: Reflections on the Origin and Spread of Nationalism* (London: Verso).
Anderson, Bridget and Davidson, Julia O'Connell (2004) *Trafficking – A Demand Led Problem?* (Stockholm: Save the Children Sweden).
Ashley, Jackie (2002) 'We Really Can Have It All – With a Little Bit of Help', *The Guardian*, 24 April: 16.
Ashwin, Sarah and Bowers, Elaine (1997) 'Do Russian Women Want to Work?' in Mary Buckley (ed.) *Post-Soviet Women: From the Baltic to Central Asia* (Cambridge: Cambridge University Press), pp. 21–37.
Attwood, Lynne (1999) *Creating the New Soviet Woman: Women's Magazines as Engineers of Female Identity 1922–53* (Basingstoke: Macmillan).
Attwood, Lynne (1997) ' "She Was Asking For It": Rape and Domestic Violence against Women', in Mary Buckley (ed.) *Post-Soviet Women: From the Baltic to Central Asia* (Cambridge: Cambridge University Press), pp. 99–118.
Attwood, Lynne (1996) 'The Post-Soviet Woman in the Move to the Market: A Return to Domesticity and Dependence?' in Rosalind Marsh (ed.) *Women in Russia and Ukraine* (Cambridge: Cambridge University Press), pp. 255–68.
Attwood, Lynne (1993) 'Sex and the Cinema', in Igor Kon and James Riordan (eds) *Sex and Russian Society* (Bloomington, IN and Indianapolis: Indiana University Press), pp. 64–88.
Băban, Adriana (2000) 'Women's Sexuality and Reproductive Behaviour in Post-Ceausescu Romania: A Psychological Approach', in Susan Gal and Gail Kligman

(eds) *Reproducing Gender: Politics, Publics, and Everyday Life after Socialism* (Princeton, NJ: Princeton University Press), pp. 225–56.

B.a.B.e. (Be active. Be emancipated) (1997) Croatian NGO Report to CEDAW on the Status of Women in Croatia, accessed 4 September 2005 from http://www.babe.hr.eng/reports/cedaw-rep.htm

Baden, Sally and Goetz, Anne Marie (1998) 'Who Needs [Sex] When You Can Have [Gender]? Conflicting Discourses on Gender at Beijing', in Cecile Jackson and Ruth Pearson (eds) *Feminist Visions of Development: Gender, Analysis and Policy* (London and New York: Routledge), pp. 19–38.

Ballentine, Karen (2002) 'International Assistance and the Development of Independent Mass Media in the Czech and Slovak Republics', in Sarah E. Mendelson and John K. Glenn (eds) *The Power and Limits of NGOs: A Critical Look at Building Democracy in Eastern Europe and Eurasia* (New York: Columbia University Press), pp. 91–125.

Barendt, Regina (2002) 'Women for Europe and Europe for Women: Karat Coalition Lobby-Building, Network Creation, Building Alliances and Gaining Power', Paper presented to the conference 'Europe's Daughters: Traditions, Expectations and Strategies of European Women's Movements', Berlin, June.

Barry, Jane (2005) *Rising Up in Response: Women's Rights Activism in Conflict* (Canada: Urgent Action Fund for Women's Human Rights).

Baskakova, Marina (2000) 'Gender Aspects of Pension Reform in Russia', in Marnia Lazreg (ed.) *Making the Transition Work for Women in Europe and Central Asia*, World Bank Discussion Paper no. 411 (Washington: The World Bank), pp. 61–8.

Bassnett, Susan (1992) 'Crossing Cultural Boundaries: or How I Became an Expert in East European Women Overnight', *Women's Studies International Forum*, 15 (1): 11–15.

Bast-Haider, Kerstin (1995) 'The Economic Dimension of Social Change: Women in the East German Clothing Industry', *Social Politics*, 2 (1): 51–61.

Basu, Amrita (1995) 'Introduction', in Amrita Basu (ed.) *The Challenge of Local Feminisms: Women's Movements in Global Perspective* (Boulder, CO, San Francisco and Oxford: Westview Press), pp. 1–24.

Bauman, Zygmunt (1995) *Life in Fragments: Essays in Postmodern Morality* (Oxford: Blackwell).

Beck, Julie A. (2000) '(Re)negotiating Selfhood and Citizenship in the Post-Communist Czech Republic: Five Women Activists Speak about Transition and Feminism', in Marianne H. Marchand and Anne Sisson Runyan (eds) *Gender and Global Governance: Sightings, Sites and Resistances* (London and New York: Routledge), pp. 176–93.

Becker, Bettina (1998) 'Warum ostdeutsche Frauen auf dem Wunsch nach Erwerbsarbeit beharren – eine Betrachtung von Biographien', in Hans Bertram, Wolfgang Kreher and Irene Müller-Hartmann (eds) *Systemwechsel zwischen Projekt und Prozess: Analysen zu den Umbrüchen in Ostdeutschland* (Opladen: Leske + Budrich), pp. 319–52.

Beckwith, Karen (2000) 'Beyond Compare? Women's Movements in Comparative Perspective', *European Journal of Political Research*, 37(4): 431–68.

Begenau, Jutta and Helfferich, Cornelia (1997) 'Kinder oder keine? Zu Kontrazeption, Schwangerschaftsabbrüchen und Familienplanung in Ost- und Westdeutschland' ('To Have or Not to Have Children? On Contraception, Abortion and Family Planning in East and West Germany'), in Cornelia

Helfferich and Jutta Begenau (eds) *Frauen in Ost und West: Zwei Kulturen, zwei Gesellschaften, zwei Gesundheiten? (Women in East and West: Two Cultures, Two Societies, Two Levels of Health?)* (Freiburg: jos fritz), pp. 32–59.

Behrend, Hanna (1995) 'East German Women and the *Wende*', *European Journal of Women's Studies*, 2 (2): 237–56.

Benn, Melissa (1993) 'Women and Democracy: Thoughts on the Last Ten Years' *Women: A Cultural Review*, 4 (3): 233–9.

Benton, Sarah (1998) 'Founding Fathers and Earth Mothers: Women's Place at the "Birth" of Nations', in Nickie Charles and Helen Hintjens (eds) *Gender, Ethnicity and Political Ideologies* (London: Routledge), pp. 27–45.

Berghahn, Sabine (1995) 'Gender in the Legal Discourse in Post-Unification Germany: Old and New Lines of Conflict', *Social Politics*, 2 (1): 37–50.

Bhambra, Gurminder K. (2005) 'De-Territorialising Human Rights and the Politics of Identity: From Origins to Beginnings', Paper presented to the conference on 'Pathways to Reconciliation and Global Human Rights', Sarajevo, Bosnia-Herzegovina, 16–19 August.

Bhavnani, Kum-Kum (1993/97) 'Women's Studies and its Interaction with "Race", Ethnicity and Sexuality', in Victoria Robinson and Diane Richardson (eds) *Introduction to Women's Studies: Feminist Theory and Practice* (Basingstoke: Macmillan), pp. 27–53.

Bijelić, Biljana (2001) 'Karat's Regional Recommendations on the Implementation of the Beijing Platform for Action', in Karat Coalition for Gender Equality *Beijing + 5 Process: Strategies and Demands of Central and Eastern Europe*, Warsaw, June.

Bitušiková, Alexandra (2005a) 'Gender Mainstreaming: Slovakia Country Report' for the European Vth Framework-supported project on 'Enlargement, Gender and Governance: The Civic and Political Participation and Representation of Women in the EU Candidate Countries'.

Bitušiková, Alexandra (2005b) '(In)Visible Women in Political Life in Slovakia', Paper presented to the final conference of the European Vth Framework-supported project on 'Enlargement, Gender and Governance: The Civic and Political Participation and Representation of Women in the EU Candidate Countries', Prague, 20 June.

Bitušiková, Alexandra (2005c) 'What Women (Don't) Want: Mechanisms to Improve Women's Political Representation in Slovakia', Paper presented to the final conference of the European Commission-supported Network for European Women's Rights, University of Birmingham, 30 June.

Bolz, Norbert (2002) 'In Fact You Have No Choice, So Cast Your Vote!', *Der Tagesspiegel*, Berlin, August: 25.

Bönker, Frank, Müller, Klaus and Pickel, Andreas (eds) (2002) *Postcommunist Transformation and the Social Sciences: Cross-Disciplinary Approaches* (Oxford and Lanham, MD: Rowman and Littlefield).

Bono, Paola (2000) 'Looking Back, Looking Forward: Looking at Italian Feminism/s', in Anna Bull, Hanna Diamond, and Rosalind Marsh (eds) *Feminism and Women's Movements in Contemporary Europe* (Basingstoke: Macmillan), pp. 166–79.

Bono, Paola and Kemp, Sandra (eds) (1993) *Italian Perspectives on Feminist Theory* (London and New York: Routledge).

Borić, Rada and Desnica, Mica Mladineo (1996) 'Croatia: Three Years After', in Chris Corrin (ed.) *Women in a Violent World: Feminist Analyses and Resistance Across 'Europe'* (Edinburgh: Edinburgh University Press), pp. 133–52.

Borić, Rada and Jelavić, Željka (2003) 'Between "Re-Patriarchalization" and European Union Standards on Women's Human Rights: Political Participation of Women in Croatia', accessed 25 June 2005 from http://www.newr.bham.ac.uk/pdfs/Political/Croatia.pol.pdf

Bourdieu, Pierre (1984) *Distinctions: A Social Critique of the Judgement of Taste* (London: Routledge).

Božinović, Neda, Zajović, Staša and Žarković, Rada (eds) (1998) *Women for Peace* (Belgrade: Pink Press).

Bracewell, Wendy (1996) 'Women, Motherhood and Contemporary Serbian Nationalism', *Women's Studies International Forum*, Special Issue on *Links across Differences: Gender, Ethnicity, and Nationalism*, 19 (1–2): 25–34.

Bretherton, Charlotte (2001) 'Gender Mainstreaming and EU Enlargement: Swimming against the Tide?' *Journal of European Public Policy*, 8 (1): 60–81.

Bridger, Sue (2000a) 'Rural Women in Russia: What Does Private Farming Mean?' in Marnia Lazreg (ed.) *Making the Transition Work for Women in Europe and Central Asia*, World Bank Discussion Paper 411 (Washington, DC: The World Bank), pp. 42–50.

Bridger, Sue (2000b) ' "Something Unnatural": Attitudes to Feminism in Russia', in Anna Bull, Hanna Diamond and Rosalind Marsh (eds) *Feminism and Women's Movements in Contemporary Europe* (Basingstoke: Macmillan), pp. 118–34.

Bridger, Sue (1996) 'The Return of the Family Farm: A Future for Women?' in Rosalind Marsh (ed.) *Women in Russia and Ukraine* (Cambridge: Cambridge University Press), pp. 241–54.

Bridger, Sue, Kay, Rebecca and Pinnick, Kathryn (1996) *No More Heroines? Russian Women and the Market* (London and New York: Routledge).

Broad, Robin (2004) 'The Washington Consensus Meets the Global Backlash: Shifting Debates and Policies', *Globalizations*, 1 (2): 129–54.

Brodie, Janine (1994) 'Shifting the Boundaries: Gender and the Politics of Restructuring', in Isabella Bakker (ed.) *The Strategic Silence: Gender and National Identities in Conflict* (London: Zed Books), pp. 46–60.

Bruno, Marta (1998) 'Playing the Co-operation Game: Strategies around International Aid in Post-Socialist Russia', in Sue Bridger and Frances Pine (eds) *Surviving Post-Socialism: Local Strategies and Regional Responses in Eastern Europe and the Former Soviet Union* (London and New York: Routledge), pp. 170–87.

Bruno, Marta (1997) 'Women and the Culture of Entrepreneurship', in Mary Buckley (ed.) *Post-Soviet Women: From the Baltic to Central Asia* (Cambridge: Cambridge University Press), pp. 56–74.

Bryant, Christopher G.A. and Mokrzycki, Edmund (eds) (1994) *The New Great Transformation? Change and Continuity in East-Central Europe* (London and New York: Routledge).

Bryson, Valerie (1999) *Feminist Debates: Issues of Theory and Political Practice* (Basingstoke: Macmillan).

Buchowska, Stanislava (2000) 'Trafficking in Women: Breaking the Vicious Cycle', in Marnia Lazreg (ed.) *Making the Transition Work for Women in Europe and Central Asia*, World Bank Discussion Paper 411 (Washington, DC: The World Bank), pp. 85–8.

Buckley, Mary (1997) 'Adaptation of the Soviet Women's Committee: Deputies' Voices from "Women of Russia" ', in Mary Buckley (ed.) *Post-Soviet Women: From the Baltic to Central Asia* (Cambridge: Cambridge University Press), pp. 157–85.

Buckley, Mary (ed.) (1992) *Perestroika and Soviet Women* (Cambridge: Cambridge University Press).
Bulgarian Gender Research Foundation (2003) 'Gender Assessment of the Impact of EU Accession on the Status of Women in the Labour Market in CEE: National Study on Bulgaria', Report for Karat Coalition as part of a region-wide UNIFEM-supported project (accessed via www.KARAT.org).
Bulgarian Gender Research Foundation (2000) *Equal Rights and Equal Opportunities for Women's Participation in Political Life in Bulgaria*, Sofia.
Bulgarian National Public Opinion Centre (2000) *Bulgarian Women: Social Status and Political Participation*, Sofia, July.
Burawoy, Michael and Verdery, Katherine (1998) *Uncertain Transition: Ethnographies of Change in the Postsocialist World* (Lanham, MD: Rowman and Littlefield).
Busheikin, Laura (1997) 'Is Sisterhood Really Global? Western Feminism in Eastern Europe', in Tanya Renne (ed.) *Ana's Land: Sisterhood in Eastern Europe* (Boulder, CO: Westview Press), pp. 12–21.
Butler, Judith (1990) *Gender Trouble: Feminism and the Subversion of Identity* (London and New York: Routledge).
Bystydzienski, Jill M. (2001) 'The Feminist Movement in Poland: Why So Slow?' *Women's Studies International Forum*, 24 (5): 501–11.
Bystydzienski, Jill M. (ed.) (1992) *Women Transforming Politics: Worldwide Strategies for Empowerment* (Bloomington, MN and Indianapolis: Indiana University Press).
Cannan, Crescy (1996) 'A Europe of the Citizen, A Europe of Solidarity? Social Policy in the European Union', in Barbara Einhorn, Mary Kaldor, and Zdenek Kavan (eds) *Citizenship and Democratic Control in Contemporary Europe* (Cheltenham; Brookfield, IL: Edward Elgar), pp. 134–49.
Cannan, Crescy (1995) 'From Dependence to Enterprise? Women and Western Welfare States', in Barbara Einhorn and Eileen Janes Yeo (eds) *Women and Market Societies: Crisis and Opportunity* (Aldershot, and Brookfield, IL: Edward Elgar), pp. 160–75.
Čermáková Marie, Hašková, Hana, Křížková, Alena, Linková, Marcela, Maríková, Hana, Musilová, Martina (2000) *Relations and Changes of Gender Differences in the Czech Society of the 90s* (Prague: Institute of Sociology, Academy of Sciences of the Czech Republic).
Chamberlayne, Prue (1995) 'Gender and the Private Sphere: A Touchstone of Misunderstanding between Eastern and Western Germany?' *Social Politics*, 2 (1): 25–36.
Chamberlayne, Prue (1990) 'Neighbourhood and Tenant Participation in the GDR', in Bob Deacon and Júlia Szalai (eds) *Social Policy in the New Eastern Europe: What Future for Socialist Welfare?* (Aldershot: Avebury), pp. 145–63.
Chang, Ha-Joon (2002) 'History Debunks the Free Trade Myth', *The Guardian*, 24 June.
Childers, Mary and hooks, bell (1990) 'A Conversation about Race and Class', in Marianne Hirsch and Evelyn Fox Keller (eds) *Conflicts in Feminism* (London and New York: Routledge), pp. 60–81.
Chimiak, Galia (2003) 'Bulgarian and Polish Women in the Public Sphere: A Comparative Analysis', *International Feminist Journal of Politics*, 5 (1): 3–27.
Chołuj, Bożena (2003) 'Die Situation der Frauen-NGOs in Polen an der Schwelle zum EU-Beitritt' ('The Situation of Women's NGOs in Poland on the Threshold of EU-Accession'), in Ingrid Miethe and Silke Roth (eds) *Europas Töchter: Traditionen, Erwartungen und Strategien von Frauenbewegungen in Europa (Europe's*

Daughters: European Women's Movements Traditions, Expectations and Strategies) (Opladen: Leske+Budrich), pp. 203–24.

Clements, Elizabeth (1994) 'The Abortion Debate in Unified Germany', in Elizabeth Boa and Janet Wharton (eds) *Women and the Wende: Social Effects and Cultural Reflections of the German Unification Process* (Amsterdam and Atlanta, GA: Rodopi), pp. 38–52.

Cockburn, Cynthia (2004) *The Line: Women, Partition and the Gender Order in Cyprus* (London and New York: Zed Books).

Cockburn, Cynthia (2000) 'The Anti-Essentialist Choice: Nationalism and Feminism in the Interaction Between Two Women's Projects', *Nations and Nationalism*, 6 (4): 611–29.

Cockburn, Cynthia (1998) *The Space Between Us: Negotiating Gender and National Identities in Conflict* (London and New York: Zed Books).

Cockburn, Cynthia and Žarkov, Dubravka (eds) (2002) *The Postwar Moment: Militaries, Masculinities and International Peacekeeping* (London: Lawrence and Wishart).

Cockburn, Cynthia with Stakić-Domuz, Rada and Hubić, Meliha (2001) *Women Organizing for Change: A Study of Women's Local Integrative Organizations and the Pursuit of Democracy in Bosnia-Herzegovina* (Zenica: Medica Infoteka).

Cohen, Robin and Rai, Shirin M. (2000) 'Global Social Movements: Towards a Cosmopolitan Politics', in Robin Cohen and Shirin M. Rai (eds) *Global Social Movements* (London and New Brunswick, NJ: The Athlone Press), pp. 1–17.

Collins, Patricia Hill (1990) *Black Feminist Thought: Knowledge, Consciousness, and the Politics of Empowerment* (Boston, MA: Unwin Hyman).

Copelon, Rhonda (1994/1998) 'Surfacing Gender: Reconceptualizing Crimes Against Women in Time of War', in Alexandra Stiglmayer (ed.) *Mass Rape: The War Against Women in Bosnia-Herzegovina* (Lincoln, NE and London: University of Nebraska Press), pp. 197–218; reprinted in Lois Ann Lorentzen and Jennifer Turpin (eds) (1998) *The Women and War Reader* (New York and London: New York University Press), pp. 63–79.

Corrin, Chris (ed.) (1999) *Gender and Identity in Central and Eastern Europe* (London: Frank Cass).

Corrin, Chris (ed.) (1996) *Women in a Violent World: Feminist Analyses and Resistance across 'Europe'* (Edinburgh: Edinburgh University Press).

Corrin, Chris (ed.) (1992) *Superwoman and the Double Burden: Women's Experience of Change in Central and Eastern Europe and the Former Soviet Union* (London: Scarlet Press).

Craske, Nikki (1998) 'Remasculinisation and the Neoliberal State in Latin America', in Vicky Randall and Georgina Waylen (eds) *Gender, Politics and the State* (London and New York: Routledge), pp. 100–20.

Crompton, Rosemary (2002) 'Employment, Flexible Working and the Family', *British Journal of Sociology*, 53 (4): 537–58.

Cronberg, Tarja (1997) 'The Feeling of Home: Russian Women in the Defence Industry and the Transformation of their Identities', *European Journal of Women's Studies*, 4 (3): 263–82.

Curtis, Polly and Branigan, Tania (2006) 'Young Women Told to Raise Their Sights on Pay', *The Guardian*, 28 February.

Dahlerup, Drude (1994) 'Learning to Live with the State: State, Market and Civil Society: Women's Need for State Intervention in East and West', *Women's Studies International Forum*, 17 (2–3): 117–27.

Dahlerup, Drude and Freidenvall, Lenita (2005) 'Quotas as a "Fast Track" to Equal Representation for Women: Why Scandinavia is No Longer the Model', *International Feminist Journal of Politics*, 7 (1): 26–48.
Daskalova, Krassimira (2003) 'Citizenship and Women's Political Participation in Bulgaria', accessed 25 June 2005 from http://www.newr.bham.ac.uk/pdfs/Political/Bulgaria.pol.pdf
Daskalova, Krassimira (2001) 'Manipulated Emancipation: Representations of Women in Post-Communist Bulgaria', in Gabriele Jähnert, Jana Gohrisch, Daphne Hahn, Hildegard Maria Nickel, Iris Peinl and Katrin Schäfgen (eds) *Gender in Transition in Eastern and Central Europe: Proceedings* (Berlin: trafo verlag), pp. 246–53.
Daskalova, Krassimira (2000) 'Women's Problems, Women's Discourses in Bulgaria', in Susan Gal and Gail Kligman (eds) *Reproducing Gender: Politics, Publics, and Everyday Life after Socialism* (Princeton, NJ: Princeton University Press), pp. 337–69.
Daskalova, Krassimira (1997) 'The Women's Movement in Bulgaria After Communism', in Joan W. Scott, Cora Kaplan and Debra Keates (eds) *Transitions, Environments, Translations: Feminisms in International Politics* (New York and London: Routledge), pp. 162–75.
Davidson, Julia O'Connell (2003) 'The Trouble with "Trafficking" ', Paper presented to the Launch Workshop of the Network for European Women's Rights (NEWR), Centre for Global Ethics, University of Birmingham, UK, 29 January.
Dawisha, Karen and Parrott, Bruce (eds) (1997) *Democratic Changes and Authoritarian Reactions in Russia, Ukraine, Belarus and Moldava* (Cambridge: Cambridge University Press).
Dawson, Elsa L. (1998) 'Assessing the Impact: NGOs and Empowerment', in Haleh Afshar (ed.) *Women and Empowerment: Illustrations from the Third World* (London and Basingstoke: Macmillan), pp. 189–209.
de Haan, Francisca, Daskalova, Krassimira and Loutfi, Anna (eds) (2006) *A Biographical Dictionary of Women's Movements and Feminisms: Central, Eastern, and South Eastern Europe, 19th and 20th Centuries* (Budapest and New York: Central European University Press).
Derbyshire, Helen (2002) *Gender Manual: A Practical Guide for Development Policymakers and Practitioners* (London: Department for International Development, DFID, UK), accessed 31 August 2005 from http://www.siyanda.org/docs_gem/index_implementation/genderman.htm
Dixon, Jay (1999) *The Romance Fiction of Mills and Boon, 1909–1990s* (London: UCL Press).
Dölling, Irene (2001) 'Ten Years After: Gender Relations in a Changed World – New Challenges for Women's and Gender Studies', in Gabriele Jähnert, Jana Gohrisch, Daphne Hahn, Hildegard Maria Nickel, Iris Peinl and Katrin Schäfgen (eds) *Gender in Transition in Eastern and Central Europe: Proceedings* (Berlin: trafo verlag), pp. 57–65.
Dölling, Irene (1994a) 'Women's Experience "Above" and "Below": How East German Women Experience and Interpret Their Situation after the Unification of the Two German States', *European Journal of Women's Studies*, 1 (1): 29–42.
Dölling, Irene (1994b) 'On the Development of Women's Studies in Eastern Germany', *Signs*, 19 (3): 739–52.

Dölling, Irene (1993a) 'Gespaltenes Bewusstsein – Frauen- und Männerbilder in der DDR' ('Divided Consciousness – Images of Men and Women in the GDR'), in Gisela Helwig and Hildegard Maria Nickel (eds) *Frauen in Deutschland 1945–1992 (Women in Germany 1945–1992)* (Bonn: Bundeszentrale für politische Bildung), pp. 23–52.

Dölling, Irene (1993b) ' "But the Pictures Stay the Same ..." The Image of Women in the Journal *Für Dich* Before and After the "Turning Point" ', in Nanette Funk and Magda Mueller (eds) *Gender Politics and Post-Communism: Reflections from Eastern Europe and the Former Soviet Union* (New York and London: Routledge), pp. 168–79.

Dölling, Irene (1992) ' "Man lebt jetzt regelrecht von Tag zu Tag, weil nichts mehr sicher ist" – Tagebücher als Dokumente eines gesellschaftlichen Umbruchs' (' "You Really Live from Day to Day Now, Because Nothing is Certain Any Longer" – Diaries as Documents of a Social Transformation'), *Berliner Journal für Soziologie*, Heft 1: 103–11.

Dölling, Irene (1991) 'Between Hope and Helplessness: Women in the GDR after the Turning Point', *Feminist Review* Special Issue on *Shifting Territories: Feminism and Europe*, 39: 3–15.

Dölling, Irene, Hahn, Daphne and Scholz, Sylka (2000) 'Birth Strike in the New Federal States: Is Sterilization an Act of Resistance?' in Susan Gal and Gail Kligman (eds) *Reproducing Gender: Politics, Publics, and Everyday Life after Socialism* (Princeton, NJ: Princeton University Press), pp. 118–47.

Dölling, Irene, Kuhlmey-Oehlert, Adelheid und Seibt, Gabriela (eds) (1992) *Unsere Haut: Tagebücher von Frauen aus dem Herbst 1990 (Our Skin: Women's Diaries From Autumn 1990)* (Berlin: Dietz Verlag).

Draga-Alexandru, Maria-Sabina (2000) 'Exiles from Power: Marginality and the Female Self in Postcommunist and Postcolonial Spaces', *European Journal of Women's Studies*, 7 (3): 355–66.

Drakulić, Slavenka (1992) *How We Survived Communism and Even Laughed* (London: Hutchinson).

du Plessix Gray, Francine (1991) *Soviet Women: Walking the Tightrope* (London: Virago).

du Plessis, Rachel and Snitow, Ann (eds) (1998) *The Feminist Memoir Project: Voices from Women's Liberation* (New York: Three Rivers).

Duchen, Claire (2000) 'Feminism and the Parity Debate in France', in Anna Bull, Hanna Diamond and Rosalind Marsh (eds) *Feminism and Women's Movements in Contemporary Europe* (Basingstoke: Macmillan), pp. 152–65.

Duchen, Claire (1994) *Women's Rights and Women's Lives in France, 1944–1968* (London: Routledge).

Duchen, Claire (1986) *Feminism in France: From May '68 to Mitterand* (London, Boston and Henley: Routledge and Kegan Paul).

Duffy, Diane M. (2000) 'Social Identity and Its Influence on Women's Roles in East Central Europe', *International Feminist Journal of Politics*, 2 (2): 214–43.

Duhaček, Daša (1998a) 'Eastern Europe', in Alison M. Jaggar and Iris Marion Young (eds) *A Companion to Feminist Philosophy* Blackwell Companions to Philosophy (Malden, US and Oxford, UK: Blackwell), pp. 128–36; last accessed 12 March 2006 from Women's/Gender Studies Association of Countries in Transition Electronic Library, http://www.zenskestudie.edu.yu/wgsact/e-library/e-lib0009.html

Duhaček, Daša (1998b) 'Belgrade Women's Studies Centre', *European Journal of Women's Studies*, 5 (3–4): 489–97.

Duhaček, Daša (1993) 'Women's Time in the Former Yugoslavia', in Nanette Funk and Magda Mueller (eds) *Gender Politics and Post-Communism: Reflections from Eastern Europe and the Former Soviet Union* (New York and London: Routledge), pp. 131–7.

Economist, The (2002) 'Doubt Inside the Barricades: Special Report on the IMF', 26 September.

Edmondson, Linda (1996) 'Equality and Difference in Women's History: Where Does Russia Fit In?' in Rosalind Marsh (ed.) *Women in Russia and Ukraine* (Cambridge: Cambridge University Press), pp. 94–110.

Edmondson, Linda (1984) *Feminism in Russia 1900–1917* (Stanford, CA: Stanford University Press).

Einhorn, Barbara (2000a) 'Gender and Citizenship in the Context of Democratisation and Economic Reform in East Central Europe', in Shirin M. Rai (ed.) *International Perspectives on Gender and Democratisation* (London and Basingstoke: Macmillan), pp. 103–24.

Einhorn, Barbara (2000b) 'Discussant's Comments' in Marnia Lazreg (ed.) *Making the Transition Work for Women in Europe and Central Asia*, World Bank Discussion Paper no. 411 (Washington, DC: The World Bank), pp. 107–10.

Einhorn, Barbara (1997) 'The Impact of the Transition from Centrally Planned to Market-Based Economies on Women's Employment in East Central Europe', in Eugenia Date-Bah (ed.), *Promoting Gender Equality at Work: Turning Vision into Reality for the Twenty-First Century* (London and New York: Zed Books), pp. 59–84.

Einhorn, Barbara (1996) 'Gender and Citizenship in East Central Europe After the End of State Socialist Policies for Women's "Emancipation"', in Barbara Einhorn, Mary Kaldor and Zdenek Kavan (eds) *Citizenship and Democratic Control in Contemporary Europe* (Cheltenham and Brookfield, IL : Edward Elgar), pp. 69–86.

Einhorn, Barbara (1995a) 'Ironies of History: Citizenship Issues in the New Market Economies of East Central Europe', in Barbara Einhorn and Eileen Janes Yeo (eds) *Women and Market Societies: Crisis and Opportunity* (Aldershot and Brookfield, IL: Edward Elgar), pp. 217–33.

Einhorn, Barbara (1995b) 'Feminism in Crisis: The East German Women's Movement in the "New Europe"', *Australian Journal of Politics and History*, Special Issue on *A New Europe?*, 41 (1): 14–28.

Einhorn, Barbara (1993) *Cinderella Goes to Market: Citizenship, Gender and Women's Movements in East Central Europe* (London and New York: Verso).

Einhorn, Barbara (1992) 'Emancipated Women or Hardworking Mothers? Women in the Former GDR', in Chris Corrin (ed.) *Superwoman and the Double Burden: Women's Experience of Change in Central and Eastern Europe and the Former Soviet Union* (London: Scarlet Press), pp. 125–54.

Einhorn, Barbara (1991) 'Where Have all the Women Gone? Women and the Women's Movement in East Central Europe', *Feminist Review*, Special Issue on *Shifting Territories: Feminism and Europe*, 39: 16–36.

Einhorn, Barbara and Sever, Charlotte (2005) 'Gender, Civil Society and Women's Movements in Central and Eastern Europe', in Jude Howell and Diane Mulligan (eds) *Gender and Civil Society: Transcending Boundaries* (London and New York: Routledge), pp. 23–53.

Einhorn, Barbara and Sever, Charlotte (2003) 'Gender and Civil Society in Central and Eastern Europe' *International Feminist Journal of Politics*, 5 (2): 163–90.

Eisenstein, Zillah (1993) 'Eastern European Male Democracies: A Problem of Unequal Equality', in Nanette Funk and Magda Mueller (eds) *Gender Politics and Post-Communism: Reflections from Eastern Europe and the Former Soviet Union* (New York and London : Routledge), pp. 303–17.

Elson, Diane (2002) 'Gender Justice, Human Rights, and Neo-Liberal Economic Policies', in Maxine Molyneux and Shahra Razavi (eds) *Gender Justice, Development, and Rights* (Oxford: Oxford University Press), pp. 78–114.

Elson, Diane (1999) 'Gender-Neutral, Gender-Blind, or Gender-Sensitive Budgets? Changing the Conceptual Framework to Include Women's Empowerment and the Economy of Care', in Diane Elson, *Gender Budget Initiative: Background Papers* (London: Commonwealth Secretariat), pp. 3–11.

Elson, Diane (1991, 2nd edn. 1995) 'Male Bias in Macro-Economics: The Case of Structural Adjustment', in Diane Elson (ed.) *Male Bias in the Development Process* (Manchester and New York: Manchester University Press), pp. 164–90.

Enloe, Cynthia (1998/2004) 'All the Men Are in the Militias, All the Women Are Victims: The Politics of Masculinity and Femininity in Nationalist Wars', in Lois Ann Lorentzen and Jennifer Turpin (eds) (1998) *The Women and War Reader* (New York and London: New York University Press), pp. 50–62; reprinted in Enloe, Cynthia (2004) *The Curious Feminist: Searching for Women in a New Age of Empire* (Berkeley and Los Angeles: University of California Press), pp. 99–118.

Enloe, Cynthia (1993) *The Morning After: Sexual Politics at the End of the Cold War* (Berkeley, CA: University of California Press).

Esping-Andersen, Gösta (1990) *The Three Worlds of Welfare Capitalism* (Cambridge: Polity Press).

European Commission (2005a) *Civil Society Dialogue between the EU and Candidate Countries* (Brussels: EC, 29 June 05), accessed 31 August 2005 from http://europa.eu.int/comm/enlargement/index_eu.html

European Commission (2005b) *Gender Equality Mission Statement* (Brussels: EC Unit for Equal Opportunities for Women and Men), accessed 31 August 2005 from http://europa.eu.int/comm/employment_social/gender_equality/index_en.html

Fábian, Katalin (2003) 'Cacophony of Voices: Interpretations of Feminism and Its Consequences for Political Action among Hungarian Women's Groups', *European Journal of Women's Studies*, 9 (3): 269–90.

Feijoó, María del Carmen (1998) 'Democratic Participation and Women in Argentina' in Jane S. Jaquette and Sharon L. Wolchik (eds) *Women and Democracy: Latin America and Central and Eastern Europe* (Baltimore, MD and London: The John Hopkins University Press), pp. 29–46.

Ferree, Myra Marx (1995) 'Patriarchies and Feminisms: The Two Women's Movements of Post-Unification Germany', *Social Politics*, 2 (1), 10–24; reprinted in Barbara Hobson (ed.) (2000) *Gender and Citizenship in Transition* (Basingstoke and London: Macmillan), pp. 156–72.

Ferree, Myra Marx (1993) 'The Rise and Fall of "Mommy Politics": Feminism and Unification in (East) Germany', *Feminist Studies*, 19: 89–115.

Ferree, Myra Marx, Risman, Barbara, Sperling, Valerie, Gurikova, Tatiana and Hyde, Katherine (1999) 'The Russian Women's Movement: Activists' Strategies and Identities', *Women and Politics*, 20 (3): 83–109.

Fodor, Éva (2005) 'Women at Work: The Status of Women in the Labour Markets of the Czech Republic, Hungary and Poland', Occasional Paper 3, Geneva: United Nations Research Institute for Social Development (UNRISD).

Fodor, Éva (2003) *Working Difference: Women's Working Lives in Hungary and Austria, 1945–1995* (Durham, NC and London: Duke University Press).

Fodor, Éva (2002) 'Smiling Women And Fighting Men: The Gender of the Communist Subject in State Socialist Hungary', *Gender and Society*, 16 (2): 240–63.

Fodor, Éva (1997) 'Gender in Transition: Unemployment in Hungary, Poland and Slovakia', *East European Politics and Societies*, 11 (3): 470–500.

Fong, Monica and Paul, Gillian (1993) 'Women's Economic Status in the Restructuring of Eastern Europe', in Valentine M. Moghadam (ed.) *Democratic Reform and the Position of Women in Transitional Economies* (Oxford: Clarendon Press), pp. 217–47.

Fong, Monica and Paul, Gillian (1992) 'The Changing Role of Women in Employment in Eastern Europe', World Bank, Europe and Central Asia Region, Population and Human Resources Division, Report No. 8213.

Foucault, Michel (1979) *The History of Sexuality: An Introduction*, vol. 1, transl. Robert Hurley (London: Allen Lane).

Fraser, Nancy (2005) 'Democratic Justice in a Globalizing Age: Thematizing the Problem of the Frame', Paper presented to a Symposium organized by the Centre for Critical Social Theory, University of Sussex, UK, 7 March.

Fraser, Nancy (1995/1997/1998) 'From Redistribution to Recognition? Dilemmas of Justice in a "Post-Socialist" Age', *New Left Review*, 212, July/August, 68–93; reprinted in Nancy Fraser (1997) *Justice Interruptus: Critical Reflections on the 'Postsocialist' Condition* (New York and London: Routledge), pp. 11–40; also reproduced in Anne Phillips (ed.) (1998) *Feminism and Politics* (Oxford and New York: Oxford University Press), pp. 430–60.

Funk, Nanette and Mueller, Magda (eds) (1993) *Gender Politics and Post-Communism: Reflections from Eastern Europe and the Former Soviet Union* (New York and London: Routledge).

Fuszara, Małgorzata (2001) 'Gender Studies at Warsaw University', in Gabriele Jähnert, Jana Gohrisch, Daphne Hahn, Hildegard Maria Nickel, Iris Peinl and Katrin Schäfgen (eds) *Gender in Transition in Eastern and Central Europe: Proceedings* (Berlin: trafo verlag), pp. 335–8.

Fuszara, Małgorzata (2000) 'New Gender Relations in Poland in the 1990s', in Susan Gal and Gail Kligman (eds) *Reproducing Gender: Politics, Publics and Everyday Life After Socialism* (Princeton, NJ: Princeton University Press), pp. 259–85.

Fuszara, Małgorzata (1997) 'Women's Movements in Poland', in Joan W. Scott, Cora Kaplan and Debra Keates (eds) *Transitions, Environments, Translations: Feminisms in International Politics* (New York and London: Routledge), pp. 128–42.

Fuszara, Małgorzata (1993) 'Abortion and the Formation of the Public Sphere in Poland' in Nanette Funk and Magda Mueller (eds) *Gender Politics and Post-Communism: Reflections from Eastern Europe and the Former Soviet Union* (New York and London: Routledge), pp. 241–52.

Gaber, Milica Antić (2003) 'The Lack of Positive Measures Which Would Support Women's Entrance into Politics in Slovenia', Country report for the Helsinki Workshop of NEWR, September.

Gaber, Milica Antić (1997) 'Politics in Transition', in Joan W. Scott, Cora Kaplan and Debra Keates (eds) *Transitions, Environments, Translations: Feminisms in International Politics* (New York and London: Routledge), pp. 143–52.

Gal, Susan (1997) 'Feminism and Civil Society', in Joan W. Scott, Cora Kaplan and Debra Keates (eds) *Transitions, Environments, Translations: Feminisms in International Politics* (New York and London: Routledge), pp. 30–45.

Gal, Susan (1994) 'Gender in the Post-Socialist Transition: The Abortion Debate in Hungary', *East European Politics and Societies*, 8 (2): 256–87.

Gal, Susan and Kligman, Gail (2000a) *The Politics of Gender After Socialism* (Princeton, NJ and Chichester: Princeton University Press).

Gal, Susan and Kligman, Gail (eds) (2000b) *Reproducing Gender: Politics, Publics and Everyday Life After Socialism* (Princeton, NJ and Chichester: Princeton University Press).

Gapova, Elena (2002) 'On Nation, Gender, and Class Formation in Belarus ... and Elsewhere in the Post-Soviet World', *Nationalities Papers*, 30 (4): 639–62.

Gapova, Elena (2001) 'Understanding the Other: A Response to Tiffany Petros' Article', *Central Europe Review* 3 (2), www.ce-review.org, accessed 11 July 2005 from Women's/ Gender Studies Association of Countries in Transition Electronic Library, http://www.zenskestudie.edu.yu/wgsact/e-library/e-lib0007.html

Gapova, Elena (1998) 'Women in the National Discourse in Belarus', *European Journal of Women's Studies, Special Issue on the Idea of Europe*, 5 (3–4): 477–88.

Gerhard, Ute (2003) 'Frauenbewegung in Deutschland – Gemeinsame und geteilte Geschichte' ('The German Women's Movement – Shared and Separate History'), in Ingrid Miethe and Silke Roth (eds) *Europas Töchter: Traditionen, Erwartungen und Strategien von Frauenbewegungen in Europa (Europe's Daughters: European Women's Movement Traditions, Expectations, and Strategies* (Opladen: Leske+Budrich), pp. 81–100.

Gheaus, Anca (2001) 'Feminism and the Public-Private Distinction in Romanian Society', in Gabriele Jähnert, Jana Gohrisch, Daphne Hahn, Hildegard Maria Nickel, Iris Peinl and Katrin Schäfgen (eds) *Gender in Transition in Eastern and Central Europe: Proceedings* (Berlin: trafo verlag), pp. 182–89.

Gill, Stephen (2003) *Power and Resistance in the New World Order* (Basingstoke: Palgrave Macmillan).

Global Database of Quotas for Women (2005) Joint Project of International IDEA and Stockholm University, accessed 22 July 2005 from http://www.quotaproject.org/dislayCountry.cfm?CountryCode=HU

Goetz, Anne Marie (2003) 'National Women's Machinery: State-Based Institutions to Advocate for Gender Equality', in Shirin M. Rai (ed.) *Mainstreaming Gender, Democratizing the State? Institutional Mechanisms for the Advancement of Women* (Manchester and New York: Manchester University Press for the United Nations), pp. 69–95.

Goetz, Anne Marie and Hassim, Shireen (2002) 'In and Against the Party: Women's Representation and Constituency-Building in Uganda and South Africa', in Maxine Molyneux and Shahra Razavi (eds) *Gender Justice, Development, and Rights* (Oxford: Oxford University Press), pp. 306–46.

Goven, Joanna (2000) 'New Parliament, Old Discourse? The Parental Leave Debate in Hungary', in Susan Gal and Gail Kligman (eds) *Reproducing Gender: Politics, Publics, and Everyday Life After Socialism* (Princeton, NJ and Chichester: Princeton University Press), pp. 286–306.

Graff, Agnieszka (2002) 'Lost Between the Waves? The Paradoxes of Feminist Chronology and Activism in Contemporary Poland', Paper presented to the conference on 'Third Wave Feminism', University of Exeter, UK, July.

Graham Ann and Regulska Joanna (1997) 'Expanding Political Space for Women in Poland : An Analysis of Three Communities', *Communist and Post-Communist Studies*, 30 (1): 65–82.

Grewal, Inderpal and Kaplan, Caren (eds) (1994) *Scattered Hegemonies: Postmodernity and Transnational Feminist Practices* (Minneapolis, MN: University of Minnesota Press).

Grunberg, Laura (2000) 'Women's NGOs in Romania', in Susan Gal and Gail Kligman (eds) *Reproducing Gender: Politics, Publics, and Everyday Life After Socialism* (Princeton, NJ and Chichester: Princeton University Press), pp. 307–36.

Grünell, Marianne (1998) 'Women's Studies in Russia: An Interview with Anastasia Posadskaya-Vanderbeck', *European Journal of Women's Studies, Special Issue on the Idea of Europe*, 5 (3–4), 499–512.

Grünell, Marianne (1995) 'Feminism Meets Scepticism: Women's Studies in the Czech Republic', *European Journal of Women's Studies*, 2 (1): 101–12.

Guardian, The (2005) 'Corporate Sexism is Still Rife', Business editorial, 5 August: 21.

Guichon, Audrey and Hellsten, Sirkku (2005) *NEWR (Network for European Women's Rights) State of the Art Report on Women's Political Participation and Citizenship*, accessed 15 July 2005 from www.newr.bham.ac.uk

Hague, Euan (1997) 'Rape, Power and Masculinity: The Construction of Gender and National Identities in the War in Bosnia-Herzegovina', in Ronit Lentin (ed.) *Gender and Catastrophe* (London: Zed Books), pp. 50–63.

Hall, Stuart (ed.) (1997) *Representation: Cultural Representations and Signifying Practices* (London: Sage with the Open University).

Haney, Lynne (2002) *Inventing the Needy: Gender and the Politics of Welfare in Hungary* (Berkeley, CA, Los Angeles and London: University of California Press).

Hann, Chris and Dunn, Elizabeth (eds) (1996) *Civil Society: Challenging Western Models* (London: Routledge).

Hansen, Lene (2001) 'Gender, Nation, Rape: Bosnia and the Construction of Security', *International Feminist Journal of Politics*, 3 (1): 55–77.

Harris, Colette (2004) *Control and Subversion: Gender Relations in Tajikistan* (London and East Haven, CT: Pluto Press).

Harsanyi, Doina Pasca (1993) 'Women in Romania', in Nanette Funk and Magda Mueller (eds) *Gender Politics* and *Post-Communism: Reflections from Eastern Europe and the Former Soviet Union* (New York and London: Routledge), pp. 39–52.

Hartmann, Petra (1998) 'Arbeitsteilung im Haushalt' ('The Household Division of Labour'), in Michael Braun und Peter Ph. Mohler (eds) *Blickpunkt Gesellchaft 4: Soziale Ungleichheit in Deutschland* (*Focus on Society 4: Social Inequality in Germany*) (Opladen: Westdeutscher Verlag), pp. 139–72.

Hašková, Hana (2005) 'Feminist Mobilization in the Czech Republic', Paper presented to the European Commission-funded conference 'Gendering Democracy in an Enlarged Europe', Prague, 20 June.

Hašková, Hana and Křížková, Alena (eds) (2003) *Women's Civic and Political Participation in the Czech Republic and the Role of European Union Gender Equality and Accession Policies* (Prague: Institute of Sociology, Academy of Sciences of the Czech Republic), Sociological Papers, 03: 9.

Hašková, Hana and Kolařová, Marta (2003) 'Women's NGOs and Women's Groups in Left- and Right-Wing Social Movements', in Hana Hašková and Alena Křížková (eds) *Women's Civic and Political Participation in the Czech Republic and the Role of EU Gender Equality and Accession Policies* (Prague:

Institute of Sociology, Academy of Sciences of the Czech Republic), Sociological Papers, 03: 9, pp. 45–57.
Havelková, Hana (2000) 'Abstract Citizenship? Women and Power in the Czech Republic', in Barbara Hobson (ed.) *Gender and Citizenship in Transition* (London: MacMillan), pp. 118–38.
Havelková, Hana (1997) 'Transitory and Persistent Differences: Feminism East and West', in Joan W. Scott, Cora Kaplan and Debra Keates (eds) *Transitions, Environments, Translations: Feminisms in International Politics* (London and New York: Routledge), pp. 56–62.
Havelková, Hana (1993) 'A Few Pre-Feminist Thoughts', in Nanette Funk and Magda Mueller (eds) *Gender Politics and Post-Communism: Reflections from Eastern Europe and the Former Soviet Union* (New York and London: Routledge), pp. 62–73.
Heinen, Jacqueline (1995) 'Unemployment and Women's Attitudes in Poland', *Social Politics*, 2 (1): 91–110.
Heinen, Jacqueline (1992) ' "Polish Democracy is a Male Democracy" ', *Women's Studies International Forum* 15 (1): 129–38.
Heinen, Jacqueline and Portet, Stephane (2002) 'Political and Social Citizenship: An Examination of the Case of Poland', in Maxine Molyneux and Shahra Razavi (eds) *Gender Justice, Development, and Rights* (Oxford: Oxford University Press), pp. 141–69.
Heitlinger, Alena (1993) 'The Impact of the Transition from Communism on the Status of Women in the Czech and Slovak Republics', in Nanette Funk and Magda Mueller (eds) *Gender Politics and Post-Communism: Reflections from Eastern Europe and the Former Soviet Union* (New York and London: Routledge), pp. 95–108.
Hinsliff, Gaby (2006) 'Why the Pay Gap Never Went Away', *The Observer*, 26 February.
Hobsbawm, Eric (1983) 'Inventing Traditions', Introduction to Eric J. Hobsbawm and Terence O. Ranger (eds) *The Invention of Tradition* (Cambridge: Cambridge University Press), pp. 1–14.
hooks, bell (1981) *Ain't I A Woman? Black Women and Feminism* (London and Boston, MA: South End Press).
Hornig, Daphne (1995) 'Sterben die Ostdeutschen aus? Untersuchung zu irreversibler Schwangerschaftsverhütung in Ostdeutschland' ('Are the East Germans Dying Out? Investigating Sterilisation as a Form of Contraception in East Germany'), *Differente Sexualitäten (Differing Sexualities)*, Sondernummer (Special issue) *MKF (Mitteilungen aus der kulturwissenschaftlichen Forschung (Cultural Theory Research Reports)*, 18 (36): 183–87.
Hoskyns, Catherine (1996) *Integrating Gender: Women, Law and Politics in the European Union* (London and New York: Verso).
Hoskyns, Catherine and Rai, Shirin M. (1998) 'Gender, Class and Representation: India and the European Union', *European Journal of Women's Studies*, Special Issue on *The Idea of Europe*, 5 (3–4): 345–66.
Howell, Jude (1998) 'Gender, Civil Society and the State in China', in Vicky Randall and Georgina Waylen (eds) *Gender, Politics and the State* (London and New York: Routledge), pp. 166–84.
Howell, Jude and Pearce, Jenny (2001) *Civil Society and Development: A Critical Exploration* (Boulder, CO and London: Lynne Rienner Publishers).
International Helsinki Federation for Human Rights (IHF) (2000) *Women 2000: An Investigation Into the Status of Women's Rights in Central and South-Eastern Europe and the Newly Independent States* (Vienna: IHF).

International Labour Organization (ILO) (2002) 'Getting at the Roots: Stopping Exploitation of Migrant Workers by Organized Crime', ILO Paper presented to International Symposium on the UN Convention against Transnational Organized Crime: Requirments for Effective Implementation, Turin, 22–23 February.

International Labour Organization (ILO) (1999) 'Ukraine: Country Employment Policy Review' (Geneva: ILO).

Inter-Parliamentary Union (IPU) (2005) Data on the political representation of women, accessed 22 July 2005 from http://www.ipu.org/wmn-e/classif.htm

Ishkanian, Armine (2003) 'Is the Personal Political? The Development of Armenia's NGO Sector During the Post-Soviet Period', *Berkeley Program in Soviet and Post-Soviet Studies*, posted at the eScholarship Repository, University of California, Berkeley, accessible from http://repositories.cdlib.org/iseees/bps/2003_03-ishk

Iveković, Rada (2001) 'Where Gender and "National/Ethnic" Difference Meet', in Gabriele Jähnert, Jana Gohrisch, Daphne Hahn, Hildegard Maria Nickel, Iris Peinl and Katrin Schäfgen (eds) (2001) *Gender in Transition in Eastern and Central Europe: Proceedings* (Berlin: trafo verlag), pp. 312–18.

Jähnert, Gabriele, Gohrisch, Jana, Hahn, Daphne, Nickel, Hildegard Maria, Peinl, Iris and Schäfgen, Katrin (eds) (2001) *Gender in Transition in Eastern and Central Europe: Proceedings* (Berlin: trafo verlag).

Jalušič, Vlasta (2002) 'Between the Social and the Political: Feminism, Citizenship and the Possibilities of an Arendtian Perspective in Eastern Europe', *European Journal of Women's Studies*, 9 (2): 103–22.

Jalušič, Vlasta (1997) 'It's a Shame! The Campaign for Constitutional Reproductive Rights in Slovenia', in Tanya Renne (ed.) *Ana's Land: Sisterhood in Eastern Europe* (Boulder, CO: Westview Press), pp. 212–17.

Jankowska, Hanna (1991) 'Abortion, Church and Politics in Poland', *Feminist Review*, Special Issue on *Shifting Territories: Feminism and Europe*, 39: 174–81.

Janova, Mira and Sineau, Mariette (1992) 'Women's Participation in Political Power in Europe: An Essay in East-West Comparison', *Women's Studies International Forum*, 15 (1): 115–28.

Jaquette, Jane S. (ed.) (1994; 2nd edn) *The Women's Movement in Latin America: Participation and Democracy* (Boulder, CO, San Francisco and Oxford: Westview Press).

Jaquette, Jane S. (ed.) (1989) *The Women's Movement in Latin America: Feminism and the Transition to Democracy* (Boston, MA: Unwin Hyman).

Jaquette, Jane S. and Wolchik, Sharon L. (eds) (1998) *Women and Democracy: Latin America and Central and Eastern Europe* (Baltimore, MD; London: John Hopkins University Press).

Jezerska, Zuzana (2003) 'Gender Awareness and the National Machineries in the Countries of Central and Eastern Europe', in Shirin M. Rai (ed.) *Mainstreaming Gender, Democratizing the State? Institutional Mechanisms for the Advancement of Women* (Manchester and New York: Manchester University Press), pp. 167–83.

Kaldor, Mary (1991) 'After the Cold War' *Feminist Review* Special Issue on *Shifting Territories: Feminism and Europe*, 39: 109–14.

Kaldor, Mary and Vejvoda, Ivan (eds) (1999/2002) *Democratization in Central and Eastern Europe* (London and New York: Continuum).

Kandiyoti, Deniz (1991) 'Identity and Its Discontents: Women and the Nation', *Millennium*, 20 (3): 429–33.
Kapur, Ratna (2002) 'The Tragedy of Victimization Rhetoric: Resurrecting the "Native" Subject in International/Post-Colonial Feminist Legal Politics', *Harvard Human Rights Journal*, 15, Spring: 1–38.
Karat (2005a) 'Women in the Labour Market in Bulgaria, Georgia, Macedonia, Poland, Serbia & Montenegro and Slovenia', Infosheet (edited by Anita Seibert) for the 49th UN CSW session, New York, 28 February–11 March, accessed 29 July 2005 from www.karat.org/documents/infosheet_Labour_popr.pdf
Karat (2005b) 'Institutional Mechanisms for Gender Equality: Despite a Formal Progress – Still Very Weak', Infosheet (edited by Stanimira Kadjimitova, Kinga Lohmann and Aleksandra Solik) for 49th UN CSW session, New York, 28 February–11 March (Warsaw: Karat Coalition).
Karat (2005c) 'New Financial Instruments are Gender-Blind', Press Release, Brussels, 20 June, accessed 29 July 2005 from www.karat.org
Karat (2005d) 'Garment Industry in Poland – Monitoring of Working Conditions', Report posted 07 April 2005 at http://www.womenslabour.org
Karat (2001) *Beijing + 5: Strategies and Demands of Central and Eastern Europe*, Warsaw, June.
Kašić, Biljana (2004) 'Feminist Cross-Mainstreaming Within "East-West" Mapping: A Postsocialist Perspective', *European Journal of Women's Studies*,11 (4): 473–86.
Kašić, Biljana (2001) 'Women's Studies: Ideological Images, Common Problems and Dilemmas', in Gabriele Jähnert, Jana Gohrisch, Daphne Hahn, Hildegard Maria Nickel, Iris Peinl and Katrin Schäfgen (eds) *Gender in Transition in Eastern and Central Europe: Proceedings* (Berlin: trafo verlag), pp. 356–60.
Kay, Rebecca (2000) *Russian Women and Their Organizations: Gender, Discrimination and Grassroots Women's Organizations, 1991–96* (Basingstoke: Macmillan and New York: St. Martin's Press).
Kay, Rebecca (1997) 'Images of an Ideal Woman: Perceptions of Russian Womanhood through the Media, Education and Women's Own Eyes', in Mary Buckley (ed.) *Post-Soviet Women: From the Baltic to Central Asia* (Cambridge: Cambridge University Press), pp. 77–98.
Keane, John (1998) *Civil Society: Old Images, New Visions* (Oxford: Polity Press).
Keane, John (ed.) (1988) *Civil Society and the State: New European Perspectives* (London and New York: Verso).
Kesić, Vesna (2002/2004) 'Gender and Ethnic Identities in Transition', in Rada Iveković and Julie Mostov (eds) *From Gender to Nation* (Ravanna: A Longo Editore); reprinted and here quoted from 2004 edition (New Delhi: Zubaan, an associate of Kali for Women), pp. 63–80.
Khan, Nighat Said (2000) 'The Women's Movement Revisited: Areas of Concern for the Future', in Suki Ali, Kelly Coate and Wangui wa Goro (eds) *Global Feminist Politics: Identities in a Changing World* (London: Routledge), pp. 5–10.
Khodyreva, Natalia (1996) 'Sexism and Sexual Abuse in Russia', in Chris Corrin (ed.) *Women in a Violent World: Feminist Analyses and Resistance Across 'Europe'* (Edinburgh: Edinburgh University Press), pp. 27–40.
Khotkina, Zoya A. (2001) 'Ten Years of Gender Studies in Russia: We Have Been Able to Accomplish a Lot and Look Forward with Optimism', in Gabriele

Jähnert, Jana Gohrisch, Daphne Hahn, Hildegard Maria Nickel, Iris Peinl and Katrin Schäfgen (eds) *Gender in Transition in Eastern and Central Europe: Proceedings* (Berlin: trafo verlag), pp. 345–49.

Khotkina, Zoya (1994) 'Women in the Labour Market: Yesterday, Today and Tomorrow', in Anastasia Posadskaya (ed.) *Women in Russia: A New Era in Russian Feminism* (London: Verso), pp. 85–108.

Kiss, Yudit (2002) 'System Changes, Export-Oriented Growth and Women in Hungary', ms.

Kligman, Gail (1998) *The Politics of Duplicity: Controlling Reproduction in Ceausescu's Romania* (Berkeley: University of California Press).

Kligman, Gail, (1996) 'Women and the Negotiation of Identity in Post-Communist Eastern Europe', in Victoria E. Bonnell (ed.) *Identities in Transition: Eastern Europe and Russia after the Collapse of Communism* (Berkeley: University of California Press), pp. 68–91.

Kligman, Gail and Limoncelli, Stephanie (2005) 'Trafficking Women after Socialism: To, Through, and From Eastern Europe', *Social Politics*, 12 (1): 118–40.

Knothe, Maria Anna (2005) 'Gender Dimensions in Labour Market Flexibility and Employment Security in Central and Eastern Europe and the Baltic States: Are Women Secure on a Flexible Labour Market?' Paper presented to the final conference of the Network of European Women's Rights (NEWR), University of Birmingham, 30 June–1 July.

Kobelyanska, Larysa (2000) 'Violence and Trafficking in Women in Ukraine', in Lazreg, Marnia (ed.) *Making the Transition Work for Women in Europe and Central Asia* (Washington: World Bank) Discussion paper no. 411, pp. 76–84.

Kofman, Eleonore, Phizacklea, Annie, Raghuram, Parvati and Sales, Rosemary (2000) *Gender and International Migration in Europe: Employment, Welfare and Politics* (London and New York: Routledge).

Kofman, Eleonore and Sales, Rosemary (1998) 'Migrant Women and Exclusion in Europe', *European Journal of Women's Studies*, Special Issue on *The Idea of Europe*, 5(3–4): 381–98.

Kolozova, Katerina (2001) 'Dilemmas of Institutionalization and their Context/s', in Gabriele Jähnert, Jana Gohrisch, Daphne Hahn, Hildegard Maria Nickel, Iris Peinl and Katrin Schäfgen (eds) *Gender in Transition in Eastern and Central Europe: Proceedings* (Berlin: trafo verlag), pp. 361–64.

Koncz, Katalin (2000) 'Transitional Period and Labor Market Characteristics in Hungary', in Marnia Lazreg (ed.) *Making the Transition Work for Women in Europe and Central Asia*, World Bank Discussion Paper no. 411 (Washington, DC: The World Bank), pp. 26–41.

Korać, Maja (1999) 'Refugee Women in Serbia: Their Experiences of War, Nationalism and State Building', in Nira Yuval-Davis and Pnina Werbner (eds) *Women, Citizenship and Difference* (London and New York: Zed Books), pp. 192–204.

Korać, Maja (1996) 'Understanding Ethnic-National Identity and Its Meaning: Questions from a Woman's Experience', *Women's Studies International Forum*, Special Issue on *Links across Differences: Gender, Ethnicity and Nationalism*, 19 (1–2): 133–44.

Kostova, Dobrinka (1998) 'Women in Bulgaria: Changes in Employment and Political Involvement', in Jane S. Jaquette and Sharon L. Wolchik (eds) *Women and Democracy: Latin America and Central and Eastern Europe* (Baltimore, MD and London: The John Hopkins University Press), pp. 203–21.

Kostova, Dobrinka (1994) 'Similar or Different? Women in Postcommunist Bulgaria', in Marilyn Rueschemeyer (ed.) *Women in the Politics of Postcommunist Eastern Europe* (New York and London: M.E. Sharpe, Inc.), pp. 117–32.

Kotowska, Irena E. (1995) 'Discrimination Against Women in the Labor Market in Poland During the Transition to a Market Economy', *Social Politics*, 2 (1), 76–90.

Kovács, Katalin and Váradi, Mónika (2000) 'Women's Life Trajectories and Class Formation in Hungary', in Susan Gal and Gail Kligman (eds) *Reproducing Gender: Politics, Publics, and Everyday Life After Socialism* (Princeton, NJ: Princeton University Press), pp. 176–99.

Kramer, Anne-Marie (2006) 'The Abortion Debate in Poland: Opinion Polls, Ideological Politics, Citizenship and the Erasure of Gender as a Category of Analysis', in Janet E. Johnson and Jean C. Robinson (eds) *Living Gender after Communism* (Bloomington, IN: Indiana University Press).

Kramer, Anne-Marie (2005) 'Gender, Nation and the Abortion Debate in the Polish Media', in Vera Tolz and Stephenie Booth (eds) *Nation and Gender in Contemporary Europe* (Manchester and New York: Manchester University Press), pp. 130–48.

Kramer, Anne-Marie (2004) 'Reproduction and the Making of Politics in the "New Poland": Gender, Nation and Democracy in the Polish Abortion Debate', unpublished Ph.D thesis, University of Warwick, UK.

Krause, Ellen (2001) 'The State is a Man Who Protects the Nation – Gender Relations and the Concept of State and Nation in Eastern and Central Europe', in Gabriele Jähnert, Jana Gohrisch, Daphne Hahn, Hildegard Maria Nickel, Iris Peinl and Katrin Schäfgen (eds) *Gender in Transition in Eastern and Central Europe: Proceedings* (Berlin: trafo verlag), pp. 303–11.

Křížková, Alena and Václavíková-Helšusová, Lenka (2003) 'Women's Participation and Representation in Local Politics', in Hana Hašková and Alena Křížková (eds) *Women's Civic and Political Participation in the Czech Republic and the Role of EU Gender Equality and Accession Policies* (Prague: Institute of Sociology, Academy of Sciences of the Czech Republic), Sociological Papers, 03: 9, pp. 26–31.

Kulczycki, Andrevzej (1999) *The Abortion Debate in the World Arena* (London and Basingstoke: Macmillan).

Kulke, Christine (2001) 'Impacts of Globalization on Gender Politics and Gender Arrangements', in Gabriele Jähnert, Jana Gohrisch, Daphne Hahn, Hildegard Maria Nickel, Iris Peinl and Katrin Schäfgen (eds) *Gender in Transition in Eastern and Central Europe: Proceedings* (Berlin: trafo verlag), pp. 75–83.

Kupryashkina, Svetlana V. (1997) 'The Limits of Research: Women's Studies in Ukraine', in Joan W. Scott, Cora Kaplan and Debra Keates (eds) *Transitions, Environments, Translations: Feminisms in International Politics* (New York and London: Routledge), pp. 383–89.

Laclau, Ernesto and Mouffe, Chantal (1985) *Hegemony and Socialist Strategy: Towards a Radical Democratic Politics* (London: Verso).

Lang, Sabine (1997) 'The NGOization of Feminism', in Joan W. Scott, Cora Kaplan and Debra Keates (eds) *Transitions, Environments, Translations: Feminisms in International Politics* (New York and London: Routledge), pp. 101–20.

Lazreg, Marnia (ed.) (2000) *Making the Transition Work for Women in Europe and Central Asia*, World Bank Discussion Paper no. 411 (Washington, DC: The World Bank).

Lennox, Sara (1995) 'Divided Feminism: Women, Racism, and German National Identity', *German Studies Review*, XVIII (3): 481–502.

Lentin, Ronit (1999) 'The Rape of the Nation: Women Narrativising Genocide', *Sociological Research Online*, 4 (2), available at http://www.socresonline.org.uk/socresonline/4/2/lentin.html

Lépinard, Éléonore (2005) 'Ambivalent Categories and Problematic Outcomes of Gender Qutoas: The Struggle Over the Definition of Gender Equality in the French Parity Debate', Paper presented to the final conference of the European Commission-supported Network for European Women's Rights (NEWR), University of Birmingham, 30 June–1 July.

Lewis, Jane (2003) 'Economic Citizenship: A Comment', *Social Politics*, 10 (2): 176–85.

Lewis, Jane (1997) 'Gender and Welfare Regimes: Some Further Thoughts' *Social Politics*, 4 (2): 160–207.

Lewis, Jane (ed.) (1993) *Women and Social Policies in Europe: Work, Family and the State* (Aldershot: Edward Elgar).

Lewis, Jane (1992) 'Gender and the Development of Welfare Regimes', *Journal of European Social Policy*, 2 (3): 159–73.

Lindsey, Rose (2002) 'From Atrocity to Data: Historiographies of Rape in Former Yugoslavia and the Gendering of Genocide', *Patterns of Prejudice* 26 (4): 59–78.

Lipovskaya, Olga (2001) 'Institutionalization of Gender/Women's Studies in Russia/St. Petersburg', in Gabriele Jähnert, Jana Gohrisch, Daphne Hahn, Hildegard Maria Nickel, Iris Peinl and Katrin Schäfgen (eds) *Gender in Transition in Eastern and Central Europe: Proceedings* (Berlin: trafo verlag), pp. 350–5.

Lisyutkina, Larissa (2003) 'Ein "Sorgenkind" im Fernen Osten Europas: Die Russische Frauenbewegung und Genderforschung zwischen Hoffnung und Verzweiflung' ('A "Problem Child" in Europe's Far East: The Russian Women's Movement and Gender Research Between Hope and Despair'), in Ingrid Miethe and Silke Roth (eds) (2003) *Europas Töchter: Traditionen, Erwartungen und Strategien von Frauenbewegungen in Europa (Europe's Daughters: European Women's Movement Traditions, Expectations and Strategies)* (Opladen: Leske+ Budrich), pp. 225–56.

Lisyutkina, Larissa (1993) 'Soviet Women at the Crossroads of Perestroika', in Nanette Funk and Magda Mueller (eds) *Gender Politics and Post-Communism: Reflections from Eastern Europe and the Former Soviet Union* (New York and London: Routledge), pp. 274–86.

Lister, Ruth (2000) 'Dilemmas in Engendering Citizenship', in Barbara Hobson (ed.) *Gender and Citizenship in Transition* (Basingstoke and London: Macmillan), pp. 33–83; originally published in *Economy and Society*, 21 (1) (1995): 1–40.

Lister, Ruth (1997) *Citizenship: Feminist Perspectives* (Basingstoke: Macmillan).

Lister, Ruth (1993) 'Tracing the Contours of Women's Citizenship' *Policy and Politics*, 21 (1); 3–16.

Lithuanian Women's Information Centre (1999) *Politics Towards Women and Women in Politics* (Vilnius: Lithuanian Women's Information Centre).

Litričin, Vera and Mladenović, Lepa (1997) 'Belgrade Feminists: Separation, Guilt, and Identity Crisis', in Tanya Renne (ed.) *Ana's Land: Sisterhood in Eastern Europe* (Boulder, CO: Westview Press), pp. 179–85.

Lohmann, Kinga (2005) 'The Impact of Enlargement on the Civic Participation of Women in Central and Eastern Europe', Paper presented to the conference 'Gendering Democracy in an Enlarged Europe', Prague, 20 June.

Lohmann, Kinga and Seibert, Anita (eds) (2003) *Gender Assessment of the Impact of EU Accession on the Status of Women in the Labour Market in CEE: National Study: Poland* (Warsaw: Karat Coalition with support from Norwegian Ministry of Foreign Affairs and Polish Ministry of Economy, Labour and Social Policy).

Lokar, Sonja (ed) (2005) *From Quota to Parity: Social Democratic Women in Action 1995–2005* (Budapest, Ljubljana, Tallinn: CEE Network for Gender Issues).

Lokar, Sonja (2003) *Women Can Do It: Integration of Gender Equality Issues in Parliamentary Parties' Work in South East Europe* (Novi Sad, Vojvodina/Serbia and Montenegro: Stability Pact Gender Task Force Project Report).

Lokar, Sonja (2000) 'Gender Aspects of Employment and Unemployment in Central and Eastern Europe', in Marnia Lazreg (ed.) *Making the Transition Work for Women in Europe and Central Asia*, World Bank Discussion paper no. 411 (Washington, DC: IBRD/The World Bank), pp. 12–25.

Lorenz-Meyer, Dagmar (2003) 'Policy Initiatives and Tools to Promote the Participation of Women and Gender Equality in the Process of the Czech Republic's Accession to the European Union', in Hana Hašková and Alena Křížková (eds) *Women's Civic and Political Participation in the Czech Republic and the Role of EU Gender Equality and Accession Policies* (Prague: Institute of Sociology, Academy of Sciences of the Czech Republic), Sociological Papers, 03: 9, pp. 61–85.

Lovenduski, Joni (2001) 'Women and Politics: Minority Representation or Critical Mass?' *Parliamentary Affairs*, 54: 743–58.

Lovenduski, Joni (1999) 'Sexing Political Behaviour in Britain', in Sylvia Walby (ed.) *New Agendas for Women* (Basingstoke: Macmillan), pp. 190–209.

Lovenduski, Joni (1996) 'Sex, Gender and British Politics', in Joni Lovenduski and Pippa Norris (eds) *Women in Politics* (Oxford: Oxford University Press), pp. 3–18.

Lovenduski, Joni and Norris, Pippa (1993) *Gender and Party Politics* (London: Sage).

Lukić, Jasmina (2000) 'Media Representations of Men and Women in Times of War and Crisis: The Case of Serbia', in Susan Gal and Gail Kligman (eds) *Reproducing Gender: Politics, Publics, and Everyday Life After Socialism* (Princeton, NJ: Princeton University Press), pp. 393–423.

Mackie, Vera (2001) 'The Language of Globalization, Transnationality and Feminism', *International Feminist Journal of Politics*, 3 (2): 180–206.

Macková, Darina (2000) *Women in Transition: The Situation of Women in Present Slovakia*, unpublished MA in Gender and International Development dissertation, University of Warwick, UK.

Maier, Friederike (1993) 'The Labour Market for Women and Employment Perspectives in the Aftermath of German Unification', *Cambridge Journal of Economics*, 17: 267–80.

Maleck-Lewy, Eva (1997) 'The East German Women's Movement After Unification', in Joan W. Scott, Cora Kaplan and Debra Keates (eds) *Transitions, Environments, Translations: Feminisms in International Politics* (London and New York: Routledge), pp. 121–7.

Maleck-Lewy, Eva (1995) 'Between Self-Determination and State Supervision: Women and the Abortion Law in Post-Unification Germany', *Social Politics*, 2 (1), 62–75.

Maleck-Lewy, Eva and Ferree, Myra Marx (2000) 'Talking About Women and Wombs: The Discourse of Abortion and Reproductive Rights in the GDR During and After the *Wende*', in Susan Gal and Gail Kligman (eds) *Reproducing Gender: Politics, Publics, and Everyday Life After Socialism* (Princeton, NJ: Princeton University Press), pp. 92–117.

Malicka, Magdalena (2000) 'Pregnancy: Unwanted in the Workplace', *Warsaw Voice*, no. 38, 17 September.

Mansbridge, Jane (2003) 'Anti-Statism and Difference Feminism in International Social Movements', *International Feminist Journal of Politics*, 5 (3): 355–60.

Margolies, David (1982–83) 'Mills & Boon: Guilt Without Sex', *Red Letters*, 14: 5–13.

Marinova, Jivka, Gencheva, Mariya and Tisheva, Genoveva (eds) (2003) *Gender Assessment of the Impact of EU Accession on the Status of Women in the Labour Market in CEE: National Study: Bulgaria* (Sofia: Bulgarian Gender Research Foundation supported by UNIFEM and coordinated by Karat Coalition).

Marksová-Tominová, Michaela (ed.) (2003) *Gender Assessment of the Impact of EU Accession on the Status of Women in the Labour Market in CEE: National Study:Czech Republic* (Prague: Gender Studies o.p.s. with the support of UNIFEM and coordinated by Karat Coalition).

Marody, Mira (1992) 'Why I Am Not a Feminist? Some Remarks on the Problem of Gender Identity in the USA and Poland', ms.

Marody, Mira (1991) 'On Polish Political Attitudes', *Telos*, 89: 112–13.

Marody, Mira (1990) 'Perception of Politics in Polish Society', *Social Research: An International Quarterly of the Social Sciences*, 57 (2): 257–74.

Marody, Mira and Giza-Połeszczuk, Anna (2000) 'Changing Images of Identity in Poland: From the Self-Sacrificing to the Self-Investing Woman?' in Susan Gal and Gail Kligman (eds) *Reproducing Gender: Politics, Publics, and Everyday Life After Socialism* (Princeton, NJ: Princeton University Press), pp. 151–75.

Marsh, Rosalind (1996) 'The Russian Women's Movement: Anastasiia Posadskaia, the Dubna Forum and the Independent Women's Movement in Russia', in Rosalind Marsh (ed.) *Women in Russia and Ukraine* (Cambridge: Cambridge University Press), pp. 286–97.

Matynia, Elżbieta (1995) 'Finding a Voice: Women in Postcommunist Central Europe', in Amrita Basu (ed.) *The Challenge of Local Feminisms: Women's Movements in Global Perspective* (Boulder, CO: Westview Press), pp. 374–404.

Mayer, Tamar (2000) 'Gender Ironies of Nationalism: Setting the Stage', in Tamar Mayer (ed.) *Gender Ironies of Nationalism: Sexing the Nation* (London and New York: Routledge), pp. 1–24.

Mazey, Sonia (2000) 'Integrating Gender – Intellectual and "Real World" Mainstreaming' *Journal of European Public Policy*, 7 (3): 333–45.

McClintock, Anne (1993/1995/1997) 'Family Feuds: Gender, Nationalism and the Family', *Feminist Review*, 44 (1993): 61–80; reproduced as ' "No Longer in a Future Heaven": Nationalism, Gender and Race', in Anne McClintock (1995) *Imperial Leather: Race, Gender and Sexuality in the Colonial Contest* (New York and London: Routledge), pp. 352–89; and in Anne McClintock, Aamir Mufti and Ella Shohat (eds) (1997) *Dangerous Liaisons: Gender, Nation, and Postcolonial Perspectives* (Minneapolis, MN and London: University of Minnesota Press), pp. 89–112.

McMahon, Patrice C. (2002) 'International Actors and Women's NGOs in Poland and Hungary', in Sarah E. Mendelson and John K. Glenn (eds) *The Power and Limits of NGOs: A Critical Look at Building Democracy in Eastern Europe and Eurasia* (New York: Columbia University Press), pp. 29–53.

Meznarić, Silva (1994) 'Gender As An Ethno-Marker: Rape, War and Identity Politics in the Former Yugoslavia', in Valentine M. Moghadam (ed.) *Identity Politics and Women: Cultural Reassertions and Feminism in International Perspective* (Oxford: Westview Press), pp. 76–97.

Milić, Anđelka (1993) 'Women and Nationalism in the Former Yugoslavia', in Nanette Funk and Magda Mueller (eds) *Gender Politics and Post-Communism: Reflections from Eastern Europe and the Former Soviet Union* (New York and London: Routledge), pp. 109–22.

Miroiu, Mihaela (2004) 'State Men, Market Women: The Effects of Left Conservatism on Gender Politics in Romanian Transition', in Krassimira Daskalova and Kornelia Slavova (eds) *Women's Identities in the Balkans* (Sofia: Polis Publishers, in Bulgarian), pp. 95–112.

Miszlivetz, Ferenc (1997) 'Civil Society', Lecture to Sussex European Institute, University of Sussex, 18 February.

Mlađenović, Lepa and Matijašević, Divna (1996) 'SOS Belgrade July 1993–1995: Dirty Streets', in Chris Corrin (ed.) *Women in a Violent World: Feminist Analyses and Resistance Across 'Europe'* (Edinburgh: Edinburgh University Press), pp. 119–32.

Moghadam, Valentine M. (ed.) (1993) *Democratic Reform and the Position of Women in Transitional Economies* (Oxford: Clarendon Press).

Mohanty, Chandra Talpade (2003) ' "Under Western Eyes" Revisited: Feminist Solidarity through Anticapitalist Struggles', *Signs: Journal of Women in Culture and Society*, 28 (2); also in Chandra Talpade Mohanty (2003) *Feminism Without Borders: Decolonizing Theory, Practicing Solidarity* (Durham, NC and London: Duke University Press), pp. 221–52.

Mohanty, Chandra Talpade (1984/1991) 'Under Western Eyes: Feminist Scholarship and Colonial Discourses' in Chandra Talpade Mohanty, Ann Russo and Lourdes Torres (eds) *Third World Women and the Politics of Feminism* (Bloomington, IN: Indiana University Press), pp. 51–80; originally in *Boundary 2*, 12 no. 3/13 no. 1 (Spring/Fall): 338–58; reprinted in *Feminist Review*, no. 30, Autumn 1988; extracted in Mary Eagleton (ed.) (1996) *Feminist Literary Theory: A Reader*, 2nd edn (Oxford: Basil Blackwell), pp. 388–93; also reprinted in Stevi Jackson and Sue Scott (eds) (2002) *Gender: A Sociological Reader*; reprinted in Chandra Talpade Mohanty (2003) *Feminism without Borders: Decolonizing Theory, Practicing Solidarity* (Durham, NC and London: Duke University Press), pp. 17–42.

Molyneux, Maxine (1988/1998/2001) 'Analysing Women's Movements', *Development and Change*, 29 (2), 1988; reprinted in Cecile Jackson and Ruth Pearson (eds) (1998) *Feminist Visions of Development: Gender Analysis and Policy* (London and New York: Routledge), pp. 65–88; also in Maxine Molyneux (2001) *Women's Movements in International Perspective: Latin America and Beyond* (Basingstoke: Palgrave), pp. 140–62.

Molyneux, Maxine (1990) 'The "Woman Question" in the Age of Perestroika', *New Left Review*, 183: 23–49.

Molyneux, Maxine (1985) 'Mobilisation Without Emancipation? Women's Interests, the State, and Revolution in Nicaragua', *Feminist Studies*, 11 (2): 227–54.

Monbiot, George (2003) 'Poisoned Chalice: Wherever It Is Prescribed, A Dose of IMF Medicine Only Compounds Economic Crisis', *The Guardian*, 19 August.

Morgner, Irmtraud (1974/1984) 'Das Seil' ('The Rope'), translated by Karin R. Achberger (abridged) in Edith H. Altbach, Jeanette Clausen, Dagmar Schultz and Naomi Stephan. (eds) *German Feminism: Readings in Politics and Literature* (Albany, NY: State University of New York Press), pp. 215–19; originally an integral part of Morgner's novel *Leben und Abenteuer der Trobadora Beatriz nach Zeugnissen ihrer Spielfrau Laura* (*The Life and Adventures of the Female Trobadour Beatrice According to Testimony by her Accompanist Laura*) (Berlin and Weimar: Aufbau Verlag) (1974), pp. 594–603.

Morokvašić, Mirjana (1998) 'The Logics of Exclusion: Nationalism, Sexism and the Yugoslav War', in Nickie Charles and Helen Hintjens (eds) *Gender, Ethnicity and Political Ideologies* (London and New York: Routledge), pp. 65–90.

Mosse, George (1985) *Nationalism and Sexuality: Middle Class Morality and Sexual Norms in Modern Europe* (Madison: University of Wisconsin Press).

Mostov, Julie (2000) 'Sexing the Nation/Desexing the Body: Politics of National Identity in the Former Yugoslavia', in Tamar Mayer (ed.) *Gender Ironies of Nationalism: Sexing the Nation* (London and New York: Routledge), pp. 89–112.

Mouffe, Chantal (1992/1993) 'Feminism, Citizenship and Radical Democratic Politics', in Judith Butler and Joan W. Scott (eds) *Feminists Theorize the Political* (New York and London: Routledge), pp. 369–84; reprinted in Chantal Mouffe (1993), *The Return of the Political* (London and New York: Verso).

Mršević, Zorica (2001) 'In Search for the Lost (Taken Away) Identity', in Gabriele Jähnert, Jana Gohrisch, Daphne Hahn, Hildegard Maria Nickel, Iris Peinl and Katrin Schäfgen (eds) *Gender in Transition in Eastern and Central Europe: Proceedings* (Berlin: trafo verlag), pp. 261–67.

Mršević, Zorica (2000) 'Belgrade's SOS Hotline for Women and Children Victims of Violence: A Report', in Susan Gal and Gail Kligman (eds) *Reproducing Gender: Politics, Publics, and Everyday Life After Socialism* (Princeton, NJ: Princeton University Press), pp. 370–92.

Nagel, Joanne (1998) 'Masculinity and Nationalism: Gender and Sexuality in the Making of Nations', *Ethnic and Racial Studies*, 21 (2): 242–69.

Nagy, Ponrac (2003) *From Command to Market Economy in Hungary under the Guidance of the IMF* (Budapest: Akademiai Kiado).

Nash, Rebecca (2003) 'Exhaustion from Explanation: Reading Czech Gender Studies in the 1990s', *European Journal of Women's Studies*, 9 (3): 291–310.

Nesporova, Alena (2002) 'Unemployment in the Transition Countries', Paper presented to the UN Economic Commission for Europe (UNECE) Ad Hoc Meeting of Experts on Gender and Macroeconomics, 5 July, Palais des Nations, Geneva.

NEWW-Polska (Network of East–West Women-Polska, 2006). Letter to the Prime Minister, received via personal communication from Małgorzata Tarasiewicz, Director of NEWW-Polska. Accessible at http://www.neww.org.pl/en.php/news/news/1.html?&nw = 2032&re = 4

Network Women's Program, Open Society Institute (NWP/OSI) (2002) *Bending the Bow: Targeting Women's Human Rights and Opportunities* (New York: Open Society Institute).

Nicholson, Linda (ed.) (1990) *Feminism – Postmodernism* (New York: Routledge).

Nickel, Hildegard Maria (2002) 'The Future of Female Employment – A Gendered Gap in Political Discourse', in Eva Kolinsky and Hildegard Maria Nickel (eds) *Reinventing Gender: Women in Eastern Germany Since Unification* (London and Portland, OR: Frank Cass), pp. 31–52.

Nickel, Hildegard Maria (2001) 'ZiF – the Centre for Interdisciplinary Women's Studies. A Paradigm for the Institutionalisation of Women's and Gender Studies', in Gabriele Jähnert, Jana Gohrisch, Daphne Hahn, Hildegard Maria

Nickel, Iris Peinl and Katrin Schäfgen (eds) *Gender in Transition in Eastern and Central Europe: Proceedings* (Berlin: trafo verlag), pp. 66–74.
Nickel, Hildegard Maria (2000) 'Employment, Gender and the Dual Transformation in Germany', in Chris Flockton, Eva Kolinsky and Rosalind Pritchard (eds) *The New Germany in the East: Policy Agendas and Social Developments since Unification* (London and Oregon: Frank Cass), pp. 106–22.
Nickel, Hildegard Maria (1993) 'Women in the German Democratic Republic and in the New Federal States: Looking Backward and Forward (Five Theses)' in Nanette Funk and Magda Mueller (eds) *Gender Politics and Post-Communism: Reflections from Eastern Europe and the Former Soviet Union* (London and New York: Routledge), pp. 138–50.
Nicolaescu, Madalina (2001a) 'Generating New Definitions of Feminine Identity', in Gabriele Jähnert, Jana Gohrisch, Daphne Hahn, Hildegard Maria Nickel, Iris Peinl and Katrin Schäfgen (eds) *Gender in Transition in Eastern and Central Europe: Proceedings* (Berlin: trafo verlag), pp. 268–73.
Nicolaescu, Madalina (2001b) *Fashioning Global Identities* (Bucharest: Editura Universitatii din Bucuresti).
Nikolić-Ristanović, Vesna (2001) 'The Construction of Identities in Media Images of Violence against Women', in Gabriele Jähnert, Jana Gohrisch, Daphne Hahn, Hildegard Maria Nickel, Iris Peinl and Katrin Schäfgen (eds) *Gender in Transition in Eastern and Central Europe: Proceedings* (Berlin: trafo verlag), pp. 284–94.
Nikolić-Ristanović, Vesna (1998) 'War, Nationalism, and Mothers in the Former Yugoslavia', in Lois Ann Lorentzen and Jennifer Turpin (eds) (1998) *The Women and War Reader* (New York and London: New York University Press), pp. 234–39.
Novikova, Irina (2001) 'East European Feminisms – in Rooms of Our Own? On the Problems of Feminist Theorising and Integrating Women's/Gender Studies in the Baltics/Latvia', in Gabriele Jähnert, Jana Gohrisch, Daphne Hahn, Hildegard Maria Nickel, Iris Peinl and Katrin Schäfgen (eds) *Gender in Transition in Eastern and Central Europe: Proceedings* (Berlin: trafo verlag), pp. 325–9.
Nowakowska, Urszula and Jablonska, Magdalena (2000), 'Violence Against Women', in Women's Rights Centre, *Polish Women in the 90s* (Warsaw: Women's Rights Centre), pp. 147–86.
Nowakowska, Urszula and Korzeniewska, Maja (2000), 'Women's Reproductive Rights', in Women's Rights Centre, *Polish Women in the 90s* (Warsaw: Women's Rights Centre), pp. 219–48.
Nowakowska, Urszula and Piwnik, Emilia (2000), 'Women in the Family', in Women's Rights Centre, *Polish Women in the 90s* (Warsaw: Women's Rights Centre), pp. 105–46.
Nowakowska, Urszula and Swedrowska, Anna (2000) 'Women in the Labour Market', in Women's Rights Centre, *Polish Women in the 90s* (Warsaw: Women's Rights Centre), pp. 41–80.
Nowicka, Wanda (2000), 'Reproductive Health and the Rights of Women', in Marnia Lazreg (ed.), *Making the Transition Work for Women in Europe and Central Asia*, World Bank Discussion paper no. 411 (Washington, DC: IBRD/The World Bank), pp. 69–75.
NRO Frauenforum and Karat Coalition (2003) 'Expanding Rights, Creating Space for Action? EU Reform and Enlargement from a Gender Perspective', Position Paper presented to the conference 'Expanding Rights? EU Reform and Enlargement from a Gender Perspective', Berlin, 11–12 December.

Nussbaum, Martha C. (2002) 'Women's Capabilities and Social Justice', in Maxine Molyneux and Shahra Razavi (eds) *Gender Justice, Development, and Rights* (Oxford: Oxford University Press), pp. 45–77.
Nussbaum, Martha C. (2000) *Women and Human Development: The Capabilities Approach* (Cambridge: Cambridge University Press).
Nussbaum, Martha C. (1995) 'Human Capabilities: Female Human Beings', in Martha C. Nussbaum and Jonathan Glover (eds) *Women, Culture and Development: Study of Human Capabilities*, Study Prepared for the World Institute for Development Economics Research (WIDER) of the United Nations University (UNU) (Oxford: Clarendon Press), pp. 61–104.
Oates-Indruchová, Libora (2001) 'Discourses of Gender in the Post-1989 Czech Republic: A Textual Perspective', in Gabriele Jähnert, Jana Gohrisch, Daphne Hahn, Hildegard Maria Nickel, Iris Peinl and Katrin Schäfgen (eds) *Gender in Transition in Eastern and Central Europe: Proceedings* (Berlin: trafo verlag), pp. 118–23.
Offe, Claus and Bönker, Frank (1996) *Varieties of Transition: The Eastern European and East German Experiences* (Cambridge: Polity).
Open Society Institute (OSI) (2002) *Monitoring the EU Accession Process: Equal Opportunities for Women and Men in Poland*, Warsaw.
Ostrowska, Elżbieta (1998) 'Filmic Representations of the "Polish Mother" in Post-Second World War Polish Cinema', *European Journal of Women's Studies*, Special Issue on *The Idea of Europe*, 5 (3–4): 419–36.
Outhwaite, William and Ray, Larry (2005) *Social Theory and Postcommunism* (Malden, MA; Oxford; Carlton, Aus: Blackwell Publishing).
Outshoorn, Joyce (2005) 'The Political Debates on Prostitution and Trafficking of Women', *Social Politics*, 12 (1): 141–55.
Paci, Pierella (2002) *Gender in Transition* (Washington: The World Bank).
Papanek, Hanna (1990) 'To Each Less Than She Needs, From Each More Than She Can Do: Allocations, Entitlements, and Value', in Irene Tinker (ed.) *Persistent Inequalities: Women and World Development* (New York and Oxford: Oxford University Press), pp. 162–81.
Papić, Žarana (2002) 'Europe after 1989: Ethnic Wars, the Fascistization of Civil Society and Body Politics in Serbia', in Gabriele Griffin and Rosi Braidotti (eds) *Thinking Differently: A Reader in European Women's Studies* (London and New York: Zed Books), pp. 127–44.
Papić, Žarana (1994) 'Nationalism, Patriarchy and War', *Women's History Review*, 3 (1): 115–17.
Paukert, Liba (1995) *Economic Transition and Women's Employment in Four Central European Countries, 1989–1994* (Geneva: International Labour Organization), Labour Market Papers no. 7.
Pavlychko, Solomea (2000) 'Women's Discordant Voices in the Context of the 1998 Parliamentary Election in Ukraine', in Anna Bull, Hanna Diamond and Rosalind Marsh (eds) *Feminisms and Women's Movements in Contemporary Europe* (Basingstoke: Macmillan), pp. 244–61.
Pavlychko, Solomea (1997) 'Progress on Hold: The Conservative Faces of Women in Ukraine', in Mary Buckley (ed.) *Post-Soviet Women: From the Baltic to Central Asia* (Cambridge: Cambridge University Press), pp. 219–34.
Pavlychko, Solomea (1996) 'Feminism in Post-Communist Ukrainian Society', in Marsh, Rosalind (ed.) *Women in Russia and Ukraine* (Cambridge: Cambridge University Press), pp. 305–14.

Pavlychko, Solomea (1992) 'Between Feminism and Nationalism: New Women's Groups in Ukraine', in Mary Buckley (ed.) *Perestroika and Soviet Women* (Cambridge: Cambridge University Press), pp. 72–96.
Peinl, Iris (2001) 'Beyond the Gender-Hierarchical Monotony? Ambivalent Gender Relations in East German Branches of Deutsche Bahn AG (German Railways plc)', in Gabriele Jähnert, Jana Gohrisch, Daphne Hahn, Hildegard Maria Nickel, Iris Peinl and Katrin Schäfgen (eds) *Gender in Transition in Eastern and Central Europe: Proceedings* (Berlin: trafo verlag), pp. 231–40.
Petchesky, Rosalind Pollack (2003) *Global Prescriptions: Gendering Health and Human Rights* (London and New York: Zed Books in association with UNRISD).
Peterson, V. Spike (1999) 'Sexing Political Identities/Nationalism as Heterosexism', *International Journal of Feminist Politics*, 1 (1): 34–65.
Peterson, V. Spike (1996) 'The Politics of Identification in the Context of Globalisation', *Women's Studies International Forum*, Special Issue on *Links across Differences: Gender, Ethnicity and Nationalism*, 19 (1–2): 5–16.
Peterson, V. Spike (1994) 'Gendered Nationalism', *Peace Review*, Special Issue on *Nationalism and Ethnic Conflict*, 6 (1): 77–84.
Petkova, Bianca and Griffin, Chris (1998) 'Bulgarian Women and Discourses about Work', *European Journal of Women's Studies*, Special Issue on *The Idea of Europe*, 5 (3–4): 437–52.
Petö, Andrea (2003) ' "Angebot ohne Nachfrage": Ungarische Frauen als Bürgerinnen eines EU-Beitrittlandes' (' "Supply without Demand": Hungarian Women as Citizens of an EU Accession Country'), in Ingrid Miethe and Silke Roth (eds) *Europas Töchter: Traditionen, Erwartungen und Strategien von Frauenbewegungen in Europa (Europe's Daughters: European Women's Movement Traditions, Expectations and Strategies)* (Opladen: Leske+Budrich), pp. 183–202.
Petö, Andrea (2002) 'The History of the Hungarian Women's Movement', in Gabriele Griffin and Rosi Braidotti (eds) *Thinking Differently: A Reader in European Women's Studies* (London and New York: Zed Books), pp. 361–71.
Petö, Andrea (1997) 'Hungarian Women in Politics', Joan W. Scott, Cora Kaplan and Debra Keates (eds) *Transitions, Environments, Translations: Feminisms in International Politics* (New York and London: Routledge), pp. 153–61.
Petrova, Dimitrina (1997) 'The Farewell Dance: Women in the Bulgarian Transition', in Eileen Janes Yeo (ed.) *Mary Wollstonecraft and 200 Years of Feminisms* (London and New York: Rivers Oram Press), pp. 180–92.
Petrović, Jasna A. (2002) *The Male Face of Trade Unions in Central and Eastern Europe: The Secret of Invisible Women* (Zagreb and Brussels: International Confederation of Free Trade Unions (ICFTU) with ICFTU Women's Network for Central and Eastern Europe).
Phillips, Anne (2002) 'Multiculturalism, Universalism, and the Claims of Democracy', in: Maxine Molyneux and Shahra Razavi (eds) *Gender Justice, Development, and Rights* (Oxford: Oxford University Press), pp.115–40.
Phillips, Anne (1999) *Which Equalities Matter?* Cambridge and Malden, MA: Polity Press.
Phillips, Anne (1995) *The Politics of Presence* (Oxford: Clarendon Press).
Phillips, Anne (1993) *Democracy and Difference* (Pennsylvania: Pennsylvania State University Press).
Pine, Frances (1994) 'Privatisation in Post-Socialist Poland: Peasant Women, Work, and the Restructuring of the Public Sphere', *Cambridge Anthropology*, 17 (3): 19–42.

Pollert, Anna (1999) *Transformation at Work in the New Market Economies of Central Eastern Europe* (London, Thousand Oaks and New Delhi: Sage Publications).
Posadskaya, Anastasia (1994) 'A Feminist Critique of Policy, Legislation and Social Consciousness in Post-Socialist Russia', in Anastasia Posadskaya, (ed.) *Women in Russia: A New Era in Russian Feminism* (London: Verso), pp. 164–82.
Posadskaya, Anastasia (1991) An Interview with Anastasya Posadskaya by Maxine Molyneux, *Feminist Review*, Special Issue on *Shifting Territories: Feminism and Europe*, 39: 133–40.
Posadskaya-Vanderbeck, Anastasia (2002) 'Without Women, Democracy Fails', Director's Message in Open Society Institute Network Women's Program, *Bending the Bow: Targeting Women's Human Rights and Opportunities* (New York: Open Society Institute), pp. 6–7.
Posadskaya-Vanderbeck, Anastasia (1997) 'On the Threshold of the Classroom: Dilemmas for Post-Soviet Russian Feminism', in Joan W. Scott, Cora Kaplan and Debra Keates (eds) *Transitions, Environments, Translations: Feminisms in International Politics* (New York and London: Routledge), pp. 373–82.
Pringle, Rosemary and Watson, Sophie (1992) 'Women's Interests and the Post-Structuralist State', in Michèle Barrett and Anne Phillips (eds) *Destabilizing Theory: Contemporary Feminist Debates* (Cambridge and Oxford: Polity Press), pp. 53–73.
Prützel-Thomas, Monika (1995) 'The Abortion Issue since Unification: Are Women the Losers?' *Debatte: Review of Contemporary German Affairs*, 3 (2): 105–20.
Pupavac, Vanessa (2005) 'Empowering Women? An Assessment of International Gender Policies in Bosnia', *International Peacekeeping*, 12 (3): 391–405.
Purvaneckiene, Giedre (2003) 'Low Political Participation of Women in Lithuania', accessed 25 June 2005 from http://www.newr.bham.ac.uk/pdfs/Political/Lithuania.pol.pdf
Rai, Shirin M. (2004) 'Gendering Global Governance', *International Feminist Journal of Politics*, 6 (4): 579–602.
Rai, Shirin M. (2003) 'Institutional Mechanisms for the Advancement of Women: Mainstreaming Gender, Democratizing the State?' in Shirin M. Rai (ed.) *Mainstreaming Gender, Democratizing the State? Institutional Mechanisms for the Advancement of Women* (Manchester and New York: Manchester University Press for and on behalf of the UN), pp. 15–39.
Rai, Shirin M. (ed.) (2000) *International Perspectives on Gender and Democratisation* (London and Basingstoke: Macmillan; New York: St. Martin's Press).
Rai, Shirin M. (1996) 'Women and the State in the Third World: Some Issues for Debate', in Shirin M. Rai and Geraldine Lievesley (eds) *Women and the State: International Perspectives* (London; Bristol, PA: Taylor and Francis), pp.5–22.
Rai, Shirin, Pilkington, Hilary and Phizacklea, Annie (eds) (1992) *Women in the Face of Change: The Soviet Union, Eastern Europe and China* (London and New York: Routledge).
Rakušanová, Petra (2003) 'Women's Participation in Formal National Political Structures', in Hana Hašková and Alena Křížková (eds) *Women's Civic and Political Participation in the Czech Republic and the Role of EU Gender Equality and Accession Policies* (Prague: Institute of Sociology, Academy of Sciences of the Czech Republic), Sociological Papers, 03: 9, pp. 17–25.
Randall, Vicky (2000) 'British Feminism in the 1990s', in Anna Bull, Hanna Diamond and Rosalind Marsh (eds) *Feminisms and Women's Movements in Contemporary Europe* (Basingstoke: Macmillan), pp. 135–51.

Randall, Vicky (1998) 'Gender and Power: Women Engage the State', in Vicky Randall and Georgina Waylen (eds) *Gender, Politics and the State* (London and New York: Routledge), pp. 185–205.
Reading, Anna (1992) *Polish Women, Solidarity and Feminism* (London and Basingstoke: Macmillan).
Rees, Teresa (2002) 'The Politics of "Mainstreaming" Gender Equality', in Esther Breitenbach, Alice Brown, Fiona Mackay and Janette Webb (eds) *The Changing Politics of Gender Equality in Britain* (Basingstoke and New York: Palgrave), pp. 45-69.
Rees, Teresa (1998) *Mainstreaming Gender Equality in the European Union* (London and New York: Routledge).
Reeves, Hazel and Baden, Sally (2000) *Gender and Development: Concepts and Definitions*, BRIDGE Report no. 55 (Brighton: BRIDGE/IDS), accessed 31 August 2005 from http://www.bridge.ids.ac.uk/reports/re55.pdf
Regulska, Joanna (2002) 'Women's Agency and Supranational Political Spaces: The European Union and Eastern Enlargement', Paper presented at the Annual Meeting of the American Association of Geographers, Los Angeles, USA, 20–24 March.
Regulska, Joanna (2001) 'Gendered Integration of Europe: New Boundaries of Exclusion' in Gabriele Jähnert, Jana Gohrisch, Daphne Hahn, Hildegard Maria Nickel, Iris Peinl and Katrin Schäfgen (eds) *Gender in Transition in Eastern and Central Europe: Proceedings* (Berlin: trafo verlag), pp. 84–96.
Renc-Roe, Joanna (2003) 'The Representation of Women in the Political Decision-Making Process in Poland: Existing Problems and Advocated Solutions', Paper prepared for the ECPR Joint Session: 'Changing Constitutions, Building Institutions and (Re)defining Gender Relations', Edinburgh, 28 March–2 April, accessed 1 December 2004 from http://www.essex.ac.uk/ecpr/events/jointsessions/paperarchive/edinburgh/ws23/RencRoe.pdf
Renne, Tanya (ed.) (1997) 'Disparaging Digressions: Sisterhood in East-Central Europe', in Tanya Renne (ed.) *Ana's Land: Sisterhood in Eastern Europe* (Boulder, CO: Westview Press), pp. 1–11.
Riszovannij, Mihaly (2001) 'Media Discourses on Homosexuality in Hungary', in Gabriele Jähnert, Jana Gohrisch, Daphne Hahn, Hildegard Maria Nickel, Iris Peinl and Katrin Schäfgen (eds) *Gender in Transition in Eastern and Central Europe: Proceedings* (Berlin: trafo verlag), pp. 254–60.
Rittossa, Dalida (2005) 'Taking the Right to Abortion in Croatia Seriously: One of the Basic Constitutional Rights or a Rudiment of Reproductive Rights?' Paper presented to the final conference of the EC-funded Network of European Women's Rights (NEWR) project, University of Birmingham, 30 June–1 July.
Rodrik, Dani (2002) 'After Neoliberalism What?' Presentation to the Oxfam Conference 'Alternatives to Neoliberalism', Washington, DC, 23 May.
Roman, Denise (2001) 'Gendering Eastern Europe: Pre–Feminism, Prejudice and East–West Dialogues in Post-Communist Romania', *Women's Studies International Forum*, 24 (1): 53–66.
Romaniuk, Tamara (1998) 'Women at Labour Market: Problems of Gender Discrimination', Paper presented to the National Tripartite Conference 'Women in the Labour Market in Ukraine', supported by the ILO, Kiev, 17–18 February.
Rosen, Ruth (1990) 'Male Democracies, Female Dissidents', *Tikkun*, 5(6): 11–12, 100–1.

Rosenberg, Dorothy (1996) 'Distant Relations: Class, "Race", and National Origin in the German Women's Movement', *Women's Studies International Forum*, Special Issue on *Links Across Differences: Gender, Ethnicity and Nationalism*, 19 (1–2): 145–54.

Rosenberg, Dorothy (1993) 'The New Home Economics: Women, Work and Family in the United Germany', *Debatte: Review of Contemporary German Affairs*, 1 (1): 111–34.

Rosenberg, Dorothy (1991) 'Shock Therapy: GDR Women in Transition from a Socialist Welfare State to a Social Market Economy', *Signs*, 17 (1): 129–51.

Roseneil, Sasha (2000) *Common Women, Uncommon Practices: The Queer Feminisms of Greenham* (London: Cassell).

Roseneil Sasha (1995) *Disarming Patriarchy: Feminism and Political Action at Greenham* (Buckingham: Open University Press).

Roth, Silke (2002) 'Opportunities and Obstacles–Screening the EU-Enlargement Process from a Gender Perspective', Paper presented at the conference 'Euroland and Eastern Europe: Assessing the New Integration Processes', University of Pennsylvania, Philadelphia, 22 March.

Rothschild, Cynthia (2005) *Written Out: How Sexuality is Used to Attack Women's Organizing*, New York and New Brunswick, NJ: International Gay and Lesbian Human Rights Commission (IGLHRC) and Center for Women's Global Leadership (CWGL), accessed 4 September 2005 from http://www.iglhrc.org/files/iglhrc/WrittenOut.pdf

Rowbotham, Sheila (1998) 'Weapons of the Weak: Homeworkers' Networking in Europe', *European Journal of Women's Studies*, 5 (3–4): 453–64.

Rowbotham, Sheila (1997) *A Century of Women: The History of Women in Britain and the United States* (London: Viking).

Rowbotham, Sheila (1989) *The Past Is Before Us: Feminism in Action Since the 1960s* (London: Penguin).

Rowlands, Jo (1998) 'A Word of the Times, But What Does it Mean? Empowerment in the Discourse and Practice of Development', in Haleh Afshar (ed.) *Women and Empowerment: Illustrations from the Third World* (Basingstoke and London: Macmillan), pp. 11–34.

Rubchak, Marian J. (2001) 'In Search of a Model: Evolution of a Feminist Consciousness in Ukraine and Russia', *European Journal of Women's Studies*, 8 (2): 149–60.

Rubchak, Marian J. (1996) 'Christian Virgin or Pagan Goddess: Feminism versus the Eternally Feminine in Ukraine', in Rosalind Marsh (ed.) *Women in Russia and Ukraine* (Cambridge: Cambridge University Press), pp. 315–30.

Rubery, Jill, Smith, Mark and Fagan, Colette (1999) *Women's Employment in Europe: Trends and Prospects* (London and New York: Routledge).

Rueschemeyer, Marilyn (2001) 'Women in the Political Life of Eastern Europe: Ten Years After the End of Communism', in Gabriele Jähnert, Jana Gohrisch, Daphne Hahn, Hildegard Maria Nickel, Iris Peinl and Katrin Schäfgen (eds) *Gender in Transition in Eastern and Central Europe: Proceedings* (Berlin: trafo verlag), pp. 167–75.

Rueschemeyer, Marilyn (ed.) (1994/1998) *Women in the Politics of Postcommunist Eastern Europe* (New York and London: M.E.Sharpe Inc.).

Ruminska-Zimny, Eva (2002) 'Gender Aspects of Changes in the Labour Markets in Transition Economies', Paper presented to the UN Economic Commission for Europe (UNECE) Ad Hoc Meeting of Experts on Gender and Macro-Economics, Paris, July.

Ruminska-Zimny, Eva (1999) 'Globalisation and Gender in Transition Economies', in UNCTAD (ed.) *Trade, Sustainable Development and Gender*, Papers from the Expert Workshop (Geneva: UNCTAD; New York: United Nations).

Salecl, Renata (1994) *The Spoils of Freedom: Psychoanalysis and Feminism After the Fall of Socialism* (London and New York: Routledge).

Sali-Terzić, Sevima (2001) 'Civil Society', in Žarko Papić (ed.) *International Support Policies to South-East European Countries. Lessons (not) Learned in Bosnia and Herzegovina* (Sarajevo: Müller), pp. 138–58.

Sauer, Birgit (2001) ' "Normalized Masculinities": Constructing Gender in Theories of Political Transition and Democratic Consolidation', in Gabriele Jähnert, Jana Gohrisch, Daphne Hahn, Hildegard Maria Nickel, Iris Peinl and Katrin Schäfgen (eds) *Gender in Transition in Eastern and Central Europe: Proceedings* (Berlin: trafo verlag), pp. 26–36.

Schäfgen, Katrin (2001) 'Gender Studies at Humboldt University. The Process of Institutionalization in Germany' in Gabriele Jähnert, Jana Gohrisch, Daphne Hahn, Hildegard Maria Nickel, Iris Peinl and Katrin Schäfgen (eds) *Gender in Transition in Eastern and Central Europe: Proceedings* (Berlin: trafo verlag), pp. 330–34.

Schendler, Revan (2001) *Remembering State Socialism in the Czech Republic*, unpublished doctoral thesis, Essex University, UK.

Schenk, Sabine (2001) 'Re-Construction of Gender Stratification: About Men, Women and Families in Changing Employment Structures – the Case of East Germany', in Gabriele Jähnert, Jana Gohrisch, Daphne Hahn, Hildegard Maria Nickel, Iris Peinl and Katrin Schäfgen (eds) *Gender in Transition in Eastern and Central Europe: Proceedings* (Berlin: trafo verlag), pp. 214–30.

Schoepp-Schilling, Hanna Beate (2005) 'Comments on the Network for European Women's Rights Report on Political Participation and Citizenship, Paper delivered at the final conference of the Network of European Women's Rights (NEWR), Birmingham, 30 June.

Schöpflin, George (2000) *Nations, Identity and Power: The New Politics of Europe* (London: C. Hurst).

Scott, Joan W., Kaplan, Cora and Keates, Debra (eds) (1997) *Transitions, Environments, Translations: Feminisms in International Politics* (New York and London: Routledge).

Segal, Lynne (1999) *Why Feminism? Gender, Psychology, Politics* (Cambridge: Polity Press).

Segal, Lynne (1987) *Is the Future Female? Troubled Thoughts on Contemporary Feminism* (London: Virago).

Seifert, Ruth (1996) 'The Second Front: The Logic of Sexual Violence in Wars', *Women's Studies International Forum*, Special Issue on *Links across Differences: Gender, Ethnicity and Nationalism*, 19 (1–2): 35–44.

Sen, Amartya (1999) 'Women's Agency and Social Change', in Amartya Sen, *Development as Freedom* (Oxford: Oxford University Press), pp. 189–203.

Sen, Amartya (1995) 'Gender Inequality and Theories of Justice', in Martha Nussbaum and Jonathan Glover (eds) *Women, Culture and Development: A Study of Human Capabilities*, Study prepared for the World Institute for Development Economics Research (WIDER) of the United Nations University (UNU) (Oxford: Clarendon Press), pp. 259–73.

Sen, Amartya (1990) 'Gender and Cooperative Conflicts', in Irene Tinker (ed.) *Persistent Inequalities: Women and World Development* (New York: Oxford University Press), pp. 123–49.

Sen, Amartya (1981) *Poverty and Famines: An Essay on Entitlement and Deprivation* (Oxford: Clarendon Press).
Shohat, Ella (ed.) (1998) *Talking Visions: Multicultural Feminism in a Transnational Age* (New York: New Museum of Contemporary Art).
Sidorenko, Ewa (2000) 'Feminism? How Do You Spell It? Associability in the (Post)communist Order', Paper presented to the Gender Studies Conference, Polish Academy of Sciences, Warsaw.
Sieghart, Mary Ann (2003) 'A Fairer World for Women? We're on the Nursery Slopes', *The Times*, 3 January: 20.
Siemieńska, Renata (1998) 'Consequences of Economic and Political Changes for Women in Poland', in Jane S. Jaquette and Sharon L. Wolchik (eds) *Women and Democracy: Latin America and Central and Eastern Europe* (Baltimore, MD and London: The John Hopkins University Press), pp. 125–53.
Šiklová, Jiřina (1993) 'Are Women in Central and Eastern Europe Conservative?' in Nanette Funk and Magda Mueller (eds) *Gender Politics and Post-Communism: Reflections from Eastern Europe and the Former Soviet Union* (London and New York: Routledge), pp. 74–83.
Slapšak, Svetlana (1997) 'Nationalist and Women's Discourse in Post-Yugoslavia', in Joan W. Scott, Cora Kaplan and Debra Keates (eds) *Transitions, Environments, Translations: Feminisms in International Politics* (New York and London: Routledge), pp. 72–8.
Slavova, Kornelia (2006) 'After the Future: The Paradoxes of Postcommunism and Postmodernism', Paper presented to the conference on 'Migrating Feminisms', Central European University, Budapest, 27 January.
Sluga, Glenda (1996) 'Cold War Casualties: Ethnicity, Gender and the Writing of History', *Women's Studies International Forum*, Special Issue on *Links Across Differences: Gender, Ethnicity and Nationalism*, 19 (1–2): 75–86.
Šmejkalová, Jiřina (2001) 'Gender as an Analytical Category of Post-Communist Studies', in Gabriele Jähnert, Jana Gohrisch, Daphne Hahn, Hildegard Maria Nickel, Iris Peinl and Katrin Schäfgen (eds) *Gender in Transition in Eastern and Central Europe: Proceedings* (Berlin: trafo verlag), pp. 49–56.
Smiljanić, Natassja (2001) 'Women's Human Rights in War: Outside the Law?' in Gabriele Jähnert, Jana Gohrisch, Daphne Hahn, Hildegard Maria Nickel, Iris Peinl and Katrin Schäfgen (eds) *Gender in Transition in Eastern and Central Europe: Proceedings* (Berlin: trafo verlag), pp. 319–24.
Soley-Beltran, Patricia (2004) 'Modelling Femininity', *European Journal of Women's Studies*, 11 (3): 309–26.
Somers, Margaret R. (2005) 'Let Them Eat Social Capital: Socializing the Market versus Marketizing the Social', *Thesis Eleven*, 81 (May): 5–19.
Somers, Margaret R. (1995) 'Narrating and Naturalizing Civil Society and Citizenship Theory: The Place of Political Culture and the Public Sphere', *Sociological Theory*, 13 (3): 229–74.
Sperling, Valerie (2000) 'The New "Sexism": Images of Russian Women During the Transition', in Mark Field and Judyth Twigg (eds) *Russia's Torn Safety Nets: Health and Social Welfare During the Transition* (New York: St. Martin's Press), pp. 173–89.
Sperling, Valerie (1999) *Organizing Women in Contemporary Russia: Engendering Transition* (Cambridge: Cambridge University Press).

Sperling, Valerie (1998) 'Gender, Politics and the State during Russia's Transition Period', in Vicky Randall and Georgina Waylen (eds) *Gender, Politics and the State* (London and New York: Routledge), pp. 143–65.

Sperling, Valerie (1996) '"Democracy Without Women is Not Democracy": The Struggle over Women's Status and Identity during Russia's Transition', in Victoria E. Bonnell (ed.) *Identities in Transition: Eastern Europe and Russia After the Collapse of Communism* (Berkeley: University of California Press), pp. 45–67.

Sperling, Valerie, Ferree, Myra Marx and Risman, Barbara (2001) 'Constructing Global Feminism: Transnational Advocacy Networks and Russian Women's Activism', *Signs: Journal of Women in Culture and Society*, 26 (4): 1155–86.

Spurek, Sylwia (2002) *Women Parties Elections* (Łódź: Women's Rights Centre Foundation).

Šribar, Renata (2002) 'Lacking Integration: The Relationship Between the Women's Movement and Gender/Women's Studies in Transitional Slovenia', in Gabriele Griffin and Rosi Braidotti (eds) *Thinking Differently: A Reader in European Women's Studies* (London and New York: Zed Books), pp. 372–7.

Staudt, Kathleen (2003) 'Gender Mainstreaming: Conceptual Links to Institutional Machineries', in Shirin M. Rai (ed.) *Mainstreaming Gender, Democratizing the State? Institutional Machineries for the Advancement of Women* (Manchester and New York: Manchester University Press for the UN), pp. 40–66.

Steans, Jill (1998) *Gender and International Relations: An Introduction* (Cambridge and Oxford: Polity Press).

Steinhilber, Silke (2006) 'Gender and Post-Socialist Welfare States in Central Eastern Europe: Family Policy Reforms in Poland and the Czech Republic Compared', in Shireen Hassim and Shahra Razavi (eds) *Gender and Social Policy* (UNRISD/Geneva and London: Palgrave Macmillan).

Steinhilber, Silke (2002a) 'Women's Rights and Gender Equality in the EU Enlargement. An Opportunity for Progress', WIDE (Network Women in Development Europe), Briefing Paper, October.

Steinhilber, Silke (2002b) 'The Gender Impact of Pension Reforms: Case Studies of the Czech Republic, Hungary and Poland', Paper presented at the OECD conference on 'Practical Lessons in Pension Reform: Sharing the Experiences of Transition and OECD Countries', Warsaw, 27–28 May.

Steinhilber, Silke (2001) 'Gender Relations and Labour Market Transformation: Status Quo and Policy Responses in Central and Eastern Europe', in Gabriele Jähnert, Jana Gohrisch, Daphne Hahn, Hildegard Maria Nickel, Iris Peinl and Katrin Schäfgen (eds) *Gender in Transition in Eastern and Central Europe: Proceedings* (Berlin: trafo verlag), pp. 210–13.

Stenvoll, D. (2002) 'From Russia with Love? Newspaper Coverage of Cross-Border Prostitution in Northern Norway, 1990–2001', *European Journal of Women's Studies*, 9 (2): 143–62.

Stephenson, Mary-Ann (2004) *Gender and Democracy: What Works? Strategies to Increase Women's Representation* (Manchester: The British Council).

Stewart, Ann (1996) 'Should Women Give Up on the State? – The African Experience', in Shirin M. Rai and Geraldine Lievesley (eds) *Women and the State: International Perspectives* (London: Taylor & Francis), pp. 23–44.

Stiglmayer, Alexandra (ed.) (1994) *Mass Rape: The War Against Women in Bosnia-Herzegovina* (Lincoln, NE and London: University of Nebraska Press).
Stiglitz, Joseph E. (2002) *Globalization and Its Discontents* (London: Penguin Books).
Stratigaki, Maria (2005) 'Gender Mainstreaming vs Positive Action: An Ongoing Conflict in EU Gender Equality Policy', *European Journal of Women's Studies*, 12 (2): 165–86.
Sutherland, Margaret (1990) 'Women's Studies and the Social Position of Women in Eastern and Western Europe', ENWS (European Network for Women's Studies) Seminar Report, The Hague, November.
Szabó, Szilvia (ed.) (2003) *Gender Assessment of the Impact of EU Accession on the Status of Women in the Labour Market in CEE: National Study: Hungary* (Budapest: Social Innovation Foundation supported by UNIFEM and coordinated by Karat Coalition).
Szalai, Júlia (2005) 'Cultural Diversity or Social Disintegration? "Cultural Otherness" and Roma Rights in Contemporary Hungary', Paper presented to the conference on 'Gender Equality, Cultural Diversity: European Comparisons and Lessons', London, 27–28 May.
Szalai, Júlia (2000) 'From Informal Labor to Paid Occupations: Marketization from Below in Hungarian Women's Work', in Susan Gal and Gail Kligman (eds) *Reproducing Gender: Politics, Publics, and Everyday Life After Socialism* (Princeton, NJ: Princeton University Press), pp. 200–24.
Szalai, Júlia, John Keane and others (1990) 'Social Policy and Socialism: Citizenship, the Working Class, Women and Welfare: An East-West Dialogue' in Bob Deacon and Júlia Szalai (eds) *Social Policy in the New Eastern Europe: What Future for Socialist Welfare?* (Aldershot: Avebury), pp. 27–50.
Szalay, Kriszta (1996) 'Domestic Violence against Women in Hungary', in Chris Corrin (ed.) *Women in a Violent World: Feminist Analyses and Resistance Across 'Europe'* (Edinburgh: Edinburgh University Press), pp. 41–52.
Tarasiewicz, Małgorzata (1991) 'Women in Poland: Choices to be Made', *Feminist Review* Special Issue on *Shifting Territories: Feminism and Europe*, 39: 182–85.
Teschner, Julia (2000) 'Conflicting Conceptions of Feminism in United Germany', in Anna Bull, Hanna Diamond and Rosalind Marsh (eds) *Feminisms and Women's Movements in Contemporary Europe* (Basingstoke: Macmillan), pp. 194–210.
Teschner, Julia (1997) *The Demokratischer Frauenbund Deutschlands: Study of a GDR Mass Organisation in Transition*, unpublished doctoral dissertation, University of Liverpool, UK.
Thompson, Kenneth (1998/2001) *Moral Panics* (London and New York: Routledge).
Tinker, Irene (1999) 'Nongovernmental Organizations: An Alternative Power Base for Women?' in Mary K. Meyer and Elisabeth Prügl (eds) *Gender Politics in Global Governance* (Lanham, MD: Rowman and Littlefield), pp. 88–104.
Titkow, Anna (1993) 'Political Change in Poland: Cause, Modifier or Barrier to Gender Equality?' in Nanette Funk and Magda Mueller (eds) *Gender Politics and Post-Communism: Reflections from Eastern Europe and the Former Soviet Union* (New York and London: Routledge), pp. 253–56.
True, Jacqui (2003a) *Gender, Globalization, and Postsocialism: The Czech Republic After Communism* (New York and Chichester: Columbia University Press).
True, Jacqui (2003b) 'Mainstreaming Gender in Global Public Policy', *International Feminist Journal of Politics*, 5 (3): 368–96.

True, Jacqui (2000) 'Gendering Post-Socialist Transitions', in Marianne H. Marchand and Anne Sisson Runyan (eds) *Gender and Global Restructuring: Sightings, Sites and Resistances* (London and New York: Routledge), pp. 74–94.

True, Jacqui and Mintrom, Michael (2001) 'Transnational Networks and Policy Diffusion: The Case of Gender Mainstreaming', *International Studies Quarterly*, 45: 27–57.

True, Jacqueline, Shore, Marci, and Vesinova, Eva (eds) (1999) *Gender and Re-Membering Communism: Narrative/Archive/Trace* (Tokyo: Sylff – Ryoichi Sasakawa Young Leaders Fellowship Fund Program), Working Papers, no. 10.

Ugrešić, Dubravka (1998a) *The Culture of Lies: Antipolitical Essays*, transl. Celia Hawkesworth (London: Phoenix House).

Ugrešić, Dubravka (1998b) 'Nice People Don't Mention Such Things', *European Journal of Women's Studies*, 5 (3–4): 297–310; also in Ugresic,1998a, pp. 236–51.

Ule, Mirjana and Rener, Tanja (1997) 'Nationalism and Gender in Postsocialist Societies: Is Nationalism Female?' in Tanya Renne (ed.) *Ana's Land: Sisterhood in Eastern Europe* (Boulder, CO: Westview Press), pp. 220–33.

United Nations (UN) (2000) *The World's Women: Trends and Statistics*, Department of Economic and Social Affairs, Social Statistics and Indicators Series K, no. 16 (New York: United Nations).

United Nations (UN) (1995), 'Productive Employment', Chapter 3 in UN, *Women in a Changing Global Economy: 1994 Survey on the Role of Women in Development* (New York: United Nations), pp. 48–77.

UN CEDAW (1979) United Nations Convention on the Elimination of All Forms of Discrimination Against Women (New York: UN).

United Nations Development Programme (UNDP) and National Commission for Statistics Romania (2000) *Women and Men in Romania*, Bucharest.

United Nations Department of Economic and Social Affairs, Division for the Advancement of Women (1999) *World Survey on the Role of Women in Development: Globalization, Gender and Work* (New York: United Nations).

UNICEF (1999) *Women in Transition: The MONEE Project* – CEE/CIS/Baltics, Regional Monitoring Report no. 6 (Florence: UNICEF).

United Nations Research Institute for Social Development (UNRISD) (2005) *Gender Equality: Striving for Justice in an Unequal World* (Paris: UNRISD/GPR/05/1).

van Hoven-Iganski, Bettina (2000) *Made in the GDR: The Changing Geographies of Women in the Post-Socialist Rural Society in Mecklenburg-West Pommerania*, Nederlandse Geografische Studies 262 (Utrecht: Groningen).

Verdery, Kahterine (1996) *What Was Socialism and What Comes Next?* (Princeton, NJ: Princeton University Press).

Verloo, Mieke (2002) 'The Development of Gender Mainstreaming as a Political Concept for Europe', Keynote Address to International Gender Mainstreaming Conference, Leipzig, 6–8 September.

Věšinová-Kalivodová, Eva (2005) 'Czech Society in Between the Waves', *European Journal of Women's Studies* 12(4): 421–36.

Věšinová-Kalivodová, Eva and Šiklová, Jiřina (2001) 'The Status of Women's and Gender Studies at Universities in Post-Communist Countries: The Example of the Czech Republic. Experiences from the First Ten Years After the Change', in Gabriele Jähnert, Jana Gohrisch, Daphne Hahn, Hildegard Maria Nickel, Iris Peinl and Katrin Schäfgen (eds) *Gender in Transition in Eastern and Central Europe: Proceedings* (Berlin: trafo verlag), pp. 339–44.

Vogel, Ursula (1991) 'Is Citizenship Gender-Specific?' in Ursula Vogel and Michael Moran (eds) *The Frontiers of Citizenship* (Basingstoke and London: Macmillan), pp. 58–85.

WAD (2002) *NGO Advocacy – Advocacy NGOs*, Summary of Conclusions of a Report on Women's and Feminist NGOs in Albania, Bulgaria, Croatia and Romania.

Wade, Robert (1990) *Governing the Market: Economic Theory and the Role of Government in East Asian Industrialization* (Princeton, NJ: Princeton University Press).

Walby, Sylvia (2003) 'The Myth of the Nation-State: Theorizing Society and Polities in a Global Era', *Sociology*, 37 (3): 529–46.

Walsh, Martha (1998) 'Mind the Gap: Where Feminist Theory Failed to Meet Development Practice – A Missed Opportunity in Bosnia and Herzegovina', *European Journal of Women's Studies*, Special Issue on *The Idea of Europe*, 5 (3–4): 329–43.

Waters, Elizabeth (1991) 'The Female Form in Soviet Political Iconography, 1917–32', in Barbara Evans Clements, Barbara Alpern Engel and Christine D. Worobec (eds) *Russia's Women: Accommodation, Resistance, Transformation* (Berkeley and Oxford: University of California Press), pp. 225–42.

Waters, Elizabeth and Posadskaya, Anastasia (1995) 'Democracy Without Women is No Democracy: Women's Struggles in Postcommunist Russia', in Amrita Basu (ed.) *The Challenge of Local Feminisms: Women's Movements in Global Perspective* (Boulder,CO, San Francisco and Oxford: Westview Press), pp. 351–73.

Watson, Peggy (2001) 'Gender and Politics in Postcommunism', in Gabriele Jähnert, Jana Gohrisch, Daphne Hahn, Hildegard Maria Nickel, Iris Peinl and Katrin Schäfgen (eds) *Gender in Transition in Eastern and Central Europe: Proceedings* (Berlin: trafo verlag), pp. 37–48.

Watson, Peggy (2000a) 'Re-thinking Transition: Globalism, Gender and Class', *International Feminist Journal of Politics*, 2 (2): 185–213.

Watson, Peggy (2000b) 'Politics, Policy and Identity: EU Eastern Enlargement and East-West Differences', *Journal of European Public Policy*, 7 (3): 369–84.

Watson, Peggy (1997) 'Civil Society and the Politics of Difference in Eastern Europe', in Joan W. Scott, Cora Kaplan and Debra Keates (eds) *Transitions, Environments, Translations: Feminisms in International Politics* (London and New York: Routledge), pp. 21–9.

Watson, Peggy (1995) 'Explaining Rising Mortality Among Men in Eastern Europe', *Social Science and Medicine*, 41 (7): 923–34.

Watson, Peggy (1993) 'The Rise of Masculinism in Eastern Europe', *New Left Review*, 198: 71–82.

Waylen, Georgina (1998) 'Gender, Feminism and the State: An Overview', in Vicky Randall and Georgina Waylen (eds) *Gender, Politics, and the State* (London and New York: Routledge), pp. 1–17.

Waylen, Georgina and Rai, Shirin M. (eds) (2004) 'Gender, Governance and Globalization: An Overview', Introduction to Special Issue of *International Feminist Journal of Politics*, 6 (4): 553–7.

Weedon, Chris (1987) *Feminist Practice and Poststructuralist Theory* (Oxford: Blackwell).

White, Anne (2000) 'New Mothers' Campaigning Organizations in Russia', in Anna Bull, Hanna Diamond and Rosalind Marsh (eds) *Feminisms and Women's Movements in Contemporary Europe* (Basingstoke: Macmillan), pp. 211–27.

White, Stephen, Batt, Judy and Lewis, Paul (eds) (1993) *Developments in East European Politics* (Basingstoke: Macmillan).
Więckowska, Katarzyna (2001) 'Universal Woman – Questions of Identity, Representation and Difference', in Gabriele Jähnert, Jana Gohrisch, Daphne Hahn, Hildegard Maria Nickel, Iris Peinl and Katrin Schäfgen (eds) *Gender in Transition in Eastern and Central Europe: Proceedings* (Berlin: trafo verlag), pp. 241–45.
Wolchik, Sharon L. (2000) 'Reproductive Policies in the Czech and Slovak Republics', in Susan Gal and Gail Kligman (eds) *Reproducing Gender: Politics, Publics, and Everyday Life After Socialism* (Princeton, NJ: Princeton University Press), pp. 58–91.
Wolchik, Sharon L. (1998) 'Gender and the Politics of Transition in the Czech Republic and Slovakia', in Jane S. Jaquette and Sharon L. Wolchik (eds) *Women and Democracy: Latin America and Central and Eastern Europe* (Baltimore, MD and London: The John Hopkins University Press), pp. 153–84.
Women's/ Gender Studies Association of Countries in Transition Electronic Library, accessible at http://www.zenskestudie.edu.yu/wgsact/electronic-library.html
Women in Black (2001) 'Women in Black', *Peace News*, 2443: 22–25.
Women in Black (1998) *Women for Peace* (Belgrade: Pink Press).
Woodward, Kathryn (ed.) (1997) *Identity and Difference* (London: Sage with the Open University).
Young, Brigitte (1999) 'The East and West German Women's Movements and the German State', in Brigitte Young, *Triumph of the Fatherland: German Unification and the Marginalization of Women* (Ann Arbor, MI: University of Michigan Press), pp. 199–221.
Young, Kate (1993) *Planning Development with Women* (London: Macmillan).
Yuval-Davis (1999) 'The "Multi-Layered Citizen": Citizenship in the Age of "Glocalization" ', *International Feminist Journal of Politics*, 1 (1): 119–37.
Yuval-Davis, Nira (1998) 'Beyond Differences: Women, Empowerment and Coalition Politics', in Nickie Charles and Helen Hintjens (eds) *Gender, Ethnicity and Political Ideologies* (London: Routledge), pp. 168–89.
Yuval-Davis, Nira (1997a) *Gender and Nation* (London, Thousand Oaks and New Delhi: Sage Publications).
Yuval-Davis, Nira (1997b) 'Women, Citizenship and Difference', *Feminist Review*, Special Issue on *Citizenship: Pushing the Boundaries*, 57: 4–27.
Yuval-Davis, Nira (1996) 'Women and the Biological Reproduction of "The Nation" ', *Women's Studies International Forum*, Special Issue on *Links across Differences: Gender, Ethnicity and Nationalism*, 19 (1–2): 17–24.
Yuval-Davis, Nira and Werbner, Pnina (eds) (1999) *Women, Citizenship and Difference* (London and New York: Zed Books).
Zajović, Staša (2005) 'Women in Black: War, Feminism and Antimilitarism', in Stasa Zajović (ed.) *Women for Peace* (Belgrade: Women in Black), pp. 13–21.
Zajović, Staša (1997) 'Nationalism and Serb Women', in Tanya Renne (ed.) *Ana's Land: Sisterhood in Eastern Europe* (Boulder, CO: Westview Press), pp. 169–72.
Žarkov, Dubravka (1997) 'Pictures of the Wall of Love: Motherhood, Womanhood and Nationhood in Croatian Media', *European Journal of Women's Studies*, 4 (3): 305–39.
Žarkov, Dubravka (1995) 'Gender, Orientialism and the History of Ethnic Hatred in the Former Yugoslavia', in Helga Lutz, Ann Phoenix and Nira Yuval-Davis

(eds) *Crossfires: Nationalism, Racism and Gender in Europe* (London and East Haven, CT: Pluto Press), pp. 105–20.

Zherebkina, Irina (2001) ' "Who is Afraid of Feminism" in Ukraine? How Feminism is Possible as a Post-Soviet Political Project?' in Gabriele Jähnert, Jana Gohrisch, Daphne Hahn, Hildegard Maria Nickel, Iris Peinl and Katrin Schäfgen (eds) *Gender in Transition in Eastern and Central Europe: Proceedings* (Berlin: trafo verlag), pp. 142–47.

Zhurzhenko, Tatiana (2001a) 'Free Market Ideology and New Women's Identities in Post-Socialist Ukraine', *European Journal of Women's Studies*, 8 (1): 29–49.

Zhurzhenko, Tatiana (2001b) '(Anti)National Feminisms, Post-Soviet Gender Studies: Women's Voices of Transition and Nation-Building in Ukraine' *Österreichische Osthefte*, 43 (4): 503–24.

Zhurzhenko, Tatiana (2001c) 'Ukrainian Feminism(s): Between Nationalist Myth and Anti-Nationalist Critique', Institut für die Wissenschaften vom Menschen (Institute for Human Sciences), Vienna, IWM Working Paper no. 4/2001.

Zielińska, Eleonora (2000) 'Between Ideologies, Politics and Common Sense: The Discourse of Reproductive Rights in Poland', in Susan Gal and Gail Kligman (eds) *Reproducing Gender: Politics, Publics, and Everyday Life after Socialism* (Princeton, NJ: Princeton University Press), pp. 23–57.

Index

abortions, right to abortion, 54, 67, 94, 96, 107, 109, 110, 112–18 *see also* reproductive rights
affirmative action, 26, 35–36, 57, 59, 168, 181
agency, 62, 84, 106, 143, 179–86
Alvarez, Sonia, 75
Amnesty International, 122
Asia-Pacific region
transnational feminism, 87
Austria, 140
authoritarian regimes, authoritarianism, 66, 137

Bában, Adriana, 114
Baltic States, 33
Baranskaya, Natalya
A Week Like any Other, 126
Barendt, Regina, 34, 90, 177
Beijing Platform for Action, 24, 32, 36, 82, 87, 88–89
Belarus
abortions, 114
femininity, 137
Belgrade
Autonomous Women's Centre against Sexual Violence, 86
homosexuality, 111
violence against women, 121
Women in Black, 85–86
Berehynia, 136–7
Berlin Wall, fall of, 1, 15, 33, 49, 118, 124
'birth strike', 106–8
Bosnia-Herzegovina, 13, 189
donor priorities and economic restructuring, mismatch, 84
Medica Women's Therapy Centre, Zenica, 86, 93
violence against women, 120
war, 13
women's NGOs, 196n12
Žena BiH, 86
BRIDGE, 24
Broad, Robin, 6, 7

Bulgaria
abortions, 113–14
Communist Party, 77
Democratic Union of Women (DUW), 77
European Union membership, 16, 33, 200n2
female representation in politics, 51, 55
gender unequal regime, 95
gender wage gap, 202n12
media images of femininity, 132, 135
National Assembly, 177
private property rights, 163
quotas, 58
sexual harassment, 201n8
social policy change, 167
Socialist Party, 77
'Women Can Do It', 195n8
women's employment, 151, 154
women's movement, 182
women's non-governmental organizations (NGOs), 75–76, 89, 195n8
Bulgarian Gender Research Foundation (BGRF), 58, 72
Bulgarian National Public Opinion Centre, 58, 201n8, 201n9
Bulgarian Women's Association, 76
Busheikin, Laura, 3

capabilities, theory of, 172, 178–86
capitalism, *see* market
'care in the community', 100, 175
career and motherhood, choice, 129
Catholic Church, 79, 109, 110, 114–15, 117, 128, 141
CEDAW, 15, 57, 115, 120, 180–81, 195n7, 199n4, 199n9, 199n11, 199n12
Central and Eastern Europe, 1, 2, 3, 16, 19, 24, 124, 149, 190
abortion rate, 113
childcare, 106, 108
civil society, 30–31, 67, 172, 173

Central and Eastern Europe – *continued*
consumerism, 142
cultural differences, 187–88
democratization, 48, 179
economy, 147, 161
family, 100
female representation in politics/
  legislature, 26, 39, 40, 45, 193n4
feminists/feminism, 4, 25, 62, 64,
  69–73
  within global context, 87–90
gender relations, 21, 29, 33–34,
  36–37, 48, 49, 62, 74, 125
gender wage gap, 160–61
integration into global market, 127
labour market, 101, 162
lack of political will, 41
market fundamentalism, 7, 179
media images of femininity, 135
organizational change, 68
political dimensions as a
  pre-condition for EU
  accession, 47
political, economic and social
  structure, 94
privatization, 6
prostitutes, 2
public-private divide, 97, 100–1
quotas, 57, 59
social policy 110
transformation process, 5, 8, 10, 15,
  21–22, 26, 32, 42, 43, 65,
  171–72, 180, 186, 187–88,
  192n7, 197n3
women, 34, 140
women's employment, 151
women's non-governmental
  organizations (NGOs), 31, 88,
  173, 189
women, worker-mother-citizen,
  triple role, 125
Central and Eastern European
  Network for Gender Issues, 59
Chamberlayne, Prue, 68
childcare and childrearing
  responsibilities, 27, 67, 74, 96, 99,
    101–4, 108, 129, 181
  demographic shift and, 104–8
  privatization of, 167
CIDA-Canada, 86
CIS region, 146
citizens, social roles and
  responsibilities, 9

citizenship, 5, 7, 8, 14–16, 20, 23, 46,
  123, 188
  entire charge & agency or
    capabilities, rights or
    entitlements, 178–86
  gendered nature, 122
  rights, 28
  shift in conceptions, 100
  status, 29
civic republicanism, 179
civil rights, 22, 179, 183, 187
civil society, 11, 15, 18, 41, 45, 48, 82,
  84–85, 90, 93, 109, 145, 172, 176
  activism/mobilization, 5, 8, 16, 17,
    21, 45, 49, 60, 66, 81, 82, 98, 174
  anti-politics, 65
  degradation of concept, 8
  discursive focus on, 46–47
  four types, 66–67
  'gap', 18, 32–33, 82, 173–75
  and gender, 64–69
  and language of empowerment,
    172–75
  political strategy, 30–33
  'projectization', 84
  'trap', 18, 31–32, 174, 177
class differentials, 2, 95, 111, 128, 130,
  146, 171–73
coalition politics, 20, 93, 189
Cockburn, Cynthia, 189, 203n4
Cold War, 1, 4, 19, 33, 65, 69, 124,
  125, 161, 181
collective action, collectivism, 45, 68,
  126–27
commodification, 186
communism, communists, 6, 25, 29,
  141–43
  and gender differentiation, 50
comparative advantage, 158
competition, 147, 190
conscience, 98, 109
consensus, 52
consumerism, consumerist culture,
  19, 127, 128, 132, 133, 140,
  142–43, 145, 171
continuity, element of, 47, 197n3
contraceptives, access and use, 110,
  113, 114
Convention on the Elimination of All
  Forms of Discrimination Against
  Women (CEDAW), 15, 57, 115,
  120, 180–81, 195n7, 199n4,
  199n9, 199n11, 199n12

convergence theory, 22
cooperation, 60
Cosmopolitan, 133, 134, 142
Council of Europe, 45
Croatia, Croatian
  abortion law, 115–16
  B.a.B.e. (Be active, Be emancipated), 86
  Catholic Church, influence, 114
  female political representation, 55, 122, 195n8
  homosexuality, 111
  HDZ (Hrvatska Demokratska Zajednica), 115, 123
  National Programme for Demographic Renewal, 115
  women's employment/ unemployment, 151–54
  Women's Network, 116
cultural, culture, 70, 90, 97, 184
  changes, 43, 48
  continuity, 121
  devaluation of labour, 165
  of female sacrifice, 184
  identity/distinctiveness, 13, 121, 187
  otherness, 29
  politics, 188
  traditions, 63
Cyprus, 189
Czech Republic
  abortions, 113
  anti-discriminatory legislation, 156
  childcare, 105
  contraceptives, use of, 113
  Czech Union of Women, 76
  domestic labour, 102
  domestic violence, 119
  European Union membership, 192n8, 200n2
  female representation in politics, 45, 51, 52, 53, 55, 58, 193n4, 195n8
  feminism, 63
  funding sources, 88
  gender bias/inequality, 39, 146, 150, 153, 168, 201n12
  Gender Studies, 39
  Government Council for Equal Opportunities for Men and Women, 53
  Labour Law, 1999, 34
  market economy, 158
  media images of femininity, 133–35
  Ministry of Labour and Social Affairs, 102
  mix of neo-liberal and social democratic elements of reform, 22
  National Training Fund, 39
  Permanent Commission on the Family and Equal Opportunities in the Chamber of Deputies, 34
  Prague Mothers, 78
  privatization, 156
  quotas for women, 58
  Social Democratic Party, 58
  social policy regime, 22, 167
  South Bohemian Mothers, 78
  women's employment status/unemployment, 149, 151–54, 157, 159–61, 163–64, 200n6
  women's non-governmental organizations (NGO), 39, 45, 75, 76, 85, 89
  Women's Shadow Cabinet, 53
Czechoslovakia:
  Charta, 77, 65
  dissolution, 51
  gender unequal regime, 95

Dahlerup, Drude and Freidenvall, Lenita, 26
Daskalova, Krassimira, 136, 182
Davidson, Julia O'Connell, 3
decision-making process, 14, 53, 82
democracy, 7, 8, 13, 14, 19, 25, 30, 32, 50, 65, 78, 87, 94, 96, 99, 109–10, 118, 122, 123, 137, 171, 176, 179, 182, 189–90
democratization, 7, 8, 9, 11, 14, 17, 42, 46, 48, 50–51, 62, 81, 93, 136, 144, 179, 180, 188
demographic shift and childcare, 104–108
de-politicization, 126
deregulation, 6
de-skilling, 165
development, centrality of gender, 87
discrimination, 10, 13, 22, 26, 74, 79, 123, 134, 136, 145, 169, 182
  see also gender, women
diversity, 86

divorce, 118
Dölling, Irane, 73, 126, 182
domestic labour, 96
  and childcare, socialization, 99
  gendered division, 101–104, 122, 147
domestic sphere, state intervention, 98
domestic violence, see violence against women
domesticity, 126
donor dependency, 31–32, 82, 84–85
donor focus, 62, 88, 92, 174
donors and recipients, relationship, 82
Drakulil, Slavenka, 12
Duhaček, Daša, 71

East-to-West migration, 3
East-West:
  divide/relations, 1–3, 73, 90, 124–25, 161
  feminist dialogue, 62–64, 69–73, 92, 189
Eastern Europe, see Central and Eastern Europe
economic reforms, 6, 19, 47, 48
economic restructuring/transformation, 6, 12, 16, 19, 22, 51, 62, 69, 94, 127, 145–48, 152, 165, 178, 188
  disadvantaging women, 107
  donors' influence, 84
  gender inequality in/male bias, 5, 148–51
  industrial to post-industrial, 10
economic rights, 73, 179, 180, 181, 183, 186
economy, economic issues, 3, 5, 8–9, 22–23, 27, 36, 83, 122, 166
  market-based, 119
  planned, 118
  pre-dominance over politics, 47, 51
egalitarianism, 13, 22, 95, 125, 127
Elle, 133
Elson, Diāne, 149, 181 184
empowerment, 20, 42, 69, 137
  civil society initiatives, 172–75
entitlements, theory of, 20, 26–27, 30, 67, 69, 148, 178–86
  failure, 183, 184
environmental degradation/protection, 6, 76, 78
equality of opportunity, 24

essentialism, 132
Estonia
  abortions, 114
  European Union membership, 192n8, 200n2
  gender wage gap, 202n12
  women's employment status, 151, 153
ethnic conflicts, ethnicity, 2, 22, 78–79, 111, 112, 123, 146, 172–73, 187, 203n4
European Commission, 35
European Court of Human Rights, 23, 29, 176, 181
European Court of Justice, 23, 27, 176
European Parliament, 26, 59, 197n12
  Women's Committee, 90
European Union (EU), 13, 15, 17, 22, 48, 53, 55, 59, 65, 84, 85, 88, 92, 123, 164, 172, 174, 176, 177–78
  abortion rates, 113, 117, 168
  dialogue on civil society, 8
  enlargement, 2, 5, 16, 25, 27–28, 71, 89, 90, 148, 161, 172, 189
  Equal Opportunities Unit, 35
  focus on trafficking, 3
  gender equality directives, 18, 21, 23, 25, 33–40, 85
  and gender mainstreaming, 33–40

family, 9, 65, 78, 132, 145, 164–65, 187
  altered social policy models, 99–104
  breakdown, 99
  dislocation, 119
  economic function, 163
  and friendship networks, 11
  gender relations in, 96–97
  gendered division of labour, 101–103
  social arrangements, 18
  values, 110
  women's role, 96–97
female asylum seekers, 30
female bodies, use to sell commodities, 134
female labour force participation, 11, 145–47, 151, 163–65
female political participation/representation, 17, 21, 23, 25–27, 33, 39–40, 48–50, 55, 60, 67, 81, 122, 178

femininity, 5, 9, 10, 13–14, 19, 70, 77, 97, 99, 101, 110, 187
  hegemonic, 139–43
  and maternity, 141
feminists, feminism, 4, 17, 22–24, 29, 48, 62–64, 75, 80, 86, 92, 189, 94, 123, 188
  East-European, within global context, 87–90
  in East-West dialogue, 62–64, 69–73, 92, 189
  feminist 'foremothers', 72
  NGOization of, 31, 80, 84, 174
  prospects for citizenship, 14–16
fertility decline, 106–108
Fodor, Éva, 50
Ford Foundation, 117
Foucault, Michel, 136
Fraser, Nancy, 28, 188
Fuszara, Małgorzata, 48, 49

Gal, Susan, 68
Gal, Susan and Kligman, Gail, 109
Gapova, Elena, 137
Gay Pride, 110–111
gender, gender issues, 2–4, 10–12, 14, 18, 26, 29, 53–56, 78, 90, 99, 120–21, 123, 128, 130, 142, 146, 149, 171
  balance, 43, 72
  and civil society, 64–69
  discrimination and male bias, 50, 54, 56, 74, 169, 184
  and domestic labour, 101–104
  equality/equity, 4–5, 7, 16–20, 23, 33–36, 40–41, 43, 47, 49, 55–56, 66, 75, 80, 84, 89, 97, 103, 105, 110, 118, 130, 143, 145, 171–72, 190
  equitable citizenship, strategies for, 23–27
  hierarchy, 9, 94, 98, 100, 101, 110, 127
  identities, 79, 166
  inequalities, 5, 62, 68, 77, 91, 96, 168, 173, 178, 187–88
  in labour market access, 151–56, 159–60
  justice, 81, 83, 122, 172, 187, 188

  mainstreaming, 16–17, 21, 23–25, 29, 32, 47, 80
    European Union enlargement and, 33–40
    political limitations, 37
    in mainstream politics, 47–56
    from margin to centre, the quota debate, 56–59
  and national identity, 136–39
  relations, 19, 64, 73, 71, 74, 98, 132, 136, 140, 147
  continuity and change, 95–96
  roles, 74, 94, 103–104, 119, 128, 131
  as a social determinant, 80
  stereotypes, 9–11, 127
  as a structuring dynamic of transformation, 6
  in transformation/transforming gender, 8–12
  wage gap, 30, 156, 160–61, 168
Gender and Economic Justice in European Accession and Integration, 89
Gender Studies as an academic discipline, 72
gendered discourses, 137
gendered entitlements, 184
gendered nationalism, 12–14, 190
gendered symbolism, 187
Gerhard, Ute, 35
German-German dialogue, 70
Germany
  abortion issue/law, 108–109, 115
  domestic labour, 103
  Equal Opportunities Officers, 80
  family, 101
  female political representation, decline, 49–50
  gender discrimination, 166
  gender mainstreaming, 35–36
  market economy, 159
  Unification, 1, 14, 40, 147, 155, 158
  violence against women, 120
  women's emancipation, 129–30
Germany, East
  Communist party, 80
  economic restructuring, 150
  Independent Women's Association (UFV), 79–80
  Party of Democratic Socialism (PDS), 80
  transformation process, 147

Germany, East – *continued*
  women's employment status/
    unemployment, 155, 159–60,
    163–66
  Women for Peace, 198n4
  women, 'losers of unification', 158
Germany, West
  occupational segregation,
    158–59, 166
  'glamour puss' and the market,
    131–36
global capital accumulation, 7
global citizenship, 176
global development theory and
  practice, 6
global economy, 168
globalization, 5, 7, 22, 28, 29, 33, 71,
  89, 147, 189
'glocalization', 190
grassroots activism/movements, 41,
  49, 66, 73, 74–87, 92, 173, 177
Grewal, Inderpal and Kaplan, Caren, 87
Grunberg, Laura, 66

Harlequin, 133, 134
Havel, Václav, 46
Havelková, Hana, 4, 11, 71
heterosexuality, 125
Hobsbawm, Eric, 95
Holocaust, 117
Hollywood, 140
home-workers, international
  networking, 87
homogeneity, 136, 139, 187, 189
homophobia, 111, 125
homosexuality, 110–12, 138
housewife-mothers, 101
human agency, 178–79, 182
human rights, 7, 8, 28, 30, 48, 62, 86,
  109, 118, 123, 172, 179, 180–82
Hungarian Feminist Network, 75, 80
Hungarian Socialist Party, 58
Hungary
  abortion law, 113
  Communist Party, 50
  Democratic Opposition, 65
  domestic labour, 103
  domestic violence, 119
  demographic shift and childcare,
    104–105
  European Union membership,
    192n8, 200n2
  female representation in politics,
    45, 52, 55, 193n4, 194n3,
    195n6, 196n8
  feminism, 63, 80
  gender differentiation and male
    bias, 50, 95, 150, 153, 168,
    202n12
  gendered labour market
    relations, 146
  homophobia, 125
  quotas, 58
  social policy change, 26, 167
  social welfare regime, 28–29, 166
  women's employment status/
    unemployment, 151, 153–54,
    164–65
  women's non-governmental
    organizations (NGO),
    74–76, 89

identity, identities, 1, 2, 5, 9, 15, 19,
  77, 78, 95, 126–27, 135, 137,
  139–40, 142, 145
  differences and the capacity for
    joint political strategies, 93,
    186–90
immiseration process, 154
individual autonomy, 12, 66, 109
individualism, individuality, 126–27,
  132, 134, 141
inequalities, inequality, 6, 8, 30, 35,
  145, 186
information technology (IT), 10, 149
institutional structures, 44, 69
international agencies, 8, 82
International Confederation of Trade
  Unions (ICFTU), 156
international donor agencies, 32,
  46, 71
*International Feminist Journal of
  Politics*, 29
international human rights law, 176
International Labour Organization
  (ILO), 10, 83, 148, 151, 154, 162,
  164, 168, 176
International Monetary Fund (IMF), 6,
  22, 89, 149, 167, 176
International War Crimes Tribunal, 181
intra-household conflict, 66
Italy
  abortion policy, 115
  Catholic Church, 114, 115

Jaruga-Nowacka, Izabela, 37
Jezerska, Zuzana, 41

Kaczynska, Elżbieta, 71
Karat Coalition, 29, 31, 32, 34, 36, 59, 88–92, 152, 161–62, 175, 177–78, 189
Kay, Rebecca, 84
Keynesian-Westphalian frame, 28
kinship and friendship networks, 66, 68
Klaus, Václav, 149
Koch, Father Jerzy, 111
Konrad, György, 46
Korać, Maja, 121
Korea
   violence against women, 14, 120
Kosor, Jadranka, 116
Kosovo
   donor priorities and economic restructuring, mismatch, 84
Kováčová, Emilia, 164
Kramer, Anne-Marie, 117–18
Kubik, Jan, 66

La Strada, Poland, 87
labour market, 3, 16, 23, 26, 34, 36, 81, 128, 149, 169, 177
   female success, 126
   gender inequality/gendered division, 5, 10–11, 54, 76, 103, 145–48, 150, 151–56, 167, 168
   impact of social policy changes, 166–68
   impact of transformation, 144
   public sphere, 129
   unregulated, 101
labour migration, 2, 83
Laclau, Ernesto, 202n3
Lang, Sabine, 80, 84
Latin America: democratic regimes, 78
Latvia
   European Union membership, 192n8, 200n2
   women activists, 25
   women's employment, 151, 152
Lenin, Vladimir I., 2
lesbian rights, 30
lesbian, gay, bisexual and transgender people (LGBT), 111, 172
Lewis, Jane, 148
liberal democratic theory,
   see democracy

liberalization, 6, 17, 180
life expectancy, 155
Lister, Ruth, 175–76, 178–79, 182, 188, 202n2
Lisyutkina, Larissa, 97, 128
Lithuania
   contraceptives, use of, 113
   European Union membership, 192n8, 200n2
   female representation in politics, 54, 55, 195n6
   Ombudsperson for Gender Equality, 39
   Sex Discrimination Act (2006), 39
   women's unemployment, 152, 153
lobbying, 41, 55–56, 59, 86, 89, 91, 120, 175
Lohmann, Kinga, 31, 90

Macedonia
   elections, 196n12
   Women's Lobby, 196n12
Mackie, Vera, 72, 87
Macková, Darina, 51
male bias in economic restructuring, 148–51, 157
male-breadwinner model, 9, 54, 100, 108, 164, 166, 184, 186
male culture, 50, 100, 112, 122, 128, 143
male-dominance in political bodies/state/legislatures, 10, 49, 55, 82, 92, 96, 110
Man of Iron, (1981), 141
Man of Marble (1977), 141
marginalization, 22, 44, 52, 54, 77, 81
market, market forces, 9, 47, 65, 127, 131–36, 147, 171
   capitalism, 5, 89, 127, 143, 145, 158, 168
   economy, 6, 147
   fundamentalism, 7
   privileged over state, 99, 144
   as the sole regulator of society, 8, 145, 183
   and state, imbalance, 32
marketization, 7, 10, 11, 14, 22, 42, 73, 81, 105, 119, 136, 149, 179, 180, 188
   and occupational segregation, 156–63
   as privatization, 6

Marody, Mira and Giza-Połeszczuk, Anna 128–29, 131–32, 136, 142
Marosan, György, 45
Marxist feminism, 71
masculinity, 5, 9–10, 13–14, 50, 94, 97, 99, 101, 110–11, 122, 131–32, 136, 137, 139, 142, 171, 187
material values, materialism, 1, 99
Matka Krolow (*Mother of the Kings*), 142
McMahon, Patrice, 74
Mecklenburg-Westpommerania labour market, 166
media, 2, 16, 54, 79, 107, 121, 125
  images of femininity, 19, 131–33, 135, 139–40
  and market realities, 126–29
Medica Women's Therapy Centre, Zenica, 86, 93
Michnik, Adam, 46
Mickiewicz, Adam, 140
migration, migrants, 21
  forced, 83
  illegal, 3
  treatment in receiving countries, 3
  women, rights, 30
militarism, 86, 120, 121
Mills & Boon, 199n1
Miroiu, Mihaela, 24
mistrust, 3, 70
Mohanty, Chandra Talpade, 4
Molyneux, Maxine, 74, 173
moral issues, morality, 12, 99, 117, 126
'moral panic', 2, 3, 107
Morgner, Irmtraud
  Tightrope, 126, 130
Moscow Centre for Gender Studies, 72, 73, 88
motherhood, 19, 78, 115, 129, 146–47
  dogged support for, 77–78
  feminization, 112
Motrych, Kateryna, 137
Mouffe, Chantal, 202n3
multiculturalism, 189
'myths of transition', 62, 107

nation, nation state, 5, 7
  as extended family, 112
  role in political representation, 27–30
  symbolic representation, 13–14, 79, 95, 128, 135, 137
national identity and gender, 13, 112, 136–39

National Women's Machineries, 24, 39–41, 178
nationalism, 14, 95, 112, 120, 122, 141–42, 203n4
negative political freedom, 30
neo-liberal market model, 5, 7, 9, 26, 30, 51, 58, 93, 97, 99, 100, 102, 145, 168, 171, 180, 183, 188
  negative impact, 6–7
  see also Washington Consensus, International Monetary Fund (IMF), World Bank
Network of East-West Women (NEWW), 88, 89, 111
New Left politics, 48
new social movements, 78
Newly Independent States-United States (NIS-US) Women's Consortium, 88
Nickel, Hildegard Maria, 169
Nicolaescu, Madalina, 133
non-governmental organizations (NGOs), women's networks, 15, 18, 25, 28–29, 30, 31–32, 34, 36–39, 45–46, 48, 49, 55, 59–60, 71, 72, 74–76, 80–82, 84, 88–90, 119, 173–75, 177–78
  donor dependence/focus, 62, 84–85
  NGOization of feminism, 80
  professionalization, 81
  see also civil society, Karat Coalition
non-violence, 86
Novikova, Irina, 73
Nowicka, Wanda, 117
Nussbaum, Martha, 179, 184–86

Oates-Indruchová, Libora, 126–27
occupational segregation, 19, 30, 168
  and marketization, 156–63
Open Society Institute, 86
  Network Women's Programme of the (OSI/NWP), 88
openness, 69
oral history accounts, 79
Organization for Economic Cooperation and Development (OECD), 170
organizational change, 68
Ostrowska, Elżbieta, 140, 142
Other otherness, 1, 2, 3, 28, 122, 124

Papanek, Hana, 184
Papil, Žarana, 138–39
paradigm shift, 7
parenthood, a disadvantage in job market, 154–55
patriarchy, 11, 55, 77, 100, 123, 125, 127, 134, 142, 177, 182
Paukert, Liba, 10
pension reforms, gender gap, 168
Petrova, Dimitrina, 129
Phillips, Anne, 17, 188–89
Poland, Polish
  abortion and reproductive rights, 111, 113, 116–18
  anti-discriminatory legislation, 156
  Catholic Church, influence of, 79, 114, 117
  Centre for Women's Rights, 25
  civil society, 79
  Constitution, 38
  contraceptives, use of, 113
  Democratic Left Alliance (SLD), 54, 56, 196n10
  Directory of Women's Organizations and Initiatives, 75
  domestic labour, 101–102, 103
  economic restructuring, 22, 146
  equal opportunities, 17
  Equal Status Act, 38
  European Union membership, 192n8, 200n2
  Family Consultant, 38
  Federation for Women and Family Planning, 79, 113, 117
  female representation in politics, 45, 48, 49, 51, 52–56, 194n3, 196n9, 196n10
  femininity, 142
    media images of, 131–32
  feminism, 40, 63, 71–72, 80
  Freedom Union (UW), 56, 196n10
  gay and lesbian issue, 111
  gender bias/inequality, 150–51, 168, 201n10
  La Strada, 87
  Labour Party, 54
  League of Polish Women, 76
  legislation for gender equality, 34, 37–39
  National Labour Inspectorate, 154
  National Programme to Counteract Violence in the Family, 38
  nationalism, 141
  OŚKA, 79
  Parliamentary Commission on the Equal Status of Women and Men, 37
  Parliamentary Women's Group, 37, 38
  partition, 13, 140
  Plenipotentiary for the Equal Status of Women and Men, 37–39
  Polish Agrarian Party (PSL), 56
  Polish Episcopate, 111
  Polish Feminist Association, 71, 80
  'Polish Mother' myth, 54, 109–10, 118, 140–42
  Pro-Family Policy, 110
  quotas, 58
  social welfare model, 105
  Solidarity, 56, 65, 66
  Union of Labour (UP), 56
  women activists/movements, 25, 142
  women's employment status/unemployment, 151, 154–56, 200n6, 201n7
  women's non-governmental organizations (NGOs), 38–39, 55, 74–75, 79, 89, 196n10
  Women's Pre-election Coalition, 26, 55–56
Women's Rights Centre, 117, 155
policymaking on gender equality, 55
political, politics, politicians, 3, 5, 9, 11, 13, 15, 16, 18, 22, 25, 33, 48–49, 58, 63, 65, 72, 74, 78–80, 91, 97, 100, 118, 122, 145, 172, 178, 187
  empowerment of women, 57, 58
  mobilization, 46, 188
  parliamentary politics, 49
  party politics, 32, 44
  powerlessness, 48, 51
  rights, 22, 58, 179, 180, 182, 183, 186, 187
  transformation, 6, 12, 36, 48, 62, 69, 94
  will, 17, 41, 51
Pollert, Anna, 169
pornography, 19
Posadskaya-Vanderbeck, Anastasia, 73, 88

positive discrimination programmes, 36
postcommunism, 133, 134
postfeminism, 133
post-TV News violence syndrome, 121
poverty, 8, 22, 100, 105, 119, 140, 168
  feminization of, 54
  and women, 74, 167
poverty, negative impact of neo-liberal market, 7
power relations, gendered, 15, 44, 46, 68, 75, 121, 125–26, 173, 177
  negotiation, between states, markets and citizens, 186–87
Pringle, Rosemary and Watson, Sophie, 177
private ownership economy, 183
private property, 109
private sector, 150, 161
  sexual harassment of women, 156
private sphere, 66–67, 95, 109, 129
  gender equality in, 96
privatization, 6–8, 10, 22, 42, 81, 84, 105, 119, 145, 152, 156, 161, 165, 180
professionalism, 31, 84
project focus, project-related funding, 84, 174
property rights, 183
prostitution, 76, 128, 154
  feminization, 54
  labour migration and trafficking, 83
Prussia, 140
public-private divide, 11–12, 14–16, 18, 48, 65, 68, 122, 163, 187
  debates about, 96–99
public opinion, 58
public sector, 161–62
public sphere of polity and market, 98–99, 129

quotas for women, as a gender equality mechanism, 15, 17, 25–26, 29, 51, 52, 56–59, 181

'race', 171
Rai, Shirin, 29, 40
rape in war, 120–21
Reagan, Ronald, 2
reciprocity, 2, 9, 13
regional divides, 172
regional networking, 20, 62, 91

Regulska, Joanna, 29, 34
religious, 95
  divides, 22, 172
  institutions, 67
reproductive health issues, 113
reproductive politics, 14, 18, 96, 97
  and discourses of the nation, 108–18
reproductive rights, 40, 79, 145, 181
return home, idealization, 99, 122
rhetoric and reality, gap, 11
rights, 20, 27, 28, 77, 178–86
role conflict, 126
role models, 126, 133, 166
Roma, 14, 29, 76, 79, 146, 172
Romania
  abortions, 114
  anti-discriminatory legislation, 24
  Ceausescu regime, 114
  Council for Social Dialogue among Women's NGOs, 77
  domestic labour, 103
  domestic violence, 119
  European Union, membership, 16, 24, 33, 200n2
  female political representation, 55, 196n8
  female self-sacrifice, notion of, 143
  feminism, 63
  gender relations, 64, 95
  gender wage gap, 202n12
  media images of femininity, 132, 135
  population growth, 114
  women's movements, 76
  Women's National Forum, 77
  women's non-governmental organizations (NGOs), 74–75, 77
  women's rights, 63
  women's unemployment, 152, 153
Rowlands, Jo, 173
Rubchak, Marian, 137
rule of law, 14, 31
rural-urban divide, 116
Russia, 140
  abortions, 114
  contraceptives, lack of, 114
  domestic violence, 119
  donor dependence, 84
  entrepreneurship, 161, 162–63
  failure of transition, 6
  feminism, 63
  Gender Studies, 72

Russia – *continued*
  homosexuality, 110
  kitchen, 97
  Moscow Gender Studies Centre, 72, 88
  Union of Women of Russia, 76, 77
  women's movement, 92–93
  women's non-governmental organizations (NGOs), 74–75, 78, 91
    financing, 84–85
  women's status, 128
Rwanda
  violence against women, 120

safety at work, 16
Sanader, Ivo, 115, 116
scepticism, 29, 135
Schoepp-Schilling, Hanna Beate, 195n7
'Second Wave' feminism, 48, 65, 67, 69
SEELINE study, 86
self-determination, 142–43
self-help groups, 68, 79, 134
Sen, Amartya, 179, 183–85
Serbia
  homophobia, 125
  homosexuality, 111
service sector, 10
sex industry/sex work, 2, 154
  binary of abolition versus normalization, 83
sexual harassment, 26, 134
  at workplace, 156
sexuality, 95, 110–12, 135, 173, 187
Siemieńska Renata, 52
single-issue projects, politics, 30, 79–80
single-parent households, 105
Slavova, Kornelia, 133
Slovakia
  abortions, 113
  Confederation of Trade Unions, 162, 201n9
  contraceptives, use of, 113
  domestic labour, 102, 103
  European Union, membership of, 192n8, 200n2
  female participation/representation in politics, 26, 51, 52, 55, 195n8
  gender bias, 150
  gender wage gap, 202n12
  media images of femininity, 135
  women's employment status/unemployment, 150, 152, 157, 162, 164
Slovenia
  domestic labour, 103
  European Union, membership of, 192n8, 200n2
  female representation in politics, 53, 196n12
  homosexuality, 111
  violence against women, 104
  social and economic conditions and gender relations, 128–29
social capital, 7–8, 87
social change, 3, 9, 81, 93, 107
social dislocation, 109
social entitlements, 26–27, 30, 67, 148, 172, 179–86
social hierarchies/inequalities, 24, 28, 118, 119, 154, 180
social justice, 5, 9, 21, 22, 23, 27–28, 96, 169, 179, 182, 185, 187, 190
social movements, 175, 176, 177
  and NGOs, communication, 32
social policy, 9, 22, 110, 146, 149, 169
  changes, impact on labour market, 166–68
  impact on women's lives, 49
social relations, 30, 83, 87, 119, 142
  eroticizing, 138
social reproduction, 103
social rights, 29, 33, 148, 177, 179, 180, 183, 186
social safety net, 100
social security, 152
social status quo, 81
social transformation, 6, 12, 35, 62, 69, 94
social welfare, 19, 100, 128, 147, 149
socialism, 34
Socialist International, 59
socialist regimes, collapse of, 6
solidarity, 54, 66, 86
Somers, Margaret, 7
Söros Foundation, 88
Southeastern Europe
  gender equality, 33
  Stability Pact Gender Task Force, 59
  women, political empowerment, 57, 58, 193n4
sovereignty, 110

Soviet Union, 2, 29
  disintegration, 112
  gender mainstreaming, 36
  political and economic
    hegemony, 13
Spain: influence of Catholic
  Church, 114
Sperling, Valerie, 131
Stalin, Joseph, 2
state, 20, 37, 65, 138, 177
  and citizenship, 7
  and civil society, 18, 66
  dependency, 80
  household and individual,
    relations, 110
  intervention, 6, 7, 34,
    64, 178
  market relations, 7, 110
  and household, 27, 183
  retrenchment, 31, 51, 81, 175, 177
state/socialism/socialists, 5, 9, 11, 12,
  32, 19, 46, 49, 50, 51, 62, 65, 68,
  78, 95–99, 101, 103, 109, 122,
  126, 127, 129–31, 133, 136, 148,
  171, 176–77, 182
stereotypes, 38, 124–25, 128, 134, 136
Stiglitz, Joseph, 6, 7
Stratigaki, Maria, 35, 36
structural power relations, 29, 66, 149
subservience, 126
Superwoman, 125, 126, 129–31, 132,
  135, 140, 143
Szalai, Júlia, 29, 176

Thatcher, Margaret, 100, 103, 175
top-down policy, 23–24, 25, 35, 178
totalitarian regime, 2, 97, 176
trade unions, 74
trafficking, 2–3, 82–84, 87, 154
transformation process/transition, 15, 19,
  25–26, 45, 49–50, 52, 63, 65, 68, 69,
  73, 74, 76, 78–79, 91, 93–96, 98, 103,
  106, 118, 123, 126, 128, 136, 139,
  157–58, 178, 179, 180, 192n7, 197n3
  difficulties, 5–8
  gender as a structuring principle, 5,
    14, 48, 118
  impact on labour market, 144
  myths, 62–63
  and the public-private
    relationship, 18
transnational corporate power, 7

transnational corporations (TNCs),
  27, 33
transnational organized crime,
  3, 82
transnational women's networking,
  29, 62, 87, 92
'transversal politics', 189–90
True, Jacqui, 133–34, 161, 201n9
True, Jacqui and Mintrom, Michael,
  17, 40
trust, 68
Tudjman, Franjo, 115, 123
Turkey
  European Union membership, 16

Ugrešić, Dubravka, 1, 120, 124,
  138–39
Ukraine, 72
  abortions, 114
  civil society, 79
  female identities, 135, 137
  female representation in politics,
    193n4
  male dominance, 137
  women's non-governmental
    organizations (NGOs), 74
unemployment
  female, 7, 9, 19, 51, 54, 99,
    103, 107, 119, 145–46,
    151–56, 163
  male, 104
United Kingdom
  Department for International
    Development, 24
  domestic violence, 119
  female representation in
    politics, 57
  feminism, 63, 64, 109
  gender mainstreaming, 36
  Institute for Development
    Studies, 24
  Labour Party, 57
  Sex Discrimination Act, 57,
    193n7
  welfare state end of based on
    universal entitlements, 23
United Nations (UN), 28, 65, 89, 96,
  122, 123, 152, 174, 176
  Commission on Status of Women
    (CSW), 162
  gender policy, 24, 82
  human development indicators, 184

United Nations – *continued*
  Human Development Report, 2000, 180
  Human Rights Committee, 111
  protocol on trafficking, 3
United Nations Children's Fund (UNICEF), 105, 106, 114, 150–51, 154
United Nations Development Fund for Women (UNIFEM), 86, 89, 91–92, 155–56
United Nations Development Programme (UNDP), 117
United Nations Fourth World Conference on Women, 23, 24, 28, 87
United Nations General Assembly (UNGA), 59, 178
United States of America (USA)
  feminism, 63, 64, 88
  human rights, 181
  market economy, 6
  women, 48
Universal Declaration of Human Rights, 181
universalism, 188, 189
Urgent Action Fund for Women's Human Rights, 82, 121

values, 134
  hierarchy, 98
  and religious institutions, 114
Vatican
  Family Rights Charter, 110
Verloo, Mieke, 35
violence against women, 18, 30, 73, 74, 76–77, 86, 96, 98, 118–22
virgin-whore binary, 19, 140

wages, gender discrimination, 30, 156, 160–61, 168
Wajda, Andrzej, 141
Wałęsa, Lech, 66, 111
'Washington Consensus', 5, 6, 22, 32, 81, 135
Watson, Peggy, 64
Waylen, Georgina, 177
welfare state, regimes, 3, 23, 28, 63, 103, 167, 183
  decline, 8
  dependency, 67, 182
  provision, 183
  universalism, 26
  well-being, theory of, 179
Western Europe, 2, 19, 30, 46, 82, 122, 124, 129, 149, 190
  abortion rates, 113
  demographic shift and childcare, 105
  devolution, 13
  domestic violence, 120
  economy, 147
  family structure, 98
  female political representation, 39, 48, 50, 55
  feminism/feminists, 4, 7, 12, 25, 62, 64–65, 70–72, 120, 177, 188, 198n6
    'Second Wave', 48, 65, 67, 69
  gender wage gap, 160
  labour market, 2, 101–102
  marketization, 10
  media images of femininity, 2, 132, 135
  model of part-time work, 164
  moral climate, 3
  neo-liberal paradigm, 102
  political restructuring, 21
  popular culture, 133
  public-private divide, 97, 98, 100–101
  social policy, 110
  welfare states, 28, 63, 103, 167
  women, 47–48, 108
  women's employment, 151
  women's networks, 15
Westminster Parliament, 26
Więckowska, Katarzyna, 133, 139
women, women's issues, 4, 12, 47, 67, 91
  activism/mobilization, 63, 73, 74, 78, 79, 85, 87, 92–93
  citizenship rights, 97, 108, 118, 123
  dual role as workers and mothers, 11, 77, 97, 100, 101, 102, 146
  emancipation/freedom, 51, 66
  empowerment, 42, 69, 137, 172–74
  exploitation, 34
  identity, 11
  magazines, 133, 139–40
  movements, 18, 35, 66, 68, 72, 74, 178, 198n11
  negative impact of neo-liberal market, 7, 9–10
  participation in civil society, 45, 65, 85–86

women, women's issues – *continued*
political education, 39
political subjectivity, 67
refugees, 86
reproductive role, 12, 13, 27
responsibility for private
  sphere, 52
rights, 6, 25, 63, 69, 74, 75, 76,
  109, 116
sense of self, 145
status, 12, 25, 41, 76, 98, 184
subordination, 74, 79
symbolic significance as Mother
  Earth/mother of nation, 13–14,
  79, 128, 135, 137
triple role as mother, worker and
  political activist, 129, 130
under-representation in private
  sector, 10
unpaid labour, 31, 100, 103
use of public sphere, 85
victims of war, 86
voting patterns, 44, 52, 54
Women in Black, 85–86, 121
Women's Councils, 67
Women's Studies and Gender Studies
  Association of Countries in
  Transition, 72, 189
Women's Studies and Gender Studies
  programmes, 72–73, 189
womanhood, 48, 117, 128, 139, 141
'women's work', 104
domesticated, 136
Worgitzky, Charlotte
  Farewell to a Career, 130

Workers, negative impact of
  neo-liberal market model, 7
working conditions, 27, 87
working relationships, 126
working women, 126
work-life balance, 98, 106
workplace, social context, 11
World Bank, 7, 22, 89, 149, 167,
  169–70, 176
World Conference on Women,
  Beijing, 1995, 23, 24, 28, 87
World War II, 23, 100, 139, 140

Yugoslavia, former
  Autonomous Women's Centre
    against Sexual Violence, 86
  Belgrade Women's Studies Centre, 72
  ethno-nationalist conflicts, 13, 85,
    86, 112, 139
  feminism, 88, 120
  gendered discourses, 137, 138
  male mindset, 138–39
  Parliament, 78
  sexuality and reproductive rights,
    110–11
  violence against women, 120–21
  Women in Black, 85–86, 121
  women's unemployment, 152
Yuval-Davis, Nira, 173–74, 189–90,
  203n4

Zaorski, Janusz, 142
Zielińska, Eleonora, 117
Zhurzhenko,
  Tatiana, 78, 135